Constructing Ethnopolitics in the Soviet Union: *Samizdat*, Deprivation, and the Rise of Ethnic Nationalism

Constructing Ethnopolitics in the Soviet Union: *Samizdat,* Deprivation, and the Rise of Ethnic Nationalism

Dina Zisserman-Brodsky

First published 2003 by
PALGRAVE MACMILLAN™
175 Fifth Avenue, New York, N.Y. 10010 and
Houndmills, Basingstoke, Hampshire, England RG21 6XS.
Companies and representatives throughout the world.

PALGRAVE MACMILLAN is the global academic imprint of the Palgrave Macmillan division of St. Martin's Press, LLC and of Palgrave Macmillan Ltd. Macmillan® is a registered trademark in the United States, United Kingdom and other countries. Palgrave is a registered trademark in the European Union and other countries.

ISBN 1–4039–6191–3 hardback

Library of Congress Cataloging-in-Publication Data

Zisserman-Brodsky, Dina.
  Constructing ethnopolitics in the Soviet Union : samizdat, deprivation and the rise of ethnic nationalism / by Dina Zisserman-Brodsky.
    p. cm.
  Includes bibliographical references and index.
  ISBN 1–4039–6191–3 (cloth)
    1. Soviet Union—Ethnic relations—Political aspects. 2. Soviet Union—Politics and government—1953–1985. 3. Minorities—Soviet Union—Political activity. 4. Nationalism—Soviet Union. I. Title.

DK277.Z57 2003
323.1'47'0904—dc21   2003042037

A catalogue record for this book is available from the British Library.

Design by Newgen Imaging Systems (P) Ltd., Chennai, India.

First edition: July, 2003
10 9 8 7 6 5 4 3 2 1

Printed in the United States of America.

To my daughters, Rachel and Sofia

Table of Contents

Preface

There were two crucial events in the Russian history of the twentieth century, which shocked the world: the 1917 October revolution and the 1991 breakup of the USSR. While the former gave birth to the discipline called Sovietology, the latter demonstrated the depth of its crisis. "The contemporary Sovietology," wrote A. Motyl, "represents an awkward amalgam of data collection, policy analysis and journalism that is divorced from scholarship, as sense impressions are from theory."[1]

After a short period of self-blaming, Sovietology made an elegant slip into the "Post-Soviet studies" leaving open the question *why* and *how* it happened that the Soviet polity had become the Post-Soviet one. The comprehensive examination of causes and driving forces of the collapse of the USSR seems to be one of the most stimulating tasks for present and future generations of scholars studying this area.

This book attempts to contribute to the filling of the epistemological gap. It investigates the rise and development of ethnic dissent, *samizdat* and their contribution to the reemergence of nationalism in the USSR. The book presents the first systematic comparative study of ethnonationalist ideologies developed in the period from the late 1960s to the mid-1980s. *Samizdat* publications were studied, and sometimes very carefully, by a number of scholars, however, mainly as a valuable source of information about repressions in the Soviet Union, discrimination of ethnic minorities, and opposition to the communist rule. Minimal attention was paid to alternative ideologies suggested by those activities of various nationalist movements and authors of *samizdat* publications, who, as early as in the late 1960s, began to formulate programs of ethnopolitics, which came to the fore in the late 1980s and were realized in the early 1990s. It became a common place in the scholarly discourse that dissent in general and ethnic dissent in particular played a minor, if any, role in the USSR's collapse. The book argues that dissident network (*samizdat* is considered its major component) has been the most important and the only fully independent institution of civil society in the former USSR. In this capacity dissent played a crucial role in the re-orientation of the Soviet socio-political thought and adoption of new normative standards.

I began this research at a time when the Soviet regime still was presumed as stable, and the nationalities were not considered the predominant political factor. The breakup of the USSR dotted the "i"s but did not change the concepts of this study. When the book had been practically finished I found a fascinating article by Christian Joppke spelling out what I intended to express in considerably milder form: "In Eastern Europe, succeeding generations of intellectuals have been at the forefront of first creating and then demolishing the communist regime. Because communism was ultimately based on ideas, the abandonment of these ideas by intellectuals turned dissidents as a critical factor of the regime's demise. The dissident intellectuals, powerless as they seemed to be,[2] delivered the decisive blow, when they denounced the regime's underlying ideology. The turn to dissidence as the premier mode of communist opposition politics went along with the invocation of national discourse."[3]

Additional explanations can neither accentuate the merits nor conceal failures of the book. So, I leave to others to judge. What remains here is to pay debts. The support of the Bernard Cherrick Center of the Institute of Contemporary Jewry at the Hebrew University of Jerusalem and of the Center of Russian and East European Studies at the University of Toronto made possible to finish this book. The study could not be accomplished without Anatoly Khazanov of the University of Wisconsin, Madison and Jonathan Frankel of the Hebrew University of Jerusalem, who had supervised my theses on which this book was based. Their academic advice, intellectual stimulus, challenging questions (I hope I have answered here at least part of them) and personal encouragement cannot be overestimated. I owe a particular debt to Galia Golan, Gabi Sheffer, Metta Spencer, Wolf Moskowich, Eddy Kauffman, and Theodore Friedgut from whom I have learned much. I am very thankful to John Ishiyama, Benjamin Pinkus, Zvi Gitelman, Peter Solomon, Donald Schwartz, and Liesbeth Hooghe for their valuable comments and suggestions. I wish I were able to express my deep gratitude to late Abraham Harman, the former President and Chancellor of the Hebrew University. I appreciate the exceptional expertise, insights, and support of editors David Pervin, Gabriella Pearce, Ian Steinberg, and Mukesh V.S.

I would like to acknowledge the people who contributed to this book in different ways: Leonid Praisman, Ze'ev Wolfson, Leah Cohen, Abraham Ben-Ya'akov, Mark Toltz, Danny Wool, Marina Gutgarts, Deborah Shainok, Haim Dolgopol'sky, Ida Shtein, Masha Shapiro, Mark Kipnis, Hanna Magarik,

Sergei Batovrin, Aharon Moonblith, Rachel Gedaleva, Svetlana Fisher, Jana Oldfield, Valerii Borschov, Abraham Torpusman, Yelena Lerman, Victoria Malikova, Inna Bershadsky, Yuri Bershachevsky, Ahmed Shazzo, Natasha Segev, Emil Pain, Igor Grishaev. My thanks to the students of a course on ethnic politics in the USSR I touched at the Hebrew University of Jerusalem: they were the first judges of the ideas expressed here.

Finally, I should like to mention the enormous assistance and encouragement that I have received from my husband Vladimir Brodsky. Without this support the book would never have been finished and even started.

CHAPTER 1

Introduction: Theoretical Perspective and Focus of Inquiry

The Theoretical Framework

This is a study of ethnic politics in the USSR as formulated within dissident ethnonationalist movements between 1964 and 1986. The juxtaposition of ethnic politics with nationalism (even if *ethno-nationalism*) intrinsically demands terminological clarification. Ethnic politics is often perceived as a nascent—*pre-nationalist*—stage of ethnic assertiveness, which may be progressively evolved into its higher phase—*nationalism*. It seems that such an approach narrows considerably the realm of both concepts—nationalism and ethnic politics. Therefore, a word must be said here about the meanings and theoretical interpretations of basic terms and concepts used in the book, namely, *ethnic politics, ethnic groups, nationalism, modernization, nationalist movements* and their *demands*.

For the purposes of this study, ethnic politics is defined as political self-assertiveness exhibited by ethnic groups, including the demands, strategies, orientations, political ideologies, and objectives with which they seek to alter or reinforce their status within or outside the existing state structures.

J. Rothschild elaborated on the theoretical framework for the study of ethnic politics in his seminal work, *Ethnopolitics: A Conceptual Framework*.[1] According to him, the student of ethnopolitics must explain and measure the politicization of ethnic groups (i.e., the process by which they are brought into the political arena) in terms of causes, dynamics, and specific characteristics. He argues that the processes involved in politicization will "1) render people cognitively aware of the relevance of politics to the health of their ethnic cultural values and vice versa; 2) stimulate their concern about this nexus;

3) mobilize them [the people] into self-conscious ethnic groups; and 4) direct their behavior toward activity in the political arena on the basis of this awareness, concern, and consciousness."[2]

The term "ethnic group" will be used to denote a social group within a larger cultural and social system, which claims or is accorded a special status in terms of a complex of traits, real or imagined, that it inherited or is believed to have inherited from past ages.[3] These common "ethnic" traits might be derived from cultural-religious, linguistic, or "folkloristic" characteristics, or from the geographical origins of the group's members, and so on.

Most champions of ethnic politics tend to avoid using the term "ethnic group" with reference to their own community, preferring to describe it as "nationality," "national group," "people," or "nation." The ethnic movements' documents cited throughout this book, use these terms interchangeably. In the contemporary nationalist discourse, an assumption that an ethnic group "naturally" constitutes a national community is perceived as an axiom rather than a theorem to be proven. Clearly, the prevailing ethnic politics can be described as the goal-oriented political expression of ethnonationalism, which, of course, is a phenomenon unique to the modern era. R. Szporluk who investigates the process of formation of "a new national community from an ethnic group"[4] in the nineteenth century repeatedly emphasizes two points—a novelty of ethnonational identity[5] based on the "discovered" or "invented" popular culture[6] and an active role of ethnic intelligentsia in the formation of a nation. "At an early stage, a small circle of intellectuals—students of language, history, and folklore—performs the crucial operation of *defining* a national category and thus takes the first step towards transforming that category into a nation," Szporluk pointed out.[7] Thus, by definition, the study of ethnic nationalism involves the examination of cultural, linguistic, psychological, demographic, philosophic, and other dimensions whereas the orbit of ethnopolitics includes these topics insofar as they relate to the political issues.

There is no casual or sequential nexus between ethnic politics and nationalism. It seems serviceable to regard them as two overlapping phenomena. Since a politicized ethnic group does not necessarily pursue the nationalist objectives, nationalism might be viewed as a segment of ethnic politics. At the same time, political dimension elucidates only one side of the multifaceted phenomenon of nationalism.

It has become increasingly accepted among scholars that it would be impractical to provide a "universal" definition of nationalism. As A. Smith pointed out, "There has, in fact, never been a single version of nationalism, and it is vain to search for some genuine doctrine or true movement to act as a criterion for all subsequent cases."[8] J. Coakley concurs with Smith: "The precise meanings of nationalism and of the concept of nationalist movement are notoriously difficult, and we do not propose in the present volume even to approach the question of providing universally acceptable definitions."[9]

Of course, there have been attempts to define nationalism. In the 1940s and 1950s the topic was examined primarily from a historical-ideological perspective, as is reflected in contemporary definitions. In 1944, H. Kohn wrote, "Nationalism is, first and foremost, a state of mind, an act of consciousness, which since the French Revolution, has become more and more common to mankind."[10] Ten years later, L. Snyder argued, "Nationalism is a powerful emotion that has dominated the political thought and actions of most peoples since the time of the French Revolution."[11] In *Nationalism* (1960), E. Kedourie described nationalism as "a doctrine invented in Europe at the beginning of the nineteenth century.... Briefly, the doctrine holds that humanity is naturally divided into nations, that nations are known by certain characteristics which can be ascertained, and that the only legitimate type of government is national self-government."[12] These scholars and others were completely aware that "modern nationalism has been a vital part of an extraordinary complex of economic, political, social, and intellectual developments."[13] However, until the mid-1960s mainstream studies of nationalism described it first and foremost in terms of its intellectual history, focusing on its ideological development.[14]

An important contribution to the study of nationalism was made by K. Deutsch, who offered a "functional definition of nationality" in his well-known book *Nationalism and Social Communication* (1953): "Membership in a people essentially consists of a wide complementarity over a wider range of subjects with members of one large group than with outsiders."[15] "In a competitive economy or culture," he continued, "nationality is an implied claim to privilege. It emphasizes group preference and group peculiarities, and so tends to keep out all outside competitors. It promises opportunity for it, it promises to eliminate or lessen linguistic, racial, class, or caste barriers to the social rite of individuals within it. And it promises security, for it promises to reduce the probability of outside competition for all sorts of opportunities."[16] The social communication theory offered by Deutsch "examines the patterns by which the socio-economic rationale of nationalism is translated into a political variable."[17]

This attempt to understand the relationship between the political phenomenon of nationalism and social factors has been followed over the past twenty years by E. Gellner, S. Rokkan, and P. Brass.[18] Evaluating this relationship, L. Hooghe noted that "nationalism must be seen as a politico-strategic interpretation of social changes."[19]

On the other hand, Gellner formulated what is probably the most famous contemporary definition of nationalism, employing a purely political perspective: "nationalism is primarily a political principle, which holds that the political and the national unit should be congruent. Nationalist sentiment is the feeling of anger aroused by violation of the principle or the feeling of satisfaction aroused by its fulfillment."[20] Correspondingly, a nationalist movement was defined by Gellner as "one activated by a sentiment of this kind."[21] A. Smith developed an "integrative" approach to nationalism, combining the ideological and political perspectives.[22] He regards the "nationalist enterprise," as "a political consequence of the broader historicist movement [that] emerged first in late eighteenth-century Europe and then in other areas in response to certain kinds of geo-political ethnic bases, and social bearers, whose rise to prominence or revival at these times formed the matrix for historicism and nationalism."[23] He then defined nationalism as "an ideological movement for the attainment and maintenance of autonomy, cohesion, and individuality for a social group deemed by some of its members to constitute an actual or potential nation. In other words, nationalism is both an ideology and a movement, usually a minority one, which aspires to 'nationhood' for the chosen group; and 'nationhood,' in turn, comprises three basic ideals: autonomy and self government for the group, often but not always in a sovereign state; solidarity and fraternity of the group in a recognized territory or 'home'; and third, a distinctive and preferably unique culture peculiar to the group in question."[24]

Regardless of their methodological approach—social, political, or integrative—most scholars agree that the "modernization" process plays the central role in the emergence and development of nationalism. But modernization itself has a wide range of interpretations that correlate with the different methodological perspectives. Gellner views the modernization process as the transition from agrarian to industrial society, and modernization as industrialization and its social concomitants.[25] Smith understands modernization to be, "self-sustaining economic growth, or, more generally, the increasing social utilization of scientific methods and machine-powered technology."[26] Deutsch tends to use the terms "modernization" and "Westernization" as interchangeable synonyms.[27] S. Eisenstadt specified this very approach in his book *Modernization: Protest and Change*: "Modernization is the process of change towards those types of social, economic and political systems that have developed in Western Europe and North America from the seventeenth century to the nineteenth and have then spread to other European countries and in the nineteenth and twentieth centuries, to the South American, Asian, and African continents."[28]

The *Encyclopedia of Sociology* defines the theory of modernization as a "description and explanation of the process of transformation from traditional or underdeveloped societies to modern societies. Attention has mainly been focused on the ways in which past and present pre-modern societies become modern (i.e., Westernized) through processes of economic growth and change in social, political, and cultural structures."[29] In his recent book, A. Khazanov evading Europeocentrism defines "the key concept of modernization" as "the notion of economic growth based on technological advances."[30] The degree of urbanization, high rates of literacy, secularization, birth control, political democracy, free enterprise, and the like, are usually considered to be indicators of modernization.[31]

The writers on nationalism often hold nationalism as a "reaction against the consequences of modernization."[32] Meanwhile Deutsch emphasizes that nationalism manifests itself in various types of reactions to the modernization process. It might "appear as a drive toward rapid Westernization" or, on the contrary, it might "assert its allegiance to the old ways and the old traditions."[33] Seeking to establish a link between the modernization process and the emergence of nationalism, scholars have elaborated various theoretical interpretations:

1. *The mobilization–assimilation theories* state that "there is a direct link between processes such as social mobilization and assimilation on the one hand, and political integration or disintegration and nationalism on the other."[34] According to Deutsch, if the rate of social mobilization is greater than that of assimilation to the dominant culture, the balance in a state system is disturbed.[35]

2. *The center–periphery theories* focus on the differential location of cultural, economic, and political power, suggesting that this imbalance results in tension between center and periphery. When a periphery accumulates considerable power in at least one of these three domains, and when, at the same time, the political regime fails to reflect the actual power structure, nationalism is likely to develop.[36]

3. *The uneven development theories* consider socio-economic stratification, which correlates with cultural divisions, to be a result of the unfavorable economic position of an ethnic community. "Nationalism is linked to the struggle of a people to free itself from the structures of economic oppression and hides a class conflict."[37] While "uneven development" theories assume that socio-economic stratification stems

from the objective process of differential economic development, internal colonialism theories—a variant of "uneven development" theories—regard stratification as a result of premeditated state policy. "Internal colonialist theories hold that capitalism's development from the center subordinates territories, just as European colonialism subjected territories in Africa and Asia. The result is a cultural division of labour in which class and ethnicity coincide."[38]

4. Finally, *competition theories*, premising that wealth in every state is scarce and unevenly distributed point out that modernization encourages a power struggle for the same resources.[39] "It is predicted that the ethnic revival should be stronger in more modernized areas, and that the new, rising social strata should be main actors in the revival."[40]

The forementioned theories account for different constellations of factors that bring about nationalist developments. Yet, as we have said earlier, most scholars agree that a social pattern common to all nationalist movements does not exist.[41]

There is one other plausible explanation of ethnic nationalism: the theory of relative deprivation. Although it does not provide a comprehensive theoretical approach it "can successfully function as a partial mechanism within a broader perspective."[42] The concept of deprivation was elaborated upon by Marx in terms of "absolute deprivation." By the twentieth century, this concept was transformed in sociology from absolute to relative deprivation. "The basic idea here is that social groups and their members only compare their position or fate with a limited range of other groups or individuals, those a little higher in the social scale. Although the position, material and social, of the group may have (or be) improved in absolute terms, what matters for their perceptions and actions is their progress relative to that of other, similar groups. Social movements and political action are the outcome of perceived frustrations on the part of individuals or groups, who feel disadvantaged and deprived relative to others and handicapped in the race for wealth, status, services, and power. According to this perspective, ethnic protest and ethnic nationalism are the outcome of regional relative deprivation."[43] Pointing out that in this variant the concept of relative deprivation "is clearly inadequate as an explanation of ethnic revival,"[44] Smith broadened its explanation considerably: "There are, first, several kinds of relative deprivation: economic (wealth, income, employment), services (health, education, housing, amenities), political and social (mainly status concerns) .... The existing data suggest that political and status deprivations are more closely related to political action than economic or services wants."[45]

J. Kellas utilized one understanding of relative deprivation to establish links between macro- and micro-level interpretations of nationalism. Quoting studies that examined relative deprivation and Scottish nationalism,[46] Kellas attested: "Many nationalists feel political deprivation, not for themselves necessarily, but for the nation. While they may be personally successful and feel no personal relative deprivation, they feel that the nation as a whole is deprived politically, because of its lack of independence or autonomy, and economically and socially, because they believe all national resources and opportunities are drained away to the center of the state."[47]

While social changes at a mass level constitute the main object of macro-level analyses of nationalism, the nationalist movements and their characteristics are the focus of meso-level analyses. J. Breuilly defined nationalist movements as "significant political movements, principally of opposition, which seek to gain or exercise state power and justify their objectives in terms of nationalist doctrine."[48]

Practically all students of nationalism indicate that the nationalist doctrines tend to demonstrate variability when they are examined diachronically and plurality if viewed synchronically. Smith wrote:

> From the late eighteenth century until today, the national ideal has expanded and proliferated into the most powerful yet elusive of all modern ideologies. It started life as a middle-class quest for social emancipation and community against the arbitrary rule of despots. It soon became a weapon in defence of privilege, and later a justification of state expansion and overseas imperialism. At the same time it was taken up by intelligentsias of ethnic minorities, who sought in the goal of national self-determination, to secede from vast empires and unify all those who shared their culture in a single state. In the later nineteenth century, nationalism also united with populism to preach the need for roots in the small town and countryside to a newly urbanized and uprooted population.
>
> In our own century, the national ideal has been used for various purposes and appeared in different guises. There is first the familiar anti-colonial drive for modernization associated with the westernizing intelligentsias of underdeveloped countries in Asia, Africa, and Latin America, which started in a protest for liberation and has now turned into a quest for homogeneity and integration in the new states. There is also and often in league with anti-colonial integration, the populist idea, which seeks to re-identify intelligentsias with their peasantries in these states, and through a national communism to promote their industrial modernization. In Europe we have witnessed a revival of the same national ideal in

a spate of ethnic neo-nationalisms, which hark back to the earlier ethnic secessionism but add new motifs and reflect a different phase of the political and economic cycle. And finally, there are colour and "pan"-nationalisms, still a vital force in some parts of the world.[49]

Within the broad range of nationalist developments one important trend should be indicated, namely, the shift from "civic" or "state nationalism" of the nineteenth century[50] to "ethnic" or "sub-state nationalism" of the twentieth century. "An idea of the nation as an association of citizens each possessing certain rights which should be guaranteed and safeguarded by the state"[51] dominated the nationalist doctrines of the nineteenth century. In the twentieth century, particularly in its second half, the "national unit," or nation is predominantly described in ethnic terms. "In brief, nationalism is a theory of political legitimacy, which requires that ethnic boundaries should not cut across political ones, and, in particular, that ethnic boundaries within a given state . . . should not separate the power-holders from the rest."[52] This description not so much defines nationalism, but rather traces realities of our time, indicating both ethnic stratification and politicization along ethnic lines. This is because ethnic revival has, since the late 1960s, become a worldwide phenomenon,[53] central to the political arena not only in the countries possessed of long-standing state structures, but in the newly established states of Asia and Africa, which gained their independence under the banner of anti-colonial nationalism.

Today, nationalist movements are primarily ethnic movements, which tend to be defined "as referring to the efforts of ethnic groups, which are not identified with the state to reshape state structures. . . . The first core concept in this definition is ethnicity."[54] According to the authors of *The Social Origins of Nationalist Movements*, "Nationalist movements find political expression in demands ranging from recognition of regional cultural distinctiveness, in forms varying from weakly supported pleas for autonomy or merely for basic rights to strongly or even violently expressed and generally supported demands for independence."[55]

Analyzing the political demands of ethnic minority groups, Smith indicated six types of ethnic strategies: *isolation, accommodation, communalism, autonomism, separatism,* and *irredentism.*[56] J. Elklit and O. Tonsgaard[57] similarly distinguished between the following models of political demands: (1) the secessionist model; (2) the frontier adjustment model; (3) the autonomy model; (4) the group rights model; and (5) the individual rights model. "These five models articulate a minority group perspective. From a majority point of view, a sixth model, a discrimination model, could be added."[58]

Some scholars pointed to another expression of ethnic nationalism: racialist terms and the pursuit of "conservative, anti-democratic, and often antisocialist purposes."[59] But the ethnonationalist principle can also be "asserted in ethical, universalistic spirit,"[60] and ethnonationalist movements can proclaim their commitment to the principles of liberal democracy. In any case, there is a consensus that "In modern or transitional societies politicized ethnicity has become the crucial principle of political legitimation and delegitimation of systems, states, and governments."[61]

Studies in Nationalism and Ethnic Dissent in the USSR

While generally accepting this formulation by Rothschild, most political analysts did not expect that it would be realized so soon, in its variant of "delegitimation," in the USSR. However, it can be argued that the leading factor behind the division of the Soviet Empire, during the Gorbachev era, into two irreconcilable camps was, in fact, the ethnonationalist factor. The main objective of the August 1991 putsch as well as its "dress rehearsal" in the Baltic republics in January 1991, was, it would seem, to put an end to the ethnic self-assertiveness of the non-Russian nationalities and to abrogate the concessions granted to union and autonomous republics as provided for by the new Union Treaty, and hence to reinforce the model of ethnic domination as practiced by the Soviet regime for decades.

At the same time, it was obvious that a victory for the democratic forces would definitely mean the final collapse of the Soviet Empire. The failed coup d'etat only accelerated the USSR's disintegration. But in itself, the collapse of the Soviet Empire was caused, not so much by ethnic clashes and fierce fighting as by the balanced and coordinated politics of ethnic groups, including (or, one might say, first and foremost) the Russians. Assessing the immediate consequences of the events of August 1991, the liberal Moscow weekly, *Ogonek*, wrote: "The Union of Soviet Socialist Republics, one of the most brutal empires in human history, no longer exists. Its former patrimonies have gone their own ways. The word freedom is now among the most popular terms used by the press."[62]

The growing political assertiveness of ethnic groups drew the attention of scholars from the early stages of *perestroika*. At a 1989 conference entitled *The Soviet Nations in the Gorbachev Era* (organized by the Nationality and Siberian Studies program of the W. Avril Harriman Institute for the Advanced Study of the Soviet Union, at Columbia University), P. Goble pointed to the "demise of the nationality question" as it had been understood in its traditional context and the rise of what could be called "ethnic politics."[63] The following year, at the Second Annual Conference on Soviet Nationalities' Relations in the Gorbachev Era, entitled *The Soviet Nationalities Against Gorbachev*, H. Huttenbach said: "Last year's conference ended with a general sense that national minority movements, still somewhat embryonic at the time, were seizing the initiative. This session opens with the consensus that these embryonic movements are far more mature, have aggressively taken center stage, and in varying degrees, have mounted a direct challenge to the center."[64] In discussing the process by which ethnicity had been brought into the political arena, both Goble and Huttenbach considered the development of ethnic politics a unique phenomenon of *perestroika*, though both were aware of its pre-*perestroika* origins.

Historians seeking to understand how future events emerge from the events of the past cannot simply assume that the transition from total ethnic passivity to articulated politics was a rapid, almost spontaneous phenomenon. At the same time, this apparent gap in the emergence of ethnopolitical issues cannot be bridged if official Soviet documents are given pride of place in the study of ethnic self-consciousness, concerns, orientations, and demands, and if the ethnic deviations of some local Communist leaders are assumed to be the most significant manifestations of ethnic self-assertiveness in the period preceding *perestroika*.

I argue that the primary and most relevant resource for the study of the crystallization of ethnic politics in the 1960s, 1970s, and early 1980s can be found in ethnic *samizdat*, that is, collections of uncensored documents issued by nationalist movements and their representatives. While it would be certainly wrong to assume that *samizdat*, particularly ethnic *samizdat* has been completely neglected by scholars, a certain underestimation of the *samizdat* documents must be noted. In his study of Russian nationalism, for instance, J. Dunlop emphasized only those *samizdat* principles for which official "corroboration" could be found in Soviet publications.[65]

"The protest movement may have had a deeper effect than is immediately evident," wrote G. Saunders, the editor of *Samizdat: Voices of the Soviet Opposition*, in his "Introduction."[66] While focusing on the phenomenon of resistance to the Soviet system, Saunders himself, as well as P. Reddaway and some other scholars of Soviet dissent, considered the political ideologies, aspirations, and orientations of the opposition movements to be a matter of relatively peripheral interest. Today the main emphasis in investigating *samizdat* documents ought surely to be given to the analysis of these very aspects—lest we fail to comprehend current ethnopolitical developments.

In his book, *Will the Non-Russians Rebel?*, published four years before the official breakup of the USSR, A. Motyl, a foremost student of the nationalities issues, concluded that the state would continue to "be quite stable" and that the "deprivatization of anti state attitudes" would face considerable problems since the "anti-state collectivities and elites" were unlikely to mobilize.[67] Along the same lines, by offering a new motto, "The USSR Is Our Common Home," Mikhail Gorbachev expressed his confidence that the nationality question had been resolved in the Soviet Union. Several years later, the party newspaper *Pravda* (9 September 1991) carried on its front page a different headline: "The Empire Has Collapsed."

"Ethnic strife in the Soviet Union has caught the unexpecting world by surprise," wrote R. Pipes in his "Foreword" (September 1991) to H. Carrere d'Encausse's new book, *The Great Challenge: Nationalities and the Bolshevik State 1917–1930.* "The violence in the Caucasus, Central Asia, and Moldavia, the clamor for sovereignty of the Baltic peoples and Georgians, and most unexpected of all, the separatism of Great Russians, were events for which, apart from a small body of experts, no one had been prepared. Why this was the case it is difficult to say, because the evidence of latent ethnic tension in the USSR was not invisible."[68]

The above-cited book by Motyl presented a standard view of postwar Sovietology. The patterns of industrialization, urbanization, horizontal and vertical social mobility, and migration, as well as growing standards of living, level of education, health services, and other indicators of modernization were often cited by various scholars up until the breakup of the Soviet Union to prove the absence of real grounds for nationalism in the USSR, and the successful management of the interethnic relations by the Soviet regime.[69]

In his article published in 1971, V. Lanser used the social communications theory to analyze the pattern of modernization among different nationalities in the USSR, and described the Soviet Union as a stable society with a balanced interaction between the ethnic groups and good prospects for the promotion of "universal elements, traits and patterns in culture, as well as in political life."[70]

The pioneer of such an approach, however, was W. Kolarz, whose book *Russia and Her Colonies* appeared in 1952.[71] Regarding the Soviet nationalities as passive objects of manipulation by the Soviet regime, the author did not consider that ethnopolitical self-assertiveness would be a factor in future developments. Even if "Bolshevism is to be overcome at its birthplaces, Leningrad and Moscow, the Russian people must not be under the impression that they will have to pay for liberation from communism with the dismemberment of their state."[72] In case of a non-Bolshevik future, Kolarz predicted a "genuine federation, probably without the Balts"[73] (because of the West, which did not recognize the annexations and not due to the Baltic peoples' nationalism). The author found it necessary to warn the "Western nations against becoming the splitters of Russia by attaching more importance to the local nationalities than to the Russian people."[74] He thus assumed that secessionist ideas would have to be imported into the USSR from the West and could not rise as a result of internal socio-political developments.

The first of the foremost Sovietologists to suggest an alternative approach toward the nationality question in the USSR and to attest to the great political potential of the ethnic factor was R. Pipes. In his fundamental study, *The Formation of the Soviet Union: Communism and Nationalism, 1917–1923* (its first edition was published in 1954, soon after Kolarz's book), Pipes found that the dualism of the Bolshevik "solution" to the nationality question, namely, the formation of a "unitary, centralized totalitarian state, such as the Czarist state had never been,"[75] together with the recognition of the multinational structure of the Soviet population and of the national-territorial principle—as well as the grant of extensive linguistic autonomy to the various nationalities—as a fundamental element in public administration, served as a major stimulus of nationalist sentiment among the peoples of the USSR. "This purely formal feature of the Soviet Constitution may well prove to have been, historically, one of the most consequential aspects of the formation of the Soviet Union," wrote Pipes at the end of the book.[76]

In a presentation, "Political Implications of Soviet Nationality Problems," delivered to the Seminar on Soviet Nationality Problems in 1969, Z. Brzezinski followed Pipes's lead by criticizing "American scholarship on the Soviet Union," which, "as a whole, has tended to minimize or simply to ignore" nationality problems in the USSR.[77] Brzezinski defined four strategies which might pertain to the Soviet nationalities: "biological assimilation" by the Russians; absorption by a more developed culture; socio-economic integration, combined with the preservation of a relatively exclusive highly developed national culture; and "at the far end of the spectrum, a nationalism potentially separatist in its political aspirations and attitudes."[78] Brzezinski concluded that Ukrainians and Balts "might be, potentially, the most secessionist of nationalities."[79]

An article by R. Lewis, entitled "The Mixing of Russians and Soviet Nationalities and Its Demographic Impact," which was published alongside Brzezinski's presentation in *Soviet Nationality Problems* reached a similar conclusion: "With nationalities and Russians competing for jobs and scarce resources, economic tension should grow. As the nationalities develop economically and culturally, they should make more demands upon the Soviet government. Under these circumstances Soviet nationality problems will almost certainly intensify and collectively become a dominant force shaping the future Soviet society."[80] To substantiate his projection, Lewis employed a "competition" approach; Brzezinski had offered an eclectic explanation combining elements drawn from various theories: "social communications," "center–periphery," and "uneven development."

While the opinions of Brzezinski and Lewis gained ground in the 1970s, the contrary position still dominated Soviet studies. "When sometime in the 1970s the dissident Andrei Amalrik asked whether the Soviet Union would survive until 1984,[81] this question was greeted in the West with polite or amused surprise," noted Carrere d'Encausse in her recent book, *The End of the Soviet Empire*.[82] Since that time, however, the future stability of the Soviet Union was questioned not only by Soviet dissidents and some extravagant politicians,[83] but also by prominent experts in Soviet studies. In 1975, Pipes published an article, "Reflection on the Nationality Problem in Soviet Union,"[84] in which he pointed to irreconcilable contradictions between the imperial center and its colonies. He stated that the Soviet authorities "are aware of an explosive situation, in which even moderate administrative concessions to the union and autonomous republics would inevitably lead to their demanding complete independence."[85]

In *Decline of an Empire*[86] (1978), Carrere d'Encausse employed the "assimilation-mobilization" model to indicate that the "renationalization of several nationalities"[87] (and the "nationality impasse" of Soviet policy) was due primarily to the "crisis in integration."[88] Although she made several references to the *samizdat* documents and protest actions of various ethnic movements, she did not consider these movements to be worthy of study: "The affirmation of nationalism in the USSR takes on a special character that must be emphasized. It is not a question of ethnic dissidence freely expressed and intended to assure the independence of the groups concerned. Nationalism in the USSR develops within a special context, that of Soviet ideology and its institutions, so it is futile to interpret it as a movement for national independence."[89] However, she failed to specify the particular characteristics of the Soviet nationalities, that made their nationalism so different from the nationalism experienced in the rest of the world.

Like Carrere d'Encausse, most analysts of the Soviet nationalities problem have restricted themselves to the macro-level analysis in their considerations of nationalism, while the meso-level, in which a nationalist movement as such is the basic unit of analysis, tended to be ignored.

The macro-level explanations (whether in terms of non-assimilation, asymmetrical political relationships between the center and peripheries, or others) concentrated on the potential for the emergence and development of nationalism, but failed to determine how far the incongruent relationship between cultural, political, and economic roles was perceived as such at the grass roots and how far this was causing the rise of nationalist sentiment among individuals (the micro-level explanation). The objective presence of adverse social conditions does not, after all, automatically lead to the emergence and development of political nationalism. To bridge the gap between socio-economic processes and political outcome, we have to study nationalist movements "in terms of their overall orientation, their ideological position, their domain of concern, their target support base, and their success in mobilizing this support base."[90]

Meanwhile, conceptual Sovietologists such as Motyl refused to regard dissident ethnic movements as the truly significant manifestations of nationalism in the USSR, mainly because of their numerical insignificance and relatively elitist social composition.[91] How far then is the numerical factor considered to be significant for nationalist development? Analyzing size and scale as factors in the development of national movements, Argyle reached the conclusion that "The nationalist process does not require large movements as well as lower limits for the size of nations."[92] Smith argued against the assertion that nationalism is a "crowd phenomenon," pointing out that "These so-called mass movements turn out to be surprisingly small-scale affairs, measured by the percentage of total population involved, or even by the percentage of upper or middle strata."[93]

It was only in the 1970s that ethnic dissent became a popular topic in Soviet studies, but since that time, the historiography of dissent in the USSR gave considerable prominence to the struggle of the Soviet peoples for their national rights. One must consider the studies of P. Reddaway,[94] J. Rubenstein,[95] M. Schatz,[96] L. Alexeyeva,[97] J. Chiama and J. Soulet,[98] and B. Lewytzkyj,[99] which described ethnic dissent as part of the broad spectrum of intellectual opposition to the Soviet regime and as an integral part of the multidimensional struggle for human and civil rights. Significant studies were devoted to ethnic minority movements, though the scholars' interests were unevenly distributed between them. Ukrainian dissent was examined by J. Bilocerkowycz,[100] K. Farmer,[101] Ya. Bilinsky,[102] and B. Nahaylo;[103] dissent in the Baltic republics by T. Remeikis,[104] S. Forgus,[105] and R. Taagepera;[106] and in the Transcaucasian republics by R. Suny,[107] N. Dudwick,[108] and S. Jones.[109] B. Pinkus and I. Fleischhauer studied the movement of the Soviet Germans,[110] a fundamental book edited by E. Allworth evaluated the Crimean Tatar movement,[111] and S.E. Wimbush and R. Wixman devoted their study to the Meskhetian movement.[112]

The Jewish movement and the Russian conservative movement comprise the most widely investigated topics in the study of ethnic dissent in the

USSR. The most comprehensive and systematic study of the Jewish movement in the USSR was made by Pinkus in his recently published book *Tehiyyah u-tequmah le'ummit* (National rebirth and reestablishment).[113] The book contains a virtually complete bibliography of publications devoted to the Jewish movement in the USSR.[114] Valuable contributions to the study of the Jewish movement were also made by L. Schroeter,[115] S. Ettinger,[116] D. Kowalewski,[117] and C. Shindler[118] in the 1970s. Among the more recent publications, the works of V. Zaslavsky and R. Brym,[119] L. Salitan,[120] E. Drachman,[121] N. Levin,[122] and Y. Goldstein[123] are noteworthy.

J. Dunlop[124] and A. Yanov[125] developed two major conceptual frameworks for the examination of contemporary Russian conservative nationalism and dissent, D. Pospelovsky[126] was the first to initiate the systematic study of the contemporary Russian conservative movement in the early 1970s. W. Lacqueur,[127] S. Carter,[128] and T. Parlan[129] continued these studies in the late 1980s and the 1990s.

In their studies, J. Azrael, S.E. Wimbush, R. Misiunas and R. Taagepera, D. Pospelovsky, and R. Sakwa cited ethnic dissent as a political factor in inter-ethnic relations and simultaneously as symptomatically important;[130] B. Nahaylo and V. Swoboda regarded it as a significant factor in the general historical process in the USSR.[131]

The unauthorized circulation of uncensored publications—*samizdat*—constitutes a unique socio-political phenomenon deeply rooted in Russian society's traditions. According to Saunders, an early student of this phenomenon, "*Samizdat* is a Soviet term coined by post-Stalinist dissidents for the old revolutionary practice, dating from the days of czarist censorship, of circulating uncensored materials privately, usually in manuscript form—nonconformist poetry and fiction, memoirs, historical documents, protest statements, trial records, etc. . . . Today's *samizdat* has post-October antecedents as well as pre-revolutionary ones—in the private printing and circulation of manuscripts written by the Left Opposition in the 1920s and 1930s, after it was denied the use of the party's printing facilities."[132]

Comparing the activity of the Left Opposition in distributing their documents with the *samizdat* network of the post-Stalinist period, Saunders stressed that the former "was part of the last resistance to the Thermidorian undertow in the Soviet Union" whereas "the rise of *samizdat*, its steady spread, and the deepening politicization in post-Stalinist society are part of a worldwide revolutionary upswing."[133] Though the term *samizdat* may be applied to any "practice . . . of circulating uncensored materials,"[134] it has come to refer to the dissident occurrence of the post-Stalinist period. The core of *samizdat* consists of original materials written for open uncensored distribution. In general, *samizdat* rejected anonymity: the authors and editors publicized their names, addresses, telephones, striving to create enclaves of civil society in the totally censored world.

The emergence of *samizdat* in the late 1950s, as well as all other nonformal activities, can be considered to have resulted directly from liberal changes in Soviet society. On the other hand, *samizdat* expressed public discontent with the rate and extent of socio-political changes in the country.

There was a gradual hardening of the political line after Khrushchev's fall, culminating in the arrests and trials of dissident intellectuals (1965–1968). Thus, in particular, the trial of Siniavskii and Daniel led to numerous petitions by Soviet citizens protesting repression. Saunders wrote that 1966–1967 might be considered the time when *samizdat* evolved from its cultural to a political orientation.[135]

Any student of dissident activity should note that *samizdat* comprised the major focus of activity for all opposition movements. By bringing uncensored information to public attention and expressing independent positions, different opposition movements seem to have pursued the same objectives: (1) Launching a dialogue with the ruling elite so as to influence the decision-making process; (2) Recruiting supporters in the USSR; (3) Mobilizing international public support. At different times, various dissident groups attached varying prominence to each of these three objectives, although all three were utilized by all groups. There was actually a "division of labor" between censored publications and *samizdat*. Dealing with "unauthorized" ideas, views, opinions, topics, approaches, styles, names, and so on, *samizdat* described events and circumstances with integrity. Until the emergence of a free press under *glasnost*, it successively tackled topics that had otherwise vanished from the official publications and the mass media. The issue of ethnic politics was never discussed officially—in censored publications—in the Soviet Union before *perestroika*; ethnic groups were traditionally considered subjects to be governed, not masters of independent policies. The topic seems to have resurfaced only after many of the ethnic movements' objectives had already been met. As such, the *samizdat* documents of ethnic movements comprise the most important evidence of the emergence of ethnic politics.

Structuring the Material

In their article "Nationalism and Reform in Soviet Politics," M. Beissinger and L. Hajda pointed to the shortcomings in studies of the nationality factor: "There is a nationalities factor to every component of Soviet politics. ...Unfortunately, it is also the nationalities factor that was so frequently omitted in previous models of Soviet politics and in the standard projections of the Soviet future. The traditional models of Soviet politics . . . raised nationality issues infrequently and contained little in the way of well-developed conceptions of ethnic politics. The ideas they did present generally lay outside the mainstream of studies of ethnic politics elsewhere in the world and were usually implied rather than stated directly."[136] Another problem specifically related to studies of dissent in the USSR was indicated by Pinkus: "There is still a considerable lack of comparative studies which would make it possible to establish a clear and well-founded typology of the multi-dimensional expression of dissent."[137]

The structure of this book is designed to introduce into the framework of contemporary ethnopolitical studies the issue of ethnic dissent in the USSR of the post-Stalin era. Chapter 2 discusses the patterns of Soviet nationality policy, concentrating on those of its aspects that contributed to the ethnic revival in the USSR. Chapter 3 deals with the impact of modernization on the ethnic revival in the USSR. It analyzes typical reactions of different ethnic movements to Western models of social, political, and cultural development. Chapter 4 examines the issue of relative deprivation as it found expression in *samizdat*. The chapter establishes a typology of relative deprivation: the method employed here is to discover which forms of deprivation were most frequently cited in *samizdat* documents. This aims to see which collective ethnic perceptions of "relative deprivation" were the most stable, following set patterns or models.[138] Chapter 5 evaluates the political demands, strategies, and programs of different ethnonationalist movements in their evolution toward the advanced stages of ethnopolitics. Chapter 6 examines various sources of legitimization cited by the ethnic movement to substantiate their political demands. Chapter 7 examines the value orientations of the political ideologies elaborated upon by the dissident ethnic movements. It evaluates their inclination toward either ethnocentrism or polycentrism, the choice sources, and the potential for violent conflicts. Finally, chapter 8 discusses the mobilization capacity of ethnic *samizdat*.

This study focuses on the *samizdat* documents of sixteen ethnic groups,[139] produced mainly in the period of 1964–1986, from Khrushchev's downfall until the first evidence that *glasnost* intended to deal with ethnic issues, specifically as expressed at the plenum of the Central Committee in January 1987. It is based mainly on original *samizdat* documents from the *samizdat* archives in Munich, which were collected and catalogued by the *samizdat* staff of the Radio Liberty Division. These documents were published as *Sobraniie dokumentov samizdata* (30 vols., 1972–1978). Since 1974, documents also appeared periodically in *Materialy samizdata*. Pinkus has estimated that some 6,000 documents had been listed in the Archives of

Samizdat by 1987.[140] The second major source is the *Evreiskii samizdat*—collection of Jewish *samizdat* (27 vols.) issued by the Center for Research and Documentation of the Hebrew University, Jerusalem. Petitions, letters, and appeals by Soviet Jews were published in *Petitsii i obrashcheniia evreev SSSR* (10 vols.), issued by the forementioned Center for Research and Documentation. Finally, a few documents were found in four volumes of *Vydan'ni zgurtavannia belarussiy u Vialikay Brytani* (Publications of the Union of Byelorussians in Great Britain) and in my private archives.

CHAPTER 2

Soviet Nationality Policy:
Theory and Practice

Ideology versus Pragmatism

Before examining the political principles conceived by dissident ethnic activism, it is important to review the overall Soviet nationality policy from a political perspective. Since Soviet leaders from Lenin to Gorbachev deemed it necessary to embellish their political decisions with ideological motives, scholars tend to analyze Soviet politics from an ideological perspective. As J. Dunlop stated: "From its inception, the Soviet Union has been an ideocracy.... The West confronts an unremitting threat in the form of this metastasizing ideology."[1] With closer scrutiny, however, it would seem that the impact of ideology on the decision-making process in the USSR has often been somewhat overestimated.

The Leninist nationality policy was the foremost slogan of Soviet propaganda for decades: all political decisions concerning the so-called nationality question in the Soviet Union were justified on the basis of this aspect of Marxist-Leninist theory. For example, as late as 1988, Kh. Bokov, then chair of the Supreme Soviet of the Checheno-Ingush Autonomous Republic, published an article in the party magazine *Kommunist* that defended the deportation of his own national group during World War II.[2] That same year *Kommunist* also published an article by Soviet scholar Dr. B. Zeimal, castigating Stalin's deportation policy as a criminal act.[3] Ironically, both authors cited Lenin to validate their respective positions. In fact, this is but one example of the excessive breadth with which Lenin's dialectical methodology could be applied to the nationality question, causing untold confusion to Soviet scholars and students.

There is, however, no real contradiction here. Like Marx and Engels before them, Lenin and the Bolshevik Party preoccupied themselves with converting ethnic interests into "class solidarity," placing particular emphasis on and carefully articulating their positions with regard to the nationality question. According to R. Conquest, "in adapting Marxist theory to the conditions of the multinational Russian Empire, it [the Russian Social Democratic Worker's Party] had perforce to develop a detailed program with regard to national minorities."[4] The Party's program, adopted at its Second Congress (1903), promised "equal rights for all citizens, irrespective of sex, religion, race, and nationality," as well as "the right of the population to receive an education in its own language, . . . the introduction of the native language on equal terms with the State language in all local, public, and State institutions." Finally, "the right of self-determination for all nations comprising the State" was proclaimed.[5]

Conquest was careful to point out that Lenin's sole understanding of the right to national self-determination was the right to political independence, that is, the right to secede from the empire and form separate national states. As an advocate of "a centralized large state,"[6] Lenin was vigorously opposed to any form of decentralization, whether via the establishment of a federalized state structure or the granting of cultural autonomy to non-Russian ethnic groups. He also made no secret of his belief that the right of self-determination was not valued by the Bolsheviks per se, but was included in the Party's program for pragmatic reasons, so as to mobilize the support of those ethnic minorities then seeking political independence. He was quite frank in his declaration that "the interests of the preservation of the Socialist Republic"[7] supercede the rights of national groups to self-determination and he believed that "recognition of the *right* to self-determination" did not mean that it would be guaranteed to "any one nation" automatically.[8]

The wide array of nationality rights recognized by Lenin was actually rendered impractical in view of the many restrictions that he promoted. For instance, while he asserted that national groups had the right to receive education in their own languages, he also denied them the right "to determine the content of this education."[9]

In light of this ambiguity, Lenin and the Bolsheviks found that they had considerable room for political maneuvering and for arbitrary decision-making once they had assumed power. This became evident in the wake of the February Revolution of 1917. The Revolution provided the minority nationalities of the Russian Empire with an opportunity to function as independent political actors, and independent ethnic politics led to the disintegration of the Empire reaching its zenith after the Bolshevik Revolution.

Conquest noted that from April 1917 to May 1918, eight national governments and many more national parties emerged, each of them demanding autonomy. Similarly, regional governments were established in the Don and Kuban regions and in Siberia.[10]

The Bolshevik leadership, seeking to strengthen its constituency, announced its support of these ethnic minority movements. *The Declaration of the Rights of the Peoples of Russia*, issued one week after the October Revolution, proclaimed the sovereignty and equality of all the peoples of Russia and recognized their right to self-determination (including their right to secede and create independent states),[11] while another document, an *Appeal to All Muslim Toilers of Russia and the East*, issued on 20 November 1917, called on Muslim peoples to "organize their national life, fully and without hindrance."[12] Other signs of Bolshevik goodwill included the return of several religious relics to the Ukraine and a ban on the further settlement of ethnic Russians in territories inhabited by the Kazakhs and the Kalmyks at the expense of the indigenous population.

Nevertheless, while officially espousing the right of secession for the constituent nationalities of the Russian Empire, the Bolsheviks repressed any attempts to realize that right, regardless of the ethnic group's political and ideological orientation or loyalty to the Moscow-based government. Even the temporary recognition of Georgian independence and Bashkir autonomy represented mere tactical concessions, which were repudiated by the Bolshevik government at the first opportunity. As Conquest demonstrated, the right to self-determination was achieved by ethnic minorities only when the Bolsheviks were unable to prevent it—generally as a result of a military defeat.[13] Yet, even before the February Revolution, Stalin presented what could be perceived as ideological grounds for the future regime's policies: "The so-called independence of so-called Georgia, Armenia, Poland, Finland, etc., is only an illusion and conceals the utter dependence of these apologies for states on one group of imperialists or another."[14]

Another "tactical concession" aimed at counterbalancing secessionist trends among the nationalities was the *Declaration of the Rights of the Toilers and Exploited Peoples* (1918).[15] Although, as we have already noted, Lenin had been vigorously opposed to any form of decentralization whatsoever, it was under his auspices that the *Declaration* was issued, and this document actually determined "the specific character" of Soviet federalism. Unlike federations that are more traditional, it was not the member states and autonomies that delegated a part of their plenary powers to the federal government of the Soviet Union, but the central government that received the authority to determine the spheres of competence for each autonomous republic. In fact, with the sole exception of the Bashkir autonomy, all member units of the Russian Federation were "nominated" by the center, that is, established by decrees of the VTSIK (The All-Union Central Executive).

By 1921, at the end of the Civil War, the Bolsheviks controlled the greater part of the territory of the former Russian Empire. Between 1920 and 1922 a series of treaties was signed between the RSFSR and the Soviet Republics, each of which enjoyed the status of an independent state. Formally recognizing the right of secession for all sides, these treaties formulated specific models of relationship between each republic and the Russian Federation. Thus, while the treaty with Azerbaijan stipulated this republic's subordination to the Russian Federation, the Khorezm Peoples' Republic enjoyed self-government in most areas. It was only the Union Treaty, signed by the Soviet Republics on 30 December 1922, that instituted greater uniformity among the different models, thereby confirming the subordination of all republican governments to the center. The treaty granted republican governments jurisdiction over the Commissariats of Agriculture, Internal Affairs, Justice, Education, Health, and Social Security only.

Even when signing the Union Treaty, Communist leaders of the non-Russian republics attempted to resist the growing power of the center. In the course of discussions on drafting a Constitution for the Union of Soviet Socialist Republics, representatives of three of the four republics signatory to the Union Treaty demanded greater independence. At the Twelfth Party Congress (April 1923)—the last serious attempt by ethnic minority Communist leaders to win back resources and power from the center—Ukrainian, Georgian, and Byelorussian delegates proposed amendments to the draft Constitution that would grant them republican, rather than all-Union, citizenship and control over their respective armed forces, foreign affairs, and trade. They also demanded the separation of the autonomous republics from the Russian Federation (thereby providing them with the option of joining the Soviet Union independently) and the breakup of the Transcaucasian Federation. Each proposal was rejected by the Congress.

According to Goble, the ratification of the First Constitution of the USSR by the Second Congress of Soviets of the USSR (31 January 1924) marked the demise of ethnic politics and the emergence of the nationality question. From this point onward, neither the anti-Communist rebellion in Georgia (1924), the peasant resistance movement in Central Asia, nor the individual rebellions of several local Communist leaders could bring about any significant changes in the existing situation. In the 1930s, republican leaders who expressed opposition to Moscow's policies were labeled as counterrevolutionaries and exterminated.

Of course, it would take more than repressive measures to assure stability in a multinational state, and one important means of ensuring the regime's control was ethnic domination. This was realized in two spheres: institutional and "situational." Institutional domination by the Russian majority was secured by: (1) the Communist Party's monopoly of power in the state, officially asserted by the party program of 1919, (2) the electoral system, and (3) the structure of executive power:

1. The federalist principle was flatly rejected by the party; republican and autonomous central committees "enjoyed the status of regional committees and were wholly subordinated to the central committee of the RCP (Russian Communist Party)."[16] In this way, the Moscow-based Central Committee gained unrestricted and undivided power throughout the country.
2. The procedure by which representatives were elected to the Council of Nationalities[17] of the Supreme Soviet automatically secured an overwhelming majority for the RSFSR in this chamber. Recently, Moscow attorney A. Makarov presented the Constitutional Court with party documents proving that the ethnic composition of the highest legislative body was strictly regulated by secret Politburo instructions.
3. Most republican institutions with executive power were subordinated to their respective, central, Moscow-based bodies.

Situational domination manifested itself in the overrepresentation of Russians in the party, state, and professional elites of the Union and its autonomous units. Basing himself on the Soviet periodical *Revoliutsiia i natsional'nosti* (1930), Conquest cited the following data. In 1922, Russians comprised 72 percent of the party's total membership. Although they constituted 53.6 percent of members of the Communist Party of the Ukraine, 79.4 percent of Ukrainian Communists considered Russian to be their native language. In 1929, the peoples of Daghestan accounted for only 25.3 percent of the employees at the headquarters of the Daghestan government. In 1931, Bashkirs composed 8.1 percent of the workers in the state apparatus of the Bashkir Autonomous Republic and only 10.5 percent of the labor force employed in the autonomous republic's heavy industry. Conquest also cited numerous instances of Russian discrimination against the indigenous populations of several regions: one common practice was setting lower wage rates for ethnic minority workers.[18]

While they were still seeking to consolidate their power in the multinational state, the Bolsheviks needed a loyal core of ethnic minority supporters in order to control the potentially rebellious masses. To achieve this, the Soviet authorities made concerted efforts to combat situational domination of the country by ethnic Russians in the first years of the regime: in the 1920s they launched an official campaign to nationalize the party and state apparatus and cadres (*korenizatsiia*), to combat Great Russian chauvinism, and to promote certain members of ethnic minority groups to the upper echelons of power. Nevertheless, all deviations from the political line prescribed by the center were suppressed. Institutional domination was preserved by the Soviet regime until the repeal of Article Six of the Soviet Constitution[19] and could be discerned to some degree until the breakup of the Soviet Union.

Building the System of Ethnic Stratification

Russian domination was essential to the system of ethnic stratification that was exploited to maintain effective control over the country. The Soviet federal model established different degrees of autonomy and respectively, non-equal rights for different federal units [union republics, autonomous republics, autonomous *oblasts* (regions), *okrugs* (districts)] providing legal grounds for ethnic stratification. In an analysis of the Soviet federal structure, A. Khazanov noted that higher levels of autonomy "mean the provision of certain advantages in such spheres as education and culture, in social advancement (including various types of official and non-official affirmative action), in economic development, and in simply protecting national interests."[20]

Since the 1930s, ethnic stratification gradually assumed even greater importance in the Soviet Union. With the introduction of internal passports, the nationality (i.e., ethnic origin) of the individual was recorded alongside his social origin and became an official criterion for the deprivation of rights (and, conversely, the granting of privileges). While the campaign against "Great Russian chauvinism" slowly tapered off, the struggle against "bourgeois nationalism" increased. Simultaneously, the dominant status of the Russians, previously dissembled by Soviet propaganda, received official confirmation. The Russian people emerged as the dominant group in Soviet ideological constructions and served as an example to be emulated by other nationalities. In the late 1930s—and particularly during World War II—the preeminence of traditional Russian symbols, including the symbolic representation of the Russian Orthodox Church, was restored. Perhaps the highest expression of the decision to endorse the guiding role of the Great Russian people can be found in Stalin's famous speech at a reception for Red Army commanders (1945). In this speech, Stalin defined the Russian people as "the most outstanding of all the nations within the Soviet Union,...the guiding force of the Soviet Union among all the peoples of our country."[21] In the late 1930s, a drive for cultural-linguistic russification was launched in the USSR: The Russian language was introduced as a compulsory subject in national schools (1938); languages that had previously used the Arabic script and, in the 1920s, had adopted the Latin script (in the wake of Ataturk's linguistic reform in Turkey), were forced to employ the Cyrillic script; Russian loan words were imposed on ethnic minority languages (often in place of native expressions), and so on. At the same time, "Marxist-Leninist theoretical concepts" were brought into line with current political needs. This brought about a dramatic change in official Soviet historiography. For instance, in the first years after the revolution, the annexation of ethnic minority territories by czarist Russia was regarded as "absolutely evil": by late 1940s it was considered "absolutely good." Similarly, leaders of ethnic resistance movements evolved from "revolutionary heroes" to "traitors" and "foreign agents."

It has already been noted that both ethnic and social stratification served as effective instruments in achieving control over the multitudes of ethnicities, religions, languages, and cultures, and over unevenly developed regions. In some respects, the patterns of ethnic and social (class) stratification set up by the Soviet regime were similar. The Russian people served as the "hegemonic" working class, whereas Ukrainians, Byelorussians, Georgians, and other major nationalities were analogues of the "working peasantry," whose class-consciousness could potentially reach that of the working class. In this way, ethnic, like social, stratification regulated social mobility.

Furthermore, whereas the revolutionary potential of the class struggle had been exhausted by the late 1930s, Stalin found that ethnic stratification could be a serviceable counterpart. It is worth noting that from 1941 to 1944 seven entire nationalities that had previously enjoyed autonomy were accused of collaboration with Germany and deported to Siberia or Central Asia.[22] Mass deportations had been a common practice of the Communist regime since its very inception, but all previous deportations were carried out against members of social groups (class enemies)—not against ethnic groups. By charging entire nationalities with high treason, Stalin indicated his intent to impose the model of the class struggle on the nationality question, with the deported nationalities serving as the equivalents of "exploiter classes."

During the brief but significant period of Khrushchev's "thaw," the Soviet leadership dissociated itself from the extremes of Stalin's nationality policies. Soon after Stalin's death, the vigorous anti-Semitic campaign ceased, and its surviving victims were rehabilitated. In his secret speech at the Twentieth

Party Congress, Khrushchev criticized the practice of mass deportations, and one year later, in 1957 the Supreme Soviet exonerated all the deported peoples with the exception of the Volga German and the Crimean Tatars.[23] Large groups of exiled Lithuanians, Latvians, Estonians, and Western Ukrainians were granted amnesties and allowed to return home, while more moderate views concerning Russian annexations and the national liberation movements of ethnic minorities were adopted by official Soviet historiography. Another important change ushered in by Khrushchev was a certain degree of decentralization. In 1957, republic-based Councils of National Economy, answerable to the republican governments, were established in place of ministries. Leaders of republican governments were organized in the All-Union Council of Ministers and the republics enjoyed greater independence in economic, planning, and budgetary matters.

The most powerful impetus underlying Khrushchev's nationality policy seems to have been the creation of a homogeneous Soviet society. The new *Program* of the Communist Party of the Soviet Union, adopted by the Twenty-second Congress of the CPSU (1961), emphasized that "With the victory of Communism in the USSR, the nations will draw still closer together, their unity will increase, and the Communist traits common to their spiritual make-up will develop."[24] The *Program* also recognized that much remained to be done with regard to ethnic relations: "The closer the intercourse between the nations and the greater awareness of the country-wide tasks, the more successfully can manifestations of parochialism and national egoism be overcome."[25]

The *Program* indicated that the main focuses of Khrushchev's policy were cultural-linguistic russification and internal migration. "The Russian language," stated a major section of the document, "has, in effect, become the common medium of intercourse and cooperation between all peoples of the USSR."[26] The significance of internal migration was emphasized by the Program as well: "The appearance of new industrial centers, prospecting and the development of mineral deposits, the virgin lands development project, and the growth of all modes of transport increase the mobility of the peoples of the Soviet Union. The boundaries between the constituent republics of the USSR are increasingly losing their former significance...."[27]

Yet, despite the seeming liberalism that characterized the Khrushchev era, none of these policies led to any structural modifications in the key principles of Soviet nationality politics. On the contrary, all manifestations of ethnic nationalism and efforts by republican leaders to achieve greater independence from the center were brutally repressed. In 1962, a group of young Ukrainian intellectuals was charged with high treason for writing a document that called on the Ukrainian people to realize their constitutional right to secede from the USSR. Nor were party officials exempt from charges of "nationalism" or "showing indulgences towards nationalist sentiments." Among the many who were dismissed from their positions were a Deputy Chairman of the Council of Ministers and the Chairman of the Republican Trade Union Council in Latvia, the Chairman of the Council of Ministers in Kazakhstan, and the First Secretary of the Central Committee in Armenia. Finally, in 1962, Khrushchev reversed his policy of limited decentralization in favor of renewed centralization. Soon after Khrushchev's fall (1964) the Councils of National Economy were disbanded and the industrial ministries were restored.

Khrushchev's short-lived thaw did not alter the fundamental positions of Soviet nationality politics, but its impact on the current ethnic revival in the former USSR cannot be underestimated. R. Emerson noted that "Both theory and practice amply support the belief that democracy at the imperial center is a matter of real importance for colonial political development."[28] Of course, Khrushchev's reforms by no means met the standards of a Western democracy, but by publicly discrediting Stalin's regime and castigating his policy of terror, as well as by reducing, if only partially, the complete control of the center over the country and its culture, they introduced a "human dimension" into the system of collective values that dominated Soviet society. Since that time, the totalitarian regime has been persistently challenged by public concern for human rights and civil liberties. "The growing importance of the dignity and freedom of the common man originally coincided with concern for the freedom and destiny of the nation—a concern that developed and became increasingly popular as the process of modernization developed," said I. Kamenetsky in his "Preface" to a collection of articles, *Nationalism and Human Rights.*[29]

The "Sip of Freedom": How Fatal?

In the long term, the "sip of freedom"[30] permitted after Stalin's death, proved to be fatal for the totalitarian Soviet Empire. The nationality policies of Stalin's successors were overshadowed by overt ethnic protests of various sorts, from organized and spontaneous peaceful protests to acts of violence.[31] Even more significant, as J. Azrael noted in 1978, is the fact that a considerable number of the Soviet nationalities "produced outspoken critics of official nationality policies and practices. These critics managed not only to replenish their own ranks in the face of hundreds, if not thousands of arrests, but also to establish dynamic and resilient dissident organizations, ranging from clandestine parties, through editorial boards for the preparation of regular *samizdat*, or underground journals, to networks for the public circulation of programs, petitions, and letters of protest."[32]

In response to the growing ethnic revival there were two important, interrelated concepts promoted by Brezhnev's leadership throughout the 1970s. The first was a portrayal of the "Soviet people" (*Sovietskii narod*) as a "new historical community," which emerged as a result of the shared experience and Communist ideology. The appearance of this "Soviet people" was proclaimed by Brezhnev in his report to the Twenty-fourth Party Congress in 1971. Previously, Khrushchev had regarded the "Soviet people" as a final product of a certain evolutionary development, which included two sequential stages: the drawing together of nations and their fusion into each other. In contrast, Brezhnev's dialectical formula indicated a "higher unity" of the Soviet nations that were supposed to be flowering individually and drawing together at the same time. The particular role of the Great Russian people in this process was stressed by Brezhnev: "All the nations and nationalities of our country, above all, the Great Russian people, played a role in the formation, strengthening, and development of this mighty union of equal peoples that have taken a path of socialism."[33] The second concept was that of Russian as the language of intercourse between nationalities. The Soviet leadership attributed to the Russian language the major role in the process of the "drawing together of nations."

The major idea behind the promotion of these two points was the attempt by the Soviet authorities to accelerate the cultural-linguistic homogenization of Soviet society. The results of the 1970 All-Union census indicated not only a decline in the proportion of the Russian and Slavic population[34] and a considerable increase in the proportion of the Central Asians,[35] but also an unsatisfactory growth of linguistic russification of non-Russians. In 1970, 11.5 percent of non-Russian peoples declared Russian as their mother tongue (as opposed to 10.8 percent in 1959), and 37.1 percent as their second language. Considering the drop in proportion of the Russians in the total population, the share of the native Russian-speakers has declined from 59.3 percent in 1959 to 58.7 percent in 1970.

Since the 1970s, energetic measures have been taken to promote linguistic russification. The main emphasis was on spreading and improving the teaching of Russian in the non-Russian republics, as well as on the expansion of the circulation of Russian publications, particularly periodicals. Based on the 1979 All-Union census, this policy had considerable success: 13.0 percent of non-Russians reported Russian to be their native language (an increase of 1.5 percent) and 49.1 percent reported it to be their second language (an increase of 12 percent). Beyond doubt, Russian had become the *lingua franca* of the Soviet nationalities.

The new 1977 Constitution of the USSR gave legislative expression to Brezhnev's policy of centralization. While the competence of the republics was presented in strictly limited terms defined by the Constitution of 1936, Paragraph 12 of Article 73 of the new Constitution virtually abolished whatever independence the republics enjoyed (even if only on paper), reserving for the federal government the right to resolve any questions of "federal importance." According to the 1977 Constitution, democratic centralism was the fundamental principle of state organization. Article 6 clearly determined the leadership role of the Communist Party, whereas the previous Constitution had made only vague mention of its political role. Ironically, the 1977 Constitution also preserved the federal principle in its ethnoterritorial form and the right to secession. However, as B. Nahaylo and V. Swoboda pointed out, "The facade of federalism was being maintained," while politically and economically the country was "run like a centralized, unitary state."[36]

According to M. Beissinger and L. Hajda, the main feature of the Soviet pattern of multinational society was "an ethnic division of political labor."[37] Carrere d'Encausse estimated that in the mid-1970s the Russians constituted 87.5 percent of Politburo members, while the Secretariat had no representatives of other nationalities. In 1970, the proportion of Russians and other Slavs in the Council of Ministers of the USSR was 90 percent, and the same held true for the chairmen of most of the state committees, "who have power both at the center and in the republics (*Gosplan* [State Planning Committee], State Security, etc.)."[38] Beissinger and Hajda assessed that in 1985, "85 percent of Central Committee secretaries ($n = 13$), 83 percent of USSR ministers and state committee chairmen ($n = 83$), and 88 percent of the top military commanders ($n = 17$) were Russians."[39]

On the other hand, representatives of the titular nationality predominated in party and governmental institutions of most union and autonomous republics. This fact, however, did not attest to the authority of the republican powers. Once Brezhnev's "collective leadership" assumed control, the scope of republican jurisdiction was reduced considerably and limited to questions of inferior importance, such as communal and housing services, consumer services, local transportation, social security, and a few others. The republican Supreme Soviets were subordinated to the Supreme Soviet of the USSR and, according to Carrere d'Encausse, did little more "than disseminate important decisions made at the center."[40] As for the republics' party agencies, they were formally subordinated to the central party organs and exercised the rights of regional organizations.[41]

N. Diuk and A. Karatnycky concluded, "Soviet leaders recognized the incendiary nature of national discontent and attempted to deal with it through propaganda, coercion, and repression."[42] Beginning in the early 1970s, however, the Soviet regime adopted a more flexible policy and permitted the selective emigration of sizeable groups of Jews and Volga Germans. In a similar vein, visible concessions were made to national languages, arts, and literatures in Georgia, Armenia, and the Baltic republics.

On 14 April 1978, thousands of Georgians crowded the streets of Tbilisi demanding that the Georgian language retain its official status in the Georgian SSR. Previously, the constitutions of the three Transcaucasian republics (they were in force until April 1978), unlike the constitutions of other Union republics, had stipulated that Georgian, Armenian, and Azerbaijani were official languages in their respective republics. The new draft republican constitutions, based on the 1977 Soviet Constitution, omitted those articles stipulating the official languages. "Faced with the vociferous protests, the government yielded and inserted the following provision (article 75) in the final text: 'The state language of the Georgian SSR is Georgian.' The Georgian victory in the constitutional conflict carried over to their Transcaucasian neighbors, who also obtained official confirmation of their linguistic rights."[43]

Only days later, 12,000 people demonstrated in Sukhumi, the capital of the Abkhazian ASSR—attached to the Georgian SSR—against Georgian oppression. As a result of the demonstration, "Basic grievances were recognized and they [the Abkhazians] were granted considerable cultural and economic concessions." Nonetheless, "The Abkhazian request to be transferred from Georgia to the RSFSR was rejected."[44] On the other hand, all attempts by the Ukrainians to achieve greater cultural autonomy were brutally repressed, no concessions were made to the demands of the Crimean Tatars, Volga Germans, and Meskhetian Turks to be repatriated to their homelands, and the Armenian request to normalize the incendiary situation in Nagorno-Karabakh was ignored.

Discussing the process of nationalist development, E. Gellner concluded: "Late industrial society can be expected to be one in which nationalism persists, but in a muted, less virulent form."[45] In his study of the ethnic revival in modern, industrialized society of Western Europe[46] E. Allardt pointed to the increased tendency of European governments to satisfy demands of ethnic minorities, considering this strategy quite effective in muting ethnonationalism and promoting the integration of ethnic minorities into the larger society. Considering the specific character of the modernization process in the USSR (Khazanov defines it as "incomplete"[47]) this conclusion can barely be automatically extended to Soviet society. Consequently, we can only speculate whether this inference would—given different official policies—have applied to the Communist polity. What is clear, however, is that Brezhnev's concessions to nationalist demands were always partial, inconsequential, and overshadowed by repressions, thereby hardening nationalist resolve rather than softening it.

Brezhnev's successors, Iu. Andropov, K. Chernenko, and M. Gorbachev (in the early years of his rule) did not attempt to change the lines of Soviet nationality policy. Scarce references by these leaders to the nationality problem and standard Soviet rhetoric attest to the fact that this issue was not at the top of their political preferences.[48] The concrete measures adopted by the Soviet leadership in the early 1980s left room for ambivalent interpretations by Western observers. Thus, the promotion of G. Aliev in 1982 and E. Shevardnadze in 1985 to full membership of the Politburo was commented on as "the success of the native Communists."[49] On the other hand, the creation in April 1983 of a Soviet Anti-Zionist Committee, or an "extensive purge" of local party officials in Bashkiria, who were dismissed for "ineffective ideological work and tolerating 'anti-social manifestations',"[50] was considered to indicate a toughening of Soviet policy toward national minorities.

The post-Brezhnev leadership seemed to continue to consider the formula "propaganda, coercion, and repression" to be quite effective in dealing with all kinds of so-called ethnic deviations. Like Brezhnev, they failed to realize that overt ethnic dissent (as well as dissent at large) was neither a deviation from mainstream development nor a survival of "the past" as they used to declare (and probably to think). It was the surface of an iceberg that signified the profound latent process of the politicization of the ethnic groups of the USSR.

Evaluating the determinants and parameters of post-Stalinist Soviet nationality policies, Carrere d'Encausse wrote, "Stalin's successors gave up the idea of a complete russification of all Soviet nations. Like Stalin, however, they tried to preserve a basically national and centralized state. Like Stalin, too, his successors thought that the Russian nation should play a central role in the organization of the entire system and that the Russian culture should occupy a preeminent position. What differentiated them from Stalin was their belief that societal development *per se* would lead to the desired unity, without any need to resort to force or violence."[51]

Cultural-linguistic russification and internal migration, hallmarks of Khrushchev's policy, had long played an important role in the multinational society of the USSR. The successful implementation of cultural-linguistic russification, in which Russians dominated education, cultural institutions, mass media, and the like, must be noted. In 1965, Russians constituted 55 percent of the total population of the USSR, that same year a disproportionate 76 percent of the books and brochures, published in the USSR were in Russian, and the ratio increased even further. By 1980, the Russian population had dropped to 52 percent, but 78 percent of the books published were in Russian.[52]

Did this fact signify the growing cohesion of nationalities and their progressive integration? Pipes cautioned against overestimating the significance of the linguistic russification of non-Russian nationals: "The fact that English had been, for a long time, the common language of Indian intellectuals, and since independence has become an official language of India's Parliament, did not and does not indicate a progressive *sblizheniie* [drawing together] of the English and Indians."[53] Only when it is combined with genuine affirmative action and depoliticization of ethnic identities the involvement of individuals in the dominant culture can be expected to switch a person's allegiance from an ethnic group to a multinational state. In his study of nationalism in Scotland, J. Kellas noted: "Among those involved in 'higher culture' are to be found not only the most fervent nationalists, but also the most fervent cosmopolitans."[54]

Internal migration, the second focus of the post-Stalinist nationality policy, actually proved deleterious as a means of integrating the country's disparate ethnic groups. As a result of the migration of Russian and Russian-speaking populations to ethnic minority territories between 1926 and 1979, the proportion of the native population declined in eleven of the fourteen Union republics (not including the RSFSR) and in fourteen of the sixteen autonomous republics of the RSFSR. In the Baltic republics, Central Asia, and the Caucasus, there emerged two culturally divergent, often mutually hostile communities, whose reciprocal alienation was aggravated by the persistent failure of the Russian newcomers to communicate in the languages of the native population.[55] By the late 1960s, the Russian population of the Transcaucasian and Central Asian republics actually began returning to the RSFSR. The census of 1989 indicated the numerical decline of the Russian population in all the three Transcaucasian and in three Central Asian republics (with the exception of Kirghizia, where the Russian population increased by only 5,000 between 1979 and 1989).

The Soviet Union never became a "melting pot." An element of so-called Soviet federalism, in which "national-territorial," rather than territorial, units constituted the components of the federation, automatically reproduced the structure of ethnic stratification in each federal unit. The notorious fifth paragraph in personnel questionnaires (point 3 in Soviet internal passports) obliged individuals to declare their national origins. This information continued to regulate the social advancement of individuals, both in the Khrushchev era and later.

The loss by ethnic groups of their cultural-linguistic identity, combined with the preservation of ethnic stratification, seems to have been envisaged by the Soviet elite as the most effective safeguard of political stability. At the same time, providing an effective mechanism of socio-political control tended to exacerbate the sense of relative deprivation felt by ethnic collectives and hence, to fuel their opposition to the regime.

According to Beissinger and Hajda: "One result of Soviet nationalities policy has been the growing level of education among all nationalities and the rise of national intelligentsias. The Soviet leadership did not foresee, however, that these national intelligentsias would eventually seek to promote their native cultures and to protect them from encroachments from the dominant Russian culture."[56] Another result of the Soviet nationality policy particularly under Brezhnev was indicated by Carrere d'Encausse: "The lack of national leaders at the center prevents the nations from participating on an equal footing in the decision-making process."[57]

Carrere d'Encausse pointed to a deep sociological change within the Party itself, resulting from modernization: "For a long time the Soviet system's rationality was a political rationality, and found expression in the ideological and decision-making authority granted to the Party apparatus, which subordinated other specialists for its own needs. The post-Stalinist apparatus, however, has changed dramatically because, particularly since the early 1960s, its recruitment policy has changed. Since then, the apparatus has recruited their members not only on the basis of political criteria, but also on the basis of technical competence. The consequences of this have been considerable, especially at the periphery. This new technical elite tended increasingly to hold that decision-making should be a function of reality rather than of ideology. It has demanded increasing shares of power in decision-making at the highest level, that of the Party, and has refused to content itself with a subordinate position."[58]

The blocked opportunities on the higher, federal level instigated the pragmatic national party and state nomenclature to seek that "the symbolic institutions and administrative framework of autonomy"[59] acquire real power. Similarly, the intellectuals began to hope for "liberation" from the rule of "aliens" at the center.

CHAPTER 3

The Modernization Process and Ethnonationalism

Most scholars link the rise of nationalism to the modernization process, examining the multidimensional and multidirectional effect of modernization, which is viewed as the self-sustaining economic growth, based on technological development, accompanied by social, cultural, and political changes. "The Europeans began to think of themselves—became capable to think of themselves—as members of national communities—under the influence of print-culture and the Protestant Reformation, with their profound religious, psychological, intellectual, and political consequences. After Gutenberg and Luther, a new kind of individual as well as new kind of cultural and political community emerged in Europe. The preconditions for the rise of nationalism thus appeared. The French Revolution contributed directly to the formation of nationalism when, by *design*, it created a modern nation in France and when it exerted a political and intellectual impact beyond France," R. Szporluk pointed out.[1]

Modernization is present as almost a "compulsory" element in discussing the emergence of nationalism in the former USSR. The indicators of modernization, such as mass education and health care services, rapid urbanization, secularization, and the like, used to be cited as the evidence of successful nationality policy conducted by the Soviet regime. Meanwhile, references to the modernization process often serve as rhetoric figures, failing to specify both the peculiarity of the modernization process in the USSR and the way (or ways) of its influencing the emergence of nationalism among the former Soviet peoples.

Has the process of modernization really had a prolonged direct effect on the rise of today's nationalism, or, once, by having created a new pattern of social communication, it gave the initial "push" to nationalism in and since then nationalism has been reproducing itself from its own resources? The lack of strongly motivated theoretical argument about the role of modernization in the contemporary ethnic revival in the former USSR let some students of nationalism suggest that in the USSR modernization and nationalism might be parallel processes, not necessarily related to each other.[2] There is a small doubt that the connection between modernization and nationalism in the USSR needs closer study.

Here I restrict the consideration of this issue to several remarks relevant to my particular study. The modernization theory suggests that the economic growth, based on the technological development, will be accompanied by congenial social and political changes. The Soviet variant of modernization demonstrates that the distribution of economic, social, and political resources was asymmetrical. The drive towards scientific-technological development since the late twenties brought considerable economic growth and instigated the reform (though partial) of social structures. Meanwhile, the political system not only has not been reformed toward the norms of liberal democracy but also degraded toward pre-modern backward models based on the middle-age order, cult of leader, negation of opposition, and rejection of liberal democracy as a political principle.

The modernization process seems to be structurally elastic. That makes possible relatively autonomous development of each element of the structure. At the same time the reserve of elasticity imposes the functional limits to autonomous development of each element of the asymmetric structure, so to say, requires synchronization of economic, social, and political parameters of modernization. In other words, the modernization process constitutes a systemic structure, and a prolonged misbalance between its components leads to a collapse of the whole system.

The Soviet drive toward industrialization demanded utilizing the enormous scientific resources. That could have been achieved only on the basis of mass education, which brought about the growing level of professional training and broadened the access to information. The wide stratum of intelligentsia that had emerged as a result of this process, not only served the operational needs of the technological modernization, but also adopted the new societal standards. In this respect, Khrushchev's political–legal reforms might be considered an uncompleted attempt of synchronizing the elements of the modernization process. The implementation of Khrushchev's reforms, however, failed to meet the expectations of the Soviet intelligentsia, that is, their perceived normative standards, which themselves to a great proportion had been shaped by these reforms. At the same time, the drive toward political liberalization has shaped the public awareness that an implementation of the desired normative standards is feasible.[3] Conjunction of these factors resulted in the first open public protests in the late 1950s.

The references to the modernization process could be extensively found in the ethnic *samizdat*, which positively connected the emergence of ethnic assertiveness to modernization, specifically, to such concomitants as Westernization and liberal democracy. This section will discuss the patterns of interpretation of this connection attempting to identify different ethnic reactions to the modernization process, its evolution, and political implications.

Syncretism of the Initial Period

Both the democratic and the nationalist movements in the USSR emerged from the same complex of social and political ideas that developed out of the nonconformism prevalent in the first years after Stalin's death. V. Osipov, in his short essay *The Maiakovskii Square* (1970),[4] cited Khruschev's secret speech at the Twentieth Party Congress and the de-Stalinization process that followed as crucial events in the rise of the nonconformist (or, as he called it, "non-formal") movement.

Nonconformism and public protest became, for young Soviet intellectuals, a means of settling a score with their own past. "With the hatred of deceived fanatics we assaulted our werewolf [Stalin],"[5] Osipov wrote. He himself was expelled in 1959 from the university and the Komsomol for publicly protesting against the arrest of a fellow student. According to Osipov, the nonconformists' search for "genuine Marxism" and "unspoiled socialism" played a key role in the formation of their social-political ideas and values. At that time Yugoslavia served as "a model of socialism . . . Lenin, Tito, Togliatti, together with the leaders of the Workers Opposition, Shliapnikov and Kollontai, had indisputable authority. . . ."[6]

While Osipov recognized rudiments of socialist ideology in post-Stalinist nonconformism, another author, Ivan Ruslanov (the pen-name of prominent dissident Boris Yevdokimov), in his fascinating essay, *Youth in Russian History*, written in the late 1960s,[7] credited Western literature, philosophy, and art, which "had become available with the thaw." It is a striking coincidence that both Osipov and Ruslanov described the evolution of young nonconformist "insurgents" to a nationalist philosophy. Ruslanov wrote:

By the mid-1960s yesterday's "nihilist" young leaders returned after serving terms in labor camps or mental hospitals. There were many things that they had seen, understood, experienced. . . . Rebels became revolutionaries. Their interest in Western literature and art became an interest in Russian philosophy, history, and religion, as well as in modern Western thinkers; their former cosmopolitanism was replaced by national self-consciousness. Soviet youth is becoming Russian youth again.[8]

Describing his return from a labor camp Osipov reported: "Not long ago I was a materialist, socialist, and utopianist. The labor camp rendered me a person who believes in God, Russia, and our ancestral heritage."[9]

In 1961, Osipov was tried for his "non-formal" activity together with another young leader of the "nonconformists" of the late 1950s and early 1960s, Eduard Kuznetsov—later a famous figure in the Zionist movement. *Samizdat* documents discussing the biographies of two other Zionist activists, Leonid Kolchinskii[10] and Isai Averbukh[11] reported that both began their political activity with public protests against the Soviet occupation of Czechoslovakia.

The initial period of political dissent in the USSR can be defined as a period of syncretism. But even when the first demarcation lines between the different opposition groups (specifically between "democrats" and "nationalists") were drawn, rudiments of the initial syncretism did not disappear. On the contrary, it sometimes manifested itself in rather curious forms.

In 1967, V. Chornovil, a future leader of the Ukrainian movement (and one of the most powerful politicians in independent Ukraine), was tried in Lviv for his book on the prosecution of Ukrainian intellectuals. In his final plea, he expressed his wonder at an attempt by the authorities to link him with Ukrainian nationalism: "It appears that I am a nationalist in addition to everything else. In fact, I have never dealt with the nationality question in my appeals. Such a conclusion was based solely on the fact that I wrote about violations of the law in Ukraine."[12]

A *Letter by Young Jewish Activists from Riga* addressed to students in Israel and the United States (February 1969), reported on an attempt at self-immolation committed by a nineteen-year-old mathematics student, Ilya Rips. The *Letter* explained that Rips was protesting against discrimination faced by "our people and against the infringement of our right to leave for Israel."[13] Meanwhile, a footnote found in the *Archives of Samizdat*, referring to an account of the event described in *The Chronicle of Current Events*, reported that Rips had demonstrated at the monument of freedom in Riga, holding a placard denouncing the Soviet occupation of Czechoslovakia. The *Chronicle's* version proved to be correct. Later Rips confirmed that "his self-immolation was carried out in protest against the Soviet invasion of Czechoslovakia and had nothing to do with the Jewish emigration issue or his desire for an exit visa."[14] Ironically, after serving a two-year sentence in a psychiatric prison, Rips immigrated to Israel, where he became an observant Jew.

Westernization, Democracy, and Patterns of Political Orientation

Subordinated Groups

The previous chapter demonstrated that demands for democratic change comprised a substantial part of the programs adopted by ethnic minority movements. The 1959 *Draft Program of the Ukrainian Workers and Peasants Union* came to demand secession because of the utter absence of prospects for the democratic development of Ukraine within the framework of the USSR. It considered the bureaucratic methods of management, the harmful results of central planning, the serf-like status of the peasantry, the limited rights of trade unions, and so on. The organization did not regard secession to be an independent value: it was merely a tool to gain political leverage in building a democratic society. They were, therefore, prepared to remove secession from their agenda if democratic reforms were launched in the USSR.[15]

An *Appeal* (1964) by the Initiative Committee of Ukraine's Communists discusses the lack of democratic liberties, the party's dictatorship, and the danger of the restoration of Stalinism in the country, as well as other, "general" problems more than it discusses the nationality question.[16] An early Estonian *samizdat* document entitled *To Hope or to Act?* was provoked by Andrei Sakharov's treatise, *Progress, Coexistence, and Intellectual Freedom.* This response by the Estonian intelligentsia touched on the Soviet invasion of Czechoslovakia, political trials, and a number of other political and economic issues. "Only democratic society can serve as a school of humanity,"[17] concluded the document.

Defending his desire to immigrate to Israel, Jewish activist I. Privorotskii stressed that he wanted to live in a state "with a multi-party system, where people enjoy the right to receive and spread information, to leave their country, and to return."[18] In 1965, Ukrainian philologist Ivan Dziuba emphasized the indivisible connection between the "national idea and all universal humanitarian values."[19] Pointing out that the "supremacy of the national idea is too often fraught with total disregard for other ideas," Dziuba emphasized his allegiance only to such nationalism that "does not neglect, but involves with the infinity of universal humane ideas."[20] Almost ten years later, in 1974, M. Sahaidak, the editor of the *Ukrainian Herald* (*Ukrains'kyi visnyk*)[21] confirmed the commitment of the Ukrainian movement to liberal democratic values. He found "a way out of the impasse" in "the democratization of political and social life via the transition to constitutional government, the guarantee of all human rights,...the abrogation of censorship."[22] A 1976 article in Armenian *samizdat* devoted to the tenth anniversary of the founding of the National Unification Party[23] pointed out that independent Armenia would be a multiparty liberal democracy.[24]

Almost all ethnic minority movements championed the democratization of the Soviet system. They recognized the relevance of universal human values and democratic changes to their ethnic interests. Their documents demonstrate a strong non-isolationist trend, advocating close cooperation between peoples, countries, and cultures and the exchange of information, ideas, opinions, and the like.

Levko Luk'ianenko, in his *Petition to the Chairman of the Presidium of the Ukrainian Supreme Soviet* pointed to the dangers inherent in the official policy of self-imposed isolation from the rest of the world. "In our century it is impossible to isolate people from the diversity of ideas,"[25] he warned. *A Letter by Ukrainian Political Prisoners* (O. Tykhyi and V. Romaniuk) formulated the political principles of an independent Ukrainian state. It stressed that the Ukraine "will maintain friendly and peaceful relations with all countries of the planet, and will closely cooperate with all nations in science, culture, tourism, and the economy," and in other spheres.[26] "The Georgian people is not just one of the nationalities of the USSR; it is also one of the nations constituting the world commonwealth," a *Letter by Six Georgians* to Iu. Andropov, N. Tikhonov, and major Soviet newspapers declared.[27] Lithuanian dissident Balis Gayauskas, in an article written in the Perm labor camp (1980), stated that the Lithuanian people, particularly "the youth has been isolated from the youth of the free world in order to prevent them from becoming infected with ideas of freedom."[28] An anonymous author of an Armenian *samizdat* essay mentioned that one of the political goals of the Dashnak party had been "the protection of bourgeois-democratic liberties along the European model,"[29] but that the Bolshevik regime had interrupted this. Tykhyi and Romaniuk's *Letter* expressed their conviction that "Ukraine soon would gain independence and take its proper place among the great democratic countries of the world."[30]

Very few expressions of anti-Western, anti-modernizing trends can be found in the *samizdat* documents of ethnic minorities. Nevertheless, A. Voronel and V. Iahot, the editors of the *samizdat* journal *Jews in the USSR*, accused Soviet Jews of abandoning their traditions for the benefits of modernization,[31] and the famous Ukrainian dissident V. Moroz described the cosmopolitan United States as "a chaotic and fragmented mixture of all cultures. All the elements of this 'melting pot' lose their cultural wealth."[32]

Discussing another Western democracy, Moroz wrote: "There is the English bank, but there is no English folklore.... The technological function is hyperbolized in a person at the expense of the spiritual function, and this is called progress."[33] These examples seem to comprise a more or less exhaustive list of anti-modernization statements in non-Russian ethnic *samizdat*. Nevertheless, even these very authors regarded democracy as an indisputable value.[34]

Between the 1960s and the 1980s all ethnic minority movements, regardless of their religious and ethnic identification, demonstrated strong pro-Western orientations. They not only advocated Western-style democracy for their fellow nationalities, but also expressed their allegiance to Western policy and social values and stressed the dissociation of their peoples from the Soviet regime and policies. In his *Letter to the Japanese Broadcasting Corporation*, Mustafa Dzhemilev, the leader of the Crimean Tatar movement, expressed his belief that the Soviet occupation of the Kurile Islands was illegal and described the Soviet invasion of Afghanistan as an act of aggression.[35] Estonian dissident Eric Udam, in his *Letter to Residents of All Countries of the Baltic Region* (1977), proposed the creation of a new international alliance of Baltic states (including the three Soviet Baltic republics) to control the implementation of the Helsinki agreements.[36] Behind the request in the *Open Letter* of thirty-eight Baltic activists (1981) to attach the three Soviet Baltic republics to the nuclear free zone of Northern Europe, was the belief that this area should constitute part and parcel of the Western polity.[37] The authors of these appeals could scarcely have believed that their proposals had any chance of being accepted. Their messages were apparently regarded as an affirmation of their pro-Western/pro-European and anti-Soviet/anti-Communist orientations. This was also the objective of Vasyl' Kobryn's *Appeal to the Austrian Catholic Party*, in which he noted the "close cultural, religious, and political links and the shared past of the Ukrainian and the Austrian peoples."[38] Another Ukrainian activist, I. Terelia, in his *Letter to Leaders of the Prague Spring* emphasized that the Ukrainian and Czechoslovakian peoples shared similar fates as victims of "Moscow expansionism."[39] *A Letter of Congratulations to the Leader of Solidarność, L. Walesa* (1980), signed by twenty Lithuanian and Estonian activists, accentuated the relevance of Solidarność's struggle to the Baltic republics.[40]

A number of appeals by ethnic movements were addressed to the peoples and governments of countries otherwise considered among the "bitterest enemies" of the Soviet regime. An *Open Letter to the Friends of Ukraine in China*, published in 1984 in the *Chronicle of the Ukrainian Catholic Church*, announced the Ukrainians' dissociation from the USSR's policy concerning

China: "The Ukrainian people expresses its opposition to the campaign of hostility toward the Chinese people maintained by Moscow. China is not a threat to Ukraine, and Ukrainians will not take up arms against China, notwithstanding Russian instigation against the People's Republic."[41] A *Letter by Five Georgian Dissidents* (Z. Gamsakhurdia, M. Kostava, and others) to Israeli president E. Katzir on the occasion of Israeli Independence Day pointed to the "deep roots" of friendship between Georgia and Israel and stressed that the "example of Israel inspires all enslaved peoples on the planet to believe that the holy struggle for their independence will triumph."[42] Israel, as the main target of Soviet hostility, was chosen by Iosif Terelia, the editor of the *Chronicle of the Ukrainian Catholic Church*, as his desired address in an application for citizenship.[43] "I will begin to serve my new term in the Communist camp as a citizen of the free State of Israel, which you so ferociously hate," Terelia wrote in his *Statement to the Supreme Soviet of the USSR* (1984).[44]

Ethnic minority movements considered Western democracies and their institutions as well as international organizations to be major objects of their efforts to mobilize support. They were also the main vehicles for gaining publicity. A Crimean Tatar document considered its success in attracting "the growing attention of the progressive public in the world,"[45] as one of the movement's most important achievements. Seven of the eleven appeals issued by the Crimean Tatar movement in 1969 were addressed to the United Nations, international human rights organizations, foreign Communist parties, and the world public. Nine of the sixteen petitions by the Jewish movement from the same time were addressed to these groups in addition to Jewish organizations and the Israeli public and leaders.[46]

In the 1960s and early 1970s, many of these appeals abroad were addressed to foreign Communist parties and their leaders.[47] In the later period, however, many such petitions appealed to non-Communist leaders and organizations such as the United Nations (including the General Assembly, Secretary General, the UN commissions, etc.), Amnesty International, the European Commission of Human Rights, the governments and parliaments of the United States and Western Europe, and participants of the Conferences in Helsinki, Madrid, Belgrade, and Vienna.

In their attempts to gain support, numerous appeals to Israel made by the Jewish movement aimed at portraying its allegiance, as part of the diaspora community, to the "center."[48] To some degree, similar expressions of the diaspora's loyalty to the "center" can be found in appeals made by Soviet Germans to German leaders.[49] Another attempt to employ a "diaspora-center" model is found in Meskhetian appeals to the Turkish authorities for protection.[50] On the other hand, a 1984 *Appeal* by I. Terelia to the Ukrainian emigrant community[51] and a 1986 *Letter* by the Latvian Helsinki-86 Group to *Compatriots in Foreign Lands*[52] demonstrated efforts of the "center" to exploit the ethnic solidarity of the "diaspora." Several attempts to mobilize religious solidarity can be found in *samizdat* documents dating from the 1980s. Examples include a *Letter by Twenty-five Crimean Tatars* to the Secretary General of the Islamic Conference Organization (1983)[53] and an *Appeal to Pope John-Paul II* (1986) by the Latvian Helsinki-86 Group.[54]

Appeals of this kind to leaders and organizations abroad not only called for protection, but also attempted to influence the decision-making process. Thus, M. Sahaidak in his article "Partial Détente" attempted to convince the American administration that "détente, when not accompanied by demands for the democratization of the Soviet regime, would have tragic consequences for us, the enslaved peoples."[55] A letter by three Jewish activists *To All People of Goodwill* (1977) emphasized: "The USSR needs Western loans, consumer goods, and technology. This situation can be used to protect...Jews who want to emigrate to Israel."[56] A 1979 *Appeal* by forty-four Jewish refuseniks to members of the United States Congress asked that the Jackson–Vannik amendment, linking freedom of emigration with favorable trade conditions for the USSR, be perpetuated. "The amendment restrains the Soviet authorities from extreme acts of repression," asserted the *Appeal*.[57]

It is noteworthy that ethnic movements tended to motivate the quest for support not only by the interests of their respective groups in the USSR, but also by the political interests of their addressees abroad. Thus, the *Open Letter against Russification* by Seventeen Latvian Communists, demanding that foreign Communist parties influence the Soviet Communist leadership, stated that "the present policies of the Communist Party leaders in the Soviet Union are destroying the world Communist movement."[58] A 1980 *Declaration of the Ukrainian Patriotic Movement* pointed out that an "independent Ukrainian state would faithfully protect the West from Communist expansion."[59] One year later, five German activists wrote a *Letter to Members of the Bundestag* calling on German legislators to demonstrate their resolve in advocating the right of Soviet Germans to emigrate. They warned that if the need to withstand the Soviet threat were not realized by the West, "tomorrow you might find yourselves in our current situation."[60]

The Russian Majority

To a great extent, early manifestations of contemporary Russian nationalism shared the democratic and socialist values adopted in the period of "syncretism." Though indicating that "the worldwide social crisis which has marked the entire history of capitalism and socialism,"[61] the VSKhSON (The All-Russian Social-Christian Union for the Liberation of the People) *Program* found that "the old classical capitalism is being transformed and freed of its most negative traits. Anti-trust laws regulate the economy. Many branches of the economy have been nationalized. Free labor unions are succeeding in their struggle for better working conditions and higher wages. The standard of living of Western Europe is very high and rising fast.... The [Roman] Catholic Church has proclaimed the existence of universal and eternal moral laws, which, if followed, can save both the individual and society from the impasse, which has developed. The non-Communist world is emerging from the social crisis by evolutionary means,"[62] concluded the *Program*. On the contrary, the "decaying Communist world" has no potential for the transformation. In fact, according to the *Program*, "the liberation of the people from the Communist yoke can only be achieved by armed struggle."[63]

The *Program* pointed to "the possibility and need for political cooperation by all countries in the interests of their peoples,...the need for close economic cooperation on a worldwide scale,"[64] and praised "the growing prestige of the United Nations."[65] It proclaimed the separation of powers and a wide range of political, economic, cultural, and religious liberties and human rights as the basic principles of the future "Social-Christian" state. On the other hand, the *Program* offered a variant of "market socialism" as its economic policy. Politically it asserted that:

> The Social-Christian doctrine of state sees as positively evil any system in which power becomes a prize for competing parties or is monopolized by one party. In general, the organization of state power along party lines is unacceptable from the point of view of Social-Christianity. Society should be able to participate directly in the life of the country through local self-government and the representation of peasant communes and national corporations on the highest legislative body of the country.[66]

Proclaiming the state to be "a theocratic, social, representative, and popular entity"[67] the *Program* devised extremely vague and ambiguous structures for a state organization combining elements of parliamentary and presidential republicanism and of monarchy.[68]

The next significant move away from the early values of syncretism was made by Ivan Ruslanov (B. Yevdokimov) in his essay *The Youth in Russian History*,[69] written in the latter half of the 1960s. Several of this essay's fascinating ideas were later adopted by the new wave of Russian nationalism among its main postulates. After reviewing Russian history, Ruslanov concluded that Westernization always had a negative impact on the Russian state and society: according to him, the harmony of Russian life was destroyed by Peter the Great's reforms. The influx of Western ideas challenged the people's confidence in the authority of the Russian Czar and Church, shook the "national mode of life,"[70] raised the problem of a generation gap, and separated the aristocracy from the masses. The appearance of foreigners in Russia only increased the gap between the Russian people and the Russian elite. "Many of them [foreigners] made valuable contributions in various fields," nevertheless, "being Russia's devoted servants and even dying for Russia, they did not know and did not understand the Russian people."[71] Western science and philosophy became rivals of the Russian Church. Russian politics, as well as Russian life as a whole, had lost its "national character," he contended.[72] Peter's reforms, claimed Ruslanov, not only divided Russian society: they provided the impulse for a state of unrest that has not been overcome until today.

Ruslanov's essay seems to have been the first *samizdat* piece to criticize the Russian intelligentsia as being "hostile to Russian organic statehood."[73] Calling the Russian intelligentsia "the most morbid stratum in world history," and accusing it of "full historic responsibility for the downfall of Russia," Ruslanov notes that by disregarding the role of the intelligentsia as a political factor, Russian authorities exploited its interest in "Utopian ideas: its hatred of the government had turned into hatred of Russia, cosmopolitanism, internationalism, [and] lack of comprehension of the Russian national goals."[74] He proclaimed "the Russian revolutionary idea" to be "national neither in its origins nor in its aims.... Socialism, parliamentarism, and political democracy of an arithmetical majority have been deeply alien to, and unnecessary for the Russian self-consciousness.... The Russian commune [*obshchina*], whose economic meaning stems from moral-spiritual grounds, has nothing in common with the socialist cell. The historic Assembly of the Land [*Zemskii Sobor*] was not a parliament but an expression of the idea of unity between the Czar and the people."[75] While European parliaments were elected to control governments in which the people felt no confidence, in Russia "the best people gathered together to assist the czar."[76] These "best people," said Ruslanov, were co-opted for participation in the *Zemskii Sobor* as a result of their magnanimous public service, moral stature, and the czar's confidence in them. "Mechanical elections" are alien to the Russian people. The Russian conception of state, Russian economic and societal institutions, and the Russian mentality bear testimony to the peculiarity of the Russian soul and history: "We have our own path, our own historical destiny, and our own spiritual values.... In the cultural-historical sense we are neither Europe nor Asia. We are a separate continent."[77]

Ruslanov found the most conclusive evidence for the non-Russian character of the Russian revolutionary movement in the non-Russian origins of its leaders. Sharply criticizing "all revolutionary programs" for an absence of national thinking, national sentiment, and for their "easy manner of granting independence to Russian peripheries (areas where Russian blood been spilled and which were linked to Russia economically, geographically, and spiritually),"[78] Ruslanov concluded: "It is easy to sell another's legacy, particularly if this other is not merely an exploiter but also a representative of the hated oppressing nationality."[79]

Ruslanov was one of the first dissident writers to stress the "particular role" of Jews in the Russian revolution. Noting the social-political factors for Jewish opposition to the czarist regime, he described the activity of Jews in the revolutionary movement as a struggle to attain certain ethnic objectives. He found that despite the non-Russian origins of revolutionary leaders and their Westernizing programs, the October Revolution did, in some respects, take on a national character, "in accordance with the inherent rules of development."[80] According to him, "October" was the people's rebellion against the Westernized nobility and intelligentsia—the vengeance of old Russian Moscow on European Petersburg.

Ruslanov resolved a contradiction between his statements on the popular character of the October Revolution and the non-Russian origins of its leaders and most of its participants by dividing revolutionaries into "Communists" and "Bolsheviks." While the "Communists" (internationalists) were rejected and obliterated by the revolution, the "Bolsheviks" ("Muscovite Old Russian party") "revitalized the absurdity of Old Moscow totalitarian statehood."[81] Describing the new Bolshevik state as the "Russia of Ivan the Terrible which possesses modern technologies and nuclear bombs,"[82] Ruslanov was among the first authors to note the combination of a drive for technological modernization with the backward collectivist, social-political views of Soviet Communist doctrine. At the same time he pointed out that "Russia, created by Stalin, became a great power, which raised its military might to an unprecedented level and completed the unification of Russia in its historic and natural boundaries."[83]

Having been influenced by various Russian thinkers, from the early Slavophiles via Berdiaev to Ustrialov, Ruslanov's essay formulated the main postulates of contemporary Russian nationalism, while implying ideas that differed from those offered by later Russian conservative nationalists.

Considering Western ideas—specifically Western democracy—to be unacceptable to Russia, he nevertheless praised their universal values and undeniable relevance for the West. Moreover, he failed to overcome some stereotypes about democracy adopted in the period of "syncretism." He depicted Soviet dissent as a "united front of democratic opposition"[84] and regarded himself as a part of this front. It should be mentioned that Ruslanov's essay championed technological modernization and had nothing in common with the rural nostalgia expressed by so many Russian conservatives.

The Chronicle of Current Events (no. 7, 1969)[85] reported the arrest in March–April 1968 of the so-called Fetisov group, which included economist A. Fetisov and architects M. Antonov, V. Bykov, and O. Smirnov. They had criticized the Soviet political, economic, and social system from particularly totalitarian and chauvinistic positions. Fetisov stated that Sinyavskii and Daniel should have been shot. Protesting against de-Stalinization, Fetisov left the Communist party in 1968. The struggle against "Jewish dominance" comprised a substantial facet of Fetisov's conception. He described the Jewish people as a destructive force and an embodiment of chaos, whereas Stalin and Hitler's regimes were venerated as positive and necessary historical phenomena that prevented the spread of chaos. Economically, the Fetisov group proposed a revival of the patriarchal commune and traditional Russian agriculture in the territory of European Russia and the transfer of all industrial enterprises and workers to Siberia. Unlike the "dissident" nationalism of Ruslanov or VSKhSON, the Fetisov group expressed a rightist reaction by neo-Stalinist orthodoxy to the partial liberalization of Soviet society. It then seemed as if there were no signs of a possible rapprochement between the ideological and political orientations of these two trends.

The *Manifesto of Russian Patriots (The Nation Speaks)*[86] that appeared in 1970 and the ideas of the Fetisov group (as the *Chronicle* presented them) demonstrated a kindred political ideology. "Democracy in its egalitarian variant has proved to be both the result of degeneration and simultaneously its stimulus," stated the *Manifesto*.[87] The idea of equal rights for an "honest man and a cut-throat"[88] was vigorously rejected by the authors, as was the idea that all races, ethnic groups, and the like, should be considered equal. The *Manifesto* asserted that only strong government "guided by national traditions" could resist the process of degeneration resulting from Westernization. In Russia such a government once existed, but "destructive forces" had made enormous efforts to undermine the basis of the Russian mode of life and to recreate an "untypical Russia" along Western lines.[89] But all these attempts were doomed to failure, because the Russian people had its own political ideas, which "could not be forced into the Procrustean bed of the Western liberal-democratic prosperity."[90] It was the idea of a "strong power" that was revitalized and realized by the Bolshevik party in October 1917. Though in the very beginning of Bolshevik rule certain champions of permanent chaos (possibly Jews) had tried to lead the "new societal order," they were "ruthlessly obliterated by a force whose origin they failed to recognize."[91]

Shortly before the appearance of the first issue of *Veche*, Osipov wrote an article entitled *Three Attitudes toward the Motherland*. The complex of ideas dealing with political, social, and technological modernization was defined by the author as "nihilism," and its social impact was classified as a "disaster."[92] In Osipov's opinion, Western ideas "dulled the national spirit, debased its honor and nobility, undermined the faith, depreciated life. In return for all that they brought *freedom*."[93] Declaring that "nihilism" was the main threat to Russia, Osipov's article still did not specify the image of a nihilist, but only alluded to his pro-Western orientation. Nor did the article reject the value of Western democracy—it emphasized that "neither rights nor liberties can bring positive changes: only the call to the Fatherland can do that."[94] Osipov later developed this idea. "I believe that even the problem of human rights in the USSR should be given less prominence in this concrete historical moment than the issue of the dying Russian nation," he contended in his 1972 *Letter to Vestnik RSKhD*,[95] the Russian-language emigrant journal.

In the early 1970s, the individualism asserted by the VSKhSON *Program* was replaced by a declaration of the priority of primordial collectivism: individualism came to be regarded as a serious vice, if not absolutely evil. A lengthy essay by M. Antonov serialized in the first three issues of *Veche*[96] concluded that Western man was inferior because of his individualism, whereas "human origins were grounded in collectivism."[97]

Economic and technological progress, regarded as positive by Ruslanov, provoked extremely negative feelings in Antonov: "Unrestricted industrial development comprises a part of the Western conception, but it is against the Russian mentality."[98] Osipov stated that capitalism is not in accordance with the Russian character. "Machine production is completely alien to the Russian man," he wrote in *Veche* (no. 1, 1971).[99] *Veche*'s editorial, "How Long Do We Have Left to Live?" depicted the "darkness of industry over the spaciousness of Sergei of Radonezh"[100] asserting that "technological progress, this true devil's child, had dug a pit for mankind."[101]

The famous *Letter to Soviet Leaders* by A. Solzhenitsyn (5 September 1973) cited the destruction of the environment and the depletion of natural resources as the main causes of Western civilization's impasse. This updated interpretation transformed the "spiritual impasse" of the West raised by the Slavophiles into an "ecological impasse." Although he rejected economic growth, modern technology, urban development, and the like, Solzhenitsyn did express the hope that Western countries, due to their inner dynamism, would find the way out of this impasse. The latter statement alluded to the VSKhSON *Program*, which noted the West's potential to overcome the "worldwide crisis." Like the VSKhSON *Program* and Ruslanov's essay, Solzhenitsyn's *Letter* gave prominence to the political and social ideas of Western democracy, though he questioned their relevance to Russia. Meanwhile, the conservative camp targeted Western democracy for criticism. Referring to the *Letter to Soviet Leaders*, Osipov contended: "The Russian man agonizes over the distrust that underlines an electoral system, as well as over the calculatedness and rationalism of democracy. The Russian needs the whole truth and cannot imagine that it is comprised of social-Christian, social-democratic, liberal, and other 'truths'. One simple fact must be realized: the Russian nation is not destined for Western-type democracy."[102] Claiming to interpret Solzhenitsyn's ideas, Osipov proclaimed a "law-abiding" authoritarian regime to be the most desirable in Russia.[103]

In contrast to Solzhenitsyn, an article by Shimanov, written in June 1974 (two months after Osipov's article), denounced any prospects for the "impotent and decrepit bourgeois West" to find the way out of the impasse and criticized Solzhenitsyn for his failure to disown "his democratic past."[104] The process of the social-political liberalization of the pre-revolutionary period in Russia was defined as "the inner decay," that caused the "national demise." The February Revolution "with the most democratic system in the world, was an apotheosis of this decay."[105] The anti-Western, anti-democratic position regularly expressed by *Veche*'s authors served as a "cultural code" for the "patriotic camp" from the early 1970s. *Veche*'s editorial, "The Russian Solution of the Nationality Question," devoted to the fiftieth anniversary of formation of the USSR, described the American mode of life as the "loss of national symbols, assimilation, standardization."[106] P. L'vov described the West as a "symbol of decline, darkness, and the Devil's power," and "revealed" the similarity between the "liberal democracy of the West and the permanent revolution of Bronstein-Trotskii."[107]

The major foreign policy guidelines championed by *Veche* were formulated in full accordance with the above-mentioned "cultural code." In the first issue of *Veche*, Osipov insisted that "the key point of Russian foreign policy should be non-interference in the problems of the West. We are strong enough not to look for allies, the more so as our allies have only betrayed us."[108] Describing the policy of isolationism, *Veche* focused its main concern on the Far East. *Veche* (no. 8, 1973) carried material asserting the unlawfulness of Japan's claims to the Kurile Islands: "Not a single inch of Soviet territory can serve as a subject for wrangling."[109] The "Chinese threat" described in Solzhenitsyn's *Letter* prompted expressions of anti-Chinese sentiment in conservative Russian *samizdat*. While Solzhenitsyn intended to emphasize the possibility of armed conflict between two Communist powers,[110] Osipov depicted China as the "quintessence of the most aggressive atheism,"[111] which was fighting for supremacy in the Communist camp, Asia, and the Third World. Apart from "geopolitical considerations," Osipov cited the "racial malice"[112] of the Chinese as a factor of China's expansionism.

The gradual increase in the anti-modernizing trends characteristic of contemporary Russian nationalism resulted in an articulated reaction by the liberal-democratic camp. One of the first responses was voiced by academician A. Sakharov immediately after the publication of the *Letter to Soviet Leaders*. Sakharov evaluated Solzhenitsyn's views as "religious-patriarchal romanticism" and "myth-making."[113] Vigorously rejecting Solzhenitsyn's argument that a democratic regime was unsuited to Russia, Sakharov stated: "I believe that the way of democracy is favorable for our country.... Only a democratic society can forge the people's character for normal existence in our increasingly complicated world."[114]

The most systematic response given by adherents of liberal democracy to Russian conservative nationalism can be found in Soldatov's *Letter to Russian Patriots*, entitled *The Twelve Principles of the Russian Cause*. A prominent activist of the democratic movement, Sergei Soldatov, introduced himself as a "religious believer, a democrat, and a Russian man."[115] He asserted that the situation in contemporary Russian ideology was unsatisfactory. "It seems," wrote Soldatov, "that the revitalization of archaic, authoritarian forms of government is late, whereas fostering theocratic ideas is premature. These projects are utopian, because they have no grounds in the present.... Any oppression of the right to self-determination in the name of authoritarian ambition and egoism seems to be inhumane. Our people are tired of utopianism and brutality...."[116]

Soldatov envisaged a modern, liberal-democratic political system as the single "Russian solution" to the nationality and all other questions. The liberal Russian State, according to Soldatov's program, will cooperate closely with all countries and particularly with the states of Western Europe. Considering Russia a part of Western civilization, Soldatov pointed to the necessity of rapprochement with Europe and the "creative adoption" of European culture. He also proposed a wide range of pro-ecological measures, a modernized urban transport system, and an urban economy, which Russia should learn from the West.

The *Letter to Russian Patriots* can be understood only in the context of the dialogue between Russian nationalists and democrats. It was written by a pioneer of the democratic movement (one of the principal authors of its *Program*) and had it as an obvious objective to discredit the basic premises of Russian conservative nationalism and disprove popular allegations that the democrats neglected matters of national interest.[117] Responding to Solzhenitsyn's demand that all foreign concessions in Soviet territory be liquidated, Soldatov suggested promoting joint ventures. He also envisaged a "Policy of international cooperation in the Far East and Siberia" and "consideration for the reasonable interests of China."[118] (Solzhenitsyn's anti-Chinese invectives were criticized by Sakharov as populist and exaggerated.[119])

Soldatov's program of "unification with Europe," probably the most provocative for Russian conservatives, stipulated the following points:

Reciprocally limited sovereignty within the framework of Europe;

Economic integration with Europe and joining the European Economic Community;

Political integration with Europe, the establishment of a European Commonwealth, and military cooperation if necessary;

The reorganization of the United Nations, providing it with effective international control and the right of global intervention in the affairs of those countries that violated principles formulated in the Declaration of Human Rights.[120]

Communist Ideology and the Soviet Regime

Russian Nationalism

Russian nationalist *samizdat* began with a decidedly anti-Communist and anti-Soviet position. Pointing to the "striking similarity between Communism and fascism," The *Program* of the Social-Christian Union for the Liberation of the People, adopted on 22 February 1964, stated: "The Communist attempt to build a new world and rear a new man has only resulted in the creation of an inhumane world. The Communist system has proved to be the exact opposite of the ideas toward which humanity strives."[121]

Marxism-Leninism was defined as a "doctrine of dictatorship,"[122] that "emerged as a deeply anti-moral, anti-humanist, and anti-national current,"[123] opposed to the people's interests championed by "the Russian revolutionary movement of the 19th–20th centuries."[124] The *Program* viewed "Marxism-Leninism, Stalinism, and Maoism" as "links in the same chain."

The teaching represents a logical whole and cannot be revised in part."[125] The Soviet regime was portrayed as a fulfillment of Communism that turned into a "monstrous system of oppression."[126]

In his short essay, *Life in Prison*, Ruslanov described the founder of the first socialist state as "a man who betrayed his motherland and covered it with blood." "To be a Soviet means to lose one's soul," he asserted, commenting that Communism is "Satanism according to Gogol's interpretation—banality takes the place of grand tragedy."[127]

In his March–April 1970 article "Three Attitudes toward the Motherland," Osipov disdainfully called Marxist theory a "moldy foreign food."[128] Meanwhile, another piece by Osipov, *The Maiakovskii Square*, appeared at the same time, offering a partial revision of the traditional dissident assessment of Stalin. While Ruslanov clamored against the "patriotic hysteria" and "national-chauvinist intoxication,"[129] inspired by Stalin's policies, Osipov credited Stalin's campaign for "stopping the anti-patriotic, anti-religious rage of Trotskysts and extinguishing the Russophobia of [Soviet historian, D.Z.] Pokrovsky."[130] In his article "Three Attitudes toward the Motherland," Osipov ranked the orthodox Soviet Communist between the "patriots" (an absolute good) and "Westernizers" (an absolute evil).[131] *The Manifesto of Russian Patriots* argued that the Bolshevik revolution and the Soviet regime had emancipated Russia from the "harmful" influences of the West.[132] A long essay on the Slavophiles by M. Antonov, a member of the Fetisov group, who represented a rightist nationalist opposition by a part of the Communist orthodoxy, contained a "declaration of principles" in its very title: "The Theory of Slavophilism Is the Highest Achievement of the People's Self-Conscientiousness in the Pre-Lenin Period."[133] The Bolshevik leader was described in this essay as a successor to the cause of the great empire, his ideal of "truth and justice" emanating from the old "idea of a third Rome and New Jerusalem." Antonov reproached Stalin solely for his inefficient struggle against "cosmopolitans without kith or kin" (*bezrodnyie kosmopolity*).[134] Considering Marxism to be linked to the alien Western Catholicism, and Leninism to the Russian Orthodox faith, Antonov stated that the "true *Weltanschauung* adequate to the century-old experience of the people could only be achieved by merging Russian Orthodoxy with Leninism."[135] In his capacity of editor Osipov felt the need to dissociate *Veche* from Antonov's position.[136]

Another dissenting piece by *Veche* related to an *Appeal* (1971) by two Orthodox clergymen, G. Petukhov and V. Khaibullin and an Orthodox believer P. Fomin.[137] The authors called on their correligionists to find practical ways of rapprochement with the state on the grounds of "goodwill," "mutual interests," and "patriotic duty" in order to withstand "the growing danger by the organized forces of Zionism and Satanism."[138] In his remarks, *Veche*'s editor repudiated both the invective against Zionism and the proposed "union with the atheistic state."[139] Osipov expressed his own, revised position concerning the "atheistic state" in an interview given to a correspondent of the Associated Press on 25 April 1972. "We believe that the problem of national specifications is to be and can be resolved under any type of state regime. We consider the Soviet social and political system, if based on national principles and real observance of the Soviet Constitution, completely acceptable."[140]

In his letter to the Russian-language emigrant magazine *Vestnik RSKhD* (November 1972), Osipov argued that the issue of "the dying Russian nation" must take precedence over all other problems. He concluded: "That was why I, who had, in the past, been an active member of the opposition, relinquished the political struggle with the Soviet regime."[141] While Osipov portrayed his reconciliation with the regime as a strategic concession, an anonymous *Veche* correspondent had no hesitation asserting that "patriotism and Communism are not only compatible one with the other, but in our perception, cannot exist without each other."[142]

A long article by G. Shimanov, provoked by Solzhenitsyn's *Letter to Soviet Leaders*, perceived the October Revolution enthusiastically, mainly because it put an end to the rule of "democratic idiots, who yearned for European standards."[143] The Bolshevik regime, "with its *de facto* autocratic system" was, according to him, the most appropriate for Russia. Like Antonov, Shimanov concluded that in future the Soviet authorities should adopt Russian Orthodoxy: only then would they be able to "launch a great transformation of the world."[144] As for Marxism-Leninism, it must not, as Solzhenitsyn believed, be abandoned but "transformed and gradually overcome."[145]

The growing apologia favoring consolidation with the Soviet regime seems to have been a serious point of discord between Osipov and most of *Veche*'s editorial staff. In April 1974, eleven contributors wrote a *Letter* against the editor, criticizing him from a right-wing position.[146] Osipov did not participate in *Veche*'s tenth and last issue.

In August 1974, Osipov and V. Rodionov launched a new patriotic journal, *Zemlia* (The Land). In an introduction to the first issue the editors argued against extreme manifestations of Russian nationalism warning that "nationalism is groundless without Christianity. Any form of atheistic or pagan nationalism is a devilish trick."[147] As if disowning the extremes of Osipov's *Veche*, the new journal emphasized that "the lack of *glasnost* as well as of constitutionally guaranteed human rights are obstacles to the achievement of national objectives."[148]

An example of "pagan nationalism" was quoted in the Jewish *samizdat* magazine *Jews in the USSR* (no. 8, 1974), in an article entitled, "Critical Remarks of the Russian Man on the Russian Patriotic Journal *Veche*". "The Russian people can be saved not by subverting Communism and Soviet power, but by strengthening them by cleansing them of the mold of Zionism. To reject our ideology and our regime means to open a door to the subjection of the state by Zionist capital," contended the anonymous "Russian man."[149] Warning that the single alternative to the Bolshevik regime was "Zionist rule," the author argued: "We have nothing but the Bolshevik party which, even if it does so poorly, defends us."[150]

The most comprehensive call for consolidation with the Soviet regime was given in the almanac *Mnogaia Leta* (Many Years), edited by Gennadii Shimanov. Material published in two issues of the almanac (1980 and 1981) reiterated the anti-Western, anti- democratic, anti-urban, anti-industrial, and xenophobic attitudes that appeared in Russian conservative *samizdat* throughout the 1970s.[151] Undoubtedly, the major message of *Mnogaia Leta* was the urgent need for concord with the Soviet State based on the mystical merging of the "Russian idea" with the ideological doctrine of the Soviet regime. In the final analysis, this regime served as the main legitimizing source for the political orientation and demands of contemporary Russian nationalism.

Nationalism among Ethnic Minorities

Of course, the policies of the ethnic minority movements toward the Soviet regime and ideology differed from those of conservative Russian nationalism. Most *samizdat* documents issued by these movements in the 1960s exhibited a neutral or even positive regard for both. They sought to carry on a dialogue with the former and to use the latter to legitimize their demands. Many early documents contained declarations of loyalty to the Communist ideology and system. "Our lives can serve as examples of adherence to the ideas of Communism," noted the *Appeal* by the Initiative Committee of the Ukraine's Communists.[152] "We pay tribute to the traditional internationalism of the Lithuanian Central Committee of the Communist Party," stressed the authors of a *Letter by Twenty-six Representatives of the Jewish Intelligentsia* to the Lithuanian Communist leader, A. Sniečkus.[153] The *Letter* also mentioned "the high Communist ideals of the equality of all peoples and nationalities," "proletarian internationalism,"[154] and other Soviet mottoes.

An *Appeal* by Crimean Tatars to the Twenty-third Party Congress employed such expressions as "our dear Party," "the great party of Lenin," and so on.[155] In 1965, E. Hovannisian appealed to the party leadership to promote the reunification of Armenia "in the name of Marxist-Leninist ideals."[156] Levko Luk'ianenko, in a letter to the Procurator General, stressed that the *Draft Program* of the Ukrainian Workers and Peasants Union "was grounded in Marxist-Leninist theory."[157] "We have been struggling for an independent Ukraine that would satisfy the material and spiritual needs of its citizens on the basis of a socialist economy and that would gradually evolve toward Communism," Luk'ianenko explained.[158] Another prominent Ukrainian dissident, Ivan Dziuba, commented on "the Ukrainian socialist nation" and its "contribution to the common cause of peace, democracy, and socialism."[159]

V. Chornovil in a letter to "My dear friends" from the labor camp found it necessary to refute "rumors" about his renunciation of socialism. "In spite of all allegations, I stood and stand now for socialism,"[160] he assured his supporters. Chornovil pointed to two variants of socialism. The Czechoslovakian and the Yugoslavian models represent the first, genuine socialism, while Stalin and Mao represent the second variant. "Genuine socialism," supposed Chornovil, cannot be imagined "without securing democratic liberties... without real guarantees of nationality rights in a multinational state."[161] Even while assessing Armenian Bolshevism as a "disaster to Armenian social life"[162] the anonymous author of a historical essay on Armenia proclaimed his adherence to Marxist-Leninist theory.

As a rule, non-Russian *samizdat* documents considered the October Revolution and Bolshevik power to be positive phenomena for ethnic minorities: they were officially granted wide-ranging nationality rights. The documents generally emphasized the positive impact of the October Revolution on the life of their fellow ethnic groups and the great services these nationalities gave to the Revolution and the Soviet regime. The Crimean Tatar *Appeal to the Twenty-third Party Congress* pointed to the participation of Crimean Tatars in the revolutionary underground and their struggle against the White Army. It also describes the prosperity of the autonomous republic, and so on.[163] A long article, "The Soviet Germans," which opens the *samizdat* almanac *Re-Patria*, emphasized the participation of Germans in the Civil War, as well as the patriotism and proletarian internationalism of Soviet Germans.[164]

In the 1960s and early 1970s gross violations of nationality and human rights in the USSR were interpreted by *samzdat* as "deformations" of Marxism-Leninism. Ethnic demands were often motivated by the necessity to restore the principles of "genuine Leninism." The *Open Letter against Russification* by Seventeen Latvian Communists accused the Soviet leadership of deviating from Marxist-Leninist theory, Lenin's style of work, and other fundamental "principles of Marxism-Leninism."[165] A *Statement by the Representatives of the Crimean Tatar People* claimed that the "Crimean Tatars confront permanent deviations from Lenin's nationality politics and unwillingness to find a Leninist solution to the Crimean Tatar question."[166]

Sharply criticizing Soviet leaders and their policies, ethnic minority movements did not originally question the foundations of the Soviet system. Even dissidents in the Baltic republics, with little respect for Communist ideas, avoided criticizing the Soviet doctrine. In his *Letter to the Presidium of the Supreme Soviet of the USSR*, Lithuanian political prisoner Simutis declared: "I am ready to be loyal to the Soviet regime if it will be serious in correcting previous mistakes."[167] For many ethnic dissidents, Marxist-Leninist theory served as the initial source of energy for their protests.

Being the second generation inculcated with Communist ideology, young ethnic dissidents had no ideological conceptions other than Communist theory, and began with a quest for the "unspoiled springs" of Communism. Non-Communist ideas were similarly presented as no threat to the integrity of their "Marxist-Leninist" identity. Mustafa Dzhemilev, in his 1968 *Letter to General Petr Grigorenko*, described an attempt by young Crimean Tatars to establish an ethnic organization in Tashkent. In 1963, Dzhemilev, then a student at the Technological Institute, together with two of his friends, had prepared a lecture on Crimean Tatar history for several dozen young Crimean Tatars. After the lecture, which had been received enthusiastically, participants discussed the "idea of establishing a genuine Leninist Youth Organization of Crimean Tatars."[168] The young people had worked out draft programs, statutes, and an oath for the future organization. Dzhemilev mentioned that the statutes had imitated the Communist Party rules; it had also been suggested that they depict the Crimean peninsula and a volume of Lenin's works on the membership card.[169]

Meanwhile, the Soviet rhetoric employed by early *samizdat* documents seems to have been related not only to the "Communist" identity of their authors, but equally to a sense of "goodwill," a declaration of loyalty—providing that concessions be granted to ethnic demands. In return for such concessions, the Crimean Tatar document of 1966 offered, for example, not to appeal abroad: "The Crimean Tatar people has never permitted itself and will not permit itself to appeal to anyone besides the Leninist Party and the Soviet government," stated the authors.[170] Nevertheless, two years later, in 1968, an *Appeal by the Crimean Tatar People* was addressed "To the World Public."[171]

It is worthwhile to analyze two versions of the same event offered in Crimean Tatar documents. On 21 April 1968, a large group of Crimean Tatars that had gathered in the City Park of Chirchik (Uzbekistan) was brutally dispersed by the militia and KGB forces. Two letters of protest[172] addressed to the Soviet authorities reported that they had intended to celebrate Lenin's birthday. A third letter addressed "To Foreign Communist and Labor Parties and All People of Goodwill"[173] said that the Crimean Tatars had gathered to celebrate "the national spring holiday, *Derviza*,"[174] and did not mention Lenin's birthday at all.

Appealing to the United Nation's Human Rights Committee in 1969, a Crimean Tatar woman quoted herself: "Some day you will write the story of the atrocity and lawlessness, and you will make all people of the world know what Soviet power really is, and what the true Soviet objectives are."[175]

Since the 1970s, one finds disillusionment over the responsiveness of the Soviet regime to ethnic demands. Ethnic minority *samizdat* gradually adopted anti-Soviet and anti-Communist positions. A Crimean Tatar document (1971) called the Twenty-fourth Party Congress "the banquet of rulers"[176] and described the "degeneration of the Soviet socialist system."[177] An *Appeal by the Initiative Group of Crimean Tatars*, on behalf of Reshat Dzhemilev, arrested in 1973, claimed that the Crimean Tatars' tragedy "did not result from the evil deeds of individuals such as Stalin, Beria, or Voroshilov, but is an outcome of the totalitarian system as a whole."[178] In 1974, the *Chronicle of the Catholic Church in Lithuania*, which had generally avoided commenting on Soviet ideology stated: "Alas, Marxist Communism is unable to satisfy the Lithuanian people. Our students and specialists study Marxist theory only under constraint."[179] An article by Kukshar on the suppression of Tatars and Bashkirs deemed the slogan "Workers of the World unite" to be "obsolete, as is Marxism-Leninism itself."[180] Another Tatar–Bashkir document, an *Appeal to the Non-Russian Nationalities*,[181] described Lenin as a Great Russian chauvinist, who instigated the split between the Tatars and the Bashkirs to facilitate control over these peoples by the Russian authorities. The authors called Communist slogans "false," while Communism itself was defined as a "vain dream." The Soviet socialist economy was assessed by the document as "disadventurous."

Armenian dissident E. Harutiunian, in his *Letter to the Catholicos* (the head of the Armenian Church), asserted that "socialism tended to resolve the nationality question in the spirit of oppression, subordinating ethnic minorities to the dominant ethnic groups. The main constant interest of the Soviet government is to create the world Kremlin Empire."[182]

The reconsideration of attitudes to Communist theory and its founders intensified in the late 1970s. In 1966, V. Chornovil and his coauthors demanded that the authorities "restore Leninist norms in the national life of Ukraine."[183] Eleven years later, in 1977, Ukrainian dissident B. Rebryk, in his *Appeal to Brezhnev*,[184] claimed that "the Ukrainian people sustained heavy losses in its struggle with Communist colonialism and world Communism." While Luk'ianenko and his friends wanted to realize the principles of genuine Marxism in an independent Ukrainian state, the *Declaration of the Ukrainian Patriotic Movement* (1980), proclaimed Stalinism as the culmination of Soviet Communism, and backed their separatist demands by the urgency of "helping our people escape from Communist captivity."[185] *The Chronicle of Current Events* carried an anonymous report from Armenia that in February 1979 leaflets denouncing Marx had been distributed.[186] At about the same time, Armenian political prisoner Ramzik Zograbian, arrested for burning Lenin's portrait, explained his action as a protest against the politician "who recognized Turkish sovereignty over our lands."[187]

Ukrainian activist Valerii Marchenko characterized Marx's theory of the class struggle as "the most savage apology for murder."[188] Fellow Ukrainian dissidents, O. Tykhyi and V. Romaniuk, assessed Marxism-Leninism as "the most monstrous and reactionary idea of the present time."[189] Correspondingly, in an *Open Letter to Three-times World Champion Mohammed Ali* Crimean Tatar activist R. Dzhemilev emphasized that the Crimean Tatars' deportation of 1944 was not a personal atrocity committed by Stalin but the inevitable result of the "natural evolution of the Communist idea."[190] He then described the Bolshevik regime as a successor of the imperialist Russian Empire. Latvian activist Balis Gayauskas, in his *Appeal to the Madrid Conference on European Security* (1982), described the USSR as the "Bolshevik Empire," populated by enslaved peoples.[191] The harshest definition of the Soviet system can be found in M. Sahaidak's article in the *Ukrainian Herald*: "The fascist Empire, where the rights of citizens are determined by the KGB."[192]

By the late 1970s, Communist ideology and the regime were regarded as an "absolute evil" in most documents issued by ethnic minority movements. Thus, in 1981, many Jewish activists refused to sign an *Open Letter* to the Twenty-sixth Party Congress, considering any "flirtation" with the immoral ideology unacceptable. In 1969, Jewish poet Iosif Kerler tried to convince the Soviet authorities that "many of those who applied for exit visas were sincere in their adherence to socialism."[193] By 1983, another Jewish activist, Polina Gorodetskaia, was explaining her renunciation of Soviet citizenship in that she "finally realized the bankruptcy of Soviet ideology and practice."[194]

Dissident Groups: Mutual Relations

"I recognize that the Jewish question in the USSR is inseparable from the general situation in the country," wrote M. Agurskii,[195] a prominent member of the Jewish movement, calling on his fellow Zionist activists to play a more active role in the fight for democratic reforms in the USSR. From the very beginning, the ethnic minority movements and the Russian democrats considered each other to be their natural allies and advocates of their interests. The Russian liberal-democratic movement was cited by minority *samizdat* as a model to be followed. "We need our own Bukovskiis and Amalriks," stated a Tatar–Bashkir document calling for the union of the Turkic peoples of the USSR.[196]

At his trial in Riga (1983), Latvian dissident Gunnars Astra thanked a procurator "for honor he did me by calling Sakharov my confederate."[197] *Information Bulletin* (no. 77, 1968), issued by representatives of the Crimean Tatars in Moscow, contained a letter protesting the illegal arrest of Irina Belogorodskaia. "Our people's movement cannot restrict itself to an ethnic framework. It must consolidate with the general democratic movement of our country,"[198] contended the document. A *Letter* (1969) by a group of Crimean Tatar activists reported that "thousands of Crimean Tatars had signed appeals on behalf of General Grigorenko,"[199] arrested by the KGB for dissident activity. Reshat Dzhemilev, a Crimean Tatar leader who was also active in the general democratic movement, protested against the arrest of Dremluga, Litvinov, Iakhimovich, and Grigorenko, the invasion of Czechoslovakia, and so on. Mustafa Dzhemilev, another prominent Crimean Tatar activist, sent an *Appeal to All Muslims*[200] calling on them to support academician Andrei Sakharov and his wife Elena Bonner.

The Jewish *samizdat* journal *Vestnik iskhoda* (no. 3, 1971) published an item entitled "Contact with the Democratic Movement."[201] "The Jewish movement is interested in the development of democracy in the USSR, and the democratic movement will benefit if Jews succeed in realizing their democratic rights in certain comparatively narrow spheres. I think that these two streams in Soviet societal life are not contradictory but can even help one another," stated the item's anonymous author. The same issue carried a *Letter* by six Moscow Jews (Iahot, Goldberg, Rutman, Slepak, Kliachkin, and Fedorova) protesting the trial of Vladimir Bukovskii.[202] The journal also contained an *Appeal* by three members of the democratic movement (V. Chalidze, A. Sakharov, and A. Tverdokhlebov)[203] on behalf of three Jewish activists sentenced to fifteen days of administrative detention.

In 1973, ten Moscow Jews (Azbel, Lerner, N. and A. Voronel, Brailovskii, Lunts, etc.) issued a *Declaration* protesting the campaign against Sakharov and Solzhenitsyn in the Soviet mass media. "Despite having made a decision to leave Russia, we cannot be indifferent to Russia, its people, and its culture," stated the authors.[204] In 1968, a *Letter* signed by 139 Ukrainian intellectuals[205] (among them I. Dziuba, I. Svetlychnyi, and V. Stus) protested against the secret political trials of A. Ginzburg, Iu. Galanskov, V. Lashkova, I. Gabai, and others. In 1980, an *Appeal by the Ukrainian Patriotic Movement*[206] spoke out on behalf of Vladimir Klebanov, founder of the independent trade union movement, and called on Ukrainian workers to establish independent trade unions. The *Chronicle of the Ukrainian Catholic Church* (no. 4, 1984) carried an *Appeal* by I. Terelia calling on the Ukrainian Diaspora to support Elena Sannikova, a Russian Orthodox participant in the democratic movement, who was arrested in December 1983.[207]

The *Chronicle of the Catholic Church in Lithuania* (no. 21, 1977) gave a detailed report of the trial of S. Kovalev, a founder of the Human Rights Committee in Moscow.[208] Another Lithuanian *samizdat* periodical, *Aushra* (no. 2/42, 1976), expressed solidarity with Russian dissidents.[209]

In its turn, the democratic movement was always active in advocating the rights of ethnic minorities. The *Program of the Democratic Movement* said that Ukrainians, Jews, Tatars, Baltic peoples, and others "should carry out a non-violent struggle for national liberation."[210] At the same time the *Program* pointed out that "these peoples must remember that their national struggle should be closely connected with the general fight for democracy.... National liberation will come only via civil liberation."[211]

The role of the general democratic movement in supporting ethnic minority movements and their members is well known and deserves special study. Dealing briefly with this topic we should mention petitions by General Piotr Grigorenko[212] and writer Alexei Kosterin[213] on behalf of the Crimean Tatars. In 1969, two collective documents championing the national rights of Crimean Tatars were issued by the Russian democrats: (1) An *Appeal by the Youth International Committee in Support of the Crimean Tatar Movement*,[214] and (2) an *Open Letter*, signed by "the Russian friends of the Crimean Tatars."[215] In 1972, a *Petition to the Supreme Soviet of the USSR* by the Human Rights Committee[216] demanded the full rehabilitation of all deported peoples. An *Appeal to the UN Secretary General* (1974) requesting that he promote the repatriation of the Crimean Tatars was signed by A. Sakharov, T. Velikanova, S. Kovalev, and others.[217] A *Letter* (1971) by V. Chalidze and supported by A. Sakharov and A. Tverdokhlebov protested the persecution of Jewish activists.[218] That same year Russian dissident writer Lydia Chukovskaia wrote a *Letter* in defence of Reisa Palatnik,[219] a member of the Jewish movement tried in Odessa for *samizdat*.

"Democrats" and "nationalists" occasionally reproached each other for a lack of interest in cooperation, group egoism, neglect of common objectives, and the like. Thus, *Ukrains'kyi visnyk* (*Ukrainian Herald*, no. 5, 1971),[220] published an article reviewing the attitudes of the democratic movement to the nationality question. The article was sharply critical of Sakharov's proposal to abolish the registration of nationality in Soviet identity cards, considering it "assimilatory." The *Chronicle*'s editors were blamed for neglecting nationality issues and even for seeking to preserve the *status quo* with regard to nationality policies. In turn, the democrats reproached the Ukrainian movement with underestimating the democratic movement's *Program* and pursuing narrow, selfish interests[221] and criticized the Jewish movement in the same way. A *Letter by Russian Democrats to the Jewish People*[222] noted that the democratic movement expressed strong support for Zionism and Jewish culture and religion, complaining that the Jewish movement championed nationality rights for Jews only, and not for the other peoples of Russia. "The Jewish people must remember that both they and the Russians committed the crime of Bolshevism and they must, therefore, join with us in order to overcome it," emphasized the *Letter*.

Representatives of various dissident groups signed a number of documents in defense of political prisoners. Members of the democratic, Jewish, Lithuanian, Latvian, and Ukrainian movements signed a *Letter* protesting the arrest of Andrei Tverdokhlebov, the founder of the Moscow branch of Amnesty International.[223] Letters on behalf of Anatolii Shcharanskii, a Jewish activist and member of the Moscow Helsinki Watch Committee, were signed by democrats, the Seventh Day Adventists, and Ukrainian and Jewish activists.[224] Alongside the democratic movement, Armenian, Georgian, Lithuanian, Latvian, and Jewish activists, Russian nationalists, and Baptists protested the arrests of A. Ginzburg and Iu. Orlov, prominent human rights workers.[225]

In 1977, sixty-two Soviet citizens, including representatives of the democratic, Ukrainian, Jewish, and Russian nationalist movements issued a joint *Declaration of Support of the Principles of the Czechoslovakian Charter-77*.[226] In 1979 five general democratic movement activists (M. Landa, L. Nekipelov, T. Velikanova, A. Sakharov, and Arina Ginzburg) added their signatures to an *Appeal by Representatives of the Baltic Republics* demanding that the full text of the Molotov–Ribbentrop Pact be publicized and that the pact be annulled retroactively from the moment of its signing.[227]

In some cases, members of ethnic minority movements expressed their concern with violations of the rights of other nationalities. In 1970, two Ukrainians, philologist Taras Franko and biologist Maria Lysenko, appealed to the Presidium of the Ukrainian Supreme Soviet with a proposal to restore the Crimean Tatar Autonomous Republic.[228] Armenian dissident E. Harutiunian in his *Letter to the Catholicos* called attention to the state of "the Crimean Tatars and other deported Muslim and Christian nationalities."[229] A high degree of cooperation was reached between the national movements of the Baltic republics, which issued a number of joint documents, such as the aforementioned *Appeal by Representatives of the Baltic Republics*, the *Open Letter to the Heads of Government of the USSR and the States of Northern Europe*[230] (proposing the declaration of Northern Europe and the Baltic Sea region as a nuclear-free zone), and a *Memorandum*[231] (demanding that the illegal occupation of the Baltic states be considered at a session of the United Nations). These joint documents are indicative of the Baltic movements' intent to formulate a coordinated regional policy.

In comparison with the Baltic movements, cooperation between other ethnic minority groups existed on a much smaller scale. Practically, the only attempt to issue a joint declaration of principles is found in a *Statement* issued by the Rumanian group, Revival, together with the Ukrainian National Front.[232] Apart from a declaration of the shared commitment to "win our freedom from the heel of Moscow," the two parties failed to specify their mutual political interests in more concrete forms.

At the same time, political prisoners of various dissident groups who were interned together in the labor camps demonstrated a high potential for collaboration. In 1974, more than one hundred political prisoners in the Thirty-fifth Perm Labor Camp, including all members of the democratic, Ukrainian, and Jewish movements then serving sentences there, signed *A Petition to the Soviet Authorities* demanding that basic human rights be observed in the USSR.[233] In several documents issued in labor camps, political prisoners attempted to formulate a general platform that would embrace the various demands of ethnic minorities. In the autumn of 1973, seventeen political prisoners from the Baltic republics, Ukraine, and the Caucasus signed a *Petition to the Soviet of Nationalities of the Supreme Soviet of the USSR* protesting against Russification.[234] The *Petition* put forward the following demands insisting that:

1. The language of the eponymous nationality be declared an official language in each union or autonomous republic;
2. All ethnic minorities living outside their ethnic territories be granted cultural autonomy, or alternately, Russians living in national republics be deprived of their cultural monopoly;
3. The rights of union republics be extended by granting them control over their foreign affairs and each republic be granted the right to have

independent foreign policies as well as to maintain cultural, political, and economic relations with other countries;

4. Republican military units be restored;
5. The authorities in union and autonomous republics be given control over all industrial enterprises in their territories, and equal partnership be guaranteed in economic relations between republics;
6. The power of the Communist party be restricted and all party activists be placed under state control;
7. The legal mechanism for the protection of ethnic minority rights be determined;
8. Any violation of nationality rights "automatically gives us moral grounds to exercise our constitutional right to promote secession from the USSR," and "any activity to achieve this right must not be prosecuted."[235]

This *Petition* contains what is probably the most comprehensive ethnic policy program shared by all national movements. Like most ethnic documents of its time, the program did not consider secession from the USSR to be a real objective: the aim was to advance pressing political interests in the framework of the Soviet Union. On the other hand, it is difficult to imagine how the integrity of the state would be preserved if each federal unit enjoyed the right to an independent foreign policy.

In 1978, political prisoners in the Thirty-sixth Perm Labor Camp held the "first Ten-Day-Festival of Solidarity of Peoples in their struggle against Russian-Soviet colonialism and imperialism."[236] The next year, prisoners in Chistopol prison joined them in a second Ten-Day Festival. Joint statements by participants demanded that the authorities "halt Russification and the dissolution of the ethnic roots of all peoples, including the Russian people"[237] and "liquidate national and colonial oppression" as practiced by "the Russian Soviet Empire."[238] The statements were signed by activists from the general democratic, Ukrainian, Armenian, Jewish, Lithuanian, Estonian, and Tatar movements.

Political prisoners also spoke out on behalf of their fellow prisoners from ethnic minority movements. Ukrainian political prisoner, V. Romaniuk, a priest of the Uniate Catholic Church, in his Letter of 1977 called on "Jews and all people of goodwill"[239] to fight for the release of E. Kuznetsov and his friends, tried in 1970 for a hijack attempt. In 1976, psychiatrist S. Gluzman, tried for his struggle against psychiatric abuses by the Soviet authorities for political interests, wrote a *Letter* to his Danish correspondent calling for the organization of a campaign on behalf of Latvian nationalist Ivar Grabans,[240] a longtime political prisoner.

Declarations by political prisoners must not be underestimated. Their marginal status automatically guaranteed them stature in their dissident groups and a degree of freedom from the pragmatism of their groups or movements living in the outside world. In December 1976, a famous *Letter by Political Prisoners*[241] in support of Armenian nationalists' demands to legalize the NUP (National Unification Party) and to hold a referendum on Armenian self-determination was signed by activists of the democratic, Lithuanian, Jewish, and Ukrainian movements, and by V. Osipov, the leader of the Russian nationalists. Remarkably, *Veche*'s editor, who had asserted the objective of "one, indivisible Russia," supported the separatist demands of Armenian nationalists.

Undoubtedly, the Soviet authorities considered the consolidation of various dissident groups to be a serious challenge to stability and tried to prevent any cooperation between the opposition movements. In a final plea at his 1984 trial, Mustafa Dzhemilev pointed to attempts by the KGB to split the opposition in order to weaken each movement: "Justice and freedom are inseparable notions. It is impossible to demand justice only for yourself and to silence your conscience when it is violated for others."[242] He criticized "hypocritical lectures" by certain narrow-minded members of his movement who argued that "we should deal only with our own problems and not to interfere in other issues."[243] Arguments by Dzhemilev's opponents within the Crimean Tatar movement were echoed in Jewish *samizdat* of the mid-1970s. The journal *Jews in the USSR* (1974) published an article by A. Volin entitled "Assimilation and Free Choice," in which the author claimed that the participation of Jews in any other movements provides their enemies with an "additional weapon...and threatens to produce still more discrimination."[244] In the same issue, the editor, A. Voronel, stated: "We must now remain aloof, while it is not yet too late to separate our problems from their [the Russian people's] problems. Otherwise they will solve our fate together with their problems, and this solution will be radical."[245] Nevertheless, until the late 1970s, the Jewish movement cooperated with other opposition groups. In 1976, three Moscow Jewish activists, N. Meiman, A. Shcharanskii, and V. Slepak, joined the Moscow Helsinki Watch Committee; E. Finkelstein, a Jewish activist from Vilnus, joined the Lithuanian Helsinki Watch Group, and I. and G. Goldstein, *refuseniks* from Georgia, participated in the Georgian Helsinki Group.

After severe reprisals against members of Helsinki Watch Committees in 1977 and 1978, particularly after Shcharanskii was arrested and accused of high treason cooperation between the Jewish and the democratic movements decreased dramatically. Many Jewish activists attributed Shcharanskii's terrible sentence to his having attempted to "sit on two seats," taking part in both the Jewish and the democratic movements. The inference was that Jews should not deal with "the problems of others." To no small degree, this mood seems to have resulted from manipulation by the KGB on the one hand, and the Israeli establishment on the other. Discussing the attitude of the Israeli authorities toward those Soviet immigrants who continued to demonstrate their support for the struggle for human rights in the USSR, L. Schroeter noted that "Their efforts were almost as annoying to Israeli authorities as were [their] activities in the USSR to Soviet officials.... In the USSR neither found any contradictions in working simultaneously for the rights of Jews to leave and for civil rights and liberties for all who wished to stay. In Israel the authorities treat such interest with a considerable degree of coolness."[246] Apart from a natural desire to protect the Jewish movement from repressions, the Israeli officials[247] regarded the liberal democratic movement as a challenge to Zionist objectives and as a factor behind increasing Jewish emigration to the West. Also at stake was Israel's desire to control the Jewish movement. In any event, while KGB officers used Shcharanskii's trial to intimidate Jewish activists participating in other dissident activities, Israeli representatives cautioned Leningrad *refuseniks* to keep silent about the arrest of Leonid Lubman (soon after Shcharanskii's 1978 trial), who was charged with high treason for his human rights activities. Lubman, who was closely connected with the Jewish movement before his arrest, was sentenced to thirteen years and served almost a full term in prison and labor camps. No reports of his arrest and no appeals on his behalf were issued by Jewish activists.[248] Similar attempts to dissociate Israel and the Jewish movement in the USSR from Shcharanskii were made by the Israeli establishment.

It is interesting that the preoccupation of the Ukrainian movement with human rights evoked no enthusiasm among certain circles of the Ukrainian Diaspora. Thus, the US-based Ukrainian American Congress Committee, as one of its members testified, "tried to focus the Ukrainian Helsinki Group's attention on the liberation of Ukraine from the Bolshevik yoke, and not solely on human rights."[249]

The first policy declaration by the Russian nationalist movement toward other opposition groups can be found in the *VSKhSON Program* (1964). Proclaiming the overthrow of the Communist dictatorship to be its main objective, the *Program* called for "cooperation with any organized force struggling for the common cause."[250] It has already been mentioned that Ivan Ruslanov, the author of the essay *Youth in Russian History*,[251] considered all dissident groups to be members of the united opposition front. *Veche's* editor, V. Osipov, in his 1972 interview with an Associated Press correspondent, said: "Our attitude to the democratic movement can be defined as sympathetic. *Veche* and the democrats both advocate Slavophile principles of policy—national and liberal."[252] His 1974 article, "On the Objectives and Methods of the Legal Opposition,"[253] cited a program suggested by A. Solzhenitsyn to develop the Russian North and Siberia as a platform for reconciliation and cooperation between Russian nationalists and democrats.

Meanwhile, though, the extremist wing of Russian nationalism showed overall hostility toward activists from liberal democratic dissident groups. In order to discredit the democratic movement, *Slovo Natsii* (The Manifesto of Russian Patriots) alluded to the non-Russian origins of "Russian democrats."[254] In *Veche* (no. 9, 1973), an item signed by O.M. and commenting on liberal-democratic *samizdat* stated that "the Jews wrote and continued to write *samizdat* not only as Jewish nationalists, but also as alleged 'Russians,' i.e. as cosmopolitans and Russophobes."[255] According to the author, if some Russians, influenced by Jews, had joined the democratic camp, they should be regarded as "renegades, lackeys, and mere idiots."[256] Leonid Borodin, a former *VSKhSON* member who had served six years in a labor camp, published an article (*Veche*, no. 8, 1973) devoted to the Russian intelligentsia,[257] in which he wrote appreciatively of the fortitude and integrity displayed by many activists in the democratic movement, but he nevertheless contended that the democratic idea was doomed in Russia. To prove this assumption, Borodin noted that the overwhelming majority of democratic activists were cosmopolitan Jews, unfit for creative national work.

Growing differences in orientations and objectives resulted in a particularly low degree of cooperation between the Russian nationalist movement and other dissident groups, particularly ethnic minority movements. Russian conservatives regarded political assertiveness by non-Russian peoples as constituting a struggle against the Russian nation. "National liberation movements are always good from the position of the 'rebellious' nationality but bad from that of the nation against which these movements are directed," *Veche*'s editors explained in reply to R. Mukhamediarov, who criticized the journal from a democratic position. "We cannot admire the struggle carried on against our nation. The sole thing that we consider to be acceptable is an indulgent attitude toward our antagonists."[258]

Unlike separatist claims, the demand to emigrate made by Soviet Jews and Germans was generally supported in conservative *samizdat*. Commenting on the German almanac *Re-Patria*, I. Ratmirov expressed solidarity with the Germans' "desire to return to their native lands"[259] in Germany. Ratmirov avoided dealing with the other demand formulated by *Re-Patria*, namely, the restoration of the Volga German autonomous republic in the "native lands" of the Volga area.

The modernization process constituted not merely an "objective" macro-level factor in the emergence of the opposition movements in the USSR. Its concomitants such as Westernization and liberal democracy served as a dialogical background in the dissident nationalist discourse.

The first open public protests after Stalin's death appeared as a plea for accomplishing the modernization in the social and political spheres. That time the protest reflected a rather general humanitarian drive that had neither clear political programs nor structural divisions along political lines. Since the mid-1960s we can indicate the politicization of the nonconformist movement, particularization of political interests, and as a result—the split of previously syncretic opposition into various dissident groups divided by their political objectives. The initial division between "nationalist" and "democrats" was quite vague, and to a considerable degree they shared many political-ideological values.

Examining the further evolution of ethnic movements one can indicate that ethnic minority nationalism and Russian majority nationalism developed two divergent reactions to the socio-political parameters of modernization. The former tended to express their nationalist appeal as an attempt to institute Westernized democratic society, the latter—as protest against an invasion by Western economic and socio-political standards, allegedly destructive for traditional values of Russian society. These two conflicting orientations were to no small degree shaped by the adverse political interests pursued by the ethnic majority nationalism on the one hand and the ethnic minority nationalism on the other. The evolution of the ethnic movements' attitudes toward the Soviet regime and the patterns of relationship between various dissident groups seem to have been determined by the dynamics of their political, ideological, and operative strategies.

CHAPTER 4

Relative Deprivation and the Politicization of Ethnic Groups

I n the midst of theoretical concepts and models that explain "militant sociopolitical attitudes (or nationalism)"[1] the concept of relative deprivation has received an expression (even more positively articulated than in the case of modernization) in the *samizdat* documents of the ethnic movements.

The term relative deprivation was coined in 1949 by S. Stouffer, E. Suchman et al.[2] Since the late 1950s, the formal theory of relative deprivation has been elaborated in various studies for the explanation of militant attitudes and protest behaviors, including nationalism.[3]

A considerable "push" to the development of the theory of relative deprivation was given in the late sixties by W. Runciman,[4] who proposed to distinguish between egoistic relative deprivation and fraternal relative deprivation. As S. Guimond and L. Dubè-Simard indicated, "egoistic RD is a type of personal discontent that occurs when an individual compares his or her own situation to that of others (in-group or out-group members), whereas fraternal RD is a more social discontent that occurs when an individual compares the situation of his group as a whole to that of an out-group."[5]

From its very inception *samizdat* dealt with the issue of relative deprivation, examining its effect in political, economic, environmental, territorial, cultural and linguistic, and religious spheres. The relative deprivation experienced by their fellow groups was unanimously described by the *samizdat* documents as provoking ethnic assertiveness, and became the major motif of ethnic *samizdat*.

An accordance with which both the social psychologists and nationalist actors attribute the protest behavior to the relative deprivation makes this issue particularly important for our study. An examination of the issue of relative deprivation as it was expressed in *samizdat* may help to overcome the serious discrepancy imposed by the traditional empirical methods that deal "with the feelings and emotions of an individual, while at the same time trying to account for social protest which involves the behavior of a large collectivity."[6]

Samizdat documents, the considerable part of which appeared as a result of the "shared participation" (even if symbolic) sometimes of hundreds or even thousands of individuals, exemplify an expression of collective sentiment. By no means, the *samizdat* accounts of deprivation quoted below should be viewed as "authentic" and accurate reports (though I believe that a notable part of them contains precise and faithful information). The documents' statements are examined here as "texts" reflecting rather contemplation of deprivation (or what is perceived to be deprivation), as narratives, which are inspired and shaped by both the tangible experience and supplemental narratives. Popular motifs of relative deprivation, common to the documents of various ethnic groups seem to account for the collective *perceptions* of inequality, as well as for the collective *interpretation* of this inequality.

Political Deprivation

Pointing to manifestations of relative deprivation, documents of all ethnic movements protested against the then-existing "center–periphery" relationship and, correspondingly, against the pattern of ethnic domination. The Soviet Union is commonly described as an "Empire," and national peripheries are described as its "colonies."

An early Ukrainian *samizdat* document, an *Appeal* issued in 1964 by the Initiative Committee of the Ukraine's Communists, mentioned "Moscow's policy of Russification and colonialism" and "Russian imperialism."[7] The *Appeal* stressed that the Ukraine, which was "proclaimed a sovereign state, in fact became a colonial province of the Empire. The government has no right to resolve any issues independently. Shelest [Party Chief of the Ukraine] cannot even approve the building of an underground passage without Moscow's permission. There is no chance of protecting the nation's interests: the army is demoralized, and the bureaucracy serves as a brace of Moscow's centralizing policy," continued the document.[8] Seventeen years later Georgii [Iurii] Badzio, the Ukrainian political prisoner, in his *Statement* addressed to the Twenty-sixth Congress of the CPSU (1981), blamed the "lack of national-political life in Ukrainian society" on the fictitious nature of the Ukrainian Soviet Socialist Republic's sovereignty.[9]

In order to corroborate the fictitious nature of republican sovereignty proclaimed by the Soviet Constitution, *samizdat* documents usually emphasized that union or autonomous republics did not obtain the right to form their own national armed forces or to establish diplomatic relations with foreign states. An anonymous essay from the 1960s that appeared in Armenian *samizdat* asserted: "For the Russians Armenia still remains a colony, an indivisible part of the Empire.... Is it to be considered a state if its government does not even have the authority to appoint an office cleaner without Moscow's permission? The Soviet Armenian State does not exist. There is a Soviet Armenian province of the Russian Empire."[10]

A short article on the suppression of Tatar–Bashkirs, dated April 1977 and signed by Kukshar (a pen-name), contained a vigorous protest against Russian domination and indicated that the USSR's repressive policy was an extension of the nationality policy of the Russian Empire. The document evaluated the politics of the Soviet Union as being exclusively Russian policy and stated that "so-called freedom of choice in determining their future is out of the question for the Turkic peoples as long as the power of Russian bayonets and guns exists."[11] An article in the Georgian *samizdat* magazine, *Sakartvello* (Georgia), 1982, discussing the subordinated state of the Georgian people, pointed to the failure in maintaining "normal relations between nationalities without securing real equality."[12] I. Kandyba,[13] a veteran of the Ukrainian dissident movement, wrote a letter (1967) to the Party Chief of the Ukraine, Petro Shelest. In it he cited the *Program* of the clandestine Ukrainian Workers and Peasants Union, pointing out that the republic was deprived of the right "to establish bilateral political and economic relations with the other countries of our planet."[14] An Armenian author, B. Movsisian, wrote in the late 1960s: "It is inconceivable that there will be a state without an army. Well, where is the Armenian army?"[15] The well-known *Open Letter against Russification* by Seventeen Latvian Communists written in 1971 developed a similar idea: "Today there are no separate Latvian military units, and it is intentional that Latvian youths in the military are not assigned to the Russian units stationed in Latvia but are scattered throughout the Soviet Union—as far away from Latvia as possible."[16] Ethnic movements considered the establishment of republican national military forces and the right to conduct an independent foreign policy to be the main attributes of political sovereignty.

It is interesting that Armenian *samizdat* documents employed the same paradigm of political deprivation for describing the state of affairs in Nagorno-Karabakh, with the difference that Azerbaijan was the center that practiced colonial rule. A *Letter* (1963) sent to N. Krushchev by Armenians from Nagorno-Karabakh and other regions of Azerbaijan pointed out that the Azerbaijani authorities had purposely subordinated many institutions and industrial enterprises in the Nagorno-Karabakh Autonomous *oblast* to the administration of remote Azerbaijani *rayons* (districts) located outside the *oblast*. The Armenians of Nagorno-Karabakh claimed that this was intended to deprive their autonomous status of any political meaning.[17]

While the state of political deprivation was described by most ethnic movements as "colonial dependence," *samizdat* documents by the Baltic peoples tended to describe the situation in their republics in terms of "occupation" and "aggression." The Soviet invasion of the Baltic countries in 1940 and its immediate consequences became, in the collective perception of the three peoples, the central event in determining the emotional background and character of their political assertiveness.

An impressive personal testimony describing this period can be found in the *Letter to the Presidium of the Supreme Soviet of the USSR* (1970) written by Lithuanian political prisoner Ludvikas Simutis:

I was five years old when they showed me the dead body of my father. Half of his face was swollen and dark blue. The other half was blood-red. His eyes were gouged out, the skin of his hands and legs was white and it came off his body, because it had been scalded. His tongue was pulled out and tied up with a string; his genitals were crushed, I later realized. There were many other mutilated corpses side by side. I heard my mother—and many other people I did not know—crying. They cursed the *Bolsheviks*, a term I had never heard before. My first introduction to the Bolsheviks was in the form of mutilated corpses—mutilated by Bolsheviks—and as the subject of curses: "Cannibals, monsters, freaks, dregs of mankind..." They were cursed not by propagandists, but by mothers, wives, and even by men distraught with horror and grief. It happened in June 1941, after the Red Army's retreat. I was five years old then...[18]

Several years later, Simutis joined LLKS (The Movement of Struggle for Lithuanian Liberation), the anti-Soviet underground organization. He explained that he joined the movement not out of opposition to socialist ideas, but as a result of:

[T]he excessive and criminal cruelty with which the Soviet regime dealt with anyone who did not embrace the new system. As for the LLKS, it represented well-known...and rather impressive forces that opposed the occupation of Lithuania by the Soviet Army and the Soviet regime imposed by this army.... Practically no outsiders helped these guerillas to defend their tiny motherland against this omnipotent aggressor.

For five years after the war, the fierce fighting did not stop, blood was shed, and people suffered—both Soviets and members of LLKS groups. But I knew that they were our people in the LLKS, whereas soldiers of the Red Army spoke the foreign Russian language. I knew that there had never been a revolution in Lithuania, that the Red Army was not invited to our country—they invaded it in order to establish their own regime. This was occupation.

I was certain that it was not the LLKS guerillas who made the fighting so fierce: the LLKS did not yet exist when *chekists* scalded the arms and crushed the genitals of my father while he was still alive.

I wanted to live, to study, and to play. But what kind of life is it when a murdered neighbor has been lying in the street for three days and no one is allowed to bury him? How can I study when classmates, one after another, must quit school because they and their families are being deported to Siberia in boarded-up trucks and vans? ...How can I play when adults are crying?[19]

This long quotation is a striking verbal projection of the invisible images stamped in the collective memory of subjugated peoples.

Soviet occupation is a motif common to the *samizdat* of all three Baltic peoples, irrespective of the authors' political views. An item in *The Chronicle of the Lithuanian Catholic Church* (no. 9, 1974), in describing a regular Congress of the Lithuanian Komsomol, protested against all attempts to "proclaim the Soviet occupation as a heroic deed of the Lithuanian people...Lithuanian youth," it stressed, "does not forget to celebrate Lithuanian Independence Day."[20] Speaking at his trial in Vilnius in 1974, M. Zhukauskas,[21] a medical student charged with anti-Soviet propaganda, called Soviet rule in Lithuania "an imposed occupation regime."[22] That same year, Lithuanian engineer M. Tamonis, refused to participate in the restoration of a monument to Soviet soldiers. *The Chronicle of the Lithuanian Catholic Church* (no. 10, 1974) carried Tamonis's explanation of his decision: "I consider it intolerable to lend a hand in perpetuating events that have deprived Lithuania of its statehood."[23] The first document issued by the Lithuanian Helsinki Watch Group[24] pointed out that "the present status of Lithuania must be considered the result of bringing Soviet troops into the [Lithuanian] territory."[25]

The celebrated *Open Letter against Russification* by Seventeen Latvian Communists (1971; published on 30 January 1972 in the Swedish newspaper,

Daggers Nyheter), cautiously expressed the same idea: "Before World War II, The Soviet Union forced the head of the bourgeois Latvian government, Ulmanis, to sign an agreement allowing large Red Army garrisons to be stationed in Latvia. In 1940, with Red Army cooperation, the bourgeois government was overthrown and Latvia was annexed to the Soviet Union. After World War II the CPSUCC [Central Committee of the Communist Party of the Soviet Union] set, as a goal, the development of a permanent powerbase in the territories of Latvia, Lithuania, and Estonia."[26]

To stress the illegality of Soviet rule in Latvia, two dissidents, Gunnar Rode (in 1977) and Lidia Doronina (in 1984), demanded that the Soviet authorities strip them of their Soviet citizenship. Rode, who was born in 1934 in an independent Latvia, maintained that "the fact of Latvia's occupation by the Soviet Union in 1940 cannot be regarded as grounds for an automatic change of citizenship."[27] Doronina also explained that having been born in an independent Latvia, she was "educated in accordance with the spirit and laws of my country."[28]

A *Memorandum by Representatives of the Native Populations of Estonia, Latvia, and Lithuania* (1982), addressed to leaders of Western democracies and to the United Nations Security Council expressed the belief that Soviet occupation was the single most significant factor behind the deprivations suffered by these countries' native populations. It declared: "The Soviet government still expects to resist the aspiration of the Baltic peoples to achieve self-determination.... The current Soviet regime in the Baltic states can be maintained solely because of the presence of military occupation forces."[29]

In no *samizdat* document is there any hint of the Baltic peoples' acquiescence to or reconciliation with their status. This seems to be the reason why no comment on the annexation of Vilnius and other territories, then under Polish jurisdiction, by Lithuania in 1940 (under Soviet auspices) can be found in *samizdat* literature, even though it was considered to be one positive outcome of Soviet occupation. Similarly, the Ukrainian national movement, while attaching particular importance to the reunification of the Ukrainian nation, seemingly ignored the annexation of Western territories, not seeing it as "occupation" or a form of "aggression."

Concepts such as "genocide" and "concentration camps" dominate descriptions of the political deprivations suffered by the Volga Germans, Crimean Tatars, and Meskhetian Turks—three ethnic minorities that became victims of Stalin's deportation policies of August 1941, May 1944, and November 1944, respectively. Every *samizdat* document by these peoples refers to the fatal events, describing the intolerable brutality of deportation and exile—starvation, suffering, and humiliation.

In 1966, an *Appeal* made by the Crimean Tatars to the Twenty-third Congress of the Communist Party claimed that 109,956 people died in the first eighteen months after the deportation.[30] "Anyone contending that the reservations set aside for our people became for us 'the second motherland,' should realize that this is simply a cynical mockery of ethnic minority rights.... Our true motherland has become a restricted area for us."[31] Like the loss of independence for the Baltic peoples, the loss of a homeland was, for these three deported peoples, an irredeemable deprivation from which all other forms of deprivation stem.

A *Statement* issued by representatives of the Crimean Tatars in July 1968—the twenty-fourth anniversary of the "liberation of Crimea from the Crimean Tatars"[32]—bemoaned the fact that "no economic, cultural, or political development is possible without residing in Crimea, our motherland."[33] In expressing the tragedy of deportation and ensuing deprivations, Crimean Tatar documents often employ terminology generally associated with Nazism. "What people are doing to us has a specific name—genocide," declared an *Appeal by the Crimean Tatar People to the World Public* (June 1968).[34] A later document issued by the Initiative Group of the Crimean Tatars, *Information Bulletin* (no. 2, August 1983) mentions a "final solution to the Crimean Tatars' national question."[35]

A document approved by the Meskhetian ethnic movement in 1970, the *Resolution of the Sixth People's Meeting of the Turkish Society for the Protection of the National Rights of the Turkish Meskhetian People*, equated life in the homeland with freedom; the current status of the Meskhetian people was defined as being that of "slaves in a foreign land."[36] A 1981 letter by five Volga German activists to the members of the Bundestag pointed out: "The German population of two million constitutes the largest ethnic group in the USSR with no autonomous status. This fact demonstrates the virtual inequality of the German among the other nationalities of the USSR."[37]

Like the Baltic peoples, the three deported nationalities regarded the restoration of their former homelands as the sole means of attaining national equality. Moreover, they tended to repudiate any offers of concessions, deeming them political maneuvers aimed at perpetuating the current state of affairs.

In 1972, the Chairman of the Presidium of the Supreme Soviet, A. Mikoyan, received a delegation of Volga Germans. He rejected the concept of restoring the Volga Germans' former autonomous status, but offered some cultural concessions to them. A letter by the delegation, addressed to Mikoyan and to KGB chief A. Shelepin, flatly repudiated Mikoyan's suggestions. "Our people did not send us to the government to ask permission for ethnic amateur talent shows. We have a mandate to speak on behalf of the rehabilitation of two million German people in securing their rights on an equal footing with all other peoples of the USSR."[38]

In 1972, the First Secretary of the Akkurgan District Party Committee, S.M. Tairov, in a letter to the Uzbekistani Communist leader Rashidov, touched upon the question of the Crimean Tatars. Tairov warily pointed to the lamentable state of Crimean Tatar culture and mentioned that the Tatars had no opportunities for professional and social promotion, and recommended lifting all restrictions imposed on them. Surprisingly, Tatar activists responded negatively to Tairov's letter in a document entitled *A Rebuff to Renegades of Lenin's Nationality Policy*: "Tairov presents means of keeping the Crimean Tatars in perpetual exile by offering them several concessions."[39] Alluding to Tairov's letter, another document asserted that such "ambiguous cultural arrangements have a definite goal—to deceive the people and reconcile them with their situation."[40]

More than ten years later the *Information Bulletin* (no. 2, 1983) of the Initiative Group of the Climean Tatars reported that Uzbekistani authorities intended to form an administrative territorial unit for the Crimean Tatars in the territory of two recently established *rayons*, Bakhoristan and Mubarak, inhabited primarily by ethnic Turkmens. The plan envisioned the recruitment of a local administration from the Crimean Tatars and the establishment of schools and newspapers in the Crimean Tatar language. Calling for Tatars to resist the plan, the Initiative Group explained that its realization would enable the authorities to declare that "the Crimean Tatars are satisfied with the status quo and have nothing more to demand."[41]

Whether the issue is the forcible change of a group's political status, the lack of any such status, or utter disregard of the group by the central government, ethnic movements generally regarded political deprivation as the overall root of all other forms of deprivation. Thus, the Lezghian author I. Kaziev, who wrote the *Letter to the Secretary General of the United Nations* (1980) explained infringements of Lezghian rights in different spheres by the failure of the Lezghians to achieve an autonomous status. On the division of territories populated by Lezghians between the Daghestan Autonomous Republic of the Russian SFSR and Azerbaijan, he wrote, "the people were divided into two channels of heteroethnic development."[42]

Unlike the publications of other national movements, Jewish *samizdat* expressed no interest in the political status of the Jewish Autonomous *oblast*, where Jews constituted only some 5.2 percent of the total population.[43] Instead, Jewish documents continued to refer to the lack of proper supraterritorial political organizations with which to assert the interests of the Jewish population in the Soviet Union.[44]

An *Open Letter* to the Twenty-sixth Congress of the CPSU (1981) by 126 Jews emphasized that "the Jews as a nationality were deprived of any representative institutions to formulate and present their interests and to maintain contacts with Jewish communities in other countries."[45] The lack of such organizations, the authors claimed, rendered Jews vulnerable to anti-Semitism.

Status Deprivation and the Pattern of Ethnic Domination

Although political deprivation is considered the root of all other forms of deprivation, ethnic *samizdat* does not avoid detailing all other aspects and forms of deprivation. The central government's policy of encouraging migration among the Soviet population was viewed with suspicion by ethnic movements as a means of altering the ethnic balance in the Union republics and autonomous regions and, thereby, reinforcing Russian dominance.

An *Appeal* (1964) by the Initiative Committee of the Ukraine's Communists protested against both the emigration of Ukrainian intellectuals to the center (the Russian SFSR) and the mass immigration of Russians and Russian-speakers to the Ukraine.[46] The document claimed that migration led to an immediate increase in the number of local supporters of Moscow's policies and interests and a dramatic decrease in the number of local champions of Ukrainian interests. The *Appeal* also pointed out that removing Ukrainian intellectuals from the republic to Moscow was gradually rendering the Ukrainian elite lifeless.

In discussing the nationality policy of the Soviet leadership, the document indicated that arrangements had been made to both prevent the assimilation of Russian populations in national republics and promote the assimilation of non-Russians living outside their ethnic territories. As an example, the *Appeal* noted the lack of educational and cultural facilities for the five million Ukrainians living in Russia as opposed to the schools, theaters, books, periodicals, and so on, catering to Russians in the Ukraine.

Samizdat documents generally examine two distinct dimensions of ethnic domination: (1) as a "foreign" (usually Russian) influx that lowers the proportion of the native population in their regions; and (2) as "preferential treatment" accorded to the dominant "foreign" ethnic group (mainly Russians) in exploiting national resources. An article published by V. Teren (1964) described a sacrilegious act committed near Shevchenko's monument in Kiev—an assistant professor at the Medical Institute, who had relocated from Russia not long before, urinated on the monument. Reporting that the culprit had not been punished for her crime, Teren concluded, "It is all nothing for such people.... They came to govern Ukrainians, to obliterate our people, our language, our spiritual achievements."[47]

Prominent Ukrainian dissident Sviatoslav Karavansky in his *Appeal to the Chairman of the Soviet of Nationalities of the USSR* (1966) challenged both the influx of Russians into the Ukraine and the privileges enjoyed by the newcomers. He noted that while large groups of retired Russian officers, KGB employees, and so on, were settling in Ukrainian towns and occupying prestigious positions, the indigenous Ukrainian population was left to perform unskilled labor at low wages. "Such an unprecedented colonization of the Ukraine can result in nothing but hostility between the nationalities," declared Karavansky, concluding that the lines of social stratification in the Ukrainian SSR coincided with ethnic lines.[48]

Noting that the Russian population constituted an overwhelming majority in several major Ukrainian cities, Karavansky claimed that this was the result of a deliberate policy intended to alter the republic's ethnic composition in favor of the Russians and to thereby legitimize Russian domination. The system of registration of passports, compulsory for city dwellers, serves as an effective instrument of this policy, enabling Russian newcomers to settle in the national republics' major cities, while the native population was not free to live in the Ukraine or in the other national republics.[49] A year later, in 1967, Karavansky, in his *Petition to the Chairman of the USSR Council of Ministers*, stressed that there was "a typical colonial structure preserved in the national republics, where Russians inhabited the major cities leaving small towns and the countryside for the native population."[50] Another Ukrainian activist, political prisoner Mykhailo Horyn', in his *Appeal* (1967) to the Ukrainian foreign minister, M. Bilokos, noted that the influx of a Russian-speaking population to the Ukraine was accompanied by a vigorous expansion of Russian culture there, despite the fact that Ukrainians living in the Russian Federation were utterly deprived of ethnic and cultural institutions.[51] This theme was reiterated in a lengthy article by M. Sahaidak, "Ethnocide of the Ukrainians in the USSR" that appeared in the *Ukrainian Herald* (nos. 7–8, 1974) edited by the author. Dealing with migratory processes, Sahaidak cited Soviet censuses, interpreting unfavorable demographic trends as the result of a deliberate policy conducted by the center. The article gave the following data on specialists with a higher education per 1,000 residents in the Russian SFSR and the Ukrainian SSR (source uncertain).

	RSFSR	Ukrainian SSR
Russians	43	66
Ukrainians	73	30

The high number of specialists with a higher education among Ukrainians in the Russian Federation is interpreted by the author as a "brain drain," aimed at weakening the intellectual potential of the Ukrainian nation. At the same time, the large proportion of Russians among the total of specialists with a higher education in the Ukraine is regarded as corroboration of the author's premise that Russians in the Ukraine enjoy a privileged status. "Russians are the sole masters of the Ukraine," while Ukrainians in the RSFSR "have nothing to satisfy their [national] needs," concluded Sahaidak.[52]

An *Appeal* (1977) by ninety-six Tatars and Bashkirs addressed to the American ambassador to the United Nations and Western information services noted the unequal opportunities offered to members of different ethnic groups in the Tatar and Bashkir Autonomous Republics. "Russians and the children of mixed marriages can expect to attain quick promotion. As for Tatars and Bashkirs, the role of draught horses for mother Russia has been prepared for them."[53]

Lithuanian medical student M. Zhukauskas, whose 1974 trial was reported by the *Chronicle of the Catholic Church in Lithuania* (no. 10), stated in court that "there were much better conditions created in Lithuania for Russians than for Lithuanians."[54] He added that native Lithuanians were forced to sign contracts with enterprises in Kazakhstan for the single reason that Russian newcomers occupied most workplaces in Lithuania.

The most famous Latvian *samizdat* document, *Open Letter against Russification by Seventeen Latvian Communists*, emphasized that "high commissars" from Moscow had continually directed the republic's cadre politics so that:

All leading positions—and, mainly, all party, state, and economic department head positions—were given to Russian newcomers. These people, in turn, granted other newcomers preference in terms of registration in cities, the allotment of apartments, and appointment to better jobs. To guarantee a massive influx of Russians and Ukrainians into the Latvian SSR, federal inter-republican and zonal government departments have been set up in Latvia, and the construction of new heavy industries, as well as the expansion of existing plants, has been undertaken, disregarding any economic necessity. . . . The local population is being absorbed by the masses of Russian newcomers, and Russian and Ukrainian interests are being furthered by the establishment of massive military bases for members of the armed forces and border guards stationed on Latvian soil and the construction of dozens of medical clinics, rest homes, and tourist facilities for use by the entire Soviet Union.[55]

Like Ukrainian *samizdat* documents, the *Open Letter* referred to the progressive decrease in the ratio of Latvians per the total population of the republic:

> Whereas Latvians constituted 62 percent of the population in 1959, in 1970 they accounted for only 57 percent. Similarly, the population of Riga was 45 percent Latvian in 1959 and only 40 percent Latvian in 1970. The future of such a policy can be clearly discerned from the fate of the former Karelian SSR. It no longer exists; it has been liquidated because local nationals make up less than half of the republic's total population. A similar fate awaits the Kazakh SSR and Latvia.[56]

Noted Latvian dissident Gunnar Rode, in his *Statement* to Soviet leader Leonid Brezhnev (1977), wrote that the "full-blooded Latvian nationality was being reduced to a dying ethnic minority in its own land."[57]

The decreasing number of Latvians in Latvia was the major topic of petitions issued by the Latvian Group Helsinki-86. An *Appeal to the United Nations*[58] and a *Letter to Pope John Paul II*[59] specified complaints about the influx of Russians (Slavs) and benefits enjoyed by them and protested against the accommodation of Chernobyl survivors in Latvia. The documents stressed that victims of the nuclear catastrophe had been "brought to Latvia regardless of our people's will,"[60] and that they could easily move into new houses, whereas Latvians continued "to live penned together in slums."[61]

The theme of a Russian influx seems to be quite scarce in Georgian *samizdat* and is virtually nonexistent in Armenian documents. These two republics demonstrated a stable trend by which the indigenous population of the republics increased in proportion to the total population. Thus, native Georgians constituted 64.3 percent of the population of the Georgian SSR in 1959, 66.8 percent in 1970,[62] and 71 percent in 1979.[63] Similarly, Armenians in the Armenian SSR comprised 88 percent of the Armenian republic's total population in 1959, 88.6 percent in 1970,[64] and 90.5 percent in 1979.[65]

Although they avoid mention of a Russian influx, Georgian and Armenian *samizdat* documents do deal intensively with the topic of Russian domination. Armenian political prisoner Ramzik Zoghrabian stated in his 1975 *Letter from a Labor Camp* that the central government of the Soviet Union habitually sent "the worst representatives of the Russian people to maintain control over Armenia."[66]

A long, anonymous article, *The Review of Relations between Moscow and Georgia Before and After 1917*, commented on the unequal treatment afforded to native populations as compared with Russians in national republics. Much along the lines of the *Open Letter against Russification*, the *Review* found that the construction of local industrial projects—such as a large hydroelectric station on the Inguiry River—was undertaken with the sole purpose of prompting the immigration of Russians into Georgia.[67] While the issue of Russian domination seemed to be more or less peripheral in Georgian and Armenian *samizdat*, documents relating to the state of Armenians and Georgians residing in the adjacent republic of Azerbaijan described the above-mentioned pattern with the difference that a Russian influx was replaced by an Azerbaijani one.

The 1963 *Letter* by the Armenians to Khrushchev[68] asserted that the leadership of the Nagorno-Karabakh Autonomous Region was recruited from among ethnic Azerbaijanis. Another Armenian document, a *Letter* to the Armenian Communist Party leader, written some time after 1967 by B. Movsisian, was more specific. There had once been no Azerbaijani families in the author's village, whereas now there were seventy such families.[69] Information carried by *The Chronicle of Current Events* (nos. 6–8, 1981) concerning discrimination against the Armenian population of Nagorno-Karabakh noted that three out of the five deputies elected to the Supreme Soviet from Nagorno-Karabakh were Azerbaijanis.[70]

Numerous petitions by Georgians concerning the situation in Saingillo in northwestern Azerbaijan described an influx of Azerbaijanis into territories once predominantly Georgian. A *Letter* (1978) by Miron Gamkhareshvili and Archil Otarashvili to the secretary of the Central Committee of the Communist Party of the Georgian SSR, Kolbin, stated that the Azerbaijani authorities' policy was openly directed at the liquidation of Georgian settlements in Azerbaijan. The authors mentioned that Azerbaijani officials had adopted different tactics with regards to the religious affiliations of ethnic Georgians living in the Kakh *rayon* of Azerbaijan: Georgian Muslims were to undergo compulsory assimilation; Georgian Christians were to be forcibly repatriated to Georgia.[71]

A collective *Petition* to Brezhnev (1980), signed by Georgians living in the Kakh, Zakataly, and Belokan *rayons* of the Azerbaijani SSR emphasized that when recruiting personnel for new projects in regions populated by ethnic Georgians, the Azerbaijani authorities systematically chose Azerbaijanis living in other areas as well as Daghestani Muslims—on the condition that the latter would then register themselves as Azerbaijanis. Dealing with the distribution of power in their districts, the authors state that "all official positions are occupied by uneducated Azerbaijanis," while well-educated Georgians had no access to these positions.[72] "There are no Georgians among the regional party secretaries or chairmen of local soviets," complained a *Letter* by Georgian residents of the Kakh *rayon* to the Party Control Committee issued that same year.[73]

The motif of an influx of "foreigners" can be found in Crimean Tatar *samizdat* too. As a rule, documents mentioning the influx of foreigners do so in the context of the failure of individual Tatar attempts to return to the homeland. The Crimean Tatar movement collected and issued hundreds of documents attesting that the Crimean authorities refused to authorize the purchase of homes by Crimean Tatars or to permit them to register passports there.

A *Letter* by R. Iunusov to the academician A. Sakharov told the rather typical story of a Crimean Tatar family that had decided to return to the Crimea. The Iunusovs bought a house in the small village of Gorlinki. One day, *kolkhoz* officials headed by a local party secretary burst into the house and demanded that the family evacuate it. Some time later, as Iunusov's wife took a handicapped daughter for medical attention (and the house was, therefore, unoccupied), the house and all its contents were demolished.[74]

Another Crimean Tatar document, issued in 1967, told of a large family, including children and a seventy-eight-year-old grandmother that was kicked out of its house in the Crimea. The document quoted a Chairman of the Regional Executive Committee of the Crimean Region as saying to family members: "There will never be a place for you in the Crimea."[75] The following year, in 1968, a *Letter* by Crimean Tatars to the Soviet authorities mentioned instructions given to Crimean officials, ordering them to prevent the return of Crimean Tatars to "their native soil."[76]

A document entitled *The Bloody Sunday* discussed events that occurred in 1968. Several Crimean Tatar families arrived in a Crimean village and made a request for employment to the village council. By nightfall, trucks drove up to the site where these families were spending the night, and militiamen seized the sleeping people and flung them into the trucks. Children were snatched from their mothers' arms, the document claimed.[77]

The 1967 *Letter to Brezhnev*, by Crimean Tatar activist Iu. Osmanov claimed that three thousand Crimean Tatars attempting to return to their homeland were forcibly expelled. At the same time, forty thousand people from various regions of the Ukraine had been settled and employed there.[78] A document dedicated to the Twenty-fourth Party Congress (1971) stated, "During the last twenty-seven years, our lands have been squandered and distributed among officers, pensioners, and other foreigners of Russian and Ukrainian origin."[79] The main focus of the Crimean Tatar *Appeal to the Belgrade Conference on European Security* (1977) was the massive influx of Slavs into the Crimea.[80]

Unlike the Crimean Tatars, the Meskhetian Turks and Volga Germans refrained from addressing the issue of a massive influx of foreigners into their respective territories. Thus, an *Appeal to the Twenty-fourth Party Congress* by four members of the Turkish Society for the Protection of the National Rights of the Turkish Meskhetian People[81] quoted statistics on the number of Meskhetian families that had attempted to return to their homeland but were expelled by the Georgian authorities throughout the period 1960–1969,[82] while no mention of a Georgian influx into the region is present in this and other Meskhetian documents. In seeking the support of Georgian public opinion, the Meskhetian national movement chose not to dwell on what they considered a delicate issue.

Volga Germans never constituted the majority population of their autonomous republic; in fact, only a quarter of the German population of the Soviet Union lived there at any time. Therefore, they did not make use of statistics concerning the migration of non-Germans to the republic. They did, however, attach prominence to the political role provided by autonomy as "an effective weapon in the struggle against discrimination."[83]

In dealing with the pattern of ethnic domination, the dispersed ethnic groups tended to accentuate their inferior status among the peoples of the Soviet Union. Other ethnic groups favored pointing to the system by which ethnic Russians were granted preferred status and privileges in their national territories.

In the aforementioned *Appeal* by the Crimean Tatars to the Twenty-third Party Congress one finds an example of the unequal status accorded to the Crimean Tatar people. A 1946 decree by the Supreme Soviet of the USSR branding the Crimean Tatar people "traitors" was issued simultaneously with another decree enabling all ethnic Russians living abroad to return to the Soviet Union and have their citizenship restored automatically. "If you are a Russian, it is enough to obtain clemency for your anti-Soviet activities and your membership in a hostile organization will be forgotten," stated the document. But for anyone unlucky enough to be born a Crimean Tatar, "You and your children and your children's children will be regarded as traitors."[84] The document cited numerous restrictions placed by the Supreme Soviets of the USSR and the union republics on enrollment by Crimean Tatars in the Communist Party and institutions of higher learning. Restrictions also prevented Crimean Tatars from entering various prestigious professions, from traveling abroad, and so on.

A *Resolution of the Sixth People's Assembly of Meskhetian Turks* (1970) emphasized that there were no scientists among the Meskhetians. In all matters pertaining to education, the document claimed, the situation of the Meskhetian Turks was "much worse than that of the African-American population."[85] In his article, *Thoughts about the State of Volga German Citizens* of the USSR, Volga German activist K. Vukkert, claimed that Germans were not nominated to various political positions such as secretaries of regional and district party committees, public procurators, the militia, and KGB officials.[86] Other documents indicated that Soviet Germans were discriminated against in facilities of higher education.[87]

The first known original document of Jewish *samizdat*, the *Letter by Twenty-six Representatives of the Jewish Intelligentsia* (1968) to Lithuanian Communist leader A. Sniečkus, pointed out that no Jews held high official state or party positions in the republic and that Jewish youth did not enjoy equal opportunities in access to higher education.[88] An anonymous article entitled *The Jewish Question in the USSR*, referred to a certain official circular in which comments were made on how it was "undesirable" to appoint Jews to high positions in the defense, rocket, and atomic industries. The article also noted that Jews could not make careers for themselves in the diplomatic service or the party, that they met with more restrictions than other nationalities in making tourist, business, or scientific trips abroad, and so on.[89]

Another article, "About Assimilation," published in the first issue (1970) of the Riga-based Jewish *samizdat* magazine *Iton* (*Iton Aleph*) emphasized that Soviet authorities generally registered children born of mixed marriages as members of the dominant ethnic group. This did not, however, protect the children of such mixed marriages from being discriminated against as Jews in various fields.[90]

The *samizdat* documents of all the aforementioned ethnic groups (Crimean Tatars, Meskhetians, Volga Germans, and Jews) indicate that Soviet authorities generally attributed the personal achievements of members of these minority groups to a dominant ethnic group, while these celebrities were not regarded as "equal" to celebrities actually belonging to dominant groups. The *Appeal by the Crimean Tatars to the Twenty-third Party Congress* said: "They call Zulfira Asanova [the famous dancer] a daughter of the Tajik people, but refused her a visa to participate in a concert tour abroad because she is a Crimean Tatar."[91]

Samizdat of the dispersed ethnic groups expressed serious concerns about the negative stereotypes of Jews, Germans, and Crimean Tatars in the public consciousness. Official Soviet propaganda was blamed as a factor instigating negative feelings toward these minorities. In his *Letter to Brezhnev* (1967) Osmanov, a leader of the Crimean Tatar movement, complained of systematic, hostile propaganda toward the Crimean Tatars in the Soviet mass media and literature and accused specific authors, among them, Pavlenko, Perventsev, Vergasov, Sel'vinskii, and Kozlov of maintaining this negative image.[92] An "Appeal to the Chairman of the Presidium of the Supreme

Soviet of the USSR, N. Podgornyi" by the German couple, the Ruppels, says:

Until the present time, the word "German" invites feelings of hostility and hatred. Soviet Germans are considered enemies. The mass media aggravates preexisting negative emotions by portraying Germans as cruel, hide-bound degenerates.[93]

An essay on Soviet Germans appearing in the *samizdat* magazine, *Re-Patria*, cited a *Course of History of the USSR for Secondary Schools*, edited by Pankratova, in which the Volga German peasantry was called the most reactionary element of the rural population—one that displayed animosity and mistrust to the Russian peasantry.[94] An *Open Letter* (1969) to Soviet Prime Minister A. Kosygin by three Jewish activists (Kleizmer, Borukhovich, and Shlaen) states that all achievements made by Jews have been hushed up, and that the sole available information about Jews coincides with the imaginative inventions of the Black Hundreds' anti-Semitic propaganda. Like the aforementioned Crimean Tatar document, the *Open Letter* named those authors who had exhibited lurid anti-Semitism in their writings, including Kichko, Ivanov, Shevtsov, and others.[95]

Jewish *samizdat* documents interpreted Soviet support for the Arab position since the early 1950s as an additional manifestation of official anti-Semitism. M. Dymshits, a leading defendant at the hijackers' trial (1970), said that anti-Semitism and the Soviet Middle East policy were the primary factors that influenced his decision to emigrate.[96] In the 1968 *Letter by Twenty-six Representatives of the Jewish Intelligentsia* to Lithuanian Communist leader A. Snieckus, there was mention of anti-Israel propaganda in the Soviet press that was provoking popular anti-Semitism.[97] Two later Jewish documents, an *Open Letter* to the Twenty-sixth Party Congress (1981),[98] signed by eighty-one Jews, and an *Appeal to the Delegates of the Twenty-seventh Party Congress* (1985),[99] signed by 140 Jews, described the potentially harmful effects of so-called anti-Zionist publications. "Concentrated propaganda against Jewish nationalism could reanimate anti-Semitism, even if there were no anti-Semitic tradition," claimed the *Open Letter to the Twenty-seventh Party Congress*.[100]

Many *samizdat* documents were written by political prisoners, who viewed the Soviet penitentiary system as a symbol of the great "zone"—the Soviet Communist state. In his letter from the Mordovian labor camp, Ukrainian political prisoner Mykhailo Masiutko contended that different criteria were employed in assessing the gravity of crimes committed by Russians and Ukrainians. He referred to a certain M. Zadorozhnyi, an active participant in the "chauvinistic uprising" of 1957 in Groznyi, where Russian rebels displayed such slogans as "Down with Checheno-Ingush autonomy," "Kill the Chechens," and so on.[101] Reporting that Zadorozhnyi was sentenced to four years in a labor camp, Masiutko countered that participants and supporters of the Ukrainian resistance (1945–1952) were sentenced to no less than twenty-five years. His letter also contended that Ukrainian political prisoners constituted 60–70 percent of the total number of prisoners in the Mordovian "strict-regime" camp, while Russians comprised only about 10 percent. Both Ukrainian and Jewish authors asserted that the conditions and attitudes in the labor camps were far worse for their fellow prisoners than for prisoners of other nationalities.[102]

In 1967, Ukrainian political prisoner M. Horyn', in his letter to the Ukrainian foreign minister, M. Bilokos, defined the practice of having Ukrainian prisoners serve their sentences in Russia as an infringement of their human and national rights.[103] Since then, "foreign captivity" has been a regular motif in the *samizdat* of various national movements. A 1979 *Statement* by six political prisoners in Chistopol prison and nine from the Sosnovka labor camp (both in Mordovia) referred to the practice of sending political prisoners to serve sentences in the remote regions of the Russian Federation as "an instrument in the suppression and extermination of non-Russian peoples, making a mockery of the union republics' institution of citizenship."[104] The *Statement* was signed by activists from the Armenian, Ukrainian, Lithuanian, and Jewish movements, as well as by Russians democrats.

The portrayal of Russians in Soviet propaganda was, to ethnic minorities, an additional proof of Russian domination and, therefore, provoked an extremely negative reaction. Responding to such ideological cliches as "Russian forests," "Russian flax," "Russian beauty," "Russian daring," "Russian fervor," "Russian spaciousness," and so on, prominent Latvian activist Gunnars Astra noted ironically that nobody ever imagines that the word, "Russian" can be replaced by "Latvian" in all these combinations.[105] M. Sahaidak, editor of the *Ukrainian Herald* (Ukrains'kyi Visnyk, nos. 7–8) stated that official Soviet ideology asserted the dominant status of Russians by describing them and their particular "role" as a "peculiar, messianic people." From this, the author contended, to Hitler's theory of an exclusive role for the German people, the distance is not great.[106] "Can it be true that only Russian comrades are not infected by bourgeois ideology? Is this to be considered their national exclusiveness? So why have the Russians never been criticized for Great Russian chauvinism?" asked a *Letter* by young Ukrainian intellectuals from Dnepropetrovsk to *Pravda* in 1968.[107]

Economic Deprivation

Considering economic deprivation to be the result of political subordination, *samizdat* documents by ethnic minorities dealt with the issue in terms of "colonial robbery." Ukrainian activist I. Kandyba, in his *Appeal* from the Mordovian labor camp to Republican Party Secretary P. Shelest, defined the Ukrainian republic as a "colonial appendage of Russia" and asserted that two-thirds of the Ukrainian national wealth is regularly misappropriated by Russia.[108]

M. Sahaidak's essay, "Ethnocide of the Ukrainians in the USSR," appraised Soviet economic policy as "predatory." It specified that the Ukraine contributed 23 percent of all Soviet exports; its share in imports, however, did not exceed 15 percent.[109] At his trial in March 1975, Ukrainian dissident B. Rebryk blamed "Russian colonialism" for "the robbery of the Ukrainian soil, and the unpaid exploitation of natural resources belonging to the Ukrainian people."[110]

A *Letter by Twenty-six Tatars and Bashkirs*[111] alluded to the misappropriation of land, natural resources, and industrial potential by the central government, while another document, an *Appeal to Non-Russian Nationalities*,[112] also issued by Tatar and Bashkir representatives, noted that while the price of meat in Moscow remained stable, in Tataria and Bashkiria, regions that supplied meat to the center, prices had risen by as much as 250 percent. An *Appeal to the United Nations* by the Latvian Group Helsinki-86 attributed the deteriorating living standards in Latvia to the "export of all consumer goods from the republic."[113]

Lezghian writer I. Kaziev pointed to the uneven development of North Daghestan, populated primarily by Avars (the largest of the ten indigenous ethnic groups of Daghestan), and South Daghestan, populated by Lezghians (the second most populous ethnic group in Daghestan). "In North Daghestan high capacity electric power stations, big cities, roads, and modern industry have been established, but South Daghestan remains an agrarian adjunct," he wrote.[114]

Armenian documents generally considered the economic deprivations suffered by Armenians in Nagorno-Karabakh as part of an articulated plan devised by Azerbaijani authorities to oust the local Armenian population from the area. A 1963 *Letter to Khrushchev* accused the Azerbaijani government of imposing restrictions and "creating unfavorable conditions" for economic development in Nagorno-Karabakh and, in particular, of obstructing the development of local agriculture.[115] In discussing the excessive delivery rates imposed by the state on *kolkhozes* in Nagorno-Karabakh, the *Letter* described how people had been forced to take the down from their pillows to fill their quotas. The *Letter* also claimed that the Nagorno-Karabakh Autonomous *oblast* was deprived of access to reservoirs along Karabakh rivers, the exploitation of these waters being permitted solely to Azerbaijani villagers living beyond the *oblast*'s borders. The document cited the trend in which industrial enterprises are transferred from Nagorno-Karabakh to Azerbaijani areas and new projects are frozen, resulting in a rising rate of unemployment among the Armenian population.

Similar claims are found in Georgian *samizdat* dealing with the situation in East Kakhetia (Saingillo). A 1978 *Letter* by M. Gamhareshvili and A. Otarashvili to the Secretary of the Central Committee of the Communist Party of Georgia, Kolbin, noted that some 40 percent of the fertile land belonging to Georgian villages had been confiscated and given to Azerbaijani villages since 1940.[116] A *Petition* by Georgians living in the Kakh, Zakataly, and Belokan *rayons* of Azerbaijan complained that Georgian settlements were deprived of access to water resources in Azerbaijan.[117]

While the theme of economic deprivation was much less prominent in the *samizdat* of dispersed ethnic groups, Crimean Tatar and Meskhetian documents emphasized that the personal property and real estate of the deported peoples had been confiscated illegally. A *Resolution of the Sixth Meeting of the Turkish Society for the Protection of the National Rights of the Turkish Meskhetian People* (1970) reported that in 1956, when the police regime was repealed, Meskhetians were forced by the authorities to relinquish in writing all rights and claims to their confiscated properties.[118] The damages caused by the deportation (and, therefore, the financial loss incurred by the Meskhetians) were assessed by the document at 200 million rubles. A Crimean Tatar *Appeal to the Twenty-third Party Congress* touched on extortionate loans thrust on Crimean Tatar families in exile. According to the document's estimation, these loans were given at 1000 percent interest.[119]

Jewish documents complained of severe restrictions placed on Jewish emigrants wanting to take their assets out of the country and of the inability of elderly emigrants to collect their pensions from the Soviet Union. The most vigorous protest was against an emigration tax imposed on education. In a *samizdat* article entitled *Unchristened Property*, A. Sugrobov called the tax, "a ransom on diplomas."[120]

Environmental Deprivation

There is a strong psychological motivation to translate environmental issues into ethnopolitical ones—to translate and fuse a collective perception of national territory with the idea of environment. "We strive to return to the land not only as our home, but as our breadbasket," said the *samizdat* magazine, *Zemlya*.[121] In this respect the editors, V. Osipov and V. Rodionov, showed that concern for national territory coincides with concern for the environment. While ethnic movements demonstrated a steady concern for the environment, the issue was generally neglected by the democratic movement. This disregard is seemingly rooted in the lack of direct correspondence between the political objectives of the democratic movement and ecological considerations. The 1969 *Program of the Democratic Movement of the USSR* does not mention environmental affairs,[122] whereas the *Open Letter against Russification* does discuss the issue.[123]

Nevertheless, among the nationalist movements the ethnic political factor takes precedence over the ecological issue itself. This assumption is corroborated by the fact that dispersed ethnic groups such as Jews, Crimean Tatars, and Meskhetian Turks disregarded environmental issues in those areas in which they resided,[124] while other groups, due to politicized ethnic perceptions, generally regarded any unfavorable ecological situation in their region as the result of deliberate manipulation. A short article from 1977 and signed by the pen-name, Kukshar, discussed the oppression of Tatars and Bashkirs not only in the traditional manner—as a protest against the influx of "Russian conquerors," who exploit the local natural resources, but also presented a new variation: "Note the regions where oil is extracted—Azerbaijan, the Tatar and Bashkir Autonomous Republics, and the Tiumen region. They [the Russian 'chauvinists'] first try to exhaust natural resources from regions with a Turkic population."[125] The same opposition (subordinated Georgians v. Russian conquerors) can be found in an anonymous article, *A Review of Relations Between Moscow and Georgia Before and After 1917* (1974).[126] The construction of a large hydroelectric power plant on the Inguiry River is condemned because it endangers the environment of Tbilisi and the Kolkhida lowlands. It is considered an element of the politics of russification since the station's personnel are predominantly Russian. As further evidence of the unfavorable policy toward ethnic Georgians, the article cited an allegation that neighboring republics, but not Georgia, would benefit from the power station. The famous *Letter to Gorbachev*, signed by 350 Armenian intellectuals, described the environmental situation in Armenia caused by chemical and nuclear plants.[127] It emphasized that raw materials for the harmful chemical plants were imported from neighboring Azerbaijan, while the neighboring republics and Turkey would benefit from the Armenian nuclear plant.[128]

Territorial Deprivation

Documents of several national movements discussed territorial deprivation. The 1966 *Appeal* by S. Karavansky[129] to the Chairman of the Soviet of Nationalities contained an enumeration of "deliberate mistakes" in drawing boundary lines between republics, namely:

1. Some areas of the Smolensk and Briansk *oblasts* populated by Byelorussians were not allocated to Byelorussia;
2. The Krasnodar *Krai* (Territory), parts of the Voronezh and Belgorod *oblasts* and Taganrog (Rostov *oblast*) were not included in the Ukrainian SSR;
3. Some Moldavian territory was included in the Odessa *oblast* of the Ukraine;
4. Nagorno-Karabakh was not included in Armenia;
5. Some Mordovian and Udmurt territories constituted districts of the Penza and Kirov *oblasts* respectively, Vyborg was not included under Karelian autonomy, and so on;
6. The Ulyanovsk and Orenburg *oblasts* populated by Tatars did not constitute part of the Tatar Autonomous Republic.[130]

Another Ukrainian author, M. Sahaidak, asserted that "Ukrainian ethnic territories such as the western part of the Kuban (the Black Sea coast) and some regions of the Kursk, Voronezh, and Don (he probably meant the Rostov) *oblasts* (regions) were given to the Russian Federation."[131]

The problem of territorial deprivation was much better articulated in the *samizdat* of the Armenian and Georgian movements. E. Hovannisian in his *Letter to the CPSU Central Committee*, said that "Stalin resolved the Armenian question by annexing the areas of Karabakh, Zangezur, and Nakhichevan to Azerbaijan. Roughly, Armenian territory has been decreased threefold."[132] An anonymous Armenian author noted that the transfer, by the Soviet authorities, of Armenian lands to Azerbaijan was in violation of their own resolutions. As a result, Armenian agricultural lands were both extremely limited and unarable.[133]

The *Review of Relations Between Moscow and Georgia* blamed Ordzhonikidze for giving the most fertile soil in northeastern Georgia (Saingillo) and some eastern territories (near David-Garedge) to Azerbaijan.[134] The *Petition to Brezhnev* by Georgians living in the Kakhetia, Zakataly, and Belokan *rayons* of Azerbaijan stressed that these areas had been illegally annexed to the Azerbaijan SSR despite the fact that "this was Georgian land" and that "Georgians constituted the majority of the population."[135]

Cultural and Linguistic Deprivation

Permanent infringements of nationality rights in the cultural and linguistic spheres, as well as high rates of linguistic assimilation among certain ethnic groups, created grounds for the politicization of this issue on the one hand and overestimating the role of language in the survival of ethnic groups on the other hand. "If the language disappears, the culture and nationality itself will disappear too," stated a 1964 leaflet issued to parents of Ukrainian pupils.[136] "The strength of a people is its language," wrote Jewish activist V. Shiffer in a letter to *Izvestia*.[137]

Language was sometimes described as a purely political idea, beyond its communicative function. In his essay, "Ethnocide of Ukrainians in the USSR," M. Sahaidak contended that "a man may not know his language, but if he has a sense of national self-consciousness, he should nonetheless regard the language of his ancestors as his mother tongue."[138] In *Jews in the USSR*, A. Temkin argues: "Probably, my native language is not a language that I know best, but a language in which my ancestors have expressed their thoughts.... It is native not because I can speak it, but because I feel it as being native."[139]

With these sentiments translated into political concepts, the use of native languages became a political issue. In his *Letter to the Administration of the Labor Camp*, Lithuanian political prisoner P. Plumpa described his decision to speak only Lithuanian with the camp's authorities as a means of protesting against being forbidden to use his native language during meetings with relatives—an infringement of his national rights.[140] In contrast, Armenian activist E. Harutiunian mentioned in his petition to the Armenian Catholicos Vazghen that he had sworn an oath "not to speak Armenian pending the reunification of Nagorno-Karabakh with Armenia."[141] *The Chronicle of Current Events* reported that S. Karavansky refused to speak Russian at his trial and demanded an interpreter.[142] His example was later followed by some Jewish activists, who demanded Hebrew interpreters at their trials, notwithstanding their having only a basic knowledge of the language.

Practically, all ethnic movements began to assert themselves politically with expressions of concern over the fate of their national languages and cultures. Even the scanty manifestations of Byelorussian nationalist activity revealed dissatisfaction with the progressively decreasing role played by the Byelorussian language in the republic. The famous Byelorussian dissident Mikhail Kukobaka described his impressions upon returning to his native town after serving several years in a labor camp:

I sighted an inscription on a turnpike. Twenty-five years ago it was written in Byelorussian with the Russian translation below. Now the

Byelorussian phrase has disappeared. To my surprise, this offended me. Suddenly I realized that I am a Byelorussian. From time immemorial my forefathers have lived here, and this land consists of the remains of count-less generations of my kinsmen. I, their descendant, have an undeniable right not only to this land but also to my native language, the right to be Byelorussian.[143]

In the mid-1960s philologist Vasyl' Lobko, a veteran of Ukrainian *samizdat*, published his correspondence with the famous Ukrainian poet, Maxym Ryl'skyi, dating from the years 1960–1964, under the title, *Documents of the Struggle for the Ukrainian Language in the Ukrainian SSR.*[144] Lobko indicated that only 5 percent of all scientific literature published in the Ukrainian SSR was in the Ukrainian language and pointed out that Ukrainian communities in the Kuban, the Soviet Far East, and Siberia had no access to their native language and culture. Examining so-called Russian-national bilingualism, the author assessed it as "a means of obliterating national languages."[145]

As in many other documents published by ethnic movements, Lobko's letters emphasized the advantages enjoyed by the Russian language, enabling its unhindered development. A 1964 leaflet containing an appeal to parents of school-aged children[146] protested against the compulsory inclusion of the "foreign Russian language" in school curricula.[147] The leaflet complained that while Ukrainian parents were deprived of the right to decide whether their children were to study Russian, Russian parents enjoyed the right to determine whether their children would study Ukrainian.

In 1965, S. Karavansky wrote a *samizdat* article, *About One Political Mistake*, in which he discussed the 1959 law, "On the Connection of Schools with Life," according to which pupils of Russian schools in national republics would study the local languages only at their parents request. "Is there an equality of rights if the language of one nationality is compulsory while the language of the other, that of the majority population of the republic is stud-ied only at a parent's request?" the author asked.[148] The *Letter by Young Intellectuals of Dnepropetrovsk* claimed that the town, with a population of one-half million, does not have a single school, kindergarten, or nursery in which Ukrainian is the language of instruction.[149] A 1966 letter by three Ukrainian activists, P. Skochok, V. Chornovil, and L. Sheremet'eva, con-cluded that there was a "constriction of the area of Ukrainian culture and its replacement by Russian culture," in the Ukraine.[150] Iurii Badzio, in a letter to the Chairman of the Union of Ukrainian Writers, noted the meager pro-fessionalism found in the Ukrainian-language press, explaining this in terms of inferior status accorded to the Ukrainian language.[151] M. Sahaidak's essay pointed to the feeble efforts made in teaching Ukrainian language and literature in the schools and universities of the Ukrainian SSR. To confirm his claim of total official disregard for the Ukrainian language, Sahaidak told how at the University of Dnepropetrovsk some courses in Ukrainian literature were given in Russian.[152]

The proximity of the Russian and Ukrainian languages rendered extremely favorable conditions for Ukrainians to enter the Russian cultural-linguistic sphere. In 1979 about 4 million of the 36.5 million Ukrainians living in the Ukrainian SSR regarded Russian as their mother tongue, while only 1.5 million of the 3.7 million Ukrainians then living in the Russian SFSR considered Ukrainian their mother tongue.[153] In other words, the linguistic assimilation of Ukrainians in the Ukraine was about 11 percent while in the Russian SFSR it approached 60 percent. High rates of cultural-linguistic assimilation seem to have created a negative attitude toward Russian among Ukrainian nationalists who spurned the idea of Ukrainians contributing to the culture of the dominant majority.

The issue of cultural-linguistic deprivation is equally prevalent in Latvian *samizdat*. While explicit manifestations of this deprivation coincide with those in the Ukraine, they can be described as two distinct phenomena. Unlike the Ukraine, the rate of linguistic assimilation of the native population of Latvia reached only 2.2 percent (approximately 29,000 out of a population of 1.34 million); however, the assimilation of ethnic Latvians living in Russia reached 45.7 percent. At the same time, there was a marked increase in the Russian-speaking population of Latvia during the period 1959–1970, which grew by 5.2 percent, second only to Estonia with 6.4 percent.[154] The difference between Ukrainians and Latvians is, therefore, that while the diminishing ethnic-cultural realm is portrayed in Ukrainian documents as being the result of the cultural-linguistic assimilation of Ukrainians, Latvian *samizdat* considers the extent of "cultural aggression" to be congruent with the extent of the Russian influx into Latvia and the phenomenon itself to be the result of compliance with demands made by the "Russian conquerors." The *Open Letter against Russification* by Seventeen Latvian Communists argued:

> The arrivals' demands for increased Russian-language radio and television programming have been met . . . . Some two-thirds of radio and television broadcasts are in Russian. Jelinskis, the former director of Riga's broadcasting center, resisted the arrivals' demands and was fired . . . About half of all periodicals issued in Latvia are in Russian. In Latvia there is a shortage of paper hindering the publication of Latvian literary works and schoolbooks; however, the works of Russian writers and Russian schoolbooks are published.[155]

The *Letter* claimed that Russian had become the spoken language in the major social, political, and economic spheres. "Even if there is only one Russian in the collective, his demand that meetings be held in Russian is met," said the *Letter*.[156] It also indicated that locally derived Latvian toponyms had been dropped, and administrative regions, streets, and the like, had been given new Russian names. Like Ukrainian documents, the *Letter* discussed the russification of the educational system, pointing to a growing number of Russian-language schools and kindergartens, and the intensive study programs in Russian offered in schools and institutions of higher learning. More than a decade later, in 1983, Latvian dissident, Gunnars Astra, in a final plea at his trial, employed themes from the *Letter by Seventeen Communists* to describe the total replacement of Latvian by Russian in all spheres. Astra contended that the overwhelming majority of the Russians in Latvia neither knew nor were studying the Latvian language: Russians felt no need to learn Latvian, but Latvians were required to know Russian.[157]

This motif was reiterated in documents of the Latvian Group Helsinki-86: "Despite having lived for decades among our people, Russians are unable to say even 'please' or 'thank you' in Latvian, but they are first to exploit the wealth created by our people."[158] The document also complains of the "contamination" of Latvian with Russian obscenities.

Giving new "Russian" names to local toponyms provoked harsh reactions among several ethnic minorities. Their documents unanimously regarded this trend as a deliberate policy envisaged to "exterminate all obvious manifestations of ethnic historical survival,"[159] and to assert the "Russian right" to the ethnic minorities' territories. An article by Kukshar on the suppression of Tatar-Bashkirs expressed frustration with the new, Russian names given to streets, parks, *kolkhozes*, and the like, in the Tatar and Bashkir Autonomous Republics.[160] Gunnars Astra noted that renaming the main street in Riga was a reflection of the historical collisions of our century: Alexander [II], Briervas (Freedom), Adolf Hitler, and V.I. Lenin.[161]

A 1971 *Statement by the Crimean Tatars* in connection with the Twenty-fourth Party Congress described the custom of renaming local toponyms as being "in accordance with the test of the colonizer": it was practiced by the czarist, Nazi, and Soviet regimes.[162] Thus, Ak'iar was renamed Sevastopol by the czarist regime and Theodorichshafen by the fascists. The village of Buiuk-Ozenbash, which was razed to the ground by fascists, was renamed Schastlivoie (fortunate). "Indeed, nobody can imagine better fortune for the jingoistic Black-Hundreder," concluded the statement.[163]

It must be mentioned that the *samizdat* documents of different ethnic movements offered a more or less common pattern in monitoring cultural-linguistic deprivation. A 1977 *Report* by the Armenian Helsinki group to the Belgrade Conference on European Security asserted that the original culture and language of the Armenian people was "on the verge of annihilation."[164] The *Report* said that on average, one school in which Armenian was the language of instruction was closed and one Russian-language school was opened, annually. The document also mentioned that Russian-language schools and kindergartens usually had better qualified personnel and secured better financing, that Russian had become the language of official correspondence in Armenia, that translations to Armenian from other languages were intentionally impeded, and so on. An Armenian authoress, in an address to the Writers' Congress (1981), stated that Armenian-language education was generally considered inferior, and that Armenian schools were hard-pressed to recruit pupils. Her main focus, however, were areas outside the Armenian SSR populated by Armenians (such as Krasnodar, Kharkov, and some regions in Central Asia), where all Armenian-language schools, newspapers, and other ethnic institutions were closed after World War II.[165]

Georgian *samizdat* expressed particular concern with the status of Georgian language and culture in Saingillo (Eastern Kakhetia), a part of the Azerbaijan SSR, where authorities had adopted the policy of utterly isolating ethnic Georgians from their native language and culture. Steps taken by the Azerbaijani officials included a ban on performances by concert groups from Tbilisi, and on visits to the region by linguistic and ethnographic expeditions from Georgia. Georgian parents were forbidden to give their children Georgian names, books by Georgian writers were withdrawn from libraries, and portraits of Georgian writers were removed from schools.[166] As with other ethnic *samizdat*, Georgian documents protested the dramatic increase in time spent studying the Russian language in Georgian schools.[167] A famous 1980 collective *Letter to Leonid Brezhnev and Eduard Shevardnadze* (then first Secretary of the Georgian Communist Party) by 365 Georgians (among them film directors Gogoberidze and Ioseliani, actress Vera Andzhaparidze, associate member of the USSR Academy of Science Shanidze, and others) emphasized that the promotion of bilingualism had undermined the role of the Georgian language and resulted in faulty knowledge of both Russian and Georgian.[168] In the final analysis, they contended, this would result in the deterioration of the "creative potential of the nation."[169] The *Letter's* main focus was the adoption, in 1975, of Paragraph 83 of VAK (certifying commission) regulations for submitting Ph.D. theses for approval only in Russian. This decision was described as a negation of the legitimacy of "the Georgian language in science."[170] This opinion is shared by the

Armenian authoress, who stated that the move to have dissertations submitted solely in Russian would deny Armenians access to scientific careers, except for those ready to abandon their native language.[171]

Documents, issued by the Tatar–Bashkir movement, deal intensively with the problems of cultural-linguistic deprivation. Kukshar's short article claimed that the Russian population of both autonomous republics was insulted when they heard the Tatar or Bashkir languages in public places.[172] Another document, the *Appeal* by ninety-six Tatars and Bashkirs, described how the authorities shut national schools in the towns and even in the countryside on the pretext of heeding the alleged "request of parents."[173] As a result, graduation certificates were given to people who knew neither Russian nor the native language and culture. The *Appeal* asserted that the study of foreign languages at an early age is harmful for children and, because of learning Russian, "the nation loses many great talents."[174]

Another Tatar–Bashkir document, an *Appeal to Non-Russian Nationalities* (1977),[175] like the 1965 *Letter* by Ukrainian S. Karavansky,[176] saw in the demand that candidates must pass university entrance examinations in Russian, a deliberate attempt to weed out non-Russian candidates. The *Appeal* also discussed the abandonment of the Arabic script for the Roman one in the 1920s, and the Roman for the Cyrillic in the 1930s, considering this to be a means of isolating younger generations of Tatars and Bashkirs from their cultural-historical heritage, so as to "create a utopian land of cattle-like people."[177]

An *Appeal to Compatriots* by Ahmed Shazzo, a young historian, appeared in Adygei *samizdat* in 1977. He indicated that the adoption of the Cyrillic script by Adygei had not only isolated the people from their culture and religion, but also impeded communication with related groups abroad.[178]

The problem of cultural and linguistic deprivation received its most acute expression in the *samizdat* of dispersed ethnic groups, as a result of their high rate of linguistic assimilation. In 1979, 57 percent of Volga Germans (75 percent in 1959 and 66.8 percent in 1970) and 14 percent of Jews (21.5 percent in 1959 and 17.7 percent in 1970)[179] called German and Yiddish their native languages.[180]

The Crimean Tatar *Appeal to the Twenty-third Party Congress* noted a dramatic decrease in the number of books published in the Crimean Tatar language: in 1940, there were 218 titles, but from 1944 to 1966, only ten titles were published.[181] As for the problem of education, the *Appeal* mentioned that in 1940 there were 427 schools in which Crimean Tatar was the language of instruction: in contrast, throughout the years of exile not a single such school had been opened. *An Appeal by Crimean Tatars to the Politburo, Soviet Government, and All Peoples of the USSR* estimated that "70 percent of the Crimean Tatars are illiterate in their native language."[182] "My people has been deprived not only of the Crimea, its motherland, but of its mother tongue as well," concluded Crimean Tatar activist Aishe Seitmuratova in her 1977 *Appeal to the Belgrade Conference on European Security*.[183] A *Letter* by four Meskhetians (E. Odabashev and others) to the Soviet leadership (1971) drew attention to the dangers of losing ethnic identity inherent in an alien cultural-linguistic environment.[184]

The first document of the German movement, a *Statement* by the delegation of Soviet Germans (9 January 1965), pointed to the lack of national schools and cultural institutions, "poor" teaching of German as the vernacular, and so on.[185] Ia. Damm in his 1973 petition to OVIR (the department for visa and registrations) cited the lack of national schools and cultural institutions for the Soviet Germans as a major factor behind his decision to emigrate.[186] A long essay, entitled "The Soviet Germans," published in the *samizdat* Almanac *Re-Patria* found that only a small anthology of Soviet German poets had been issued in twenty-three years.[187]

The Jewish movement's method of dealing with the problem of cultural-linguistic deprivation was no different from those of other dispersed groups. An *Open Letter* to A. Kosygin by G. Feigin, D. Zilberg, and R. Alexandrovich stated that Soviet Jews "were deprived of their spiritual and cultural heritage," and pointed to the closing of Jewish schools and theaters, the suppression of newspapers, the extermination of Jewish writers, and so on.[188] A 1973 article by I. Begun, entitled "On the History of the Jewish Language," described the growing suppression of the Jewish culture and language in the USSR, culminating in their total destruction in 1948–1950: since that time, the Jewish culture has never recovered.[189] The article compared the data of the 1909 census, in which 96.6 percent of Jews in the Russian Empire called Yiddish their native language, with the results of the 1970 census. But the focus of Begun's article was the ban imposed by Soviet authorities on teaching and studying Hebrew and the repressive measures taken against those Jews who dared to do so. He included his correspondence with a District Financial Department, which refused to register him as a Hebrew teacher. Numerous petitions by unofficial Hebrew teachers and students protesting against the authorities' repressions of Hebrew comprised a substantial section of Jewish *samizdat* material in the 1970s and 1980s.[190] *An Appeal by 126 Jews to the Twenty-sixth Party Congress* commented that Jews had established an all-Union record in linguistic and cultural assimilation, with Yiddish dying out and Hebrew subjected to severe repressions.[191]

The disregard, or "hushing up," of "national history" and historic monuments comprised another regular motif in ethnic *samizdat* concerned with cultural deprivation. Levko Luk'ianenko, in his *Petition to the Chairman of the Presidium of the Ukrainian Supreme Soviet*, D. Korotchenko, pointed out that "Ukrainian pupils study the history of Russian czars, not the history of our own people."[192] Luk'ianenko accused the Soviet authorities of intending to conceal "from new generations the rich spirituality of our ancestors," in order to cultivate the idea that "nothing in our past is to be considered worthy of notice."[193] S. Karavansky, in his *Petition to the Chairman of the USSR Council of Ministers*, protested against "the distortion of history" and "the humiliation of national heroes" in official Soviet historiography.[194]

A *Petition* by Lithuanian Catholics to the Committee for Religious Affairs (1973), signed by 16,498 citizens, complained against one-sided, biased interpretations of Lithuanian history by school textbooks.[195] It noted that while the textbook for the study of Lithuanian history consisted of only 148 pages, the textbook for Soviet history contained 650 pages. "Pupils are well informed about Pugachev and Peter the Great, but know nothing about the glorious past of Lithuania," said the *Petition*.[196] Similarly, the *Letter to Brezhnev and Shevardnadze*, signed by 365 Georgians, mentioned that only one-quarter of all school history lessons were devoted to Georgian history.[197]

The Estonian *samizdat* magazine *Izekiri* (no. 2, 1983) complained about the coverage of the 350th anniversary of the University of Tartu in the Soviet press.[198] The jubilee of the oldest university in the USSR, which counted among its graduates famous writers, scientists, philosophers, and politicians of international prominence, including the Russians Burdenko, Dal', Iazykov, Pirogov, Struve, Veresaev, and others, was the most important event in Estonia in 1982. At the same time, the jubilee was completely ignored by the Moscow press. The article considered this an attempt to depreciate Estonian scientific and cultural achievements and to humiliate the Estonian people.

In *Thoughts about the Status of German Citizens of the USSR*, Volga German activist K. Vukkert said that a book on historical sites in the Saratov *oblast* failed to mention ethnic Germans, as if they had not lived there for over 150 years.[199] An *Open Letter to the Twenty-sixth Party Congress* by 126 Jewish activists emphasizes that "there was, in the nineteenth century, the largest Jewish community in the world [in the former Russian Empire], but museums do not have sections dedicated to Jewish history or ethnography, and history text books fail to mention Jews."[200] Latvian G. Rode, in his *Statement to Brezhnev*, protested against "twisting the history of the Latvian people" and the "obliteration of historical and cultural values."[201]

Issues concerning historical monuments were also examined by ethnic *samizdat* from a political perspective. The state of historical relics was discussed in the official press of the 1960s and 1970s, since this was partially permitted by the Soviet authorities. However, while official publications avoided politicizing the issue, *samizdat* documents accentuated its ethnopolitical implications. An Armenian *samizdat* document stated that the Azerbaijani authorities had sanctioned the destruction of Armenian relics in Nakhichevan and Nagorno-Karabakh in order to obliterate all material proofs of Armenian settlement in these territories.[202] The same claims against the Azerbaijani authorities are expressed in Georgian documents. The essay on relations between Georgia and Russia told how the medieval fresco in the David-Garedzh monastery was blotted out and several orthodox churches and fortresses were destroyed in Georgian-populated areas of the Azerbaijan SSR. The essay asserted that in contrast, all Muslim relics were well preserved in Azerbaijan.[203]

A study by Georgian dissident Zviad Gamsakhurdia, entitled *The State of Relics of the Christian Culture in Georgia*, cited appeals made by specialists to General Shkrudnev, deputy commander of the Transcaucasian Military District, concerning damages caused to buildings of the David-Garedzh Monastery by locating firing ranges around it. "I can hardly imagine that General Shkrudnev does not know about the huge sums invested and measures taken to preserve relics in Suzdal, Novogorod, Pskov, and Vladimir. So much the more disappointing is his indifference to the cultural relics of Georgia."[204]

An *Appeal* to Brezhnev (1980) by Georgians of the Kakh, Zakataly, and Belokan *rayons* of the Azerbaijan SSR,[205] echoed the Armenian explanation of the Azerbaijani authorities' policy.[206] Azerbaijan officially pursues its objective of obliterating all Georgian relics in East Kakhetia, which would indicate that the territory is "age-old Georgian land," and "pretending that Azerbaijani culture has always existed here."[207]

A 1971 Crimean Tatar document contended that "modern Russian chauvinists consider the culture and history of the Crimean Tatar people to be an obstacle for the realization of their monstrous plans."[208] So, according to the document, they intended to eliminate "everything reminiscent of the history of the native inhabitants."[209] The document told how Crimean Tatar libraries were closed and plundered, valuable books were burned, and numerous historical-cultural monuments in Crimea were destroyed, while others survived precariously. The authors vigorously protested against the conversion of the Oriental Museum in Yalta and the celebrated palace in Bakhchisarai (containing unique exhibits of Crimean Tatar art and ethnographic collections) into "centers for the popularization of the czarist regime's history and predatory policy."[210]

In 1981, a group of Jewish activists from Moscow, Kiev, and other towns arrived in Babi Yar to commemorate the fortieth anniversary of the mass extermination of Ukrainian Jews and to lay a wreath at the site of the massacre. KGB and militia servicemen prevented the group from attending the memorial. The incident provoked a series of protest letters by Jewish activists, who blamed the Soviet authorities for hushing up the catastrophe of European Jewry and revealing insulting disregard for the victims of the massacre.[211]

The *Letter* by young Ukrainian intellectuals from Dnepropetrovsk contained an account of historical relics destroyed in the town.[212] There were no monuments in honor of prominent Ukrainians, the authors noted, but new monuments celebrating Russian writers, composers, heroes of the Great Patriotic War, and so on, had recently been erected in Dnepropetrovsk. An article by the Tatars-Bashkirs asserted that churches in Kazan had been restored beautifully, while mosques were completely and utterly neglected.[213] The *Letter by Twenty-six Representatives of the Jewish Intelligentsia* stressed that no synagogues or other Jewish historical monuments had been restored in Lithuania; at the same time, funds were regularly allotted to restore Catholic churches.[214]

Religious Deprivation

The suppression of religion and infringements of believers' rights appear in the documents of all ethnic movements as a constituent element of the general problem of relative deprivation. Ethnic *samizdat* virtually never discusses the universal, supraethnic aspects of religious systems.

In his *Letter to the Procurator General of the USSR* (1966), G. Budzinsky, a Greek Catholic priest, declared that the fabrication of a criminal case against him was striking evidence of infringements against both national and religious rights.[215] He defined the liquidation of the Greek Catholic (Uniate) Church in the Western Ukraine in 1946 as "a forcible conversion of Catholics to the Russian faith."[216] Though an Uniate priest, Budzinsky also found it necessary to mention the discrimination faced by Ukrainian Orthodox believers, doing so within an ethnic context. The affiliation of the Ukrainian Orthodox to the Russian Orthodox Church is described as the key point of religious deprivation, resulting in discrimination against Ukrainian Orthodox believers. He emphasized that, unlike the Georgian, Armenian, Polish, or Czech Orthodox Churches, the Ukrainian Orthodox Church does not exist as a national entity. "The Russian Orthodox Church rules over the

Ukraine, and refusal to be converted to the Russian faith means death," he concluded emotionally.[217] An *Appeal to the Soviet Government* by Ukrainian Catholic believers (1986) sought to advance the "rights of the Ukrainian Church."[218]

M. Sahaidak, in his essay "Ethnocide of Ukrainians in the USSR," considered the liquidation of the Ukrainian Autocephalous Church in the 1930s and of the Uniate Church in Western Ukraine in the 1940s to be stages in "Moscow's struggle against the Ukrainian Church."[219]

A letter by Georgian dissident Z. Gamsakhurdia to the *New York Times* stated that Moscow controlled all appointments to the hierarchies of the Georgian Orthodox Church, subordinating it to the Soviet Communist authorities.[220] The traditional Jewish equation of nationality and religion is preserved in Jewish *samizdat*. The lack of religious education, the closing of synagogues, the ban on producing and importing religious articles, and so on, are cited as manifestations of a discriminatory policy toward the Jewish people.[221]

An article by Christopher Doersam analyzing twenty-four issues of the *Chronicle of the Catholic Church in Lithuania* (March 1972–February 1977) concluded that "in this period the subject matter of this journal has undergone a considerable evolution. Initially a periodical reporting incidents of religious persecution, it has transformed itself into a journal increasingly reflecting all the nationality's discontents."[222] A *Memorandum* by members of the Catholic Church in Lithuania to the Secretary General of the United Nations stressed that ethnicity was an underlying factor in religious persecution. "For our believers, the liberty of conscience still does not exist."[223]

As with other forms of deprivation, ethnic *samizdat* tended to emphasize the contradiction between oppression of a "national religion" and promotion of the dominant group's religion. An anonymous author of Georgian *samizdat* noted that Azerbaijani authorities in the Kakh *rayon* forbade the opening of an Orthodox Church while the Muslim religion was welcome in the area.[224] At the same time, Kukshar, an author of Tatar–Bashkir *samizdat*, asserted that there is not a single mosque in many districts of the Tatar and Bashkir Autonomous Republics with populations of 30,000–50,000 Muslims, whereas Russian Orthodox believers enjoy all benefits that would enable them to practice their religion.[225]

Conservative Russian Samizdat and the Issue of Relative Deprivation

The motif of relative deprivation in Russian *samizdat* indicated, to no small degree, a split between the liberal democratic and Russian conservative movements. The first (1968) *samizdat* document complaining about relative deprivation suffered by Russians did not originate with the dissident movement. It circulated as a *Letter* by an anonymous resident of Ufa, the capital of Bashkir Autonomous Republic. The *Letter* was addressed to a "Dear Friend,"—an otherwise anonymous member of the Communist Party Central Committee.[226] The author, as a lecturer at the Institute of Agriculture, expressed discontent with the growing self-assertiveness of non-Russian nationalities. He claimed that the native populations of the Baltic Republics and Georgia displayed a negative attitude toward Russians; students in Latvia and Moldavia even wrote "Russians, go home!" in school auditoriums. The author was exasperated by those nationals who pretended that they did not know Russian and deliberately answered in their native language. In Ukraine, he stressed, "even executives attempt to speak Ukrainian."[227]

The author recalled an example of behavior insulting to the Russian people that occurred at the institute where he worked. In the office of the Institute's party committee, he met two nationals, one of them the Party Secretary, speaking their language. Thinking that they did not want him to understand, he asked them: "Maybe I should leave?" "No, no, you ought to study our language," said the Party Secretary. "If it is not nationalism, then it must be impertinence," concluded the author emotionally.[228] This anonymous resident of Ufa considered the poor knowledge of Russian as a sign of disrespect toward the Russian people and was infuriated at a television appearance by a Bashkir singer who "could not speak Russian."

The rise of a native intelligentsia, the advancement of local specialists, and even the "influx" of many non-Russian nationals into the sanatorium, where the author was staying were cited to prove the author's suspicions concerning the anti-Russian politics found in the national republics of the USSR. "The Great Russian people saved Tatars, Bashkirs, and all other peoples from the ignorance of slavery and lack of rights. Which way should representatives of the Great Russian people, who had done the saving go now?" the *Letter* asked in desperation.[229]

In 1970, the most famous programmatic document of Russian conservative nationalism, the *Manifesto of Russian Patriots*, entitled *Slovo natsii* (The Nation Speaks), appeared in *samizdat*.[230] Describing points of deprivation, the document claimed that, unlike other peoples of the USSR, the Russian people did not enjoy political sovereignty. To prove this, the *Manifesto* argued that by not having a separate Russian Communist party the Russians played a disproportionately small role in party politics.

Relative deprivation appeared in Russian conservative *samizdat* largely as a reaction to both the rise of non-Russian ethnonationalist movements and to the Russian Liberal Democratic movement's support for their political self-assertiveness. Yaroslav Bilinsky, in his essay "Russian Dissenters and the Nationality Question,"[231] indicated that *Slovo natsii* "engages in lengthy and bitter polemics with the preceding *Program of the Democratic Movement*, particularly on the nationality question. It is, in fact, a polemical reply to the corresponding section in that Program."[232] The *Manifesto* also alluded to claims advanced by the Ukrainian, Georgian, and Armenian movements and attempted to repudiate them.

Of all possible reactions to the self-assertiveness of subordinated ethnic groups the Russian conservative movement adopted the strategy of mirroring manifestations of the minorities' nationalism. Thus, utilizing a popular claim concerning political deprivation, *Slovo natsii* asserted that the Russian people were underrepresented in governmental structures and the All-Union Party agencies.[233]

The issue of territorial deprivation is reflected in the conservative Russian claim that entire Russian provinces such as the Crimea, Kharkov, Donetsk, Lugansk, and Zaporozhie *oblasts* were handed over to Ukrainian jurisdiction. The issue is also raised in an allegation that Kazakhstan's status is "unconstitutional" since the Kazakhs "comprise only one-third of the total population."[234] The issue of economic deprivation is mirrored by *Slovo natsii* in the allegation of unlawful redistribution of resources in favor of the Transcaucasian republics—a "parasitic growth on the body of our country," according to the document.[235]

The claim that Russians enjoy a dominant status is countered by *Slovo natsii*'s claim that Jews dominated Soviet science and culture. The Jews are described as "the new Germans, standing in the way of Russian Lomonosovs, while poor 'privileged' Russians are driven into a corner."[236] The document rejects accusations of anti-Semitism, stating that Jews enjoy a far better living standard than Russians and other peoples of the USSR.

The question of relative deprivation was originally devised by the Russian "patriotic" journal, *Veche* (The Council). This journal, edited by famous Russian dissident V. Osipov, appeared regularly from 1971. An anonymous letter published in *Veche* (no. 4) described the humiliation of Russians by "impudent aliens": A daughter of the author's friend, "an ordinary Russian woman," married a Georgian. At the wedding party Georgian relatives of the fiancé "sang their national songs, and did not permit Russians to sing their own songs." Insulted, the Russians "moved to a neighbor's room with their home-brew" to continue the celebration. "This slight incident reflects the present state of the overwhelming majority of the Russian people. This is what we have come to; in the very heart of Russia, aliens can prevent us from singing our own Russian songs. We Russians have become accustomed to trembling, to shrinking from the impudence of alien boors," contended the letter.[237]

The idea that Jews enjoyed a privileged position in the Soviet Union is presented in conservative Russian *samizdat* as part of a striking pattern of alien domination. The author, or authors, of an anonymous essay entitled "The Struggle against So-Called Russophilism, or the Way of National Suicide," (*Veche*, no. 7), stated that the youth newspaper *Komsol'skaia pravda* carried material openly written in the "spirit of Jewish exclusiveness," whereas "several patriotic sentences published in the press led to a massive campaign against patriotically-oriented writers."[238]

A short item in *Veche*, signed O.L.,[239] reviewed an article by D. Pospelovsky, "The Resurgence of Russian Nationalism in *Samizdat*," published in the British journal *Survey*.[240] The item inferred that "Jews, backed by the Western press, have obtained more rights than any other nationality."[241] In the same issue of *Veche* its editor, V. Osipov, stated that the Jewish minority had ruled over the spiritual life of the USSR for two decades.[242]

Seeking subjects conducive to political propaganda, Russian conservative *samizdat* blamed anti-Russian politics for the dire ecological situation and the miserable state of historical-cultural monuments. Two articles deal with these topics. The first, "The Fate of the Russian Capital," by an anonymous author, was published in *Veche* (no. 1, 1971).[243] The second, "The Last Day of Moscow," was written by *Veche*'s editor, V. Osipov, in 1973.[244] Both describe the total destruction of the unique historical and environmental heritage of Moscow through the demolition of its architectural masterpieces, the collapse of its geographical landscape, the destruction of its gardens, and the diversion of its rivers. These factors have all contributed to the deterioration of climatic conditions in the capital. In accordance with the chosen model, V. Osipov interprets the catastrophic ecological situation as a sequence of deliberate actions to obliterate Moscow, "to build a new Babylon on its plot," and "ruin the Russian spirit and love of the Russian people for their fatherland."[245] The same position can be found in an anonymous article that discusses a plot to destroy Russian culture and replace it with a cosmopolitan one.[246]

An anonymous article, "The Fatherland is in Peril" (1982), protested vigorously against diverting waters from both European and Siberian rivers into the North Caucasus and Soviet Central Asia.[247] One motive behind this protest is the alleged benefit it will have for non-Russian peoples. The article blamed the Soviet authorities for "neglecting the principal, pivotal people of the state," considering the project to be "a challenge to the Russian people's interests, fraught with the threat of secession of Soviet republics."[248]

Veche (no. 10) carried an article by A. Skuratov devoted to the polemics between A. Solzhenitsyn and A. Sakharov provoked by Solzhenitsyn's *Letter to Soviet Leaders*.[249] Skuratov states that in the two post-Revolutionary decades politics in the USSR were conducted "ruthlessly, obliterating Russian culture, persecuting the Russian Orthodox Church—in addition to the politics of derision and the desecration of Russian history"[250]

Russian conservative *samizdat* identified those individuals defined by Osipov as the purveyors of an anti-Russian policy. According to him, this policy was conducted by cosmopolitan authorities—people such as Stalin, Kaganovich, Khrushchev, Moscow's architect-in-chief, M. Posokhin, and others.[251] In contrast, the author of "The Fate of the Russian Capital"[252] emphasized the non-Russian origin of those people responsible for anti-Russian policy, claiming that they were ethnically and ideologically alien. He mentioned the non-Russian (primarily Jewish) names of the architects who destroyed the Moscow landscape, noting that among their predecessors were such "ideologically, extremely odious persons" as "a Free Mason and westernizer, Bazhenov, and two Germans."[253] The anonymous author of the "Response to Lev Andreev," published in *Veche* (no. 8), attributed the role of the manipulating powers that directed anti-Russian policy to the "dark forces of international Zionism, supported by a few Russians."[254]

M. Antonov,[255] in his serialized essay on Slavophiles, cited the names of "aliens" whose activity was "aimed at the destruction of the cultural heritage of the Russian people."[256] A note published in *Veche* (no. 9) in response to an article in *Survey* on Russian nationalism, offered an exhaustive explanation of the objectives envisaged by these 'alien' manipulative forces: "cultural genocide, permanent damage to the Russian genetic pool, the dispersal of allegations concerning the inferiority and depravity of Russia and Russian culture."[257]

Non-Russian documents on relative deprivation tended to base their arguments on empirical facts: Russian conservative *samizdat* finds in literary reminiscences a serviceable replacement for facts. The authors of many documents were inclined to regard the judgments of their political opponents as manifestations of the deprivation itself:[258]

> Russia is hated; it is covered with accusations, ruin is predicted for it . . . .
> But the main thing is that Russia fails to be understood. All judgments
> about her are human conjectures. . . . Russia, the greatest sufferer, slandered, and crucified.[259]

Ya. Bilinsky's article, "Russian Dissenters and the Nationality Question," found in this passage from an anonymous collection of epigrams published in *Veche* (no. 2), an allusion to Amalrik's book, *Will the Soviet Union Survive until 1984?* Russian conservative documents generally employed axiomatic methods in drawing inferences. Most were deeply rooted in primordial emotions: "Is the spiritual exhaustion of the Russian people not evident?" asked Osipov.[260] "The national humiliation of the Russian people has reached such a level that almost no one is oblivious to it. . . . We are humiliated and slandered. We are blamed for imposing a yoke that is not ours, not of us. But the yoke is regarded as our national fault, and we have been insulted for it. . . . Our state is grievous in all respects" he concluded.[261]

The Discourse of Relative Deprivation: Common Trends

In discussing relative deprivation, Russian conservative *samizdat* and the *samizdat* of ethnic minorities shared many common trends. All ethnic movements regarded deprivation as a major factor in the political mobilization of their fellow ethnic groups. An early Crimean Tatar *samizdat* document pointed out that "the crime of 1944 and all succeeding crimes are the best incentive in mobilizing and organizing the people to fight for the right to survive and develop."[262] G. Fleig, a German, in his *Letter to the Central Committee of the CPSU*, reached a similar conclusion: "Discrimination always results in the accentuation of national pride and in increased interest in the national language and cultural values of the people."[263] The author of the article *Why Am I Zionist?* assessed the impact of relative deprivation on the politicization of ethnic groups:

> Why do the most active groups of Jewish youth continue to preserve feelings of national solidarity, though they know neither the Jewish culture and tradition nor the language? The answer is simple. To a large degree we should be grateful to anti-Semitism. . . . It is only anti-Zionism/anti-Semitism that does not allow us to relax and unites us more and more closely.[264]

V. Osipov, in a letter to the Russian emigrant newspaper *Novoie Russkoie slovo*, asserted that the rise of Russian nationalism is "a protective reaction of the nation, sentenced to annihilation."[265] Ukrainian human rights activist M. Masiutko, in his *Appeal to the Supreme Soviet of the Ukrainian SSR*, indicated that "nationalism is a response to existing chauvinism. There is no nationalism without chauvinism."[266]

An essay by Ukrainian dissident Valentin Moroz, written in 1970, stated that the arrests of Ukrainian intellectuals in 1965 "have not impeded, but accelerated the Ukrainian revival."[267] In another essay by Moroz, *Instead of My Final Plea*, he warned the Soviet authorities against repressions: "You have introduced the element of supreme sacrifice. Society has already reached such a degree in its development that your repression provokes an adverse reaction. . . . You are launching a boomerang."[268] Generalizing on the experience of the dissident movement, two Ukrainian political prisoners, Olexa Tyhyi and Vasyl' Romaniuk, indicated that "the intensity of the dissident movement throughout the seventies was the result of increased pressure on the national cultures of non-Russian peoples in addition to the resurgence of Stalin's methods in dealing with differently-minded people."[269]

I have already mentioned the common tendency of non-Russian documents to cite and compare statistical data as proof of relative deprivation. M. Zhukauskas, in dealing with Soviet repressive politics, mourns the loss of three hundred thousand Lithuanians.[270] A *Memorandum by Representatives of the Native Population of Estonia, Latvia, and Lithuania* claimed that the Baltic countries lost one-third of their total population "in consequence of the policy of genocide," that is, deportations and mass executions.[271]

One Crimean Tatar document estimated that the death rate during the first few years after the deportation exceeded 50 percent of the total Crimean Tatar population.[272] Another document stated that the Crimean Tatars' mortality rate reached 46.3 percent in the first year after the deportation, while the death rate in the USSR during the Great Patriotic War reached about 2 percent per year.[273] Pointing to continuity in predatory Russian colonial policies, Crimean Tatar documents estimated that the total Crimean Tatar population declined by 7.7 million (96 percent) in 130 years (from 8 million in the seventeenth and eighteenth centuries to 320,000 in 1917).[274]

Jewish and Latvian *samizdat* documents used data on fertility, mortality, and life expectancy to prove relative deprivation among fellow ethnic groups.[275] Similarly, a long article by K. Voronov in *Veche* (no. 9), entitled "Demographic Problems of Russia"[276] noted the low fertility, high mortality, and low life expectancy in all regions of the Russian Federation populated by the Russians. Arguing against A. Iakovlev's attacks on Russian nationalism, another article in *Veche* (no. 7)[277] alleged that the Russian population of the USSR was growing at only half the rate of the rest of the country's population.[278]

The rapid increase of the Uzbek population (50 percent in eleven years) was exploited by A. Skuratov as his sole argument against Sakharov's assertion of a catastrophic environmental situation in Uzbekistan.[279] Correspondingly, he used this as proof of his own statement that the Russians suffered from a deprived status in the USSR, since the Russian population had increased only 13 percent in the same period. Skuratov, described the relative deprivation of the Russians in terms of degree emphasizing the exceptional nature of the "Russian case." In a discussion with Sakharov he stated that during the first two decades of Soviet rule, the Bolshevik government respected the traditions of all ethnic groups except the Russians: no other religion was persecuted with such cruelty as Russian Orthodoxy.[280] "All other nationalities have the right to declare and assert their national sentiments and even their hostility toward everything connected with Russia. At the same time, when the Russian movement directs its energies toward the preservation of the universal roots of Russian culture, it falls victim to allegations of racism," contended a *Statement* in *Veche* by eleven contributors.[281]

To much the same extent, non-Russian *samizdat* documents emphasized the extraordinary character (whether in quality, degree, etc.) of their peoples' deprivations: "The language of no other people has traversed such a thorny path [as the Ukrainian language]," stated V. Lobko.[282] "Why is the Georgian church deprived of elementary rights enjoyed by churches in all Union republics?" questioned Z. Gamsakhurdia in his *Appeal to Brezhnev*.[283] Another Georgian document, *The Review of Relations between Moscow and Georgia Before and after 1917*, pointed out that because of Stalin's particular hatred for Georgians, they had suffered the greatest losses.[284]

A *Letter by the Crimean Tatars to the Central Committee of the CPSU* (1972) claimed that there was an "unprecedented prosperity [enjoyed] by all national cultures" in the USSR, with the exception of the Crimean Tatar culture.[285] An *Appeal to Gorbachev* (1986) reiterated this: "The CPSU program states that the nationality question has been completely resolved in the USSR. This is true concerning many nationalities, but not the Crimean Tatar people."[286]

An appeal to N. Podgornyi by the German couple, the Ruppels, asserted that "all other peoples [except the Germans] who have been subjected to unjust repressions are now utterly rehabilitated."[287] Three Jewish activists (Klesizmer, Borukhovich, and Shlaen), in the *Letter* to Soviet Premier Alexei Kosygin (1969), complained that "Unlike other peoples living in the USSR, the Jewish people is subjected to brutal discrimination."[288] Twelve years later, an *Appeal to the Twenty-sixth Party Congress* insisted that "The state of the Jewish people cannot be compared in its gravity of deprivation with the state of other ethnic minorities."[289] The Lezghian dissident writer I. Kaziev, bemoaning the assimilation of the Lezghians and the loss of their lands, proclaimed that "The nationality question has been resolved for all the peoples of Daghestan, except for the Lezghians."[290]

A number of empirical studies[291] indicate "that fraternal RD, rather the egoistic RD, as current theories suggest, is an important factor in the explanation of protest movements."[292] The *samizdat* documents provide strong support to these findings. The references to relative deprivation in documents of the ethnic movements are expressed in terms of fraternal deprivation even if they deal with the cases of individual grievances.

These references seem to have been not merely reflections of actual material conditions but rather collective judgments on relative deprivation, the collective interpretation of the feeling of discontent. Moreover, the same "material condition" sometimes finds the antipodal interpretations by different ethnic movements (e.g., the fact of absence of the Central Committee of the Communist Party of Russian Federation in assessment by the Russian conservative movement and by the ethnic minority movements).

The data collected from *samizdat* documents support a group of empirical studies, which connect the perception and interpretation of relative deprivation to social comparison.[293] The comparison of status of the fellow ethnic group with that of others comprises an important element of the *samizdat* references to relative deprivation. Regarding the question "who these comparison others are likely to be"[294] we can indicate that in all models of relative deprivation an element of "comparison others" is present as a variable. Usually, the role of "comparison others" is attributed to the dominant ethnic group (or to a group considered to be dominant in the particular area). In some cases, the authors of documents choose to compare the status of their nationality to that of "all others" in order to stress the particularity and uniqueness of relative deprivation experienced by their fellow ethnic group.

The idea of non-social, or temporal, comparison proposed by S. Albert[295] as a plausible explanation of the perception–interpretation process has also proved to be relevant for the ethnic *samizdat*. The documents used to compare the present status of their group to that in the 'past'—both relatively recent and remote 'historical.' Sometimes the same document combines references to both social and temporal comparison.

One more type of comparison appeared to be essential for ethnic *samizdat*: that is, comparison against the normative standards, or "salient legitimate standards of fairness"[296] adopted by society. The nationality rights promoted by the Soviet Constitution, UN Covenants, Helsinki Accords and other domestic and international documents are cited by the *samizdat* documents as normative standards to which actual status of ethnic group has to be compared. Of all normative standards the ethnic movements tend to attribute the paramount significance to the right to self-determination in its variant of secession.

Andrè deCarufel who's empirical study[297] dealt with the evaluation of the outcome of improvement by disadvantages parties in relation to perceived normative standards finds "that individuals develop expectations about what they ought to receive" and "that insufficient improvement may intensify discontent" if the improvement does not match expectations.[298] The *samizdat* references to relative deprivation indicate that this conclusion may be applied to the behavior of nationalist movements as collectivities. Thus, an incomplete rehabilitation of the Soviet Germans and Crimean Tatars had only intensified their dissatisfaction sharpening the feeling of deprivation. Moreover, these movements made clear that they prefer the preservation of the existing disadvantageous status to any insufficient improvements.

Finally, it should be mentioned, that practically all studies, which touch upon various types and parameters of relative deprivation, do not exceed the framework of economic deprivation, primarily dealing with different aspects of so-called well-being. Meanwhile, "Existing data suggest that political and status deprivations are more closely related to political action than economic or service wants. Nationalists may nowadays frame their appeals in economic terms, but the core of that appeal remains psychological and political, rather than economic," argued A. Smith[299] against the tendency to place unwarranted emphasis on economic factors in the theory of relative deprivation. The present analysis of the typology of relative deprivation, drawn as it is from *samizdat* documents, indicates that the nationalist movements of the USSR formulated their appeals mainly in political terms. Indeed, ethnic documents tend to favor political and status deprivations over all other kinds of deprivation, whether economic, cultural, linguistic, environmental, and the like. Although other types of deprivation are certainly discussed, they are utterly subordinated to political deprivation.

CHAPTER 5

Ethnic Organizations, Programs, and Demands

T his chapter deals with the political demands made by various ethnonationalist movements. The demands will be examined both synchronically and diachronically: the former makes it possible to evaluate models of political demands characteristic to ethnic groups, the latter makes it possible to examine the development of ethnic demands and political objectives as they evolved over 20 years.

Relative deprivation, a regular motif in the *samizdat* documents, was the grounds for a systematic enumeration of demands: structurally, *samizdat* documents containing ethnic demands generally begin with preambles citing specific types of issues of deprivation. Ethnopolitical demands were expressed in three main ways:

1. *Personal Demands* were usually expressed in petitions by individuals seeking to alter their status. This type of demand includes appeals by Soviet Jews and Germans asking that their families be granted exit visas, or by Crimean Tatars requesting to purchase real estate in Crimea, and so on.

2. *Delegated Demands* were presented by groups or individuals on behalf of collectives (as a rule, members of the same national group). The *Letter by Ukrainian Political Prisoners* (*An Attempt at a General Conclusion*, signed by Olexa Tyhyi and Vasyl Romaniuk) on "the historic fate of the Ukraine" and "feasible forms of resistance,"[1] is an example of "delegated" demands. Personal and delegated demands were commonly combined in ethnic *samizdat* documents.

3. *Institutionalized Demands* are generally advanced by documents claiming to formulate programs or to describe the basic orientation of nationalist organizations or movements, such as the Program of *VSKhSON*[2] (the Social Christian Union for the Liberation of the People) or the *Declaration by the Crimean Tatars on the Crimean Question*, signed by fifty-five thousand people in 1971.[3]

We will discuss ethnopolitical demands, as they appeared in the *samizdat* documents of various ethnic movements.

The Ukrainian Movement

Following their late imperial predecessors, the Soviet authorities considered Ukrainian nationalism the most menacing challenge to the preservation of Empire.[4] There were some "good" reasons for the authorities' anxiety such as a large and powerful diaspora, "problematic" population inherited together with the annexed Western territories. But the main trouble was caused by elementary arithmetic: Ukrainians comprised about one-sixth of the total population of the USSR. That is why self-assertiveness of the "second Soviet nation" has been scrutinized through "a magnifying glass" of fear and suppressed with an exceptional virulence. To a considerable degree Ukraine became a "firing ground" where new repressive strategies and methods of dealing with dissidents were hammered out.

Ukrainian *samizdat* offered, probably, the most elaborate structure for forging ethnopolitical demands. The earliest known expression of systematic demands was made by the Ukrainian Workers and Peasants Union (URSS— *Ukrains'ka Robitnycho-Selians'ka Spilka*) established in 1959 by several young Ukrainian intellectuals, primarily jurists, from Lviv and other towns in Western Ukraine. In 1961, seven participants of this unauthorized organization were tried in Lviv for high treason (Article 56 of the Ukrainian Penal Code) and anti-Soviet propaganda (Article 62 of the Ukrainian Penal Code). The judges found that the union struggled against the Soviet regime, the Communist Party, and the Soviet government in order to separate the Ukrainian republic from the Soviet Union. One defendant, Levko Luk'ianenko, a lawyer from Lviv, was sentenced to death (he later obtained the clemency and served 15 years in prison and labor camps), while the others were sentenced to varying terms of imprisonment—Ivan Kandyba to fifteen years and Luts'kiv and Libovik to ten years.[5]

The single document that incriminated the defendants was a *Draft Program of the URSS*. An *Appeal*[6] by I. Kandyba to P. Shelest describes the contents of this document. Outlining points of relative deprivation in its preamble, the *Draft* concluded that "for its normal development, the Ukraine should secede from the USSR, on the grounds of Article 14 of the Ukrainian Constitution and Article 17 of the Constitution of the USSR, and form an independent state."[7] In order to achieve this, the *Draft Program* suggested the establishment of institutions to popularize the idea of secession in accordance with these constitutional guarantees. If the idea of independence did not gain the support of the majority of Ukrainian citizens, secessionist propaganda would stop and all secessionist institutions would be disbanded. Kandyba's *Appeal* noted that the *Draft Program* had been rejected by most of the Union's members, and at the general meeting it was decided to remove secession from the platform and concentrate on the Ukrainization and democratization of Ukrainian society.[8]

The overwhelming majority of Ukrainian documents issued in the mid-1960s contained cultural-linguistic demands. In 1964, ten Ukrainian intellectuals (V. Lobko and others) addressed a document entitled *Our Proposals* to the Ukrainian Supreme Soviet. It put forward the following demands:

1. The use of the Ukrainian language be reinforced in kindergartens, day care centers, schools, colleges, universities, and so on.
2. "In accordance with Lenin's behest," Ukrainian be introduced in all spheres.
3. Ukrainian institutions be established in regions containing large Ukrainian populations beyond the borders of the Ukrainian SSR (mainly in the Russian Federation and Kazakhstan.[9]

An *Appeal to the Chairman of the Soviet of Nationalities* (1966), by prominent Ukrainian dissident Sviatoslav Karavansky, demanded a halt to the Russification of the educational system in the Ukraine.[10] The *Chronicle of Current Events* (no. 5)[11] reported that in March 1968, leaflets calling for a struggle against Russification were scattered at the University and the Agricultural Academy in Kiev. During this period, the quest for Ukrainization seemed to have been the most powerful idea mobilizing Ukrainians for mass action. Several *samizdat* documents reported public demonstrations at Shevchenko's monument in Kanev in 1964 and 1967.[12]

A complaint about the conduct of militiamen signed by sixty-four citizens stated that on 22 July, the day Shevchenko's remains were transferred to Kanev, hundreds of Ukrainians gathered by the monument to commemorate the event. They laid wreaths on the grave, recited his poetry, and chanted slogans in praise of Ukrainian culture. The demonstration was broken up brutally by the police, army, and KGB forces.[13] Without reference to a broader historical context, the behavior of both parties is usually met by perplexity. Indeed, why have the memorials of the most "canonical" in the USSR Ukrainian writer been chosen for the non-official gatherings? Why have these definitely non-political convocations exasperated the authorities? In fact, such gatherings emulated Shevchenko's anniversaries, which had been commemorated by the Ukrainian cultural nationalists since the 1860 provoking the suspicions and animosity of the Russian authorities.[14] Hence, the apparently innocuous Soviet-style assemblages bore the profound symbolic meaning for each side. Symptomatically, the reaction of the Soviet Communist administration to the gatherings emulated that of the infamous czarist Minister of Interior P. Valuiev.

At the same time as cultural-linguistic demands were being made, a wide spectrum of demands dealing with various political spheres was advanced by documents of Ukrainian *samizdat*. Karavansky's *Appeal* of 1966 to the Chairman of the Soviet of Nationalities of the Supreme Soviet of the USSR demanded a halt to the further settlement of ethnic Russians in the territories of national republics and specifically, in the Ukrainian SSR.[15] The *Appeal* put forward a number of territorial claims, asserting that the existing borders between union republics of the USSR should be reconsidered so as "to restore their correspondence with ethnic borders."[16] According to Karavansky, the Krasnodar *Krai*, some areas of the Vononezh, Belgorod and the Rostov *oblasts* should be transferred to the Ukrainian SSR, and Moldavian territories illegally included into Odessa *oblast* of the Ukrainian SSR should be returned to Moldavia.[17] Karavansky mentioned those areas of the Russian Empire in which Ukrainians had been the major ethnic element since the late eighteenth century. By the late 1950s, however, most of them had assimilated into the Russian ethnicity. Karavansky also mentioned the territory of the former Moldavian Autonomous SSR, ceded in 1940 to the Ukrainian SSR. However, he and other Ukrainian *samizdat* authors fail to mention Crimea, which was incorporated by the Ukrainian SSR in 1954.

The most articulated expression of ethnopolitical demands can be found in the *Open Letter* by Ukrainian dissident Anton Koval'. Written in April 1969, the *Letter* is formally addressed to the people's deputies of all Soviets of the Ukrainian SSR.[18] His demands focus on three topics: the economy, state politics, and culture. Koval's economic demands were:

1. All branches of the Ukrainian national economy be subordinated to the government of the Ukrainian SSR;

2. The Ukrainian government be granted exclusive authority in distributing the national income of the republic;
3. Industrial enterprises be self-governing;
4. Data concerning the economic aid given by the Ukraine to other Soviet Republics and foreign states be publicized and discussed openly.

His economic program also combined typical trade-unionist demands: a rise in wages, and the curtailment of the gap in wages of different employee categories.

With regard to state politics, Koval' focused on the need to adopt a new constitution for the Ukrainian SSR, simultaneously devising a wide range of political demands. He believed that the basic law should provide a mechanism establishing the Ukrainian Republic as a sovereign state with a multiparty system. He also considered it necessary to establish a Ukrainian Defense Ministry and to subordinate those Soviet army divisions to be recruited from the Ukrainian Republic to this ministry. The political section includes demands for the establishment of a constitutional court, the repeal of political articles (62 and 187-1) in the Ukrainian penal code, an end to censorship, the disbanding of the KGB, and the release of political prisoners.

The third section of Koval's program outlines popular cultural-linguistic demands:

1. The use of Ukrainian in all the republic's institutions;
2. The Ukrainization of secondary schools in the republic;
3. The abolition of all discriminatory measures concerning the cultural heritage of the Ukrainian people, including reductions in the publication of Ukrainian classics and publications bans against modern Ukrainian writers;
4. The five million Ukrainians living in the Russian Federation be granted the same conditions for free national development as Russians enjoy in the Ukrainian SSR.

Advocating independence in political, cultural, and economic spheres neither Koval's program nor most other available documents from the sixties contained explicit separatist demands. At the same time, however, *samizdat* reports of the period alluded to groups that were likely to have claims that are more radical.

Levko Luk'ianenko, in his *Petition to the Chairman of the Presidium of the Supreme Soviet of the Ukrainian SSR*, D. Korotchenko, written in the Mordovian labor camp in 1967, dealt with the repression of Ukrainian nationalists.[19]

He reported on the trials of five defendants from the M. Apostol group (1961) and five from the B. Hohus' group and six from the M. Protsiv group in 1962. Two leaders, M. Protsiv and B. Hohus' were sentenced to death. Several trials of Ukrainian nationalists were reported by I. Kandyba in his *Appeal* to P. Shelest.[20] In March 1959, a group of young workers and students were brought to trial in Ivano-Frankivs'k for establishing the United Party for the Liberation of the Ukraine. Participants were sentenced to seven to ten years in prison. In December 1959, twenty members of the so-called Ukrainian National Committee were brought to trial: two of them, Ivan Koval' and Bohdan Hrytsyna, were sentenced to death. Kandyba said that the Ukrainian National Committee championed secession from the USSR.[21]

An anonymous document (1968) on the prosecution of Ukrainian activists described a group calling itself the Ukrainian National Front.[22] The document reported that the group was formed in 1964, that it regarded itself as a successor of the OUN,[23] and to a large degree, copied the OUN's program. The National Front considered the "liberation of the Ukraine as the main goal of its activity," and called on Ukrainians to "consolidate all national forces" around a strong organization for the liberation of the Ukraine.[24]

The document reported that the National Front had published the *samizdat* journal *Volia i Bat'kivshyna* (Freedom and Fatherland), and that several issues of this journal had already been printed. The journal contained original articles written by the National Front's members, as well as reprints from the OUN magazine, *Ideia i Chyn* (Idea and Means), and material from the OUN's archives. According to the document, the circulation of National Front publications was in the hundreds.[25]

The Front's members were sentenced to long terms of imprisonment (D. Kvets'ko, the National Front's leader, fifteen years; M. D'iak, thirteen years; and Z. Krasyvs'ky,[26] twelve years). The document noted that some participants had already served prison terms in the 1940s, 1950s, and 1960s. It can be assumed that several of them had been connected with the OUN.

"The Most Important Case" was the name of the report in the *Chronicle of Current Events* (no. 17, December 1970) on the National Front members' trial. It explained how the National Front's members were brought to trial for high treason (Article 56 of the Ukrainian Penal Code) and anti-Soviet propaganda (Article 62).[27] The report also mentioned that the first issue of *Volia i Bat'kivshyna* carried a document entitled "Demands of the Ukrainian National Front" and the second issue published an article entitled "Tactics of the UNF." With Ukrainian independence as its political objective, UNF documents stressed the need to concentrate on the group's activity on secession.

By late 1980, an anonymous report *Some More from the History of the UNF*[28] told how the trials of UNF members were carried out in Lviv and Ivano-Frankivs'k in 1967. It was noted that the UNF recommenced its activities in the mid-1970s, launching a new round of repressions against its members by the KGB. Indicating that the National Front of the 1970s had about forty members, the report proceeded to name several, including M. Krainyk, V. Zvarych, and I. Mandryk. The UNF of the 1970s called for the consolidation of all forces "supporting the concept of Ukrainian independence and speaking against all forms of national or social oppression."[29] The report also mentioned attempts by the National Front to publish an almanac, *Prozrinnia* (Insight),[30] and a journal, *Ukrains'kyi Visnyk* (Ukrainian Herald).

The *Ukrainian Herald*, that reappeared in 1974 (nos. 7–8), edited by M. Sahaidak (Stepan Khmara), adopted a "much more radical tone,"[31] which can be attributed, to a certain degree, to the influence of "a more nationalistic position" of the Ukrainian National Front.[32] Sahaidak's study, "Ethnocide of Ukrainians in the USSR," was, in fact, an emotional account of the urgent need to obliterate "Soviet Russian colonialism"[33] and proclaimed the struggle for Ukrainian statehood to be the nation's major goal.

Olexa Tyhyi and Vasyl' Romaniuk, in their *Letter by Ukrainian Political Prisoners* (1977), stated that "the Ukraine would become an independent, democratic, welfare state with an advanced educational system, modern science, and a culture that would be national in its form, content, and essence."[34] The *Letter* articulated a program of non-violent resistance, and called on Ukrainians to commit themselves to:

Using only Ukrainian and refusing to use Russian in all spheres;
Refusing to work outside the Ukraine;
Refusing to work in any institution in which the Ukrainian language, national traditions, and human rights are slighted;
Asserting human rights and sovereignty in the Ukraine, and so on.[35]

Despite the vigorous separatist demands of the 1960s and early 1970s, the mainstream Ukrainian dissident movement generally regarded secession as being merely the vaguely possible outcome of distant political developments or even as a political extreme. From the mid-1970s, however, there was a radicalization of Ukrainian ethnic strategy and demands. One significant example of this is Ukrainian mathematician Leonid Pliushch. In an interview with *Le Monde* (4 February 1976) this prominent spokesperson for the general liberal democratic movement said: " . . . I am for the separation of the Ukraine from Russia. For it is only in an independent Ukraine that the building of socialism and the preservation of Ukrainian culture would be possible."[36] Similarly, the program formulated in the *Declaration of the Ukrainian Patriotic Movement* (1980) was unambiguous: "We declare our desire to secede from the USSR and to take our people out of Communist captivity. Secession is the sole chance for national salvation."[37] The *Declaration* appealed to "the Ukrainian people, the international community, and the United Nations" to hold a referendum on Ukrainian secession under the auspices of UN representatives.

Documents by the Ukrainian National Front reappeared in 1984. An *Appeal* to the new party leader Iu. Andropov, co-issued by the Front and the Romanian Group of Revival, was published by the *Chronicle of the Ukrainian Catholic Church*.[38] Although the authors were not identified, it can be assumed that the *Chronicle*'s editors, I. Terelia, V. Kobryn, and G. Budzinsky, were involved in preparing this document.

In the first paragraphs of the *Appeal*, the Romanian Group of Revival called for the reunification of the Moldavian SSR with "mother-Romania."[39] Although the *Appeal* declared that both the Ukrainian and Romanian (Moldavian) movements were committed to a common struggle for liberation "from under Moscow's heel,"[40] one cannot reach any conclusions about the identity of the Romanian Group's members or supporters. The remainder of the *Appeal* advanced a number of demands connected with the Ukraine:

> The Ukrainization of all institutions in the republic;
> The establishment of custom services on the Ukraine's borders with other Soviet republics;
> The introduction of a Ukrainian currency;
> The formation of a national army;
> The securing of religious freedom for the Ukrainian Catholic Uniate Church and the restoration of the Ukrainian Autocephaly of the Orthodox Church.

The *Appeal* explains that the realization of these goals will enable the further preservation of a "common union of the Ukrainian and Russian people."[41] It is interesting that in 1959 the Ukrainian Workers and Peasants Union issued a similar platform advocating secession from the USSR, while supporting the Ukraine's participation in a "Commonwealth of Socialist States,"[42] preserving the Soviet political regime and a common socialist economic system. The National Front's document of 1984 champions isolationism, offering in exchange, an agreement to formally preserve the republic's membership in the USSR. The Ukrainian Workers and Peasants Union demanded a fictitious divorce: the Ukrainian National Front expressed tolerance of a fictitious marriage, in which the Ukraine enjoyed full independence from its "spouse."

The Armenian Movement

The question of Nagorno-Karabakh is the main focus of modern Armenian nationalism. One of the earliest available Armenian *samizdat* documents, the *Letter to Khrushchev*, signed by 2,500 Armenians from Nagorno-Karabakh and other areas of the Azerbaijan SSR, appeared in 1963.[43] Asserting the urgency of the problem, the *Letter* demanded that it be settled immediately and offered two acceptable settlements: the reunification of Nagorno-Karabakh and all adjacent areas of Armenian settlement with the Armenian SSR, or the incorporation of these areas into the Russian Federation. In the long history of subjection–domination, ethnic minorities not infrequently preferred the direct government from a center to the rule of a provincial oppressor. After Armenians from Nagorno-Karabakh the claim to be incorporated into the Russian Federation was made by Abkhazians in the late 1970s (see correspondent section of this book). During *perestroika* the *Rusin* (Ruthenian) ethnic movement had advanced the demand to attach Ruthenia to the Russian Federation as an autonomous unit.

In many senses, the *Letter* of Armenians to Khrushchev seems to have been a plea to the central government for protection rather than an assertive demand to alter the political map of the USSR. The center's failure to respond mobilized the Armenians politically and prompted the Azerbaijani authorities to intensify their oppression of the local Armenian population.

Ethnic sentiment was similarly challenged by the official reaction to the fiftieth anniversary of the 1915 genocide of Armenians by the Turks. Attempts to hush up and even to deny the Armenian genocide were unequivocally regarded by Armenians as expressions of the Soviet government's anti-Armenian, pro-Turkish orientation. Armenian activist E. Hovannisian, in his 1965 *Letter to the CPSU Central Committee*, contended that Armenian interests were sacrificed by the Soviet leadership to the situational needs of current Soviet policy regarding Turkey.[44]

On 24 April 1965, public officials representing the Armenian Apostolic Church and delegates from the Diaspora gathered in the Spendarian State Theater for Opera and Ballet to commemorate the fiftieth anniversary of the Armenian genocide. Outside, an estimated 100,000 people were also gathered to ask the Soviet to help restore all Armenian lands seized by the Turks. The demonstration was broken up by the militia.[45] Speaking at the district party conference in autumn, 1965, Silvia Kaputikian, a famous authoress and a loyal member of the Communist Party discussed the April demonstration in Yerevan.[46] The speech was circulated in *samizdat* literature. She stressed that the demonstration should be considered a protest reaction against official disregard of the Armenian tragedy. Pointing to the deep-rootedness and complexity of ethnic sentiment, Kaputikian warned that "ignoring national interests could damage our global policy and shake people's belief in the socialist regime. History knows many examples of the disintegration of multinational states that did not manage to resolve their nationality questions."[47] Kaputikian vigorously denied the accusations of separatist tendencies leveled against the demonstrators, while emphasizing the Armenian resolution "to develop the national life, language, and culture."[48] She commented on the traditional fidelity of the Armenian people to Russia, determined by geography, history, and mentality. "But any pressure, moral or other," she continued, "could result in such a situation that this profound fidelity turns into fear, hypocrisy, and blind submission."[49]

While Kaputikian tried to translate the Armenian protest into popular Marxist terms, E. Hovannisian's *Letter to the CPSU Central Committee*[50] seemed to contain candid expression of the demonstrators' claims. Hovannisian asserted that Nagorno-Karabakh and the Shamhor, Dashkesan, and Shaumian *rayons* of the Azerbaijan SSR should be attached to the Armenian SSR. Furthermore, the territories of Kars and Ardahan, now incorporated into Turkey, should be annexed to Armenia. Hovannisian indicated that 200,000 of the 760,000 sq. km of Turkish territory should be ceded to Armenia. Apart from this irredentist claim, Hovannisian's *Letter* called on the Armenian Diaspora to return home.

Early manifestations of Armenian nationalism[51] did not advance separatist claims. They even explained Armenia's commitment to union with Russia. In 1966, however, the National Unification Party (NUP), an organization promoting Armenian independence, was formed in Yerevan.

An extensive Armenian *samizdat* document devoted *To the Tenth Anniversary of the Founding of the NUP* sketched the program and history of the party.[52] It was established in 1966 by Haikazun Khachatrian. Born in 1919, he was the NUP leader until his arrest in 1968.[53] Parouir Hairekian (born 1949) took over the NUP leadership until his arrest in 1969. According to the document, from 1967 to 1975 eighteen trials were held and more than fifty NUP members were sentenced to prison terms ranging from six months to ten years.

The NUP *Program* envisioned the solution of the Armenian question in the accomplishment of the following objectives: (1) The restoration of a national state in the entire territory of historical Armenia; (2) The return of Diaspora Armenians to their reunited homeland; (3) National revival. Unlike earlier documents, the *Program* called for "complete self-determination": that is, Armenia's secession from the USSR, as the main condition necessary in securing these national objectives and, therefore, as the primary task of the Armenian movement. Though it was claimed that the above-mentioned national objectives would be achieved by independent Armenia the NUP *Program* did not reject the possibility of a partial solution of the Armenian question in the framework of the USSR. The same document[54] reported that the party was launched as an underground anti-Communist organization, but in 1969, it removed anti-Communism from its agenda, and since 1973, it was seeking legitimization. Similar information on the NUP and its demands can be found in the final plea of Hairekian at his trial (22 November 1974).[55]

The NUP *Program* intended that the issue of independence be submitted to an all-national referendum. All Armenian citizens, as well as Armenian subjects living temporarily in other countries, would vote. The *Program* stipulated that the referendum should be held under the supervision of a special international body, empowered by the United Nations. Two preconditions must be accomplished pending the referendum: legalization of the NUP and the release of political prisoners belonging to the NUP. The *Program* stressed that nonviolence, negotiations, and compromise should be adopted as fundamental principles of NUP political strategy.

Most nationalist programs avoided describing political activity after independence. In contrast, the NUP elaborated on its policy regarding transitional periods by providing for the following stages:

Joining the United Nations and establishing diplomatic relations with other countries;

Holding elections to a constituent assembly and adopting an interim constitution;

Negotiating with Moscow on the just allocation to Armenia of its share in all Union movable and unmovable property;

Gaining the Armenian share of all-Union gold and foreign currency reserves;

Forming a provisional government;

Returning all Armenian soldiers serving in other republics to the homeland, reestablishing the Armenian National Army, and obtaining the Armenian share of all-Union military property.

According to the *Program*, the above-mentioned measures would secure the political, administrative, economic, and military independence of Armenia. At the same time, the *Program* pointed out that during the transitional period of no more than a year; United Nations forces would defend Armenia's frontiers. Touching upon the NUP's future, the *Program* emphasized that the NUP "constitutes a popular front rather than a party."[56] As such, its sole objective is securing Armenia's independence. Once independence is achieved, the NUP will split into different political parties and organizations. The first edition of the NUP *Program* was compiled by H. Khachatrian in 1967. In 1974, P. Hairekian and H. Harshekian prepared a second edition, while imprisoned in the Yerevan KGB prison.

The NUP gave particular prominence to *samizdat* activity. Two newspapers, *Paros* (The Beacon, founded: 1967) and *Yerkunk* (Birth Pangs, founded: 1969), and journals *For the Motherland* and *The Voice of the NUP*, were published by the NUP. The estimated circulation of the two newspapers reached 3,000–10,000 copies.[57]

In 1977, the Armenian Helsinki Watch Group was established in Yerevan. A *Declaration* by the Group, made on 1 April 1977, proclaimed as its objective the unification of all Armenians in a [reconstituted] Armenian SSR. To accomplish this, the document elaborated, Armenia should join the United Nations as a full and equal member.[58] The *Declaration* stated that the group was dedicated to the re-incorporation of Nagorno-Karabakh in the Armenian SSR. A final demand called for the Armenization of culture, education, and management in the republic.

This relatively moderate *Declaration* mentioned neither independence nor Western [Turkish] Armenia. At the same time, this document, like later documents of Armenian *samizdat*, showed no readiness to compromise on Nagorno-Karabakh. Armenian claims in Nagorno-Karabakh were supported by a national consensus. There were no differences of opinion between the political prisoner and labor camp veteran P. Hairekian and established writer Sergo Khanzadian, the author of *An Open Letter* to Brezhnev on the Karabakh Problem.[59]

The Georgian Movement

The Georgian movement focused its political assertiveness on cultural-linguistic demands as well as on demands seeking to reinforce or alter the status of Georgians within or outside their titular republic.

In 1976, the magazine, *Georgian Herald*, one of the two most famous Georgian *samizdat* journals (the second was *Sakartvello*—Georgia), published an article by V. Rtskhiladze titled "A Crime Against the Georgian People (A Meskhetian Tragedy)."[60] The author finds a simple solution to the Meskhetian problem—permitting their immediate repatriation to the motherland. He asserts that the Meskhetians should be considered an integral part of the Georgian people and not a distinct ethnic group.

A later document, *Claims of the Georgian People* (1981), addressed to L. Brezhnev and E. Shevardnadze,[61] then the First Secretary of the Georgian Central Committee, called for the repatriation of Meskhetians to Georgia and the conferral of official powers to the Meskhetian leaders Kuradze and Khozravanadze so that they could oversee the Meskhetian return to Georgia. The document intentionally called these two leaders by their Georgian names (Khozravanadze was widely known as Enver Odabashev), whereas Meskhetian documents usually carried their Muslim names.

Georgian *samizdat* showed a deep concern and involvement with the problems of the Georgian minority living in Saingillo (the northwestern district of the Azerbaijan SSR). In 1978 M. Gamkharashvili and A. Otarashvili in their *Letter to G. Kolbin*, Secretary of the Georgian Central Committee of the Communist Party, made demands of both the central government and the Georgian authorities regarding this issue.[62] They demanded a stop to the "policy of genocide against the Georgian population,"[63] and elaborated on concrete measures to be taken:

> The migration of Muslims from Azerbaijan and Daghestan to the predominantly Georgian district of Saingillo (East Kakhetia) be stopped;
>
> Discrimination against Georgian specialists be stopped. Only Georgians should be appointed as directors in schools where Georgian children comprise the majority of students;
>
> Newspaper and radio programs in Georgian be established to promote scientific and cultural contact between East Kakhetia and the Georgian SSR.[64]

A section addressed to the Georgian government included a request to permit Georgians from Azerbaijan to settle in the area of Tbilisi (populated by ethnic Azerbaijanis) and to grant them state housing. Yet, while this *Letter* and other documents discussing Saingillo[65] noted that Azerbaijan's incorporation of the region was illegal, they avoided irredentist claims.

Open expressions of separatist demands are also rare in Georgian documents. However, the 1974 essay, reviewing 250 years of Russian–Georgian relations, welcomed Georgian independence as proclaimed by the Menshevik government and assessed "the new annexation" in February 1921 as "a real occupation."[66] The document called on the Soviet government to abolish the colonial regime and recognize the right of peoples to self-determination. The spring 1982 issue of *Sakartvello* (Georgia) no. 1[67] was devoted to the two-hundredth anniversary of the incorporation of Georgia into the Russian Empire. A *Petition by Georgians to L. Brezhnev and E. Shevardnadze* carried by *Sakartvello*[68] called for jubilee celebrations to be cancelled and for public acknowledgment of the unlawfulness of the annexation.

The journal carried a long article entitled "Two Hundred Years of the Russian-Georgian Treaty," it was subtitled "We Reject the Czarist Jubilee."[69] Referring to Georgian historians N. Berdzenishvili and I. Dzhavahishvili and to Lenin's newspaper, *Iskra*, the journal developed the idea that "the annexation was illegal"[70] while avoiding any separatist demands. On the contrary, it even recognized a certain value in maintaining the Soviet federal structure—provided that "real equality"[71] between all nationalities be achieved.

The assertion of cultural-linguistic rights comprised the major issue in Georgian *samizdat*. In June 1980, 365 representatives of the Georgian intelligentsia, including prominent writers, scientists, artists, and others, such as leading film directors O. Ioseliani, T. Abuladze, N. Gogoberidze, actress V. Andzhaparidze, composer G. Kancheli, and member of the Soviet Academy of Science Shanidze, signed a *Letter to Brezhnev and Shevardnadze* "on the violation of the cultural rights of the Georgian people."[72] They demanded that Paragraph 83 of the VAK (Higher Certifying Committee) Instructions—requiring that all doctoral dissertations be submitted in Russian—be repealed (the paragraph was approved by the VAK on 6 December 1978). The *Letter* also demanded that all instruction that had been given in the Georgian language, but had been curtailed, be immediately restored and that Georgian history be introduced as a subject of instruction in Georgian schools. Ten months later, in March 1981, Georgian students voiced similar commands during a series of demonstrations in Tbilisi.

An anonymous *samizdat* report[73] told how ethnic disturbances were provoked by the authorities' lack of responsiveness to two Georgian petitions to Brezhnev and Shevardnadze. The first was the *Letter* by 365 intellectuals, and the second, dating from April 1980 was written by one hundred Georgians living in Abkhazia. It commented on the discrimination suffered by the Georgian majority there and demanded that their dominant status be secured.

On 23 March 1981, about one thousand students participated in a demonstration demanding the restoration of a course of studies given at the University of Tbilisi by philologist A. Bakradze (a signatory to the *Letter* by 365 Georgian intellectuals). According to the report, their demand was satisfied. One week later, on 30 March, the opening day of the Congress of the Georgian Union of Writers, another demonstration by students and intellectuals took place in Tbilisi. These demonstrators had broadened the scope of their demands considerably. They reiterated the cultural-linguistic demands of the *Letter* by 365 intellectuals but also demanded that monuments be erected to commemorate King David and Queen Tamara. They also touched on the status of Georgians in Saingillo and Abkhazia; some held placards with the inscriptions: "Stop the prosecution of Georgians in Abkhazia!" and "Release Markozia!" (the arrested leader of the Georgian movement in Abkhazia).[74] The report said that several participants were arrested, but they were soon released at the demand of the other demonstrators. It was also reported that Shevardnadze left his office to meet the demonstrators and discuss their demands.

On 18 May 1981, students launched a new demonstration. Zviad Gamsakhurdia had handed the Georgian authorities a list of demands (specifying several new points) for them to deliver to Brezhnev and Shevardnadze.[75] The demonstrators called for: legal recognition of Georgian as the state language (while considering the interests of the Russian-speaking population); the use of Georgian inscriptions on all signboards in the Georgian SSR; the expansion of the Georgian sector in all institutes of higher education, and an increase in the proportion of TV and radio programs broadcasted and books printed in the Georgian language.

In terms of the Abkhazian question, the document demanded that Georgian settlement there be intensified and that all historical monuments there be restored and registered, to prove the "historical rights" of the Georgian people to the territory of the Abkhazian Autonomous Republic. As for Saingillo, the demonstrators demanded that the ordnance yard occupying the territory of the monastery David-Garedzhe be removed, that an Orthodox church be opened, and that all violations of the human rights of the Christian population of East Kakhetia be stopped.[76]

While upholding the interests of the Georgian population outside the Georgian SSR, Georgian *samizdat* documents were virulently opposed to political assertiveness on the part of ethnic minorities living within Georgia. Documents insisted on entrenchment of the Georgians' status not only in Abkhazia, but also in other areas with considerable non-Georgian populations, such as the South Ossetian Autonomous Region or the Marneuli *rayon* near Tbilisi, populated mainly by Azerbaijanis.[77]

In September 1983, six Georgians, among them Dr. Nodar Notadze, Professor G. Tavzadze, and writer G. Kankava, wrote a *Letter* to Iu. Andropov, N. Tikhonov (the Chairman of the Council of Ministers), *Pravda* and

Izvestia[78] demanding that the "elementary rights of the Georgian population" in the Azerbaijan SSR be secured. At the same time it called for a massive influx of Georgians into all areas neighboring Tbilisi, which were then populated by Azerbaijanis. According to the *Letter* this was necessary to "protect the equal rights of the Georgians, and their "sovereignty over their national territory."[79]

The Abkhazian Movement

Information on Abkhazian assertiveness can be drawn primarily from Georgian *samizdat* documents. An *Appeal to the Population of the Georgian SSR* (1983) by Georgian political prisoner Boris Kakubava referred to Abkhazian demonstrations in 1956, 1968, and 1978. He noted that the organizers of the 1968 demonstrations were punished and their demands were declared provocative.[80]

The Western mass media reported that in December 1977 about 130 Abkhazian intellectuals signed a *Letter to the Soviet Government* protesting against "oppression of the Abkhazian nationality"[81] by the Georgian majority. The *Letter* described the massive influx of Georgians into the Abkhazian ethnic territory, compulsory studies of the Georgian language in Abkhazian schools, and the "plundering of natural resources."[82] After repressive measures were taken against those individuals who signed the *Letter* mass demonstrations were launched in Sukhumi, the capital of the Abkhazian Autonomous Republic, demanding that the signatories who had been expelled from the Communist Party be reinstated, Abkhazians be nominated to all official party and state positions in the autonomous republic, the Georgian language be withdrawn from official and public spheres in Abkhazia, Abkhazian be recognized as the official language, an Abkhazian university be established, television programs be broadcast in the Abkhazian language, and local Georgian toponyms be replaced by Abkhazian ones.

B. Kakubava's *Appeal* said that demonstrators also demanded that Abkhazia secede from the Georgian SSR and be included in the Russian Federation and that provisions be made for a new Abkhazian constitution. He also cited a demand that all ethnic Georgians be deported from Abkhazian territory, but this allegation is not corroborated in other sources, including Georgian documents dealing with the Abkhazian question.[83]

The Lezghian Movement

Lezghian ethnic claims were expressed by writer Iskander Kaziev in his 1980 *Letter to the Secretary General of the United Nations*.[84] In it he demanded the reunification of the nation in the framework of an autonomous unit.[85] Kaziev devised a program of Lezghian irredentism, in which he envisioned that the Daghestan ASSR and the Azerbaijan SSR would each cede those parts of their territories populated by Lezghians to a future Lezghian autonomous unit. The new autonomy would be federated with the RSFSR or the Azerbaijan SSR. Until that time, the Soviet authorities and the United Nations should stipulate measures to help those areas with a Lezghian population to overcome any socio-economic backwardness resulting from the policies of deprivation carried out by Daghestan and Azerbaijan.[86]

The Adygei Movement

An *Appeal to Compatriots* (1977) by A. Shazzo contained an impassioned call for "all Adygei unity,"[87] pointing out that the Adygei, together with the Circassians, Kabardinians, and some other, small related ethnic groups, constitute an artificially divided national entity sharing a common past. The author called on them to foster "the all-Adygei national identity,"[88] so as to make social and political gains. The *Appeal* did not suggest concrete means of uniting the various groups, preferring to regard their ties in terms of ethno-communalism. According to the author, the establishment of close ties with the Adygei–Circassian Diaspora is an important national goal, particularly in that it might lead to the repatriation of a considerable part of that Diaspora.

The Tatar–Bashkir Movement

Unlike Adygei documents, Tatar–Bashkir *samizdat* vigorously proclaimed separatism as its ethnic strategy: "national freedom" and "national independence"[89] were interchangeable terms. At the same time, geopolitical considerations prevented activists of the nationalist movement from demanding the secession of the Tatar or both the Tatar and Bashkir Autonomous Republics from either the Russian Federation or the USSR. According to Kukshar, the author of an article on suppression of the Tatars and Bashkirs,[90] the only way to win freedom from "Russian-Soviet colonialism" is by consolidating the ethnic forces of all Turkic peoples in a joint effort to press ethnopolitical interests. In this respect, Kukshar addressed a cautious reproach to the Crimean Tatar movement for pursuing its own objectives, while "the future unification of the Turkic peoples should be posed as the main objective."[91] An anonymously written *Appeal* (1977) to representatives of the non-Russian nationalities called on the Turkic peoples to foster a common national self-consciousness, "not worrying whether our grandchildren consider themselves Tatars, Bashkirs, Uzbeks, or Kazakhs. It is important that they be Turks. Our future lies in the unification of the Turkic peoples."[92]

The call to create a monolithic Turkic entity that could challenge the Soviet Empire appeared in Tatar–Bashkir documents as entirely politically motivated, free of references to religious, cultural, or historical factors. Declarations of the need to adopt a pro-Turkish orientation ("our nearest brother"[93]) did not go beyond strictly political considerations.

The Baltic Movements

The restoration of national independence was the major objective of all ethnic activism in the Baltic republics since their incorporation into the USSR in 1940. Reports of nonviolent, spontaneous protests by Latvians, Estonians, and Lithuanians figure prominently in the *samizdat* of the 1960s and 1970s. The *Chronicle of Current Events* (no. 11, 31 December 1969)[94] told of an unauthorized meeting near the grave of Janis. Chakste, former president of independent Latvia. Graves in the cemetery were decorated with red and white roses (the national colors during independence), participants held white and red candles, and a national flag was hoisted over the tomb. The *Chronicle* (no. 26, 5 July 1972)[95] reported on a series of self-immolations in Lithuania, done in protest against Soviet rule. On 14 May 1972, 19-year-old Romas Kalanta set fire to himself in Kaunas. His funeral (18 May) was followed by a student demonstration during which slogans demanding independence were chanted. On 28 May 1972, four young Lithuanians hoisted a national flag in Varena. Three were arrested; the fourth, V. Stonis, escaped and committed self-immolation the next day in Varian's central square. On 3 June 1972, K. Adrushkevichus committed self-immolation in Shiauliai. The *Chronicle*'s report also mentioned an attempt at self-immolation by Zalichkeuskasis on 10 June 1972.[96] In June 1972, Soviet authorities faced serious student disturbances in the Lithuanian capital. The previous year, S. Kudirka, in a final plea at his trial, demanded that Lithuania be granted independence.[97]

Early Baltic *samizdat* documents contained very discreet expressions of separatist tendencies. The famous letter by Estonian intellectuals, *To Hope or to Act* (1968), was issued in response to academician Sakharov's *Progress, Coexistence, and Intellectual Freedom*. It stressed that "the just solution to the nationality question should be found. The right of peoples to an independent national existence should be guaranteed."[98] A program adopted by the underground Estonian National Front on 10 August 1971 contained the basic principles for a future independent Estonia and its political system.[99]

It called for a referendum on self-determination and declared this to be the organization's major objective. In 1972, the Estonian National Front, together with the Estonian Democratic Movement, issued a joint *Memorandum to the UN* demanding "independence for the Baltic States."[100] In 1974, Lithuanian scientist M. Tamonis refused to participate in the restoration of a monument to Soviet soldiers. He explained that he was protesting the Soviet army's involvement in Stalin's massacre of Lithuanians. An "Explanation" sent by Tamonis to the director of his institute was published by the *Chronicle of the Catholic Church in Lithuania* (no. 10, 1974).[101] In it, the author set forth a political agenda. He insisted that the "formally proclaimed right of nations to self-determination should be specified in additional acts providing the mechanism of its implementation."[102] One such necessary measure considered by Tamonis was the legal procedures implicit in organizing a referendum on independence. Results of such a referendum, in which the people's free will is expressed, should serve as the sole determinant for any decision on secession by any Soviet Republic.

The *Chronicle of the Catholic Church in Lithuania* (1972) focused mainly on advancing the religious rights of the Lithuanian people. Petitions demanding religious freedom contained thousands of signatures. A *Memorandum by Lithuanian Catholic Believers* to L. Brezhnev was signed by 17,054 Lithuanians.[103] An *Appeal by Catholic Believers* (1973) to the Lithuanian authorities demanded that the atheist monopoly on education be broken and that religious literature be circulated freely: it contained 16,498 signatures.[104]

Besides the well-known *Chronicle of the Catholic Church in Lithuania* and the *Estonian Democrat*, other *samizdat* literature included the Lithuanian *Aushra*, *Alma Mater*, and *Perspectives* in the 1970s and the Estonian *Iezekiri* in the early 1980s. These all championed the national rights of the Baltic peoples.

From the mid-1970s, the various Baltic national movements began to consolidate so as to promote their agendas. In 1975, a *Memorandum by Baltic Democrats to the Participants of the Helsinki Conference* was issued jointly by Latvian and Estonian dissident groups.[105]

In August 1979, forty-five representatives of the Baltic republics (among them were such famous dissidents as Ziemelis, Nicklus, Terliatskas Andriyauskas, etc.) and five of their supporters from the General Democratic movement (Landa, Nekipelov, Velikanova, Sakharov, and Arina Ginzburg) issued an *Appeal to the Governments of the USSR, the Federal Republic of Germany, the German Democratic Republic, Signatory States of the Atlantic Charter, and the UN Secretary General*, in connection with the fortieth anniversary of the Molotov–Ribbentrop Pact.[106] The *Appeal* demanded that the Soviet and both German governments publish the full text of the

Molotov–Ribbentrop Pact, including all secret protocols. According to the *Appeal*, this should be followed by its nullification from the moment of its signing. The *Appeal* envisioned the creation of a joint Soviet–German commission to eliminate the negative consequences of the pact. The most pressing measure in this context was the withdrawal of "all foreign military forces from the territory of Baltic republics."[107] Rather than insist on immediate independence, the *Appeal* suggested a number of successive intermediate stages so as to force the Soviet administration to face the dilemma of whether to continue to reap the benefits of Hitler and Stalin's agreement, or to recognize that the countries had been occupied illegally, with all ensuing consequences.

While the *Appeal* focused on the illegal character of the Baltic State's incorporation into the USSR, another joint document, an *Open Letter to the Heads of Government of the USSR and the States of Northern Europe* by thirty-eight residents of the Baltic republics[108] attempted to establish that the Baltic states constituted an integral part of a geo-political entity with different political interests from those of the USSR. Allegedly expressing support for Brezhnev's proposal to proclaim the countries of Northern Europe a nuclear free zone, the *Open Letter* demanded that the three Baltic Republics be included in this zone. The document explains that this would guarantee that these countries would not be involved in any potential conflicts between the superpowers.

One year later, in 1982, a new program, the *Memorandum* by the native population of Estonia, Latvia, and Lithuania,[109] was issued. Addressed to leaders of the Western democratic countries and the UN Security Council, the *Memorandum* called self-determination "a sacred idea, . . . in the name of which conquered peoples struggle and continue to struggle."[110] It reiterated claims for independence and Soviet withdrawal from the three Baltic republics and requested that the Western states discuss Latvian, Estonian, and Lithuanian independence at the Madrid Conference and at a session of the United Nations. The *Memorandum* also asked the West to recognize a delegation of emigrants from the three Baltic states (including recent emigrants) and to enable this delegation to represent the Baltic peoples at the Madrid Conference and in discussions in the United Nations on independence for the three countries.

In the early days of *perestroika*, a dynamic and aggressive group, Helsinki-86 appeared in Liepai, Latvia. Throughout July 1986, the group issued a number of documents declaring its political orientations and claims. A *Statement of Establishment of the Group*[111] demanded that "the decision on ways of national development be left to the peoples' choice."[112] The next document, an *Appeal to Mikhail Gorbachev*, called on the new party leader "to help us exercise Latvia's right to freely secede from the USSR, in accordance with the Article 69 of the Latvian Constitution."[113] "Let us speak Latvian and be understood! Let us hold a referendum to decide on our future! Let us eat our bread and sell what remains, not the opposite! Let us meet with any people in the world, without being told whom we are allowed to meet!" demanded the document.[114]

The most complete expression of the Group's claims can be found in its *Appeal to the United Nations* (July 1986). The main element of this document was an appeal to the member states of the UN to request the Soviet Union to elaborate on the legal context of the constitutional right of secession for the republics of the USSR. Other claims discussed a "transitional period," during which Latvia would be represented in the UN as an independent state. The *Appeal* also demanded that Latvian soldiers not be assigned to serve in other republics, that Latvian be assured recognition as the official language of the republic and the sole language of instruction in all schools. The UN was also asked to send observers to monitor the situation in Latvia. Like other ethnic documents, the *Appeal* called for religious freedom and the release of all Latvian political prisoners. It also called for a UN special commission to investigate crimes against the Latvian people during the period of 1940–1945. All suspected perpetrators should then appear before a "people's court."[115] In addition, the document put forward a number of territorial claims. In the authors' opinion, a district of Arbene (now Pytalovo) and six small rural districts, misappropriated by the Russian Federation and included in Pskov *oblast* should be returned to Latvia.

One symptomatic innovation must be noted in the Helsinki-86 group's assertiveness. Although most ethnic movements in the Baltic region protested against "influx of Russians," their privileged status or disproportional influence, sometimes employing the harshest terms, no extremist suggestions concerning "Russian migrants" living in national republics can be found in documents by Baltic dissident groups. The *Appeal to the United Nations* suggested that "appropriate humanitarian conditions for the emigration [from Latvia] of those migrants who treated our language and culture with hostility and disdain"[116] be made. However, it specified neither the criterion to be used for indicating "hostility and disdain," nor the measures to be taken to encourage emigration from Latvia.

Movements of Dispersed Ethnic Groups

Crimean Tatars

"The Twentieth Party Congress, and especially Khrushchev's famous secret speech, are considered by many to be directly responsible for the vigor with which the non-Russian people of the Soviet Union have begun to voice their accumulated resentment against the injustices suffered at the hands of the Great Russian chauvinists. Of all the non-Russian groups, the Crimean Tatars have organized the most vigorous protest—a protest supported by the fact that other deported nationalities have been rehabilitated, permitted to return to their former territories, and had their autonomous status within the Soviet federation restored," wrote P. Potichny in his article, "The Struggle of the Crimean Tatars."[117]

An *Appeal by the Crimean Tatars to the Twenty-third Party Congress* (1966), sketching mass petitions by Crimean Tatars since the Twentieth Party Congress, cited the following data:

> In 1957, a *Letter to the Central Committee* was signed by 14,000 Crimean Tatars; In 1958, 28,000 Crimean Tatars signed a *Letter* that was handed to A. Mikoyan, then Chairman of Presidium of the Supreme Soviet.[118]

A nationwide protest *Declaration* (1969) was addressed to all branches of the Soviet government.[119] It noted that as of the commencement of the Twenty-third Congress (28 January 1966–18 March 1966) 14,284 individual and collective petitions had been sent by Crimean Tatars to the Central Committee. One document, an *Appeal by the Crimean Tatars to the Twenty-third Party Congress* was signed by 120,000 Crimean Tatars.

Since its inception, the Crimean Tatar movement regarded mass participation as an important instrument in pressing their ethnic interests. For this reason Crimean Tatar *samizdat* regularly reported the number of signatures on petitions. An *Appeal by the Crimean Tatar People to the World Public* (1968) assessed that "more than 3 million signatures had been collected in petitions to the Soviet leadership. This means that every adult Crimean Tatar has signed no less than ten times."[120] Five years later, the *National Inquiry*, addressed to the Politburo of the CPSU Central Committee and signed by 6,800 people, mentioned that between 1956 and 1973, sixty-six national documents with more than 4 million signatures were issued by the Crimean Tatar movement.[121]

Return to the homeland and the restoration of autonomous status constituted the key demands of Crimean Tatar documents. Practically, all collective or individual petitions contained variations of these demands. A *Statement by the Representatives of the Crimean Tatar People* (1968) called for the "restoration of national equality, as guaranteed by the Soviet Constitution."[122] The *National Inquiry* spoke of a "just solution to the nationality question,"[123] and demanded that the Crimean Tatars be allowed to return to the Crimea to restore their compact settlements there without any restrictions, and be granted autonomous status. All forms of Crimean Tatar ethnic activism are organized around the idea of homecoming.

The prominent Crimean Tatar dissident, Mustafa Dzhemilev, in his *Letter* (1968) to Petr Grigorenko, stated that in 1962 he was part of a group of young Crimean Tatars who discussed a project to establish an unauthorized organization, *The Union of the Crimean Tatar Youth for Return to the Motherland.*[124] To promote this objective an unprecedented ethnic institution—"the Crimean Tatars' Representatives in Moscow"—emerged in the late 1960. Each representative arrived in Moscow with a warrant signed by several dozens of Crimean Tatar activists, and stayed in the capital for some period of time. One representative was empowered to act by proxy for their interests.

Sobraniie documentov samizdata reprinted the text of the mandate given to Rollan Kadyev by forty-three persons living in one district of the city of Samarkand. The paper ran as follows: "Kadyev is empowered to act in the practical interests of the Communist Party, government, and the people for the restoration of the constitutional national motherland, the Crimea."[125] The mandate also specified the demands to be championed by Crimean Tatar representatives: (1) An organized return to the Crimea; (2) The restoration of the autonomous status "granted by the Revolution—by Lenin."[126] An *Appeal by the Crimean Tatar People to the World Public*[127] reported that in May 1965 about eight hundred representatives had received mandates from Crimean Tatars assembled in Moscow to hand the Soviet authorities a new petition. Almost all were arrested and deported to Tashkent, Uzbekistan, under police escort.

Crimean Tatar representatives in Moscow acted as regular delegates, engaging in various activities, including holding meetings with Soviet officials; maintaining contacts with liberal democratic movements, the foreign press, and diplomats; and organizing protest actions. A *samizdat* document mentioned that from 1956 to 1973 Crimean Tatar representatives were received "at the highest levels" fourteen times.[128]

Despite repressive measures taken by authorities, the institution of Crimean Tatar representatives in Moscow was retained throughout the 1970s and 1980s. Representatives issued regular accounts of their work in the capital[129] and reports on the situation in the provinces.

Like the Ukrainian and Baltic peoples, the Crimean Tatars also organized nonviolent, symbolic acts of protest. In October 1966, in commemoration of the forty-fifth anniversary of the establishment of Crimean Tatar autonomy, a group of young Crimean Tatars laid flowers at Lenin's monument in Tashkent. Ten demonstrators were arrested. In Andizhan a wreath inscribed

"To V.I. Lenin from the expelled Crimean Tatars"[130] was placed at Lenin's statue. A *Statement* (April 1968), signed by sixteen representatives of the Crimean Tatar people, described a peaceful demonstration of Crimean Tatars in Chirchik, Uzbekistan, on 21 April 1968: it was brutally suppressed by the police and army.[131]

A *Letter to the Central Committee*[132] reported that for twenty-five years it was a custom to go into mourning on 18 May—the anniversary of the deportation of the Crimean Tatars: commemorative ceremonies were held in Crimean Tatar cemeteries on that day. On 18 May 1969, however, the police blocked entrances to all Crimean Tatar cemeteries in Uzbekistan, disrupting commemorative ceremonies honoring the twenty-fifth anniversary of the Crimean Tatar tragedy.

Probably the most vigorous attempts to resolve ethnic demands can be found in settlement attempts by Crimean Tatars. Numerous *samizdat* documents, issued by both individuals and groups, reported on failures to successfully register a passport in Crimea and on illegal campsites established in the Crimea by Tatar activists. *Information Paper* (no. 26, 26 July 1968)[133] reported that on 26 May of that year ninety-eight activists set up tents in the suburbs of the Crimean capital of Simferopol. The next day, over 250 militiamen, accompanied by KGB staff members, arrived there and destroyed the site. All the inhabitants, including children, were thrown into trucks, robbed, and deported to Baku. Discussing a similar event, another Crimean Tatar document demanded that the persecution of Crimean Tatars, who came to the Crimea seeking employment, housing, and the like, be stopped.[134] On 23 June 1978, in the Crimean village of Donskoie, Musa Mamut committed self-immolation in protest against violations of the individual rights of the Crimean Tatars.[135]

In 1977, the Crimean Tatar movement launched a campaign for the abrogation of all decrees, instructions, and other open and secret acts adopted after the deportation. A document reporting on this campaign mentioned that from May to August 1977, two hundred appeals dealing with this issue and signed by four thousand people were sent to Brezhnev. The well-known leader of the Crimean Tatar movement, Mustafa Dzhemilev, addressed a *Statement to the Supreme Soviet* in which he demanded permission for Crimean Tatars to settle in the Crimea. He also called for the repeal of "all decrees, resolutions, and instructions infringing on the rights of the Crimean Tatars on the basis of their ethnic origins."[136]

An *Appeal to the Belgrade Conference on European Security* (1977)[137] reiterated the demand for an organized return to the Crimea. The *Appeal* also insisted that all Crimean Tatar property confiscated by the Soviet authorities after the deportation be returned and that "everything that was destroyed be restored."[138]

In the early 1980s, the so-called *Initiative Groups* appeared in various regions with dense Crimean Tatar populations to coordinate efforts in championing their ethnic interests. A *samizdat* document dated 8 March 1984 was signed by seventeen Crimean Tatar activists at a meeting in Samarkand of representatives of towns and regions of the Uzbek SSR.[139] According to the document, the following problems were discussed:

1. The state of the national movement in regions with a Crimean Tatar population;
2. Prospects for the further development of the Crimean Tatar movement;
3. The status of the Crimean Tatar language and culture.

In conclusion the delegates discussed a draft of the *Statement by the Crimean Tatar Movement*, demanding "the genuine rehabilitation"[140] of the Crimean Tatars.

Soviet Germans

The Soviet Germans launched their struggle for rehabilitation after the Twentieth Party Congress (1956). Available *samizdat* documents make it possible to trace the dramatic developments in Soviet German ethnic assertiveness since 1965.

In January 1965, a delegation of Volga Germans, introducing itself as the *Initiative Group of the Communist Party, Komsomol Members, and Nonparty Representatives* came to Moscow to advocate the restoration of the Autonomous Republic of the Volga Germans. The delegation included thirteen members who represented Soviet Germans living in various regions of the Russian Federation, Kazakhstan, and Kirghizia.[141] The delegation's members spent ten days in Moscow (2–13 January 1965) and had warrants from 660 Germans to act on their behalf. The *Initiative Group* handed the Soviet leadership a *Statement* issued on 9 January, and addressed to the recently elected General Secretary of the Communist Party, Leonid Brezhnev, and the Chairman of the Presidium of the Supreme Soviet, Anastas Mikoyan. It demanded the full rehabilitation of the Soviet German people and the restoration of their autonomous status.[142] The *Statement* emphasized that "only the restoration of the autonomous republic can secure a solution to the other urgent problems involving culture, education, religious sectarianism, and so on. Only the restoration of the German Autonomous Republic can stop the spiritual and moral degradation of the Soviet German population, who have lost their cultural and linguistic links."[143]

The second delegation, consisting of forty-three members, visited Moscow six months later (12–27 June 1965). This delegation received power of attorney from 4,498 Soviet Germans. Four representatives had an audience with A. Mikoyan, then Chairman of the Presidium of the Supreme Soviet. He explained that the Soviet authorities considered it unreasonable to raise the issue of German autonomy then. Two years later, in 1967, a new Soviet German delegation arrived in Moscow, and was received in the party Central Committee by an anonymous employee of low rank. By the late 1960s, it became obvious that meetings with Soviet officials did nothing to promote the Volga Germans' struggle for autonomy. This lack of progress compelled the German movement to seek an alternative solution to their nationality question.

Much of the material in the *samizdat* almanac *Re-Patria* of 1974 (editors: B. Grigas, L. Bauer, and F. Ruppel) indicated that since the early 1970s the restoration of autonomous status no longer constituted the single focus of Soviet German assertiveness. In a 1972 *Statement* to N. Podgornyi, Chairman of Presidium of the Supreme Soviet of the USSR, the Ruppel couple announced their decision to relinquish their Soviet citizenship. The couple also expressed their desire to obtain the citizenship of any country "that would be ready to receive us."[144] The authors cited their dramatic story as an example of the Germans' fate in the USSR. They regarded emigration as a radical form of protest against a gross violation of their national rights: they did not describe it as an independent value or even as a "national goal." Though, in the 1960s and earlier, dozens of German families applied for—and were refused—exit visas there are no demands for free emigration found in the collective petitions asserting German ethnic objectives. The Soviet German movement then attached no public prominence to the issue of emigration.

Re-Patria did equate the demand for autonomy with the demand for freedom of emigration. A "Letter to the Estonian Department of Visas" (1973), written by Ia. Damm, demanded that they "grant exit visas to all Germans who want to emigrate to Germany."[145] The almanac also reported that in late 1973 delegates of the recently established Estonian Committee of the Association of German Citizens and the Latvian Committee of Citizens of German Origin arrived in Moscow to hand the Soviet authorities a list of Germans who applied to emigrate to the Federal Republic of Germany.[146] Another item in *Re-Patria* reported that in January 1974 the Girning family from Dushanbe, Tajikistan, demonstrated with their three children near the office of the Central Committee demanding an exit visa to Germany.[147]

Failure to achieve any positive results in pressing for autonomy seems to have been the main factor in the German movement's demands. Like the

Meskhetians, the Germans "may well have been influenced by the success of several thousand Soviet Zionists in gaining permission to leave for Israel from 1968 on," P. Reddaway assessed.[148] (In 1971, 13,022 Jews and 886 Germans emigrated from the USSR; in 1972 the numbers of emigrants were 31,681 and 3,315 respectively.) Another factor that influenced this reorientation was the general deterioration of the political climate in the Soviet Union. *Samizdat* increasingly depicted the Federal Republic of Germany as the *patria* of the Soviet Germans. V. Grigas, in his 1974 *Letter*, told how he had applied for "re-patriation" and had been refused a visa to his "motherland, the Federal Republic of Germany."[149]

Konstantin Vukkert's long article, "Some Thoughts on the State of the Germans, Citizens of the USSR" (1976), considered autonomy to be an "effective weapon in the struggle against discrimination against ethnic minorities."[150] He emphasized the significance of this status for all Soviet Germans irrespective of where they lived. He described the restoration of the Volga German Autonomous Republic as a necessity, sufficient for securing equal status for the Soviet Germans. At the same time, Vukkert declared freedom of emigration to West Germany as the second goal to be achieved by the Soviet German movement. "Emigration is the only thing left for this permanently insulted and humiliated people," he contended.

Since the late 1970s, demands to emigrate dominated Soviet German documents. In 1976, Vukkert appealed to L. Brezhnev, H. Schmidt, and E. Honneker, proposing that they hold trilateral negotiations on the issue of the Soviet Germans. The author explained that because of the malicious neglect by the Soviet authorities of the Germans' claim to restore their autonomous republic, the issue of free emigration for the Germans should be a focus of international concern.[151] Similarly, a *Letter to Members of the Bundestag* by five Soviet Germans (V. Axt and others) called the emigration of Germans "the only thing left to be done."[152] A 1981 *Petition* to the Presidium of the Supreme Soviet, signed by 246 Soviet Germans,[153] advanced demands completely devoted to emigration: (1) Germans must not be refused exit visas, except in cases specified by law (e.g., individuals on trial or under judicial examination, in debt, possessing knowledge of state secrets, etc.); (2) Every applicant must receive a detailed answer to his application for an exit visa. Other demands called for an end to the persecution of Germans who applied to emigrate. A later document, an *Appeal by Fourteen Soviet Germans to the Conference on Human Rights and to the Soviet Government* (June 1984),[154] contained a single request—to promote their emigration to the Federal Republic of Germany.

Meskhetians

On November 15th 1944, the forcible deportations from Meskhetia (a southern part of Georgia) of the indigenous population took place. This population was mainly formed when, in the late 16th and early 17th centuries, the Meskhi Georgians gradually adopted the Turkish language and became converted to Islam. The all-union census of 1929 officially described them as Turks, and schools using Turkish were opened in the province.

In 1935–6 the people were suddenly renamed Azerbaijanis and teaching was transferred to the Azerbaijani language. But on November 15th 1944, they were once again stated to be Turks and deported to Central Asia and Kazakhstan. Apart from the Meskhi Georgians, the following were deported from Meskhetia: the Karapapakhi Azerbaijanis, Islamicized Khemshil Armenians, Turkicized Kurds, and the Meskhetian Turkmens, who are also calling themselves Turks. Common misfortune brought these various ethnic groups together and welded them into one people.[155]

According to Peter Reddaway, this report (appeared in *Chronicle of Current Events*, no. 7, 1969) is the first detailed account on the tragic fate of the Meskhetian people.[156]

The deportation of the Meskhetians was never officially reported. Although they were not accused of high treason or any other crime "the regime for deported exiles—the same as that for peoples accused of being 'traitors'—was imposed upon all areas where the 'temporary deported peoples' had been put."[157] While the Decrees of 1956 and 1957, promulgated by the Presidium of the Supreme Soviet of the USSR, officially lifted the regime for deported exiles, the Meskhetians were not permitted to return home.

A report in the *Chronicle*, no. 7, entitled "The Movement of the People of Meskhetia for Return to the Homeland," said that in late 1956 and early 1957 two delegations of Meskhetians went to Moscow to request permission to return to Meskhetia. "In answer the Meskhi were declared to be Azerbaijanis and were 'given permission' to 'return' to Azerbaijan." Between 1957 and 1963 a number of interviews were held with Soviet officials in Moscow and Tbilisi, the Georgian capital, but no results were achieved. A Temporary Committee for the Return of the People to their Homeland was formed to represent the Meskhetians, and members of the Committee continued to hold talks with the Soviet authorities. The *Chronicle's* report said:

On 15 February 1964 the First Meeting of the People was held in the *Leninskii Put'* kolkhoz (collective farm), in the Tashkent region of

Uzbekistan. More than six hundred delegates from Central Asia, Kazakhstan, and the Caucasus, with mandates from local assemblies of the people and representing the entire people (with a total population of 200,000) participated in the meeting. A *Petition* to the Party and Government was drawn up and a Temporary Organizing Committee for the Return of the People to the Homeland was elected. The historian Enver Odabashev (Khozravanadze) was elected president and 125 delegates were chosen to go to Moscow. A complete record of the meeting was sent to party and government leaders. Until now (1969) twenty-six meetings of representatives of the whole people have been held.[158]

The twenty-second national meeting (April 1968) in Yangiyul, Uzbekistan, was attended by more than six thousand delegates. Thirty were detained and spent two to six months in prison.

On 24 July 1968, seven thousand Meskhetian delegates demonstrated at the government house in Tbilisi, demanding a meeting with the Georgian leadership. Though the demonstration was brutally suppressed by police and army detachments, two days later, on 26 July, several Meskhetian delegates were received by the First Secretary of the Georgian Central Committee, Mzhavanadze. He promised that various regions of Georgia would accept a hundred Meskhetian families per year, but said that in order to find a general solution to the problem they should apply to the central government in Moscow. In August and November 1968, the delegates were twice received in the Central Committee by one of its officials, B. Iakovlev.

"New Persecution of the Meskhi," an account published in the *Chronicle* (no. 9, 1969), reported that B. Iakovlev finally "granted the Meskhi permission to settle in various regions of Georgia, and fifteen to thirty families were even allowed to settle in Meskhetia. Although this permission was not confirmed in writing, the Meskhi people decided to trust this indefinite form of permission."[159] The *Chronicle* described several failed attempts by Meskhi families to settle in Georgia. Even those people who found work there were soon dismissed and deported by the police. The item also reported that "by June 1969, 505 Meskhi families had arrived in Georgia. The Georgian population welcomed them as brothers and helped them to settle in. But on 7 June there was a round-up of Meskhetians who had already arrived and found work: were sent off by train in various different directions."[160]

Peter Reddaway supposes that "in some ways the Meskhetians—with up to seven thousand people assembling for national conferences—have even outdone the numerically stronger Tatars."[161] The high level of ethnic solidarity and organization shown by the Meshketians is corroborated by the following episode cited by the *Chronicle*. The President of the Temporary Organizing Committee, Enver Odabashev, a history teacher, was arrested in Saatly, Azerbaijan. When the Meskhi found out about Odabashev's arrest they "left work and came from all the village settlements in the area to gather in Saatly at the district party committee building, where they demanded the immediate release of their teacher.... When they met with refusal, the diligent Meskhi sent express telegrams to L. Brezhnev and V. Iu. Akhundov, then the Azerbajani Communist leader. The crowd did not disperse. Late in the evening of 21 April, Batayev, the secretary of the district party committee, who had been in Baku, returned in great haste.... After lengthy deliberations with representatives of the Meskhi, the district committee secretary ordered Odabashev's release."[162]

In 1969, the Meskhetian movement became increasingly radical. According to Reddaway, "the patience of the Meskhetians began to run out."[163] A *Resolution* issued by the Sixth People's Meeting of the Meskhetian people, which took place in May 1970 in the village Adygiun (Saatly District, Azerbaijan), described how 113 members of the thirty-third Meskhetian delegation visiting Moscow gathered in the reception room of the Party Central Committee, "threw down their passports and renounced their Soviet citizenship, in protest against the official answer insulting the dignity of the [Meskhetian] people."[164] The People's Meeting approved this action as "defying the policy of violence and discrimination."[165] The delegation then appealed to the Turkish embassy to permit Meskhetians to immigrate to Turkey (also approved by the Sixth People's Meeting). The *Resolution* formulated the following demands:

1. The Meskhetians be permitted to return to their original home, where they will be granted autonomy, that is, to form the Meskhetian Turkish Autonomous Republic or Region within the framework of the Georgian SSR.
2. The Meskhetians be provided with appropriate conditions for coming home and building homes, and that they be paid 200 million rubles for losses incurred as a result of the deportation plus 3 percent annual interest for twenty-six years of exile, in accordance with Soviet law.
3. To prevent confusion, the return be coordinated with the Temporary Organizing Committee. A special commission, to include representatives of the Temporary Organizing Committee, should be formed to oversee the return.

The resolution stressed that if these demands were not met the Meskhetians would seek to emigrate to Turkey. At the same time, an *Appeal to the Turkish*

Parliament called on Turkey to grant the Meskhetians Turkish citizenship.[166] The *Chronicle of Current Events* (no. 19, 30 April 1971) reported that on 15 March 1971 a list with the names of Meskhetians seeking to emigrate was passed to the Turkish embassy in Moscow.[167] The significance of emigration for the Meskhetian movement should not be overestimated. Emigration, and the Turkish factor in general, seems to have served as a trump card in pressuring the demand to return home, rather than a viable ethnic objective. In 1972, Meskhetian activist Rashit Seifatov wrote letters to the Secretary General of the Central Committee Brezhnev, UN Secretary General Kurt Waldheim, and Turkish Prime Minister Melen. His letter to Waldheim appealed for help to return home or immigrate to Turkey "for everyone who so desires."[168] At the same time, the appeals to Brezhnev and Melen focused solely on a return to Meskhetia.[169] A *Document*, no. 18, issued in January 1977 by the Moscow Helsinki Watch Group[170] quoted extremist activists of the Meskhetian movement as saying that if the problem of repatriation were not resolved, they would champion the secession of the Meskhetian territory from Georgia and its annexation by Turkey. (The document stated that Iu. Orlov, Chairman of the Helsinki Watch Group, had explained to the group that this demand contradicted international agreements signed by the Turkish government.)

Another trend, possibly influenced by Georgian dissident activities, can be found in the Meskhetian movement from the mid-1970s. In 1977, five Meskhetians issued a statement protesting the persecution of Georgian activist V. Rtskhiladze.[171] They noted that Rtskhiladze had organized the collection of Meskhetian signatures on an appeal demanding the "restoration of their Georgian nationality" and enabling them to return to Georgia. In 1982, Kh. Umarov (Gozalishvili), D. Aiubov (Abashidze), and F. Dursunov (Maniadze) wrote an *Appeal to the Georgian People by the Georgian Deported Exiles (Muslim Meskhetians)*. The *Appeal* defined the Meskhetians as part of the Georgian people, not as a particular ethnic group, and called for the "restoration of Georgia's unity."[172] Late Meskhetian *samizdat* documents seem to indicate that the Meskhetians were ready to demonstrate some restraint in ethnic self-assertiveness (specifically to omit demands for political or even cultural autonomy) to gain broader support in Georgia.

Jews

The first known original Jewish *samizdat* document, a *Letter by Twenty-six Representatives of the Jewish Intelligentsia* (15 February 1968) was addressed to the First Secretary of the Lithuanian Central Committee, A. Snieckus.[173] It contained a simple request: to stop the wave of anti-Semitism.

The Six-Day War instigated ethnic militancy among Soviet Jews. The first Jewish *samizdat* magazine, *Iton*, appeared in February 1970 in Riga: it carried dozens of appeals, statements, and petitions to the Soviet authorities, Western and Israeli leaders, and the world public, written by Soviet Jews after the Six-Day War. This material was published in a section entitled *The Jews are Stopping to Keep Silent*.[174] An editorial introduction formulates the documents' message: "It is time to voice and demand the same thing that Moses demanded from Pharaoh: 'Let My People Go.'"[175] The following month, a second Jewish *samizdat* journal, *Iskhod* (Exodus) appeared in Moscow. In 1969, a collective petition by twenty-five Jewish activists to the Secretary General of the United Nations called upon him "to resolve a problem with which we are deeply concerned, namely the problem of free emigration from the USSR."[176] *Samizdat* documents from 1969–1971 contained regular reports of protest activities organized by Jewish activists. In a single issue of another well-known *samizdat* journal, *Vestnik Iskhoda* (1971) the following events were cited:

1. A hunger strike took place on 10–11 March 1971 at the reception room of the Presidium of the USSR Supreme Soviet. About 150 Jews from nine cities participated. By the end of the second day, Soviet Minister of the Interior Shchelokov appeared and promised the demonstrators that he would reconsider their applications to emigrate. By late May 1971, most had received exit visas.[177]

2. A hunger strike by twenty-five Lithuanian Jews took place at the Central Telegraph in Moscow on 14 June 1971; a demonstration by thirty-two Georgian Jews took place on 12 July at the same location.[178]

3. On 1 August 1971, the commemoration of the thirtieth anniversary of the massacre of Jews at Babi Yar, Kiev, was marked by a hunger strike at the site. Ten participants were arrested and sentenced to fifteen days of administrative detention.[179]

4. On 24 December 1971, one year after the hijackers' trial in Leningrad, Jewish activists in several areas of the USSR supported a hunger strike by Jewish political prisoners.

It is interesting that the hijackers' attempt—it was later described as a climactic event in the Jewish struggle for emigration—provoked a very negative immediate reaction. One anonymous report in Jewish *samizdat*, written soon after 15 June 1970, called the twelve people arrested in Leningrad "a small group of irresponsible people," whereas the plan to escape the Soviet Union by hijacking an airplane was regarded as "a provocation, carefully orchestrated by the KGB."[180]

Dealing with Jewish *samizdat* in general and the journal *Iskhod* in particular, Peter Reddaway notes that the mainstream of Jewish *samizdat* "was concerned with the efforts to leave for Israel rather than to improve the cultural and religious conditions of Jewish life in the USSR."[181] While emigration undoubtedly comprised the focus of Jewish assertiveness, a certain evolution in the approach to emigration is noticeable. Emigration was already discussed in the *Letter* by twenty-six Lithuanian Jews to Snieckus. The authors stated that many Lithuanian Jews wanted to emigrate because of the rise of anti-Semitism in the republic. But the authorities created "a paradoxical situation.... They do not want us, they persecute us, but they forcibly hold us here."[182] Describing the desire of Jews to leave for Israel merely as a reaction to anti-Semitism the *Letter* does not count it among Jewish national goals. A 1968 *Appeal* by B. Kochubievskii to L. Brezhnev and P. Shelest (then First Secretary of the Ukrainian Central Committee) gave emigration ideological prominence. "I am a Jew. I want to live in the Jewish State. I want my children to go to a Jewish school. I want to read Jewish newspapers. I want to go to Jewish theaters," he declared.[183]

From its very inception, the Jewish movement that rose after the Six-Day War manifested itself as a Zionist movement completely oriented toward emigration as its main objective. Jewish documents demanded that Soviet authorities enact laws securing the legislative grounds for emigration. An *Open Letter* (1969) by twenty-five Moscow Jewish activists to the Secretary General of the United Nations demanded that he encourage a solution to the "problem stirring us so exceedingly—the problem of free emigration from the USSR."[184] The following year, in 1970, the *Appeal to the Central Committee and Leonid Brezhnev* by G. Feigin, D. Zilber, and R. Aleksandrovich described the necessity of "promulgating democratic regulations for repatriation to Israel."[185] V. Belotserkovskii, in his 1972 *Appeal to the Soviet Public and Government*, stated that the Jews, as well as other Soviet citizens, should be granted the legal "right of emigration to Israel and other countries, as well as the right to return."[186] In the late 1960s–early 1970s most Jewish documents calling for emigration to Israel considered it to be a universal human right that any citizen could leave any country, including his/her own.

Demand for free emigration was often accompanied by many varied cultural, linguistic, and political claims. The *Appeal* by Feigin, Zilberg, and Aleksandrovich demanded a stop to anti-Semitic and anti-Israel propaganda and the restoration of Jewish culture. The authors claimed that "Jews should be granted the right to form communal institutions to protect their interests and to speak up on their behalf."[187] Considering the traditionally negative attitudes of the Soviet Communist elite toward so-called "national cultural autonomy" (associated historically with the Austro-Marxists[188] and Bund), the idea of ethnocommunalism suggested by the *Appeal* seems to have been particularly provocative; however, it remained underdeveloped in later Jewish *samizdat* documents.

In order to reduce anti-Semitism in the USSR, V. Belotserkovskii suggested abolishing the so-called "fifth point," that is, registration of nationality in Soviet identity documents.[189] Rejecting allegations that this would accelerate assimilation, Belotserkovskii responded that securing freedom of Jewish culture and religion would prevent assimilation. He pointed out that "full and objective information on Jewish history, struggle, suffering, and achievements" could reduce anti-Semitism in the USSR considerably.

A. Voronel, co-editor of the most popular Jewish *samizdat* journal, *Jews in the USSR*, supposed that a comprehensive solution of the Jewish question should be based on providing Jews with three main options: (1) Emigration; (2) Assimilation; (3) The unhindered development of Jewish culture in all languages, including Russian, Hebrew, Yiddish, and so on.[190] Considering the Soviet leadership's pro-Arab orientation and the so-called "anti-Zionist" campaign launched by the Soviet mass media to be both a result of and initiator for Soviet anti-Semitism, Jewish activists called on the Soviet government to abrogate the tough anti-Israeli and anti-Zionist policy and to stop all unreserved support for Arab countries in the Middle-East conflict. This message can be found in an article attributed to B. Kochubievskii, entitled "Why Am I a Zionist?"[191] and in an article written after 5 March 1970 and signed by Ahad Ha'Am (a pen-name) entitled "My Press-Conference."[192] The anonymous author of *The Jewish Question in the USSR*[193] warned that pro-Arab policies fused with pan-Islamic propaganda appealing to Muslim solidarity had exacerbated anti-Semitic sentiments among the Muslim population of the USSR.

In the mid-seventies, *samizdat* gave "official recognition" to the absolute precedence of emigration over all other goals championed by the Jewish movement. In the *Jews in the USSR* (no. 9, 1974–1975) Vitalii Rubin, a well-known Jewish activist, published a programmatic article entitled "Prospects for Russian Jewry." "*Aliyah* is the choice in favor of truth,"[194] he stated. He argued that since Jewish life in the USSR cannot be revived, emigration to Israel should be considered the Jewish question's single possible solution.

A gradual shift from universalism to particularism should be indicated as a trend in the Jewish *samizdat*'s approach to emigration. Throughout the seventies, emigration was depicted less as a universal right to leave one's own country; at the same time, emigration to Israel was increasingly described as a national obligation. Those who refused to fulfill their duty were condemned. In an essay pretentiously entitled "To Jews" (1975) Jewish activists G. Rozenshtein and V. Fain passionately reprimanded Jews emigrating to Western countries for "treason to their Jewishness."[195] "Why... should Israel pay for your voyage?" the authors asked sarcastically. In 1979, another activist, Iu. Kosharovskii, lectured on *noshrim* (Jews who left the USSR for Western countries) at a regular session of the nonofficial seminar for Hebrew teachers. He argued that *noshrim* rendered the situation worse, and actually threatened the continuation of *aliyah*. In his opinion, the Soviet authorities had a "formal pretext" to close the gates of *aliyah*: many emigrants had deceived them by using their official permission to leave for Israel in order to emigrate from the USSR to other countries. After the lecture, participants were asked to sign a letter to the Israeli president requesting that he take decisive measures to prevent the emigration of Jews to the West. The campaign against *noshrim* was encouraged, if not initiated, by the Israeli establishment, dispirited by the progressive decline in the number of people of Zionist orientation among the total (real and potential) emigrants.

Political-ideological grounds for asserting the priority of *aliyah* were formulated by A. Lerner in his programmatic article "Emigration or Civilization: What is More Important?" prepared for presentation at the 1976, unofficial (in fact, banned) symposium on Jewish culture. Material from the symposium was later published in a *samizdat* almanac (1976) entitled *The White Book on Symposium: Jewish Culture in the USSR—Perspectives and the Present Situation.*[196]

Vigorously asserting that emigration to Israel should be the main preoccupation of the Jewish movement, A. Lerner contended:

> The fact that the Jewish population of the USSR comprises over two million people, while the total number of refuseniks and prisoners of Zion reaches several thousand does not mean that the issue of Jewish culture should have priority over the issue of emigration.
>
> .... The emigration movement had been and remains the major stimulus of the revival of the national consciousness of Soviet Jewry. Every family that evades the dramatic fate of being a *refusenik* [by successfully making *aliyah*], and more so, every prisoner of Zion who emigrates to Israel will be more effective than hundreds books or speeches, no matter how well written.[197]

The main article opposed to Lerner's opinion was written by M. Zubin (the pen-name of Jewish activist and Hebrew teacher M. Chlenov). Zubin paid tribute to *aliyah* activists and their aims, but argued that the Zionists' slogan: "Let my people go," was only relevant to "several hundred *refusenik* families";[198] it had lost the nationwide validity of the early days of the Jewish movement. According to him, championing emigration to Israel had become a "narrow international campaign"[199] and could not be considered the sole Jewish cause. The revival of Jewish culture was the only objective that held universal validity for Soviet Jews. Pointing out that within Soviet Jewry, *aliyah* activists were the most educated in Jewish topics, he suggested that they lead the movement to revive Jewish culture—only mass promotion of this culture could create the necessary conditions for the continuation and extension of the "repatriation movement."[200] An article entitled "The Nearest Stage of Revival," by Jewish activists, V. Fain, V. Prestin, and others and carried in the almanac demonstrated an even more decisive position: "It is an illusion to think that *aliyah* can solve all the problems and satisfy all the needs of the national movement," stated the article. The authors attacked "some short-sighted adherents of *aliyah*, who spread myths about hundreds of thousands of applications for exit visas."[201] Both the competing sides devised specific programs for the Jewish movement. Zubin's program called for:

The legal publication of books and periodicals "for Jews and about Jews," free circulation of the world Jewish press;

The legalization of private Hebrew lessons and Hebrew instruction in universities, seminars for foreign languages, and the like; the promotion of Jewish studies, publication of Jewish archives, creation of Jewish theaters, museums, cultural societies, and so on;

The development of tourism at Jewish sites in the USSR;

Securing free contacts between Soviet Jews and their relatives, friends, and compatriots abroad, including free postal and telephone communication, visits to foreign countries, and organized tours to Israel and other countries with deep-rooted Jewish traditions;

Securing the right of emigrants to preserve their Soviet citizenship and return to the USSR.[202]

Lerner put forward his own demands:

All prisoners of Zion must be released and exit visas must be granted to all *refuseniks*;

Emigration policies must be liberalized;

Voice of Israel broadcasts must not be jammed;

Discriminatory policies against Jews and the anti-Semitic campaign in the mass media must be stopped;

Restrictions on the import of politically neutral books and periodicals devoted to Jewish topics must be lifted.

Lerner flatly rejected Zubin's belief that a dialogue should be held with the Soviet authorities in order to gain some cultural and communal indulgences. He pointed out that any cultural activity permitted by the regime would be exploited as a show-window for the West, leaving the issue of the *refuseniks* utterly neglected.[203] Viewed in its entirety, Jewish *samizdat* of the 1970s and 1980s synthesized Zubin's and Lerner's ideas. On the one hand, the enormous flowering of periodicals and almanacs dedicated to cultural-linguistic problems since the mid-1970s should be noted. In addition to *Jews in the USSR*, the journals *Tarbut, Nash Ivrit, Maggid, The Jews in the Contemporary World* (a digest of the Jewish press), and others were issued in this period. On the other hand, while appreciating that cultural-linguistic topics were important factors of ethnic mobilization, the Jewish movement never considered them self-dependent values. As a rule, references to cultural-linguistic deprivation did not culminate in cultural-linguistic demands, but in the demand of free emigration.

An *Open Letter* by 81 Jews to participants of the Belgrade Conference (1977)[204] discussed the procedure of emigration. The authors called for the repeal of instructions by visa departments (OVIR) requiring invitations from relatives in Israel, and the issuing of regulations defining the terms of emigration and grounds for possible refusal. They argued that every refusal, including refusals based on security considerations, should be given in written form and contain detailed justification of such a decision. Any person who received a refusal should be granted the legal right to appeal against the decision. It also insisted that a maximum period of secrecy and a legal, democratic procedure of ascertaining financial claims to potential emigrants be established. Finally, the *Open Letter* demanded that the compulsory military service should not be used as a pretext for delaying repatriation and that applicants for visas and *refuseniks* should not be persecuted in any way because of their desire to emigrate.

By giving priority to "repatriation to Israel," the Jewish *samizdat* inevitably gave particular prominence to the interests of *refuseniks* as a distinct group. A *Letter* (1982) by thirteen Jewish *refusenik*-scientists to Israeli President, Y. Navon, asserted their special status within the Jewish repatriation movement. "We are not concerned about our personal fate but first of all, with the tragedy of the annihilation of our learning, which has been left to rot in jail rather than being of benefit to Israel and to the whole mankind."[205] It emphasized that victims are chosen from among those "who after the catastrophe, did everything to succeed in science."[206]

As of 1984, a new drive toward particularism can be noted in the Jewish movement. On 7 February 1984, twenty *refuseniks* appealed to the Presidium of the Supreme Soviet of the USSR demanding repatriation to Israel.[207] The *Appeal* asserted that *aliyah* should not be considered in the generally accepted terms of emigration or the re-unification of families. In the authors' view, *aliyah* must be equated with return of Greek and Spanish emigrants to their original countries, which was permitted by the Soviet government. This *Appeal* was followed by symbolic acts by approximately two hundred *refuseniks* from Moscow, Leningrad, Kiev, and some other towns who publicly renounced their Soviet citizenship and appealed to the Israeli authorities for Israeli citizenship.

Later programmatic documents added procedural claims to the general demand for emigration. A *Petition to the Central Committee* (1985) by a group of Moscow Jews called upon the Soviet leadership to "establish the clear and acceptable procedures for applying for exit visas,"[208] to define the terms for considering applications, and to list the maximum periods in which exit visas can be postponed because of the applicant's access to state secret. The *Petition* also demanded an end to all forms of persecution of Jewish activists and an end to negative propaganda about Jews wanting to emigrate.

An *Appeal* by 140 Jewish activists to delegates of the Twenty-seventh Congress of the CPSU[209] demanded that all prisoners of Zion be released and granted exit visas. It also demanded, that all-longtime *refuseniks* (more than five years) be granted visas and that the maximum period of "refusal" not exceed five years. Finally, it called for the publication of documents regulating emigration from the USSR and the signing of a bilateral Soviet–Israeli treaty on the repatriation of Soviet Jews.

Russians: The Conservative and General Democratic Movements

"On February 2 1964 an important clandestine military-political organization made its appearance in Leningrad. Its declared aim: the formation of an 'underground liberation army,' which would 'overthrow the [Soviet] dictatorship and destroy the defensive forces of the oligarchy.' " Calling itself the All-Russian Social-Christian Union for the Liberation of the People, or more commonly, *VSKhSON*—the Russian acronym for the organization's somewhat ponderous title—this underground union succeeded in recruiting almost thirty members before it was uncovered by the KGB in 1967. Another thirty candidates "were being prepared for membership" wrote J. Dunlop, a prominent student of Russian nationalism, in his book, *The New Russian Revolutionaries*.[210]

Once VSKhSON's documents became available in the West, scholars unanimously considered the organization to be the first "opposition [movement] based on Russian nationalism"[211] in the post-Stalin era. Undoubtedly, VSKhSON's program had a crucial impact on the political-ideological conception of modern Russian nationalism. On the other hand, VSKhSON's nationalism was based on the broad concept of a "nation" united by the moral values of Christian universalism, whereas mainstream contemporary Russian nationalism was deeply rooted in ethnic particularism.

The *Program* begins: "The Union for the Liberation of the People considers itself a patriotic organization, whose members are selfless representatives of all the nationalities of Great Russia. It is struggling for the interest of the entire populace and is not a party, either in the class or totalitarian sense of the word."[212] "Universal Christianity is in the process of laying religious-cultural foundations for supra-national unity. Tomorrow's world will be founded on Christian ideals. Social-Christianity affirms the freedom of the individual, the sacredness of the family, brotherly relations among men, and the unity of all nations. Social-Christianity stands for personalized economics, politics, and culture based on the lawful rights and interests of the individual," the *Program* proclaimed.[213]

After Christian universalism, individualism comprised the second substantial difference between VSKhSON's *Program* and those of later Russian conservative nationalists. Calling for the formation of a state and society based on the principles of social-Christianity, the VSKhSON *Program* detailed points that were generally beyond the considerations of other ethnic minority movements. Thus, the *Program* determined forms of ownership ("national, state, communal, and personalistic"[214]) and specified that land must be national property, not subject to sale or any other form of alienation, which "citizens, communes, and the state may use only on the basis of limited holdings."[215] According to the *Program*, "industrial enterprises and service industries must be owned and directed by the collectives which work or finance them."[216]

The *Program* said, "a broad system of national credit must become the basis our socio-economic policy."[217] "Banking should not be a government monopoly. It should also not be in the hands of private individuals. Corporation banks should function side by side with the State Bank in the handling of corporation and private funds. Commerce should be free. In the interest of society, the state must retain the right to set a ceiling on the prices of basic commodities and to maintain control over foreign trade."[218] This system is defined by the *Program* as a "free market."

When discussing the organization of the state, the *Program* stressed that "society should be able to participate directly in the life of the country through local self government and the representation of peasant communes and national corporations (the latter large unions of those engaged in physical and mental labor) on the highest legislative body of the country.... Social Christianity strives to create a society in which man will not be exploited by man and where mutual relations will be based upon solidarity."[219]

At the same time, the *Program* vigorously rejected the idea of private property and the multi-party system. Proclaiming broad, liberal individual, cultural, and religious rights, the VSKhSON *Program* nevertheless declared that "Christian culture bears an inherently supra-national character, which will play a decisive role in our era in bringing peoples together into one pan-human family."[220]

Considering the Russian state, rather than ethnicity, to be the focus of its interests, and offering benevolent paternalism to non-Russian minorities, the All-Russian Social-Christian Union for the Liberation of the People was an example of unchallenged nationalism. It was utterly unaware of the resourcefulness and potential of ethnic minorities' nationalism.

Russians from non-Russian peripheries were the first to express a nationalistic reaction to manifestations of ethnic minorities' assertiveness. An anonymous *Letter* (1968) addressed to a "Dear Friend," an otherwise unspecified official of the Central Committee, is a striking example of this reaction.[221] The fact that "even high officials attempt to speak Ukrainian"[222] in the Ukrainian SSR provoked indignation in our author.

A contrary political response to ethnic self-assertiveness was offered by the *Program of the Democratic Movement of the USSR* (1969).[223] The *Program* described the USSR as a "forcible union of peoples around the Great Russian national core."[224] Expressing "full solidarity" with the ethnic minorities' struggle against "Russian colonialism," the *Program* formulated the democratic movement's approach to the so-called "nationality question" with the following principles:

> The choice of political self-determination by means of all-national referendums to be supervised by the United Nations;
> The offer of cultural or economic autonomy to nations that have chosen not to secede from the Union of Democratic Republics (political entity to supplant the USSR);
> The resolution of territorial questions only with the help of an arbitration committee of the United Nations;

The restitution of all moral, cultural, territorial, and material losses of all the nationalities incurred under Great Power hegemony;

The right of each small people to restrict the number of foreigners in their territory according to a norm acceptable for its ethnic existence;

Noninterference by the Union of Democratic Republics in the domestic affairs of the nations that secede;

Friendship, cooperation, and mutual respect between the seceding republics and the Union of Democratic Republics within the framework of the United Nations.[225]

To some degree, the Democratic Movement's *Program* anticipated the demands and objectives of the ethnic minorities.

The *Manifesto of Russian Patriots*, widely known as *Slovo Natsii* (The Nation Speaks, or Word of the Nation), appeared in 1970,[226] soon after the Democratic Movement's *Program*. *Slovo Natsii* expressed the nationalist reaction both to the *Program* and to non-Russian political assertiveness. Seeking to reinforce the Russians' dominant status, which "Russian patriots" felt had been challenged, they demanded a stop to all patronizing of the "nonexistent cultures" of small ethnic groups and attacked the democrats' proposal to impose restrictions on Russian migration to the national territories of ethnic minorities. "Since when have we become foreigners in our land?" the *Manifesto* demanded. It asserted the preservation of "one, indivisible Russia" and the Russian people's inherent right to the entire territory of the USSR. It was natural enough that a strong, centralized state was necessary to secure these goals. "Only such a state," stressed the *Manifesto*, "meets the expectations and traditions of the Russian people."[227]

In January 1971, *Veche*, "the first Russian patriotic journal,"[228] edited by former political prisoner V. Osipov, was launched in Moscow. "The only thing we want is to strengthen Russian national culture and its patriotic traditions in the spirit of the Slavophiles and Dostoievskii, and to prove the greatness and originality of Russia," Osipov explained in a declaration of principles.[229]

One year later, in an interview with a correspondent from Associated Press, Osipov listed *Veche's* goals:

The protection of monuments to material and spiritual creative work;
The fostering of respect to our sacred national values—to our national dignity;
The promotion of a revival of Russian culture;
The fostering of love of the Motherland, the Russian Orthodox Church, and so on.[230]

"We have taken the responsibility of being a voice of the national aspirations of our people," Osipov states.[231]

Although every movement finds ideological bases for political demands, the ideological oversaturation of *Veche*'s programmatic declarations, as well as its failure to formulate any concrete socio-political ideas—apart from demands to reinforce the dominant status of Russians throughout the USSR and to preserve the Russian Empire—is unprecedented.

An editorial entitled "The Russian solution to the Nationality Question" prepared on the occasion of the fiftieth anniversary of the formation of the USSR, praised the Soviet government for "wise nationality politics" enabling it to maintain the integrity of the "great state."[232] Another *Veche* editorial, written as a polemical response to the sensational article by A. Iakovlev[233] (the acting chief of the ideological department of the party's Central Committee, who sharply criticized Great Russian chauvinism) proclaimed "the preservation of the multi-national state without prejudice to the national interests of other peoples" to be a national goal.[234] As an argument for the Russians' dominant position, the article stated: "Due to their mentality, the Russian people, like no other people, are able to comprise the core of a voluntary union."[235]

A. Solzhenitsyn, in his *Letter to Soviet Leaders* (5 September 1973)[236] gave impetus to nationalist assertiveness. Theodore Shabad, the first analyst of Solzhenitsyn's *Letter*, called his article in *The New York Times*, "Solzhenitsyn Asks Kremlin to Abandon Communism and Split up Soviet Union."[237] Solzhenitsyn proposed that the "development of the Russian North-East"[238] (Siberia and the Russian North) be adopted as a positive all-national goal and a serviceable counterpart to Soviet "political gigantism." Moreover, the *Letter to Soviet Leaders* called for disarmament, de-ideologization, and the need to "lift our trusteeship from Eastern Europe, the Baltic republics, Transcaucasia, Central Asia, and possibly even from parts of the Ukraine,"[239] indicating that on this issue Solzhenitsyn shared the position of the liberal democratic movements. However, in his criticism of modern civilization he devised the "Utopian" principles of a nonprogressive economy and industry and particularly his advocacy of an "enlightened," authoritarian regime—revealing Solzhenitsyn's strong propensity toward conservative Russian neo-Romanticism.

The ambivalent concept expressed by Solzhenitsyn in his *Letter to Soviet Leaders* garnered only minimal support, but it proved to be the basis of various political adaptations. Osipov praised the *Letter* as a "manifesto of our century,"[240] and offered his own interpretation of Solzhenitsyn's program based on the following points:

Renouncing Marxism;
Developing Siberia;
Reviving the Russian peasantry;
Restricting industrial development;
Sound isolationism;
A drastic shift from the international agenda to a domestic one.[241]

One month later, Osipov returned to the subject of "developing Siberia" describing an imaginary progression of events: "The NEP (New Economic Policy) is introduced in Siberia. Enthusiasts are rushing there to gain everything—the Fatherland, freedom of speech, press, trade, agriculture, and of all kind of crafts. Clergymen, deprived of their parishes, dissidents deprived of their public pursuits and jobs, peasants, workers, specialists [will come here]. Only Siberia can save all—freedom, the Fatherland, and Soviet ambition."[242] Interestingly, Osipov, the champion of "one, indivisible Russia," ignored Solzhenitsyn's solution of the nationality question.

I. Shafarevich, coeditor with Solzhenitsyn of *From Under the Rubble*, offered his own "revised" version of Solzhenitsyn's idea of relinquishing Russian control over national republics of the USSR. Formally supporting the right of republics to secede from the USSR, he expressed reservations, which, if accepted, would render this right impracticable.[243] Commenting on Shafarevich's statement that plebiscites should not be used to determine secession (since a majority in the disputed area is only a minority in the USSR), Ya. Bilinsky pointed out that "numerous Russians would always be able to veto the secession of any smaller republics."[244]

One example of the impact of the *Letter to Soviet Leaders* can be found in a lengthy programmatic document entitled *The 12 Principles of the Russian Cause* written in 1978 by Sergei Soldatov, a prominent democratic movement activist then interned in a Mordovian labor camp.[245] Solzhenitsyn's *Letter* served as the background for Soldatov's *12 Principles*, in which he formulated ethnic goals and strategies proceeding from liberal democratic considerations. He adopted Solzhenitsyn's appeal to preserve the environment and advanced his demand that the national economy be demilitarized. To avoid ambiguity, he specified that his main objective was the creation of a "liberal national state" based on the following points:

1. Democratization of the political regime, creating a liberal society based on the rule of law;

2. Decolonization and granting independence (by referendum) to the fourteen union republics and to the Karelian Autonomous SSR;

3. A focus on national interests, rather than "global ventures" and expansionism. The [Russian] national territory extends to the Urals: the Far East and Siberia constitute a condominium of the Russian State.[246]

According to Soldatov, the second objective of the Russian people was to gather the Russian Diaspora in Russia. Predicting that the Russian Diaspora would return from foreign countries and former Soviet republics, he stressed the need to create favorable conditions for the absorption of new immigrants. His program contained a wide spectrum of proposals dealing with cultural, religious, and environmental issues, and with international cooperation.

One year later, in 1979, Soldatov wrote an article entitled "Six Theses for Liberal National Russia," devoted to the tenth anniversary of the Democratic movement. "I support the idea of a liberal, national Russian state and reject the idea of one indivisible Russia. I am for the social democracy and national sovereignty, and I oppose imperialism and totalitarianism; I am for national self-determination and against the enslavement of nationalities,"[247] he declared. He reiterated that the frontiers of the liberal, national Russian State would take shape as the fourteen union republics gained independence. Those republics that reject secession would enjoy the right to join Russia as federal units. He also remarked that states might be denied entry to the new federation because of the violation of human rights and democratic principles.

Samizdat documents of the early 1980s indicate no substantial change in the lines of ethnic politics championed by Russian conservative nationalism and by the liberal-democratic movement. An anonymous article entitled "The Fatherland is in Peril" (1982) protested against diverting water from Russian rivers and contained an unambiguous demand to reinforce the dominant status of the "principal, pivotal people of the State."[248] A polemic by the famous Russian writer V. Astafiev with historian N. Eidelman, cynically asserted that criteria for selecting personnel for national institutions be based on the ethnic origins of the candidates. "In our 'chauvinistic' drive we can reach a state in which students of Pushkin and Lermontov will be of Russian origin (oh, it's awful [sic]),...we will control all kinds of editorial offices, theatres, the film industry..." he claims.[249]

The correspondence between Astafiev and Eidelman appeared in *samizdat* in 1986, before being published in the officially approved press. Marking a beginning of *samizdat*'s demise, this correspondence also completed a cycle in the evolution of contemporary Russian nationalism. From VSKhSON's call to create a supra-ethnic state, unified by the principles of universal Christianity, emerged a quest for ethnic purity. Thus, from championing a victory in the old global competition between Russia and the West, contemporary Russian nationalism turned its efforts to asserting the "indisputable rights" of the dominant Russian majority to preferential treatment in interethnic competition for status and resources.

Political programs of ethnic movements, being considered diachronically, tend to demonstrate a stable tendency toward gradual evolution from relatively moderate (at the early stages) to more radical (at the advanced stages) demands. Thus, in the sixties and early seventies, most of the "republic nations" movements championed "sovereignty" and national political rights primarily within the Soviet Union, or at least avoided expressing secessionist demands. ("A nationalist movement is rarely secessionist from the start," L. Hooghe noted.)[250] In the late seventies, the realization of these rights turned to be viewed mainly in terms of secession. To the same degree, a radicalization in championing the reinforcement of privileges for the "Great Russian Nation" by the Russian conservative movement can be indicated.

At the same time it should be stressed that the radicalization in demands did not bring any considerable radicalization in strategies of the ethnonationalist movements: the number of *samizdat* documents that considered violence a conceivable means of achieving objectives was negligible.

The synchronic evaluation of demands made by the ethnic movements in the USSR indicates that four of the six models of demands assessed by J. Elklit and O. Tonsgaard[251] are found extensively. The *secessionist, autonomy*, and *frontier adjustment* models were elaborated upon by the minority movements, whereas the *discrimination* model was devised by the Russian conservative movement.

Though demands to observe the human rights or suspend the discrimination of members of ethnic communities could be found in documents of various ethnic movements, the *individual rights* model, mentioned by J. Elklit and O. Tonsgaard,[252] failed to receive the systematic development in ethnic *samizdat*. The *individual rights* model holds that equal access to resources should be provided for members of the discriminated communities by the means of hindering discrimination and affirmative action. In fact, this model regards the *privatization, depoliticization* of ethnic sentiment, whereas ethnic movements in the USSR tended to promote the corporate political rights of their groups, which are viewed as political entities.

The *group rights* model—asserted primarily in terms of *consociationalism* (powersharing)[253] and *minority rights protection*[254]—which have become important dimensions in West European ethnic minorities politics is virtually ignored by the ethnic movements in the USSR (slight traces of this model found in the Jewish *samizdat* remained underdeveloped).

An absence of the two mentioned models of political demands can hardly be viewed with surprise. In Western Europe, the perception of self-determination by ethnic minorities has been significantly transformed since the early 1970s. Previously being regarded as a positive claim for secession, the idea of self-determination gradually acquired more balanced and temperate articulation. Thus, *internal* (non-secessionist—in contrast to *external*) self-determination has been acknowledged by the West European ethnic movements as valuable response to their demands. At the same time, neither the ultimate consideration of self-determination as secession nor the ethnic stratification in the USSR—the two pivotal principles of the Soviet nationality politics—have ever been questioned by the ethnic movements. To a great extent, the ethnic movements devising components of their demands anticipate not to eliminate the ethnic stratification, but rather to reconstruct the ethnic scale in favor of their fellow groups. This evaluation seems to be true also for the groups championing emigration. Thus, a former participant of the Jewish movement who had emigrated from Leningrad in the 1970s, explained her motives of "coming home": "I always wanted to belong to a dominant nationality."[255]

As for the right to secession provided by the Soviet Constitution, the ethnic movements regarded it as the highest-ranked priority and major legitimizing source of their political claims.

CHAPTER 6

Legitimizing Sources of Ethnic Politics

Over a century ago, a successful journalist and playwright from Vienna signed his book, *The Jewish State*, T. Herzl, Doctor of Law. Herzl was perhaps the first person to use an academic degree in the effort to convince public opinion that the idea of Jewish political independence should be taken as a scientifically grounded project, and not as a new Utopia. In order to mobilize the support of different forces, first among them their fellow ethnic groups, the national movements sought to substantiate their political platforms by appealing to various legitimizing sources. The selection of legitimizing sources is a multi-collinear mental construct intended to assure *entitlement* (*deserving*) of individuals or groups to the desired object. As it is unearthed in the research, feelings of entitlement stimulate the social protest. [1]

Political–Legal Legitimation

In studying the political–legal level of legitimization, we can see that ethnic minority movements as the major source of legitimization exploited Marxism-Leninism and the Soviet Constitution.

Vasyl' Lobko in his *Letter* to Ukrainian Poet M. Ryl'skyi, reported that a group of Ukrainian intellectuals was preparing an article to be entitled *Against Revisionism in the Nationality Question*,[2] in protest against Russification. A 1964 appeal to the Presidium of the Ukrainian Supreme Soviet, signed by V. Lobko and nine other Ukrainian intellectuals, demanded that the authorities "act upon Lenin's behest and make wide use of native languages in all spheres of life."[3] The *Appeal of the Crimean Tatar People to the Twenty-third Party Congress*[4] substantiated its demands by referring to Lenin's articles on the nationality question, early documents of the Soviet Bolshevik regime, materials from the Twentieth Party Congress, and the *Program of the Communist Party of the USSR* that was adopted by the Twenty-second Party Congress (1961). The *Statement* of Soviet Germans (1965), demanding the restoration of the Volga German Autonomous Republic pointed to the necessity of having current Soviet policies conform with the "Soviet Constitution and the principles of Lenin's nationality policy."[5]

Besides citing Lenin's works, ethnic minority documents cited the *Declaration of the Rights of the Peoples of Russia* (2 November 1917), which proclaimed the equality of all peoples, the right of nationalities to self-determination, the abolition of all national restrictions and privileges, the free development of ethnic minorities, and so on. Some cited the *Appeal to all Muslim Toilers in Russia* by the Council of People's Commissars, which called on Russian Muslims to organize their lives freely and without limitations. Ukrainian political prisoner M. Masiutko, in his *Letter* to the Ukrainian Supreme Soviet,[6] quoted Lenin, Sukarno, and Sun Yat-sen to prove that he had been punished for views that were not different from those of other world-renowned Communist and Third World leaders. A Meskhetian *Resolution of the Sixth People's Meeting* pointed out that Soviet policy toward the Meskhetian Turks "contradicted Lenin's nationality policy"[7] and demanded that this policy be changed in "accordance with Lenin's laws."

"All peoples of the world welcome the most humane, fair, and progressive Communist ideology that has proclaimed the nationalities' freedom of self-determination and life in their independent states."[8] This passage from a *Letter* by two Jewish activists emphasizing the right of self-determination sought to use Communist doctrine as a source of legitimization of ethnic, and even more important, separatist claims. Undoubtedly, the right of nations to self-determination as proclaimed in Soviet doctrine was more attractive, and therefore it had a broader constituency than Soviet ideology in practice.

By 1964, Ukrainian lawyer and political prisoner Levko Luk'ianenko asserted the precedence of law, and specifically, of the Soviet Constitution, over Soviet doctrine as actually implemented. In his *Appeal to the Procurator General* Luk'ianenko indicated that "Marxist-Leninist theory was not proclaimed a compulsory ideology by Soviet law and the state did not stipulate that political, economic, and other rights be granted in accordance with a pursuit of ideological convictions."[9] Attesting that Soviet laws were his major legitimizing source, Luk'ianenko attempted to reconcile conflicting points in the constitution and penal code. Thus, he argued against the Soviet court's interpretation of the term, "the territorial inviolability of the USSR." "Regarding the USSR as a union of republics with equal rights, we should understand territorial inviolability as the preservation of a republic's territory, whereas...it is interpreted by the Soviet court as the inadmissibility of secession from the USSR, he pointed out."[10] "In the Romanov Empire chauvinists could act in accordance with their laws," Luk'ianenko continued. "Now they violate the law. The right of secession does exist, and no device can change it."[11]

By the end of the 1960s, ethnic minority *samizdat* found two additional legitimizing sources: international law and international practice. The Crimean Tatars' 1968 appeal *To All People of Goodwill, Democrats, and Communists*[12] blamed the Soviet authorities for their violation of the *Charter of the United Nations*, the *Universal Declaration of Human Rights* and other international human rights covenants. The same documents were cited by Jewish *refusenik* D. Koliadnitskaia in her *Letter to the International Committee of Human Rights*.[13] The text of the *Universal Declaration of Human Rights* was carried in the *samizdat* almanac *Re-Patria*[14] issued by the Soviet German movement.

Levko Luk'ianenko may have been the first nationalist activist to cite international practice as a legitimizing source of ethnopolitical demands. In his *Petition* to D. Korotchenko, the Chairman of the Presidium of the Ukrainian Supreme Soviet, he stated that the disintegration of the world colonial system should be considered a delegitimizing factor with regard to Soviet imperialist policy.[15] Thirteen years later, Lezghian dissident writer Iskander Kaziev[16] cited the liberation of former colonies as an important argument in his demand that the Lezghians be granted autonomy. Yiddish poet and emigration activist I. Kerler stated in his 1969 *Appeal*[17] that the return of a large group of Spanish antifascists to Spain should serve as a precedent to be followed by the Soviet authorities in dealing with the Jewish emigration problem. Another Jewish document[18] cited the return of the Armenian diaspora to Armenia.

The *Final Act of the Helsinki Conference*, signed by the Soviet government, was adopted by ethnic minority movements as a legitimizing source since the late 1970s, and became one of the most quoted international documents. A letter by twenty-six Tatars and Bashkirs to the American ambassador to the United Nations[19] noted gross violations of the Helsinki agreements by the Soviet authorities. A petition by forty-six Jewish *refuseniks* from seven towns in the Soviet Union to the leaders of countries that participated in the

Helsinki conference requested that they influence the Soviet government to observe the Helsinki agreements, and specifically, to secure "contacts between people and regular meetings based on family links, the reunification of families, and the right of every nationality to live in accordance with the requirements of its historical development."[20] The *Memorandum by Representatives of the Native Populations of Estonia, Latvia, and Lithuania* (1982)[21] cited international law, the *Charter of the United Nations*, and the *Final Act of the Helsinki Conference* to substantiate their demand for secession. In the programmatic *Letter by Ukrainian Political Prisoners* O. Tykhyi and V. Romaniuk proclaimed: "We regard the *Universal Declaration of Human Rights*, and the UN covenants on sovereignty and national independence as the supreme principles of any social and national commonwealth."[22]

Lezghian writer Iskander Kaziev in his *Letter to the Secretary General of the United Nations* attempted to formulate a systematic overview of the legitimizing sources of ethnopolitical claims:

> What are the bases of the Lezghian people's demand for unification and the formation of a national autonomy within the borders of a single union republic?
> 1. Politically, it is the *Declaration of Rights of the Toilers and the Exploited People* issued in 1918.
> 2. Practically, it is experience in the political settlement of the nationality problems of other peoples, whose situation can be equated with that of the Lezgians.
> 3. As for international jurisdiction, it is the *Universal Declaration of Human Rights*.[23]

While "Lenin's nationality policy" and "Marxist-Leninist theory" gradually lost popularity as sources of legitimization throughout the late 1970s and the 1980s, the Soviet Constitution continued to be cited intensively to substantiate ethnic demands. In 1977, the Crimean Tatar movement launched a campaign for the repeal of all decrees and resolutions from the period 1944–1976 dealing with the status of the Crimean Tatar people on the grounds that they were unconstitutional.[24] The *Letter* by 365 Georgian intellectuals protested a new requirement that all Ph.D. dissertations be submitted in the Russian language, calling this decision of the supreme certifying commission a violation of the "constitutional status of the Georgian people."[25]

An article devoted to the tenth anniversary of the National Unification Party of Armenia[26] pointed out that the party's demand for secession was secured by article seventeen of the Soviet Constitution, while the demand for a referendum had support in article forty-nine. The Latvian Group Helsinki-86 in its *Appeal to M. Gorbachev* (July 1986) asked him to help the Latvian people "exercise article sixty-nine of the constitution of the Latvian SSR," conceding the right of secession.[27] While in 1977 Tykhyi and Romaniuk supposed that it was "enough to use the laws formulated in the Soviet Constitution"[28] to achieve their political goals, in 1983 another Ukrainian activist, Iu. Badzio, argued that the term, "the single union state," contained in the new Soviet Constitution of October 1977, could be used as legal grounds for annulling the right of nations to self-determination.[29]

Unlike those ethnic movements that found grounds for their separatist demands in the right to national self-determination as proclaimed by the Soviet Constitution, the three Baltic movements regarded the nullification of the Molotov–Ribbentrop Pact as their major legitimizing source, and as the crucial event in the process of the restoration of the Baltic states' sovereignty. An *Appeal* by forty-five representatives of the Baltic republics[30] found legal grounds for Latvian, Lithuanian, and Estonian independence in the official recognition of their sovereignty by the Bolshevik government in 1919 and in later bilateral peace treaties signed by the Soviet Union and each of the three Baltic states. The *Appeal* also pointed out that on 24 September 1941, the Soviet Union joined the Atlantic Charter, signed by the leaders of the United States and Great Britain, which proclaimed that any forcible territorial, political, or social changes were illegal. They stated that they would seek to restore self-government and the national rights of their peoples, who had been violently deprived of this status. Considering the Soviet annihilation of the Baltic States to be a direct result of the Molotov–Ribbentrop Pact, the *Appeal* by forty-five representatives of the Baltic republics found in the bilateral and multilateral commitments of the Soviet Union judicial grounds for deeming it null from the moment it was signed. The *Appeal* also emphasized the moral inadmissibility of collusion with the Nazi regime. In 1983, Latvian dissident Gunners Astra based his refusal to recognize the Soviet regime in his country on the fact that Soviet rule was proclaimed in Latvia on 21 July 1940, after the Soviet invasion of this country on 17 July 1940 and after the signing of the Molotov–Ribbentrop Pact on 23 August 1939. "If the Soviet regime had been proclaimed before the Soviet invasion, I would respect the fact of its existence,"[31] he concluded.

In contrast to ethnic minority movements, Russian conservatism made little use of Soviet and international legislation in dealing with the substantiation of ethnopolitical demands. The founder of the Bolshevik regime, however, was quoted as a legitimizing source. Thus, *Veche*'s editorial, "The Struggle

Against So-Called Russophilism, or the Way of National Suicide," cited Lenin's attacks on the "vulgar ideal of federative relations," as they appeared in his article, "On the National Pride of the Great Russians," and praised Lenin's "genuine internationalism and regard for the national tradition."[32]

References to Marxism, Lenin, and Soviet law by no means testify for particular "inclination" of the *samizdat* authors towards these sources. Nevertheless, that should not be regarded solely as a tactical device helping to mobilize supporters and establish a minimal level of "common language" with the Soviet authorities. The ethnonationalist groups strove to assure their *entitlement* within (not outside!) the location of political–legal resources of the Soviet society.

Historical Legitimation

By avoiding contemporary domestic and international legislation, the Russian conservative movement focused its quest for legitimizing sources on Russian history. A conceptual framework in which to place the historical myth was devised by I. Ruslanov in his essay, *The Youth in Russian History*, written in the 1960s. His ideal of this "glorious past" was Muscovite Rus', described by the author, as an idyllic national community possessed of continuity from generation to generation. Russian political goals, according to Ruslanov, were determined by Russian Orthodoxy, the "spiritual basis of national life," in addition to a "healthy national sense."[33] Ruslanov portrayed Russian conquests not only as "broadening Russian frontiers to their natural historic limits," but also as the "liberation of Christian Orthodox believers from Turkish oppression."[34] He stated that the idea of uniting all Slavic peoples under the czarist autocracy had played a crucial role in the formation of the Russian nation. The Westernizing reforms launched by Peter the Great were assessed by Ruslanov as destroying the harmony of Russian life, interrupting the spiritual continuity of generations, and provoking conflict between "fathers" and "sons." As a result, Russian society, previously monolithic, was split. Later variants of the historical myth reiterated Ruslanov's interpretation, offering the "golden past" as an unalterable model for the "bright future."

All this was derived from Slavophile doctrine, and when devising historical myths, conservative *samizdat* cited Slavophiles sources. Thus, M. Antonov[35] referred to A. Khomiakov when stating that Russia, in contrast to Western states, never indulged in political intrigue or the conquest of other peoples. Stressing the specific character of Russian history, Osipov wrote: "The Russian state has always been multi-national, but it has never been a colonial empire. The Russian Empire was logically and geographically inevitable, and serfdom constituted grounds for the consolidation of Russian and non-Russian peoples."[36]

The nationalistic perception, then, rejected any idea of the violent or even forcible character of Russian conquests. Commenting on a *Letter to Veche* by Jewish activist M. Agurskii, an editorial note claimed that the "conquests of Peter [the Great] and Catherine [II] should actually be considered the reunification of Russian lands, torn away by Sweden and Poland."[37] The note portrayed these conquests not merely as acts of historical justice, but as a service to the indigenous population in their struggle against Sweden oppression.

Dealing with territorial disputes, conservative *samizdat* substantiated the Russian right to disputed territory by "historical priority." The "Historical-Geographical Information on the Kurile Islands." carried in *Veche* no. 8[38] stated that Russians had settled there before the Japanese, and had brought prosperity to the native inhabitants, who voluntarily converted to Russian Orthodoxy and accepted Russian names. *Veche*'s editorial, "The Russian Solution to the Nationality Question" credited the czarist aristocracy with the defense of ethnic minorities. "Russian ideologists discussed only the problem of how best to secure equal rights for all nationalities in the framework of the one state,"[39] argued the editorial. Another programmatic article[40] asserting the "voluntary union" of other peoples with the Russian Empire pointed out that Russian bayonets defended peripheral peoples from menacing neighbors.

Seeking arguments against modernization, conservative *samizdat* "revealed" certain negative phenomena in Russia's "glorious past." Osipov described the government of Alexander I as apostasy from Russian traditions; he called Peter the Great "the creator of violence;"[41] Peter III, who had issued the *Manifesto* on the emancipation of the Russian gentry, thus launching the formation of Russian civil society, was defined by Osipov as a "Russophobe," and his *Manifesto* was assessed as "fatal" for Russian historical development. The czar who really commanded Osipov's sympathy was Nicholas I: "His long government brought peace and internal tranquility."[42] The spokesman of Russian nationalism, G. Shimanov, found the Tatar–Mongolian yoke to be the Lord's blessing. It had preserved Russian originality and saved the country from the "strong embraces" of the European Renaissance.[43]

In such politicized ethnic views, historical myth often played a compensatory role for a sense of deprivation. Appealing to collective sentiment, historical myth dealt with those historical events that aroused self-respect and pride. Speaking at a meeting of the unofficial Leningrad Society of Jewish

Culture, B. Vainerman lamented Soviet Jewry's isolation from their history: "Jews have never heard of the Macabees, Bar Kochba, the Warsaw Ghetto uprising, the Jewish heroes of the Soviet Union, etc."[44] Unlike Jewish children, continued Vainerman, "every child in Armenia, Georgia, Uzbekistan, and Estonia, can recount with pride the heroic past of his people.[45]

A non-heroic, inglorious past has no value for historical myth. In dealing with the subordinated status of an ethnic group in the past, the politicized ethnic perception usually pointed to heroic resistance to oppression. The *Letter against Russification* by Seventeen Latvian Communists[46] told how the ancestors of the Latvian people "lived for seven hundred years under oppressive German crusaders and barons," and later under Russian oppression. "All these conquerors tried to assimilate the local tribes, but with no success."[47] The leader of the Crimean Tatar movement, M. Dzhemilev in his *Letter to P. Grigorenko* specifically referred to historical myth as a compensatory factor. Recalling his 1962 lecture on Crimean Tatar history, Dzhemilev said: "Certainly, young people who once read the official literature in which their ancestors were described as barbarians and traitors always defeated by the valiant Russians, were pleased to hear that the celebrated Russian Czar, Peter I, suffered a crushing rout near the Prut River at the hands of Turkish-Tatar troops . . . or that the Crimean Tatars already had institutes of higher education five hundred years ago."[48] The *Letter by Ukrainian Political Prisoners* (O. Tykhyi and V. Romaniuk) focused on key points of the Ukrainian historical myth: "Ukraine was a mighty power called Rus' or Kievan Rus'. As distinct from other states of that period, Ukraine never had any plans of world domination or territorial expansion at the expense of other peoples."[49]

Armenian dissident E. Harutiunian in his *Letter to the Catholicos* wrote: "Whole states vanished without a trace, whole peoples were annihilated or died out. But we have survived. God supported us, and we did not lose our courage and determination in our struggle against enemies. . . . Our intelligence was sharper than the Turkish *yataghan* or Persian saber."[50]

State and military power comprised important and necessary elements of the "glorious past." I. Kaziev in his *Letter to the UN Secretary General*[51] described Lezghians as the dominant force in Eastern Daghestan "since the ninth century. In the thirteenth century the country called Lezghinistan was populated not only by Lezghians, but also by many other tribes of Daghestan." Kaziev stressed that Lezghinistan should be considered the first state set up by any of the local tribes in the territory of Daghestan. There the Lezghians repulsed enemies and protected other peoples. A Georgian *samizdat* essay claimed that ever since the Armenians lost their independence in the tenth century, they had suffered from Persian and Turkish oppression and "from time to time Georgia liberated them and they settled in Georgia."[52] Emphasizing the antiquity of ethnic roots was no less vital an aspect of historical myth. History should not be merely "glorious and heroic": it had to be "ancient" to no less a degree. "We have been fighting for our exodus longer than they [the superpowers] exist,"[53] declared a letter by three Zionist activists. Though the ethnogenesis of the Meskhetians actually began after their deportation, delegates of the First All-Peoples' Meeting of the Meskhetian Turks in February 1964 reportedly discussed Meskhetian history "from ancient times until today."[54]

Like Russian conservative *samizdat*, ethnic minority documents utilized history to legitimize territorial claims. A *Letter* by the Armenians of Nagorno-Karabakh to N. Khrushchev stated: "From time immemorial our territory has extended from the Kura to the Aras rivers and to Lake Sevan. This land, known in history as Artsakh, comprises an integral part of Armenia."[55] The same arguments were cited by two Georgian activists, Miron Gamkharashvili and Archil Otarashvili[56] to substantiate the Georgian right to Eastern Kakhetia. Refuting the illegal incorporation of Saingillo by Azerbaijan in 1922, the authors declared that this territory had never belonged to Azerbaijan and until the seventeenth century was populated solely by Georgians.

Ukrainian *samizdat* appealed to history for the legitimization of separatist demands by conceiving the idea of Ukraine's "primary bond" to Europe. The gifted Ukrainian *samizdat* author, E. Sverstiuk, in his 1969 essay *Kotliarevs'kyi Laughs*, analyzed Kotliarevs'kyi's paraphrase of the classic poem *Eneida*. Sverstiuk asserted that the Ukrainian "historical" model of socio-political development had always been in the framework of European tradition. Having been enslaved by Russia in the seventeenth century and disconnected from European development, the Ukrainian people, like *Eneida*'s hero, found itself on a "bewitched island."[57] Commenting on the European roots of Ukrainian culture, Iu. Badzio vigorously rejected the theory of a single, ancient Russian people as an attempt to "discredit the idea of an independent Ukrainian state both ideologically and morally."[58]

In reviewing history, *samizdat* documents dealt with bilateral agreements that could be cited as legal sources for Russian annexations. Thus, the *Letter by Ukrainian Political Prisoners* (O. Tykhyi and V. Romaniuk)[59], asserted that in 1654 the Ukraine, after beating Poland, signed an alliance with the czar in Moscow. This alliance between two equal sides had been subsequently and permanently violated by Moscow. Finally, Peter I completely neglected the alliance and Ukraine was turned into a periphery of the Russian Empire. Discussing Georgian–Russian relations, a Georgian document[60] described Russian policy in Georgia as a series of deliberately perfidious actions adopted in order to weaken the Georgian people by involving it in wars with Persia and Turkey, and then to subordinate Georgia by turning it into a province of the Russian Empire. Commenting on negotiations between Peter I and Vakhtang concerning mutual defense, the document stated that Russia purposely induced Vakhtang to invade Persia, but after the invasion it broke an agreement on military support and abandoned the Georgian army.

It should, however, also be noted that a shift in political orientation might result in amendments being introduced into historical myths. The *Statement* by the Delegation of the Soviet Germans (1965) proclaimed the restoration of the autonomous republic to be the movement's major goal. *Samizdat* documents of this period stressed the loyalty of German colonists to the Russian State, their contribution to the country's prosperity, and so on. The *Statement* denounced "the harmful idea that Soviet Germans comprised a fragment of the German, Austrian, or Swiss nations.... We are one of the many peoples of the Soviet Fatherland. Russia is the homeland of our fathers."[61] The lack of progress in the question of resettlement in the Volga German autonomous area and the deteriorating political atmosphere caused a shift in the priorities of the Soviet German movement. By the late 1970s, emigration to Germany had become its main concern. A *Letter to Members of the Bundestag*,[62] written in the early 1980s, described the history of the Germans in Russia as a series of humiliations, suffering, and oppression, culminating in the 1917 deportation edict of Nicholas II. A *Petition* (1984) signed by eighty-four Soviet German activists declared that the Soviet Germans wanted to leave "the country where after all attempts, we have not found our real homeland."[63] Just two decades after denouncing any connection with other German-speaking peoples this new document stated that "the restoration of unity is the main motive in our desire to return to our historical homeland after two centuries of survival in foreign lands."[64]

Divine Legitimation

Having little interest in theological esotericism, ethnic *samizdat* found in religion an important legitimizing source for political demands. Ethnic movements generally considered religion to be a kind of ethnic ideology. Russian conservative author, L. Borodin defined Orthodoxy as the Russian "national variant of Christianity."[65] "The Jewish national entity has been preserved and continues to be preserved by Judaism,"[66] stated a Jewish document. The role of religion in the preservation of nationhood was also stressed by the Armenian dissident, E. Harutiunian, in his *Letter to the Catholicos*.[67] "To disrupt the unity and solidarity of the national Church means to commit a crime against the nation," contended a *Letter to Veche*, signed by A.D.[68] *Samizdat* documents asserted that religious and ethnic interests coincided. An *Appeal* by Archimandrite Ihoakim contended that the Georgian Church was chosen by the authorities as the main target in the struggle against national revival.[69] An item in the *Chronicle of the Catholic Church in Lithuania* stated that the real aim in the war against Catholicism in Lithuania was "to enslave Lithuanians as human beings, and to deprive religious people of their national consciousness."[70] "To bear your cross for the faith means . . . to bear your cross for your oppressed people," stated Ukrainian activist I. Terelia in his "Easter conversation" with readers of the *Chronicle of the Ukrainian Catholic Church*.[71]

The mutual relationship between religious and ethnic sentiments was illustrated by an episode reported in an anonymous document of Ukrainian *samizdat*. In a small Ukrainian village a group of people, probably authorized by the authorities, started to remove the cross of the local church. Village residents surrounded the church and began a spontaneous rally. "Moscow's yoke and occupation have been endured enough,"[72] claimed speakers at the gathering.

Nationalist spokespersons also demonstrated an awareness of the divergence between religious and ethnonationalist goals. As Osipov put it, "I am a religious believer, and Christ's teachings mean more to me than nationalism. But I know the soul of the modern Russian man. At the present time he feels his ethnic belonging more strongly than his religious one."[73] L. Ovsishcher, a Jewish activist and former Soviet Army officer, in his attempt to use religion for political objectives, proposed that it be institutionalized as the "supreme" legitimizing source.[74] He argued that political pluralism in Israeli society comprised a serious obstacle to Jewish unification. In order to overcome this situation he suggested that all spheres of life in Israel be subordinated to Judaism.

If a religious tradition "resisted" being used as a legitimizing source, divine legitimization was proclaimed to be an "immediate" emanation from the will of God. The image of a sinner chosen by God to implement His will appeared in various forms in Russian conservative *samizdat*. "Russia repudiated God in the name of His ideals . . . Europe preserved God in order to repudiate His ideals and enjoy comfort," L. Borodin contended in his article, "Vestnik RSKhD and the Russian Intelligentsia."[75]

In marginal cases, if religion was considered to be incompatible with the "national idea," the former was unambiguously rejected. An item entitled "Critical Notes by a Russian Man on the Russian Patriotic Journal *Veche*" stated that the Russian Orthodox Church played the role of Judas the traitor with respect to the Russian national self-consciousness.[76]

There are three sources of legitimation cited by *samizdat* to substantiate the ethnic claims: political–legal, historical and divine legitimation. Each of these sources is present in the *samizdat* documents of every ethnic group as a variable. It might be assessed that minority's movements tended to appeal to political–legal legitimation, while the Russian nationalism's legitimization was "overloaded" by references to God and History.

Structurally, the mentioned sources frame three mutually complementary "legitimizing narratives" in nationalist discourse. Semantically, they manifest two divergent reactions: the first one, referring to normative standards of modern society, is based on rational choice, while the two others, appealing to tale, originated from primordial emotion. Being displayed as "uninterrupted text," the political–legal, historical and divine legitimizing narratives are intermingled constituting the body of "national myth." In a final analysis, the "universal" *right of nations to self-determination* comprises not less "organic" part of contemporary national mythology than *the glorious past*.

The combination of the legitimizing sources seems to have reflected the ambivalence of nationalistic reaction to the modernization process: it expresses the drive towards modernization and simultaneously—nostalgic rejection of its consequences.

CHAPTER 7

The Problem of Orientation: Ethnocentrism–Polycentrism

Polymorphism of nationalist expression in terms of goals, strategies, orientations, and ideologies provides a wide range of options for typologization. The propensities of ethnic movements towards liberal (polycentric) or illiberal (ethnocentric) nationalism seem to be counted among their important qualitative characteristics. The most famous definition of ethnocentrism was given by W.G. Sumner in 1906: it is a view of things in which "one's own group is the center of everything and all others are scaled and rated with reference to it."[1] Correspondingly, polycentrism ought to be defined as a view of things in which every group including one's own, has equal and independent value.

"For an *'ethnocentric'* nationalist, both 'power' and 'value' inhere in his cultural group. Indeed, these dimensions are inseparable. My group is the vessel of wisdom, beauty, holiness, culture; hence, power automatically belongs as an attribute to my group," A. Smith describes.[2] "*'Polycentric'* nationalism, by contrast, resembles the dialogue of many actors on a common stage. ... This kind of nationalism starts from the premise that there are many centers of *real* power; other groups do have valuable and genuinely noble ideas and institutions which we would do well to borrow or adapt.... It seeks to join the 'family of nations,' the international drama of status equals, to find its appropriate identity and part."[3]

In this chapter, the issue of polycentrism–ethnocentrism in the orientations of ethnic movements will be examined within two contexts:

1. How did ethnic movements describe the role (both then and in the future) of their fellow ethnic groups in the interplay of ethnopolitical forces?

2. What strategies did ethnic movements adopt toward other ethnic groups, and in particularly toward those groups with whom they shared territory?

While the former indicates the explicit trends, the latter reveals the implicit propensities.

Russian Nationalism

Seeking to assert Russian dominance, Russian conservative *samizdat* emphasized its "natural" or even "divine" character. *Slovo natsii* (*The Manifesto of Russian Patriots*) declared that ethnic and racial discrimination should be the basis of political and legal stratification. "Is it reasonable that nations that are not mature enough to enjoy independence have been granted by the United Nations equal rights with the cultured nations?" it asked.[4] Its authors believed that no republic seeking to secede from the USSR could possess any vital capacity as an independent state.

Avoiding the extremes of the *Manifesto*, *Veche* used the stereotype of the "elder brother" or "father" in describing the status of the dominant Russian majority. "Peoples feel an enormous respect toward the Russians, and abroad the representatives of non-Russian nationalities [of the USSR] introduce themselves as Russians," stated I. Starodzhubaiev, in his *Letter* to *Veche*.[5] Another *Veche* author, G. Shimanov, contended: "The Soviet Union is not a mechanical conglomeration of different ethnic groups. It is a mystical organism that consists of mutually complementary nationalities, headed by the Russian people: it constitutes a microcosm of humanity."[6] He rejected any speculations about "the liberation of a part from the whole" as being "immoral in essence."[7] In an interview with the Jewish *samizdat* journal *Evrei v SSSR*, he developed the concept of benevolent Russian dominance: Russification had an "extremely beneficial" influence on all peoples of the USSR, since it gave them access to "the superior categories of the worldwide historic drama."[8] The Russian people, Shimanov stressed, "came to other peoples not as a conqueror or a bourgeois colonizer, but as the elder brother in their worldwide historical fate."[9] With this he explained the "wonderful stability of so-called Russian colonialism," which in fact "has nothing in common with colonialism," but should be regarded as the "joining of other peoples to the birth throes of Russia, chosen by God to give birth to a new Christian civilization."[10] Russia's dominant status was also perceived as favorable for ethnic minorities by authors who otherwise seemed free of Russian messianic objectives. Solzhenitsyn's *Letter to the Soviet Leaders* upheld the status of Russians in Siberia with the assertion that they were sustaining the way of life and very existence of the region's smaller peoples.

Russian nationalist *samizdat* regarded as being entirely reasonable the "right" of the Russian people in its capacity as a dominant group to set up an "ethnic order," in which every nationality had its "proper" place. An answer by *Veche*'s editorial staff to one of its correspondents asserted that the "so-called Ukrainians and Byelorussians comprise a historical misunderstanding."[11] *Veche*'s editor, V. Osipov, said in his interview with the Associated Press: "We do not distinguish Ukrainians and Byelorussians from Russians."[12] Similar views on the Ukrainian and Byelorussian peoples were expressed by Solzhenitsyn in his *Letter to the Soviet Leaders* and by I. Shafarevich in an article entitled "Separation or Reconciliation."[13] In his interview to the *Jews in the USSR*, Shimanov described a "desirable" pattern of "ideal" relations between the dominant and subordinate ethnic groups. "It is important that the nationality which bears the highest truth influence the others and not the reverse. It is unreasonable to be afraid of such an influence, but it is criminal not to resist the influence of lower cultures."[14]

Viewing the acculturation of ethnic minorities into the "superior" Russian culture as a positive phenomenon, Russian conservative *samizdat* nonetheless expressed considerable opposition to allowing non-Russians to play any active role in Russian culture. Protesting the penetration of "alien" elements into Russian culture, *Veche*'s editorial staff argued: "As far as Tatars, for example, become Russified, we will become Tatarized to the same extent. . . . What is the real value of cultural phenomena such as Chinghiz Aitmatov, the so-called 'great Kirghiz writer,' although he writes solely in Russian?"[15] A *Letter* by T. Novikov to *Veche* expressed indignation at the definition of B. Pasternak and O. Mandelshtam as "great Russian writers."[16]

Russian nationalism, therefore, resisted not only alien cultural influences, but also the "contamination" of the ethnic environment by "alien" blood. "The installation of alien ethnicities in a settled cultural environment goads us to break our long-formulated traditions and behavioral standards," declared Osipov, explaining his negative attitude toward mixed marriages.[17] "People should concern themselves with remaining close to their own nationalities and avoid unnecessary contacts with strangers. Ethnic borders must be impermeable. This is the sign of healthy nationhood," contended another of *Veche*'s author[18] who called mixed marriages "the scourge of modern mankind," that destroys its "national structure."[19] Touching on the issue of "half-breeds" the author claimed that they "tended only to complicate relations. They are neither aliens, nor ours but often have not reached a stage where they can be members of any nationality."[20] In the same issue of *Veche* M. Sergeev[21] mentioned the "practical" implications of mixed marriages: he claimed that the apologists for mixed marriages were still "intimidated by the appearance of their own pygmy grandchildren." Sergeev pointed positively to "foreign experience," praising Israel for conducting a "quite perfect racial policy."[22]

John Dunlop, the author of several books on modern Russian nationalism, has concluded that contemporary Russian nationalism is polycentric. He finds a major argument for this extravagant assumption in Solzhenitsyn's *Letter to the Soviet Leaders* and Shafarevich's "Separation or Reconciliation." Both Solzhenitsyn and Shafarevich shared the belief that national republics had the right to secede from the USSR, but this was what made their conception so unpopular among Russian nationalists, notwithstanding the high regard for these writers. Conservatives cited Solzhenitsyn's overall liberalism as the main reason why they criticized the major idea of his *Letter*. As for Shafarevich's article, which was written during his transition from a liberal to a conservative orientation, an analysis by Yaroslav Bilinsky pointed to the discrepancy between Shafarevich's avowed support for the right of nationalities to self-determination and his conviction that "plebiscites should not be used to determine secession: for even a majority in the disputed area is but a minority in the state as a whole. This means that the numerous Russians would always be able to veto the secession of any smaller republics."[23]

An explanation of Shafarevich's dramatic shift from the democratic to the nationalistic camp can probably be found in his failure to accept an important principle of the contemporary liberal democratic *Weltansicht*—securing minority rights, including those of ethnic minorities, and protecting minorities from the majority's arbitrariness—that derives from the structurally asymmetrical power relationship between the majority and minority groups. In this respect he is not different from other ethnic majorities' nationalists. In his *Statement*[24] on the publication in the West of the 1974 book *From Under the Rubble*, Shafarevich criticized the Democrats for perverting their position by advocating the right of emigration, while for most Soviet peoples, the right had no value. During the next fifteen years this thesis evolved into a "theory" of the so-called "small people," as expounded in Shafarevich's essay, *Russophobia*. In this essay the preoccupation of the Soviet liberal intelligentsia with the rights of minorities provoked the author's irritated perplexity. "The issue of free exit abroad has resulted in an enormous wave of emotions. Although it seems relevant to only several hundred thousand people,... the plight of the Crimean Tatars attracts much more interest than that of the Ukrainians, while the fate of the Ukrainians attracts more attention than that of the Russians.... Reporting on the oppression of religious believers, they

[the democrats] tend to deal with relatively small religious groups....
Touching on the problem of prisoners, they hardly concentrate on more than
one percent of all prisoners."[25]

Another author of Russian nationalist *samizdat*, A. Skuratov, expressed
the same approach in 1974 in his comments on Sakharov's polemical retort
to the *Letter to the Soviet Leaders*. Asserting the paramount significance of the
Russian people, Skuratov found improper Sakharov's demand to "put on the
same level the many-million victims from among the Russian people and
the troubles of Uzbek pupils on cotton plantations."[26] "Sakharov forgot the
deportation of millions of Russian peasants during the collectivization,
and remembered only the Crimean Tatars, Kalmyks, Chechens, Ingushi, and
others, which together do not reach the total of deported Russians."[27]

Unlike Dunlop, I cannot regard Shafarevich's position as evidence of the
irresistible inclination of Russian nationalism to polycentrism. Moreover,
I believe that championing the precedence of any dominant majority,
whether it be the "protection" of the Jewish rights above those of Arab citizens in Israel or the "defense" of German interests from Turkish immigrants
in Germany comprises a basic characteristic of ethnocentrism.[28] The evolution of Shafarevich's conception seems to testify that ethnocentrism, as
a mode of self-assertiveness is immanent within the nationalism of a dominant ethnic group, or, in other words, that the nationalism of a dominant
ethnic majority is doomed to ethnocentrism.

Pointing to the alleged polycentrism of Russian nationalism, Dunlop
referred to Shimanov's programmatic declaration dealing with the proposed
solution to the nationality question. In an article published in the second
issue of the almanac *Mnogaia Leta*, Shimanov proposed a "new type of free
association"[29] for the nationalities living in the USSR. This "free association"
according to Shimanov, would guarantee "the sovereignty of each small
nation over its territory," which "would be recognized by the large nation and
fortified by the right of each nation to leave the association."[30] Shimanov
specified neither the political-administrative structure of this "free association" nor the legal procedure of exercising the right to leave it. Dunlop
assumes that according to Shimanov's "free association with ethnic Russians,
the peoples of the USSR and Eastern Europe would enjoy national security
and the right to linguistic and cultual freedom."[31] To achieve this, Shimanov
even expressed his readiness to offer the Jews a new "national territory" with
better climactic conditions. In 1976, Shimanov described this idea in an
interview given to the journal *Jews in the USSR*. Motivating his decision to
allocate a territory for Jewish settlement, Shimanov explained that the Jews
should localize themselves within their national territory, "maintain their

autonomous national life," and not "interfere in the national lives of other peoples."[32] Interestingly, Shimanov and other spokespersons of Russian conservatism never mentioned both political and economic autonomy for ethnic minorities, powersharing, or any other form of their participation in the decision-making process. Summing up Shimanov's vague rhetoric we can infer that he intended to offer ethnic minorities in this "free association" some sort of benevolent paternalism and cultural-linguistic rights in exchange for their noninterference in "high politics." As for individual members of ethnic minorities, in Shimanov's "free association" they would enjoy the right to acculturation—without assimilation—into the adopting society. Notwithstanding all attempts by Dunlop to find liberal trends in the pattern of ethnopolitics elaborated by contemporary Russian nationalism, this nationalism, for the most part, comprised a classical example of ethnocentrism.

Ethnocentric self-assertiveness presupposes upholding the superiority of one's own ethnicity and, as a result, its right to preferential treatment. Thus, *Veche*'s author depicted *Russian man* as "a religious person with high spiritual aspirations, generosity, and ready sympathy, the man of the future."[33] Vice versa, aliens and everything related to them used to be stereotyped within the Russian nationalist discourse in negative terms. Thus, M. Antonov, in his essay on the Slavophiles, stated with reference to Khomiakov, that an inclination toward coercion constituted the major feature of the Latin and Germanic peoples.[34] According to him, Russian Orthodoxy allows for an integral reflection on the nature of the universe, while the Catholicism must be considered "a perverted Orthodoxy."[35] Protestantism was blamed by Antonov (again with reference to Khomiakov) for its emphasis on freedom and for suffering from a "lack of obligatory moral links."[36] Only the Russian people and its religion can spare the people of Europe from this "endless impasse."[37] Speaking in political terms, this enigmatic Russian messianism seems to be nothing more than a type of ethnocentrism.

Ethnocentric nationalism tends to explain negative phenomena by alien influences or even conspiracy. Thus, a *Letter to Veche*'s editor warned of the "danger of Catholicism" in Russia, noting that "Russian Orthodox clergymen of non-Russian origins"[38] advocated the dissemination of Catholicism. Regretting the split in the Russian Orthodox Church and the oppression of the Old Believers, *Veche* blamed "the three hundred year strife" on two prominent figures of the Russian Orthodox Church, Arsenii Grek, "initially a Jewish believer," and on Semion Polotskii, another alleged Jew.[39] An article in *Veche* devoted to the Kurile Islands blamed Karl Nesselrode, the Russian foreign minister from 1815 to 1856, for his underestimation of the Kurile's significance. It goes on to note that this lack of patriotism originated in Nesselrode's non-Russian origin: allegedly he was a "German Jew."[40]

Subordinate ethnic groups seek to portray the dominant ethnicity as oppressive by referring to its numerical superiority and sheer power. This approach is mirrored by Russian nationalists in their portrayal of supposed ethnic enemies as perfidious and crafty, possessed of manipulative, demonic powers. "Progressive Russian thought was obliterated during Stalin's bloody tyranny by the dark forces of world Zionism," stated an anonymous author in *Veche*.[41] A. Skuratov blamed Stalin's purges on the Jews, explaining that they hated the Russian people: after capturing all points of leverage, they conducted "a policy of genocide,"[42] by organizing the systematic annihilation of the Russian people. The anonymous author of the "Critical Notes by a Russian Man on the Russian Patriotic Journal *Veche*" described an apocalyptic picture of Zionist subversive activity and, simultaneously, of Zionist control of the world. According to the "Russian man," Jews invented Christianity and Islam to "convert all peoples to cosmopolitanism" and "to hold all people in subjection."[43]

Although expressions of ethnic assertiveness often employ the image of an enemy, in the ideology of Russian nationalism it bears particular prominence, compensating for the idea of national liberation, which is otherwise lacking. The concept of a "common enemy" comprises the major formative element in nationalistic perceptions. In this context xenophobia can be considered an important aspect of ethnocentric nationalism. Anti-Semitism and anti-Westernism are not merely "worrisome traits," as J. Dunlop supposes,[44] but actual manifestations of the indispensability of xenophobia to Russian nationalism. Commenting on Slavophiles Alexandr Herzen has noted that they confuse a "love for mate" with "hate for neighbor." The twentieth-century Russian nationalism including its Soviet dissident version has definitely inherited or failed to overcome this confusion.

In Russian nationalist discourse, the literal sense of terms used to describe an enemy is neutralized by attributing other meanings to them. Words such as Zionism, Cosmopolitanism, Free Masonry, West, Democracy, and the like, are used as interchangeable synonyms. The image of the enemy is manifested in various incarnations, and in any paradigm, the *West* can be easily replaced by *China*, by *Zionists*, by *Chechens*, and so on. What cannot be eliminated is the permanent quest for a common enemy.

Nationalism of Ethnic Minority Groups

"I want Ukraine to take its rightfully deserved place among the cultured nations of the world," wrote an editor of the Ukrainian *samizdat* journal, *The Catholic Herald*.[45] To be a people like other peoples, to be an equal member of the family of nations—is a declared objective of ethnic minority movements. "Our nationalism is not that we consider ourselves better than other peoples: it is that we have a right to consider ourselves no worse than any other nationality in the world," stated an *Appeal by Eighty-two Soviet Jews*,[46] expressing the most common motif of ethnic minority declarations.

Such documents describe self-determination as the universal right of all ethnic groups. A *Memorandum* by representatives of the native population of the Baltic republics declares that "all peoples living under Soviet oppression have the right to self-determination."[47] Demanding autonomy for the Lezghins, I. Kaziev, in his *Letter to the UN Secretary General*,[48] emphasized that autonomous status must be granted to all the indigenous ethnic groups of Daghestan. "I think the world should recognize the right of every ethnic minority to establish an independent state," said A. Temkin, author of the piece published in *Jews in the USSR*.[49]

The single example of the representative of a minority group expressing interest in the preservation of the Soviet Empire, can be found in an introduction by Jewish activist M. Agurskii to the *samizdat* collection of his articles. He declared that the Jewish people always played a "centralizing role" in Russia and called on Jews to support Russian nationalists in their struggle against "local, mainly Ukrainian, separatism."[50] To prove his thesis, Agurskii cited allegations of strong anti-Semitic trends within ethnic minority movements. Generally, all ethnic minority movements shared the position formulated by another Jewish activist, B. Panson, who wrote from the Mordovian camp: "There are Ukrainians, Armenians, Lithuanians, Latvians, Moldavians, Jews... together in the same barracks of the Mordovian concentration camps. We are really united here by common aspirations and shared suffering."[51]

A liberal, polycentric orientation was certainly adopted by non-Russian ethnic movements insofar as it provided impetus to their drive to alter their political status. In other respects, leanings toward poly- or ethnocentrism varied from movement to movement and even within each movement. Ukrainian *samizdat* produced two paradigms in its perception of "the other." The first one, found in M. Sahaidak's essay "Ethnocide of the Ukrainians in the USSR,"[52] described events that occurred in a small Ukrainian village, Volevin, in 1972, where the Church was pillaged by local authorities. Broder, a Ukrainian Jewish purveyor, was ordered by the authorities to register unique Church property as a utility. He refused and, as a result, was cruelly beaten and hospitalized. The image of the Jew (stranger) who reveals a sacrificial readiness to suffer for the Ukrainian cause receives a symbolic meaning, and at the same time contrasts not only with a corresponding image in Russian conservative *samizdat* but also with an alternative image of the stranger that is found in Ukrainian *samizdat*. V. Moroz, in his essay *The Chronicle of Resistance* expressed a vigorous protest against the work of non-Ukrainians, such as film directors Iu. Solntseva, a Russian, and S. Paradzhanov, an Armenian, "in the field of Ukrainian culture."[53] "They will never understand Ukraine," he claimed insisting that Ukrainian culture should be created solely by Ukrainians, and strangers should have no access to "national sacraments."[54]

Like Moroz, Jewish activist V. Shakhnovskii, commenting in the *samizdat* journal *Nash Ivrit* on the desirability of popularizing Hebrew throughout the world, said: "God forbid! It would be the last straw if the Chinese or others began to learn Hebrew, the intimate language of our people."[55] In the next issue of *Nash Ivrit* another Jewish activist, Iulii Kosharovskii, answered the same question about a hypothetical Chinese person seeking to learn Hebrew. "I will be happy to teach him if he wants," he wrote, pointing to the reciprocal benefit of such studies to the Jewish and Chinese peoples.[56]

Unlike Russian dissident groups, whose lines of demarcation between liberal (polycentric) and illiberal (ethnocentric) orientations were drawn in the early stages, ethnic minority movements tended to preserve their unity until their political goals were achieved. At the same time, at least some political leaders of these movements seemed to be aware of the fact that a split in their movements would be inevitable after they had achieved their political objectives. P. Hairekian, the leader of the Armenian National Unification Party, emphasized that the NUP would split into various parties of different orientations "after independence is gained."[57]

Despite their equivocal tendencies, mainstream ethnic minority movements took a positive approach to open ethnic borders, in which people would be able to join other nationalities. A *Statement* by the prominent Crimean Tatar activist, Iu. Osmanov,[58] in connection with his arrest mentioned the Byelorussian origins of his mother. Another member of the Crimean Tatar movement, M. Sarmina, in a *Letter to Podgornyi* on behalf of her Crimean Tatar husband stressed that she was a Russian by origin.[59]

Protesting the assimilation of members of their ethnic group by other nationalities via mixed marriages, non-Russian movements often welcomed the assimilation of "non-indigenous" spouses into their own ethnic groups. They also encouraged individuals to join their groups in other ways. "I met Russians, Ukrainians, Uzbeks, Ossets, and others, who had chosen the way of Torah, and hence, would be considered Jews. It does not amaze me. Being experienced in many fields they made the best choice," wrote Z. Korshun in the Jewish *samizdat* journal *Nash Ivrit*.[60] A. Volin, a contributor to another Jewish journal, *Jews in the USSR*, told of Yelizaveta Zhirkova, the daughter of a Russian clergyman, who immigrated to Palestine and became a Hebrew writer. "The new Jewish Palestine seems to be of Russian no less than of Jewish origins," concluded the author.[61] It is interesting that the first version of the National Unification Party's program stated that all Armenians and half-Armenians could join the NUP. The second version, adopted in 1974, substantially broadened access to the party, pointing out that "any adherent of Armenian independence can speak on behalf of the NUP."[62]

While Russian conservative documents described the "solitude" of the Russian people in a hostile environment ["Strangers are afraid of Russian patriotism, but similarly despise Russians for their lack of patriotism."[63]], ethnic minority movements preferred to stress manifestations of support. Thus, Crimean Tatar documents emphasized the sympathy and support their movement received from the local Russian and Ukrainian population, notwithstanding the anti-Tatar demonstrations that took place in the Crimea in the 1960s. In fact, Crimean Tatar *samizdat* did not mention these riots. *Information no. 73*,[64] issued by representatives of the Crimean Tatars in 1968, reported that in the Obil'noie *sovkhoz*, in the Dzhankoi district, most workers went on strike to protest the police raid on Crimean Tatars who had returned to the Crimea. According to the document, seventeen Russian and Ukrainian families left the *sovkhoz* in protest, while four families from the Ukraine refused to join it. Another Crimean Tatar document from this period told how during the police raid, "citizens of other nationalities surrounded Crimean Tatars and prevented their detention by the police."[65]

An anonymous Jewish *samizdat* article, *Why Am I a Zionist?* attributed to a B. Kochubievskii, pointed out that "the progressive Russian intelligentsia has always supported us."[66] A variant of this idea can be found in the article by Iosif Begun entitled "The History of the National Language of the Jews."[67] The author stressed that Russian cultural workers had supported the Jewish theater, *Ha-Bimah*, in the 1920s, while members of the Evsektsiia (the Jewish section of the CPSU) vigorously opposed it.

The specific status of the so-called "republic-nations" (that is, the dominant nationalities in the union republics) lay in their being simultaneously subordinate minorities in the Soviet state but dominant majorities with respect to their own ethnic minorities. The political behavior toward minority groups demonstrated by these nations served as the most representative indication of the tension between propensities to poly- and ethnocentric nationalism. In this respect, the patterns of Ukrainian and Georgian *samizdat* are the most significant.

The issue of ethnic minority rights was raised by Ukrainian *samizdat* in its earliest stages. The prominent Ukrainian activist S. Karavansky, in his

Letter to the Procurator of the Ukrainian SSR (1965) demanded the establishment of "schools with Jewish, Armenian, and other languages of instruction."[68] That same year, Karavansky, in his *Petition* to Polish Communist leader V. Gomulka,[69] pointed to the Stalinist regime's repression of Jewish intellectuals and asserted the urgency struggle against anti-Semitism. In his *Appeal to the Chairman of the Soviet of Nationalities* (1966)[70] he demanded that all secret instructions restricting the access of Jewish youth to higher education in the Ukraine be revoked and that Jewish cultural institutions in the republic be opened. Another Ukrainian activist, Anton Koval', in his *Letter to the People's Deputies of the Ukraine* (1969),[71] protested against the infringement of the national rights of Moldavians, Jews, Hungarians, Bulgarians, Greeks, and other ethnic minorities living in Ukraine. Sahaidak, in "The Ethnocide of Ukrainians in the USSR," emphasized the cultural and civil deprivations suffered by "775,000 Jews, 385,000 Byelorussians, and 295,000 Poles, not to mention smaller ethnic groups"[72] in the Ukraine. The *Chronicle of the Ukrainian Catholic Church* (no. 2, 1984) reported the persecution of Moldavians and Gypsies by the Ukrainian authorities.[73] I have already mentioned the *Appeal* by T. Franko and M. Lysenko concerning the reestablishment of Crimean Tatar autonomy[74] and other cases of ethnic minorities' rights being championed by members of the Ukrainian movement.

While mainstream Ukrainian nationalism advocated the interests of ethnic minorities, thereby attempting to consolidate all ethnic forces in the republic, the Georgian nationalist movement persistently repudiated all demands by ethnic minorities in Georgia. Dealing with Abkhazian unrest, writer Revas Dzhaparidze in his *Letter* (1979) to Georgian Communist leader, E. Shevardnadze (who tended to seek compromise with ethnic minorities), accused the Georgian leadership of "weakness" and "compliance."[75] The author anticipated a "reprisal by the Georgian sector" to withstand the policy of suppression conducted in Abkhazia by "an insignificant number of anti-Soviet provocateurs."[76] Another Georgian author, Boris Kakubava, expressed his vigorous opposition to the opening of the Abkhazian University and the commencement of television programming in the Abkhazian language. As his main argument he cited the numerical insignificance and cultural "underdevelopment" of the Abkhazians, pointing that this people never had a written language, and the first Abkhazian alphabet had been borrowed from the Georgians. Kakubava also added that the total number of Abkhazians in Georgia was only 70,000, and that they had never enjoyed independence.[77] A *samizdat* report (1982) on B. Kakubava's arrest said that he was punished for criticizing Georgian policy in Abkhazia.

The report described the Abkhazian demonstrations of 1977–1978 as "the violence of Abkhazian provocateurs-separabsts, inspired by the Great Russian chauvinist clique from Moscow."[78] Kakubava himself said that he demanded that leaders of the Abkhazian unrest be "arrested" and "isolated."[79]

A more favorable attitude cannot be found in Georgian *samizdat* about the ethnic claims of the Azerbaijani and Ossetian populations. In 1983, an anonymous Georgian *samizdat* document[80] reported on demonstrations by Azerbaijanis in Marneuli in February 1983, in protest against the nomination of an ethnic Georgian to the position of local party secretary there. As a result of the demonstration the secretary was replaced by another of Azerbaijani origin. Commenting on this, the document demonstrated an extremely negative response to this compliance and warned of similar political assertiveness in the South Ossetian Autonomous Region. The anonymous authors of the document pointed to "the hand of Moscow" in all manifestations of ethnic minority assertiveness in Georgia. The *Letter* to Iu. Andropov and N. Tikhonov by six Georgian intellectuals[81] asserted the urgent need to colonize the Marneuli district with ethnic Georgians. A 1981 document addressed to Brezhnev and Shevardnadze, entitled *Claims of the Georgian People*,[82] demanded that the Bzyb' canyon in the Abkhazian ASSR be settled with Georgians from the Svanetia countryside.

The treatment by Georgian *samizdat* of the Meskhetian problem sheds further light on the ethnocentric features of Georgian nationalist assertiveness. Georgian documents expressed strong support for the Meskhetians' struggle to return home, with the provision that the Meskhetians be considered a part of the Georgian ethnicity, and not a distinct ethnic group. While major Meskhetian documents employed the self-denomination "Meskhi Turks" and indicated that the Meskhetians had their own ethnopolitical consciousness, Georgian documents tended to deny or to ignore this. Thus, Z. Gamsakhurdia, in his *Letter to Newsweek*, commented on the deportation of the "Georgian Meskhetians who were erroneously called the Meskhi Turks."[83] Prominent Georgian dissident Merab Kostava in his artide, *Are Meskhetians Turks or Georgians?*[84] insisted that the term "Meskhi-Turks" is nonsense, and explained the misusage by the fact that members of genuinely Turkic ethnic groups were deported together with Georgians. According to M. Kostava, the former category of deportees called themselves Meskhi Turks and even demanded the right to emigrate from the USSR to Turkey. Meanwhile, Meskhetian *samizdat* indicated rather internal political struggle and debates on strategic interpretations of the movement's policies than split among the Meskhetian people along ethnic lines;[85] more so, Meskhetian documents emphasized the joint Georgian and Turkish roots of the Meskhetian people.

It is noteworthy that the *Claims of the Georgian People*[86] demanded that A. Kuradze and E. Khozravanadze be granted the status of official Meskhi representatives. Meanwhile, Enver Odabashev-Khozravanadze, the President of the Temporary Organizing Committee of the Turkish Society for the Protection of the National Rights of the Turkish Meskhetian People not only accepted the self-denomination, Meskhi-Turks, but also supported the demand of free emigration to Turkey, approved by the Sixth People's Meeting of Meskhetians in May 1970.[87]

Georgian nationalists felt no discrepancy between their own demands to secure the national rights of the Georgian minority in Azerbaijan and their harsh repudiation of the same demands put forward by the Azerbaijani minority in Georgia. Moreover, this double standard enabled Georgian activists to attach in their document addressed to Brezhnev and Shevardnadze the demand that the Abkhazian opposition be crushed. Ironically, the nationalists then called on the two leaders to "satisfy the demands of all nationalities living in the Georgian SSR."[88]

A *Letter to Pope John Paul II* issued by the Latvian Group Helsinki-86 group protested against accommodating the Chernobyl victims, who, as the *Letter* stated, "easily moved into new houses,"[89] while Latvians lived in slums.

Like the ethnocentrism of the Russian conservative movement, manifestations of non-Russian ethnocentrism revealed an inclination toward the externalization of the evil. An anonymous author of Georgian *samizdat*[90] accused the Armenian Catholicos of smuggling narcotics into Georgia. Z. Gamsakhurdia asserted that the overwhelming majority of speculators in Georgia were of non-Georgian origin.[91] An *Appeal to the Non-Russian Nationalities* by representatives of the Tatar–Bashkir movement explained ethnic frictions between these two groups as intrigues contrived by "inveterate Great Russian chauvinists."[92]

It should be indicated that "Great Russian chauvinism" serving in ethnic minority *samizdat* as an incarnation of the image of the enemy, was eventually equated with the Russian people. A document of the Latvian Group Helsinki-86 claimed that a certain primordial "hatred for small nationalities" was always revealed by Russians, who were "the first to exploit the values created by our people."[93]

"Religious intolerance is a typical feature of the Russian people," asserted Ukrainian dissident G. Budzins'kyi in his *Letter to the Ukrainian Newspaper, Radians'ka Ukraina*.[94] "We, Ukrainians are choked, as by the gases of war, by all things Russian—by Russian swear words, intolerance, violence, hypocrisy, insidiousness, hysteria, and permanent extremes," wrote the Ukrainian political prisoner, Ivan Hel' in his *Appeal to the UN Human Rights Committee*.[95]

A satiric essay in the Lithuanian *samizdat* journal *Aushra*, entitled "A Real Soviet Woman," pointed to various routine problems faced by an ordinary woman in Lithuania. It was estimated that "it is even worse to find yourself visiting a Russian woman doctor. She will shout and cuss like a barge operator, not only at me but at all my compatriots."[96] Even the normally cautiously worded Crimean Tatar *samizdat* mentioned the "Slavic racism" of the Russian people.[97]

While a multiparty system, free elections, independent trade unions, free press and other democratic institutions comprised the most popular demands advanced by all ethnic minority movements and shared by all elements within their movements, ethnocentric and polycentric orientations seemed to have been the only substantial point of divergence and the single token of an impending split along political lines. A discussion in Lithuanian *samizdat* on Lithuanian–Jewish relations revealed two controversial trends in the orientation of the Lithuanian dissident movement. The discussion was provoked by an article entitled "Jews and Lithuanians," written by Thomas Ventslova, a human rights pioneer in Lithuania. It discussed Lithuanian collaboration with the Nazi regime in massacring the Jewish population. "As a Lithuanian I feel obligated to speak out about Lithuanian guilt. Every sin committed elsewhere burdens the conscience of the whole nation and every member of that nation. Responsibility must not be shifted to other peoples. They themselves will deal with their problems, whereas we should realize what we have done," he wrote.[98]

The article provoked an angry response from part of the Lithuanian opposition. A retort published in *Aushra* under the pen-name Zhuvintas stated that the mass participation of Lithuanians in the massacre of Jews was a reaction to the latter's collaboration with the Soviet regime, so it must be considered a kind of punishment for sins committed by Jews against the Lithuanian people.[99] A strongly worded article by former political prisoner A. Terliatskas vigorously denounced Zhuvintas's arguments:

> In my native Krivasalis the Jews were not shot, no one from my family was soiled with innocent blood.... But throughout the years I have borne a sense of guilt.... Being concerned solely with the future of my people, I would not want Lithuanians to ever shoot innocent and defenseless people.... Our world is not secure against new, even more terrible catastrophes. Only unreserved censure of the massacre of a peaceful population can protect Lithuanians from participation in pogroms, the next time probably not against the Jews.[100]

It was quite predictable that the dominant majority nationalism (in our case the Russian conservative movement) might develop the ethnocentric orientation. The subordinated minority movements, on the other hand, asserting their right to be equal members in the family of nations, for a time being demonstrated explicit polycentric orientation, which coincided with their ultimate political goals. Meanwhile, the implicit propensities towards ethnocentrism can be detected to a various extent within each and every ethnic minority movement.

The issue of orientation had split the Russian opposition into "democrats" and "nationalists" in the early stages whereas the shared political goals pursued by all members of the ethnic minority movements made possible, for the time being, the mutual tolerance and even alliance of the contradicting propensities in orientations, as well as a successful cooperation between their proponents.

" 'And after independence, what then?' That is the question to which some of the best brains of our century have chosen not to address themselves," P. Calvert states[101] pointing out that the achievement of independence does not solve the main economic and social problems. Calvert's conclusion has probably more profound implication. Strictly speaking, the subordinated minority nationalism, which champions its goal under the slogan of national liberation ought to die immediately after the goal has been achieved. Usually, it does not happen, primarily due to the dichotomy between ideological resources of the ethnic nationalism, in which the civic idea of "national liberation" is fused with the ethnocentric eagerness of reshaping (not abolishing!) the pattern of ethnic dominance. In a word, the idea "one people–one state" tends to be implemented in its variant "one state to one dominant people." In fact, the demand of congruency between ethnic and political borders is often realized as the quest for congruency between ethnic borders and political-economic power.

When nationalist movements have achieved sovereignty, and the ideal of national liberation has become exhausted, ethnocentrism remains the major formative element of ethnic majority nationalism in the newly independent states, whereas anti-Westernism, anti-Semitism, anti-Russianism, or any other anti- seems to have been its epiphenomena.

CHAPTER 8

Samizdat and Ethnic Mobilization

Assessing the Parameters of Mobilization

"In 1985, when Mikhail Sergeevich Gorbachev came to power," wrote A. Motyl in 1990, "the Soviet state was stable by any standard. Party rule was perceived as legitimate, the population was quiescent and generally satisfied, and open opposition to the regime was minimal... [By 1990] the condition of the Soviet state had experienced a 180-degree turn. The Party was thoroughly delegitimized,... the population was in the streets, and open opposition was the order of the day.... Who or what pushed the USSR onto this slippery slope? The answer, quite simply, is Mikhail Gorbachev."[1] Predicting a "breakdown or a crackdown,"[2] as extreme variants of political developments, Motyl remarked: "I still doubt that the non-Russians, who may increasingly want to rebel, will be able to do so successfully."[3]

In 1979, long before *perestroika* began, Estonian dissident M. Nikluss wrote an essay devoted to his trip to Lithuania.[4] The author noted that the Lithuanian people were highly politicized, adhered to national cultural values, and committed to independence. Based on his own analysis, the author concluded that Lithuania would be the first of the Soviet republics to achieve independence. He was right. In 1990, the Lithuanian parliament made the unprecedented decision to secede from the USSR. This was more than just a coincidence. Beyond any doubt, *samizdat* proved to be the most significant indicator of ethnic revival in the USSR from Stalin's death until the rise of *perestroika*.

Due to the lack of any "conventional" means of championing ethnic politics—through parliamentary means, political parties, communal ethnic organizations, the mass media, and so on—*samizdat* became a social institution for the formation of ethnic politics and, at the same time, a means of conveying political ideas. During the period of stagnation, this social institution served both to mobilize ethnic groups and promote the emergence of a new ethnic elite. In itself, the appearance of ethnic *samizdat* can be considered one of the most significant manifestations of ethnic politicization.

Overly modest figures for the number of active members in dissident groups under totalitarian conditions cannot be taken at face value. Ukrainian dissident Bohdan Rebryk stated in his final plea: "Millions of Ukrainians share my views. It is only the fear of repression that keeps them silent."[5] This statement seems to be far more authentic than any assumptions of mass satisfaction with the Soviet regime.

Having made this statement, we are expected to provide some proven statistic data concerning the dynamics of participation and constituency of the nationalist movements. Specifically, we have to answer how many people took part in the ethnonationalist movements, how many "passive" supporters did they have, how many people were involved in preparing (including writing, typing, editing, and disseminating) the *samizdat* materials, and finally, how many readers did the *samizdat* have?

Alas, all these questions can hardly have definite answers. The figures of active participants can potentially be estimated by the use of references to their names in various, *samizdat* and non-*samizdat* sources. In this respect, an instructive attempt of quantitative estimation of national dissident activities between 1965 and 1981 has been undertaken by Th. Smith and Th. Oleszczuk in their study "The Brezhnev Legacy: Nationalities and Gorbachev."[6] Thus, counting references to nationalist dissident activities found in *Arkhiv Samizdata* and *The Chronicle of Current Events*, the two major sources of information on dissident activities, the scholars reached, for example, the conclusion that the Jewish movement practically stopped its activity in 1980, since there were zero reported cases by these sources. Meanwhile, 1980 should be recognized as one of the most "productive" years of the Soviet Jewish dissent. The list of *samizdat* activities alone, in this year (based on the data from *The Jewish Samizdat*[7]), includes not less than eight periodical and non-periodical issues (five titles), which contain at least thirty-five names of their authors and editors. I do not mention here the mass gathering of nonofficial Hebrew teachers in Crimea, the collective hunger strike during the Olympic Games in Moscow, and individual and collective petitions counting dozens of signatories. It is not necessary to say that every additional "lost" or "found" activity or name will dramatically change the results of quantitative analysis in this case.

The specification of all relevant sources of data (necessary and sufficient for the quantitative estimation) testifying for open dissident public activities and activists constitutes a difficult but probably practical task. At the same time, the prospects to establish satisfactory criteria for quantitative estimation of the *samizdat* circulations, or all the more, their readers or Soviet citizens who have shared in general the dissidents' position seem to come to naught. Furthermore, we should indicate that not every reader of *samizdat* might be considered a potential oppositionist, and equally, not everybody who held nonconformist attitudes necessarily read *samizdat*. Commonly, the *samizdat* editors cited from several dozen to several hundred copies but failed to refer to the precise figures of circulation of their own publications.[8]

To an even lesser degree, we can trace the path of every single piece of the *samizdat* publication. How many readers have passed through each copy? How many times have unknown volunteers reproduced it? The answers to these simple questions are unlikely to be ever found.

With regard to "consumers" of *samizdat* we have to make a difference between active and passive ones. The former might be defined as those who had direct access to *samizdat*, that is, were involved in reading and distributing the *samizdat* materials. The latter might have no direct access to the *samizdat* production, but received the information from the wide network of foreign broadcasters or to some extent from the Soviet *mass media* which carried the "unmasking" items against dissidents. In any case, the figures of recipients of the *samizdat* production seem to have been quite impressive, particularly among the Soviet intelligentsia.

Any attempt to assess the constituency of dissident activities or ideologies by carrying out an empirical research today can hardly be effective for it will reflect the contemporary attitudes to such activities and ideologies rather than provide the satisfactory data on the state of affairs then.

During the years of *perestroika* and later I was repeatedly surprised how many former loyal members of the Communist Party and even its Central Committee tended to introduce and probably perceive themselves as "dissidents". In 1989–1990, when the visits of Soviet citizens to Israel were launched there were several meetings with Soviet representatives organized by the Marjorie Mayrock Center for Soviet and East European Research at the Hebrew University of Jerusalem. One guest who represented the pro-reformist faction of the official Soviet Peace Committee, a long-time employee of this organization, had introduced himself as a "member of the nonofficial peace movement." Another guest, a journalist who since the 1960s had been working for the APN, the Soviet news agency closely associated with the KGB, told that in the late 1980s she established the first private independent news agency in the USSR. "Modestly" assessing her audience abroad to be "several times as large as that of Solzhenitsyn," she consistently recommended products of "the first independent news agency" as *samizdat*. Visualizing her personal story, the journalist emphasized that as a result of her heretic views for a long period she had been denied access to the Soviet press, and was forced to have her articles (distributed by the APN!) published solely abroad. As one could anticipate, she "delicately" failed to indicate that this kind of materials had undergone particularly stubborn censorship, as well as the fact that the APN publications had been used by the Soviet authorities as a means of disseminating the awry and deceptive information abroad.

Celebrated human rights activist and former political prisoner Semyon Gluzman, now executive secretary of the Psychiatrists Association of Ukraine, in an interview given to the Ukrainian newspaper sarcastically mentioned the growing lure of "dissident biography": "...Mythology of dissent is being forged—consciously or subconsciously.... The overwhelming majority of all these so-called dissidents—nobody has ever heard about them. Even former employees of the CPSU Central Committee and the Procuracy have turned into dissidents."[9]

Meanwhile, such "aberrations of memory", intentional or unintentional, which reflect the desire of women and men of another background to be identified with the dissident narrative that they have not shared, seem to be eloquent qualitative indicators of the significance of the Soviet dissent in general and of the *samizdat* specifically.

The sociological profile of a dissident activist who produced *samizdat* and that of an active *samizdat* consumer seem to share identical characteristics. They both belong to the generation that grew up after World War II and are supposed to be urban dwellers, primarily residents of big cities, and possess some experience of the post-secondary education (from attending several courses in college to having the Doctor of Science degree).

National movements in their nascent stages already recognized the potential for ethnic mobilization inherent in *samizdat*. A Crimean Tatar document (1968) indicated two means of pressure to advance political interests: mass demonstrations, and the collection of documents testifying to arbitrary rule by the Soviet authorities.[10]

An item devoted to the tenth anniversary of the *Chronicle of the Catholic Church in Lithuania*, written by an anonymous reader, stressed that this journal had become "the voice of all Lithuania, of all religious believers, and of all who were persecuted."[11] *Veche*'s editor, V. Osipov, said in his interview with the Associated Press: "We take upon ourselves the complete responsibility to serve as the mouthpiece of our people's national aspirations."[12]

Samizdat was the medium by which ethnic dissidents could best appeal to their fellow nationals. It would be no exaggeration to say that the ethnic dissident elite was formed via *samizdat*. The fact that virtually all the political prisoners prepared their final pleas thoroughly, although they were to be delivered before closed courts seemed to demonstrate this. Not expecting to convince the KGB-appointed judges of their innocence, political prisoners were certain that their statements would be *samizdat* "bestsellers."

"Pending Armenian independence, the prison will remain my only residence.... As for my final plea, it has not yet been delivered. You and the all Armenian people will hear it later," P. Hairekian, the Chairman of the Armenian Unification Party (NUP), stated at his trial (1974).[13] We can be sure, that there, in the courtroom, this leader spoke over the heads of his judges, to his nation and history.

Matvei Chlenov, a young Moscow scholar who examined the Jewish *samizdat* magazine *Nash Ivrit* (Our Hebrew Language) concluded that its authors tended to describe themselves as leaders of Soviet Jewry.[14] Similarly, the Lezghian author, I. Kaziev, repeatedly called himself "a leader of the Lezghian people."[15] Since the beginning of *glasnost*, numerous references to the moral authority of dissident leaders can be found in public statements at various levels. This suggests that they were recognized in the capacity of an ethnic elite not only by their dissident counterparts but also by wider circles of the intelligentsia. It is worth noting that a significant number of dissident ethnic leaders later joined the political establishment of their republics and of the newly formed independent states.[16]

As we have seen, both readers and writers of *samizdat* considered it to be a major force for mobilization. Nevertheless, ethnic mobilization can in no way be described as an immediate response to nationalist propaganda. Indicating "a sense of being deprived relative to others," (I) and "a political climate and regime which tolerates protest action" (II)[17] as prerequisites for mobilization, A. Smith pointed to the following dimensions of ethnic mobilization:

1. Those who feel deprived share "a common perception that there is a single cause of their plight, and that they possess the organizational means to overcome it";
2. "The existence of a social movement which can coordinate and organize their efforts effectively";
3. The existence of "a body of convinced nationalists with a well-thought-out ideology."[18]

Describing mobilization as "a process of accumulation of power," L. Hoogh[19] referred to the prominent social scientist S. Tarrow[20] in her classification of resources available for mobilization. "Sidney Tarrow distinguishes three major internal resources: leadership, organization, and group solidarity. Their joint weight constitutes a group's mobilization capacity. The major external resources are those aspects of the political opportunity structure that are within reach of the group and that can be manipulated to forward its aims. Tarrow lists three aspects: access to the political system, stability of political alignments, and the presence of influential allies or supporters."[21]

While Smith considers action to be part of the mobilization process, the German scholar J. Raschke distinguishes between mobilization and action: "Power is accumulated through mobilization; it is directed at an aim through action."[22] In this respect, the first prerequisite (I), the first (1) and third (3) dimensions of mobilization mentioned by Smith, as well as the "internal resources" indicated by Tarrow are related to the process of mobilization, whereas the second prerequisite (II) the second (2) dimension of mobilization, and Tarrow's "external resources" are related to "action." The distinction between mobilization and action is substantial because of the de-synchronization of these two processes in the USSR. The post-Stalinist period of ethnic dissent can be described as the time of mobilization, while *perestroika* can be described as the time of action.[23]

At the same time that ethnonationalist ideologies were being elaborated in *samizdat* publications, nationalist leaders were winning their reputations, mainly via the same publications. Did *samizdat* promote mobilization and how? Nationalist appeals on their own can hardly inspire nationalist sentiment. *Samizdat* does, however, articulate a vague feeling of deprivation relative to others and of cultural distinctiveness. It also shapes the readers' awareness that they as members of the ethnic community are *qualified* and *entitled* for gaining the objects (such as autonomy, independence, etc.) that *others* have and *they* are denied. This can be translated into set political principles. In this way, *samizdat* served as the important *indicator* of and, at the same time, as the *vehicle* for ethnic mobilization.

There are no relevant qualitative criteria for estimating ethnic mobilization in the USSR. We can, however, assume that more advanced dissident activity, including *samizdat*, signified a higher level of mobilization. Assessing ethnic mobilization through action, that is, through the activities of social movements in the *perestroika* period, seems to corroborate this assumption. At any rate, the level of "ability, strategy, tactical strength, and perseverance"[24] of the peoples' fronts in the Baltic republics or Ukraine, which previously enjoyed advanced ethnic dissent, was considerably higher than in Byelorussia, which had a weak dissident nationalist movement, or in the Central Asian republics, which failed to develop open ethnic dissent. We can also conclude that the character of current socio-political strategies and orientations of some newly independent states has been strongly predetermined by the propensities towards ethno- and polycentrism in the orientations of their nationalist movements. Thus, an adoption by the independent state of Latvia of the *discrimination* model of policy towards the so-called Russophones versus the *equality* model adopted by the independent Lithuanian state seems to have been predetermined by the developments of their fellow dissident discourses rather than by the alleged "demographic imperatives." The *equality* model of politics and strategy of cooperation with the ethnic minorities championed by the mainstream Ukrainian dissent was adopted by *Rukh*—the Ukrainian Popular Front, where dissidents played a prominent part—and afterward by all governments of the independent Ukraine. Inversely, the first democratically elected Georgian President Zviad Gamsakhurdia, former dissident and political prisoner, carefully preserved the ethnocentric orientations of his fellow movement. Considering "ethnic minorities living in Georgia the main threat to the Georgian people"[25] he hesitated neither to repudiate publicly their demands, nor to employ violence against the "dissenting" minorities groups.

Samizdat *and Potentials for Violent Conflicts*

With its glimpses into ethnic tension, *samizdat* revealed potentials for fierce ethnic conflict. One of the first Armenian *samizdat* documents, the *Letter* by Armenians of Nagorno-Karabakh to Khrushchev (1963),[26] demanded that urgent measures be taken to avoid fierce fighting between Armenians and Azerbaijanis in the region. Further developments in Nagorno-Karabakh made it clear that a rapid evolution toward a conflict situation was taking place.

Hushing up of the fiftieth anniversary of the Armenian genocide, by the Soviet authorities, provoked a wave of Armenian protests. This policy was perceived by both Armenians and Azeris as a concession to the latter and as a *carte blanche* for repressive measures against the Armenians in Nagorno-Karabakh. Two Armenian documents of the late 1960s depicted the dramatic deterioration of affairs in this autonomous *oblast*. The first, a *Letter* to an unspecified Armenian party official, was written by Benik Movsisian,[27] the father of a ten-year-old boy who was cruelly murdered by a certain Arshad Mamedov, the director of a school in Martuni, Nagorno-Karabakh. The second, an *Appeal by Armenians of Nagorno-Karabakh* was addressed to the "People, Government, Central Committee, and Public Organizations of

Armenia."[28] Both documents recollected the events of 1967, which had prompted the first *samizdat* accounts of fierce clashes between Armenians and Azeris. The boy, son of the head of a police station in Martuni had been killed and dismembered by Arshad Mamedov. B. Movsisian mentioned that one year earlier Mamedov had killed another Armenian, Grisha Sogomonian. Neither document cited the official version of the murder. The victim's father pointed out that the "Armenian case had been given to a Turk,"[29] that is, an Azeri judge. As a result, the murderer was sentenced to only ten years in prison. Armenians, infuriated by the lack of justice, rioted. The document reported that militiamen directed jets of water and opened fire on the rioters. Twelve Armenians were critically wounded; several more, including B. Movsisian, were seriously injured. In reprisal, the crowd assaulted several Azeris, killed them, and burned their bodies. Arshad Mamedov was among the dead. The *Appeal by Armenians of Nagorno-Karabakh*[30] also listed other acts of terror committed against Armenians in Nagorno-Karabakh and pointed to the immunity enjoyed by the terrorists and the visible indifference of the central authorities to dangerous developments in the region.

Analyzing Georgian *samizdat* we can find the potential for violence in several more local ethnic conflicts. I mentioned above that the Georgian Communist leadership generally demonstrated its readiness to compromise in dealing with the assertiveness of the Abkhazian and Azerbaijani minorities in Georgia. At the same time, their dissident opponents pressed a hard-line policy toward any political ambitions by ethnic minorities, denouncing their demands as utterly illegitimate. Politicized ethnic minorities in Georgia were depicted by Georgian *samizdat* as Moscow's puppets, and their claims—as provocation against the Georgian people, organized by the center. Georgian documents described the assertiveness of the Abkhazian, Ossetian, and Azerbaijani minorities as an additional manifestation of the "anti-Georgian policy in Georgia"[31] conducted by Moscow, as "the persecution of Georgians,"[32] and so on. On the other hand, the inaction—and more so, the tough political response by the dominant majority to ethnic claims by minority groups—propelled the latter to seek the support of the center. Thus, Abkhazian and Lezghian documents appealed to Russia for support, the Georgians of Eastern Kakhetia addressed their appeals to the people and government of Georgia, and Armenians in Nagorno-Karabakh tried to mobilize both Armenian and Russian support.

The prospect of third-party involvement in inter-ethnic disputes tended to aggravate ethnic tensions, particularly when the third side avoided revealing its precise stance. In such cases, any ambiguity by the third party left room for arbitrary interpretation by each opponent in its own favor and increased the potential for escalation of ethnic tensions into a violent conflict.

There are definite indications that *samizdat* has served as a factor in the mobilization of ethnic communities for political actions. Can any connection be established between reporting by *samizdat* the cases of violent or derogatory behavior signaling the potentials for violent conflicts and the outbreaks of ethnic violence?

We have no evidence that *samizdat* accounts of this kind have ever prompted the ethnic violence. It seems that the contrary is true. Due to the network of social and personal communication developed by dissidents, many of them felt adherence not only to their specific group but also to the whole "guild" of oppositionists to the Soviet regime. The dissidents who have accustomed themselves to conveying their arguments via *samizdat* seem to have little interest in using violence as a medium of communication.

Hence, we can assume that the pattern of ethnic mobilization via *samizdat* has had a "civilizing" effect on the character of actions of the upcoming mass movements. This assumption certainly demands further serious and comprehensive examination.

Conclusion

*S*amizdat in general, and ethnic *samizdat* in particular, constituted the major manifestation of Soviet dissent. Moreover, *samizdat* reports of dissident activities rendered them significant acts in the overall social and political life of the USSR. Regarding the nationalist activity in the USSR, A. Motyl concluded:

The sociological theories are inadequate to explain it.... Even if we give the sociological theories the benefit of the doubt, what they lead us to expect is all wrong. First, the nationalists are not frustrated social climbers but well-adjusted and socially successful individuals. Second, the non-Russians in general and the Balts, Ukrainians, Armenians, and Georgians in particular, have been competing very favorably with the Russians. Indeed, these groups generally enjoy living standards and educational attainments that are no worse than those of the Russians. Third, sociological theories cannot account for timing—for the rise and fall of nationalist dissent—as modernization is a continuous process. Fourth, if anything, such theories would lead us to expect nationalist sentiment to have been greatest during the 1930s, when modernization was at its peak, but dissent clearly was not. Finally, sociological theories would lead us to believe that nationalist dissent should have been substantial in the regions undergoing the most modernization and competition with Russians of late, Byelorussia and Central Asia.[1]

With reservations deriving from the specific character of the Soviet Union, the sociological theories rejected by Motyl are, in fact, not only applicable but also completely adequate in explaining the phenomenon of nationalist dissent in the USSR.

First, the social composition of nationalist movements, as described by social theories, can hardly be explained in terms of "frustrated climbers."

A. Smith stressed that "the detailed composition of the nationalist movement varies considerably. The 'intelligentsia' always contributes representatives out of proportion to its number, if by 'intelligentsia' is meant lawyers, journalists, academics, doctors and teachers, and all who possess higher education qualifications. So do clerks and civil servants, and officers, especially in this century. But we also find considerable numbers of the bourgeoisie, both wealthy capitalists and small traders and shopkeepers. [Pointing to the role of 'intelligentsia' Smith indicated that] this category is unfailingly over-represented in nationalist movements, and especially in their leadership, ... they are the most relevant group in exploring the *emergence* of nationalism, rather than its subsequent diffusion. The ideology of nationalism is born of their situation and problems."[2]

Second, now it is generally accepted that the universal macro-level theory, which is expected to account for the emergence of all patterns of nationalism, does not exist. While the unfavorable economic position may be valid for the explanation of nationalism in one ethnic community, the accumulation of considerable economic power will serve as a relevant explanation for the rise of nationalism in another one. Moreover, the economic (or "well-being") parameters may not account at all for the rise of nationalism. Despite the fact that some non-Russian ethnic groups enjoyed the same (or an even higher) standard of living and educational achievement as the Russian majority, the pattern of ethnic domination remained unchanged. As both individuals and collectives, ethnic minority representatives felt *fraternal* relative deprivation—first and foremost in the political and status spheres.

Third, sociological theories consider modernization to be a compound process involving social and political modernization as no less integral elements than technological progress. De-Stalinization as launched by Khrushchev actually marked an attempt to synchronize technological modernization with social-political modernization: a necessary component of this was the liberalization of the public consciousness. The conjuncture of social-political modernization (which brought the new normative standards into the collective perception) and relative deprivation generated nationalist dissent in the USSR.

Evaluating the drive of colonial peoples toward independence, R. Emerson noted that the most intense nationalist movements emerged in the British colonies that enjoyed more liberal rule and higher standards of living standard and educational achievement than those existing in the German or Portuguese colonies. In this respect, there was no substantial difference between developments in the Soviet republics and those in the "world at large."

From its inception, ethnic minority *samizdat* elaborated upon the motif of relative deprivation. Dealing with relative deprivation in the political, cultural-linguistic, economic, and other spheres, *samizdat* insisted that here was a major incentive to ethnic assertiveness. Every ethnic movement advanced in *samizdat* a complex of demands in accordance with its political goals. In the 1960s and early 1970s, there were already ethnic minority movements that regarded secession as a possible variant of political development. However, even *samizdat* from the Baltic republics, where separatist trends were traditionally strong, did not assert that secession was the only possible solution.

Through the 1970s, though, there was the growing rejection of the Soviet ideology followed by a radicalization of ethnic demands. While in the 1960s ethnic minority *samizdat* championed "genuine socialism" and "the restoration of Lenin's norms," by the mid-1970s virtually all ethnic minority movements had formulated anti-Soviet and anti-Communist political positions.

It is significant that the Soviet conception of federalism (as enshrined in the Constitution) became the principal source of legitimation for the ethnopolitical demands of subordinated ethnic groups. National rights were generally understood by ethnic minority movements to mean the legitimate rights of an ethnic group to a defined territory in which this group would be the dominant political, economic, and cultural factor. Collectively, politicized ethnic groups tended to adopt the concept of secession as the highest in a hierarchy of national rights and, therefore, as the best, if not the sole solution to their nationality question.

Dissident ethnic movements gave the highest prominence to the formal attributes of statehood demanding republican citizenship and control over their armed forces, foreign relations, foreign trade, and the like. By the mid-1970s ethnic movements of the so-called republic-nations had elaborated separatist platforms. At this time, documents issued by the Tatar–Bashkir movement asserted the right of self-determination, including the right of secession from the USSR, for all nationalities. While indigenous nationalities in autonomous republics demanded that their regions' status be raised to that of federal units, ethnic groups deprived of such a status struggled to attain it. Thus, a Lezghin dissident writer, in a petition to the United Nations, described the relative deprivation of his people as resulting entirely from their lack of any political status. Indeed, the concept of statehood, even in its Soviet variant, was generally considered by ethnic movements to be the major national collective value, with precedence over all other national interests.

Dissent among the Russian dominant majority demonstrated two opposite reactions to ethnic minority assertiveness. The Russian conservative movement, which had, to a considerable degree, risen as a reaction to non-Russian political assertiveness, adopted a strategy that mirrored ethnic minority claims. While some prominent supporters of the Russian conservatives, such as Solzhenitsyn and Shafarevich, accepted (albeit with some reservations) the idea of the secession of Soviet republics, the mainstream of the movement pressed for the preservation of the Soviet Union at any price.

Russian conservatism offered a set of ethnocentric ideas and denounced democratic institutions as alien and unsuitable for the Russian people. Early Russian conservative *samizdat* from the 1960s shows a markedly anti-Soviet and anti-Communist stance. In the 1970s, *Veche* declared its neutrality toward Communist ideology and its loyalty to the Soviet state. The evolution of the "Russian idea" frequently culminated in the proclamation that the Soviet Communist regime had divine sanction.

On the contrary, the general democratic movement expressed its full support of ethnic minority demands and solidarity with their goals. In their turn, all ethnic minority movements that arose as a result of the socio-political modernization of Soviet society in the post-Stalinist era championed liberal-democratic changes in the USSR and advocated Western-style democracy for their fellow ethnic groups.

Occasional "misunderstandings" between the general democratic movement and ethnic minority movements reported by *samizdat* seem to have had a minor significance at that time. In addition to the congruity of operational strategies of minority nationalists and democrats, their alliance had a solid conceptual foundation. It was a wide consensus in the dissident circles about the principle of self-determination and its "natural" affiliation with liberal democracy. "Virtually everyone... took for granted the notion that every 'people' is entitled to 'self-determination,' which includes the right to secede."[3]

In fact, this perception was neither specifically "Soviet" nor "dissident." In contemporary discourse ("not only of the formerly socialist countries but elsewhere as well"[4]), democracy has been consistently linked to self-determination. "Both the left and right portray both processes as interdependent aspects of a single progressive development, the trend toward giving human beings more control over the conditions of their own lives. Yet, despite these similarities, democracy and self-determination are two distinct projects with sometimes contradictory objects," M. Spencer argued.[5]

The general democratic movement in the USSR had designated liberal democracy with its commitment to the rule of law and human rights as the preeminent objective, whereas the ethnic minority movements striving for national sovereignty tended to regard democracy first and foremost as a vehicle for attaining their nationalist goals. I do not mean that among the nationalist activists faithful democrats cannot be found. I mean that in general nationalists' adherence to liberal democracy is rather contextual (situational), and cannot be ascertained merely by demands of the democratic reforms they made to the "center." To a considerable degree, "nationalists' sincerity" in their "promises of democracy" (in Metta Spencer's terms)[6] might be tested through formulating their policies toward other ethnic minorities in their native republics.

In this respect, *samizdat* parlance of ethnic minority movements reveals their prevalent propensity for either polycentric (inclusive) or ethnocentric (exclusive) nationalism, as well as the potential for future violent ethnic conflicts. Ethnocentric expressions, meantime, can be detected within each and every ethnic minority movement including the movements that generally display polycentric liberal orientations.

"It is always a surprise when repressed groups fail to recognize the general category from which they have just escaped. Again and again, they act as if they are the only or the last victims of repression, and they claim rights and entitlements that restrict the rights and entitlements of the groups that come next, their neighbors in minorities in their own midst," M. Walzer pointed out, calling this "kind of behavior human, all-too-human."[7]

It seems that the paradox of this "all-too-human" behavior cannot be fully explained by the lack of sincerity in intentions of ethnic minority nationalists. The dichotomy between ethnonationalist ideological resources, which manifests itself in demand for equality of a subordinated ethnic collective via attaining popular sovereignty and simultaneously in claim for dominance via altering a pattern of ethnic stratification poses serious difficulties for practicing liberal politics. In fact, efforts of ethnic elite, in newly independent states, to come to terms with both democracy and nationalism have a tendency to be implemented within the strains of political–legal arrangements described by Sammy Smooha as "Ethnic Democracy."[8] This term coined by Smooha for explication of the Israeli political system is activated in contemporary scholarly and political discourse to depict the regimes forged in the newly independent states of the former Communist block (specifically, in Latvia, Estonia[9]). In Smooha's definition, "ethnic democracy is a system, which combines the extension of civil and political rights to individuals and some collective rights to minorities, with institutionalization of majority control over the state. Driven by ethnic nationalism, the state is identified with a 'core ethnic nation,' not with its citizens. The state practices a policy of creating a homogenous nation-state, a state of and for a particular ethnic nation, and acts to promote the language, culture, numerical majority, economic well-being, and political interests of this group. Although enjoying citizenship and voting rights,[10] the minorities are treated as second-class citizens, feared as a threat, excluded from the national power structure, and placed under some control. At the same time, the minorities are allowed to conduct a democratic and peaceful struggle that yields incremental improvement in their status:"[11]

Serving as a free voice for the politically mobilized part of the nationalist intelligentsia, *samizdat* expressed the most popular ethnic claims and championed the most popular political objectives. At the same time, the social, cultural, and political values fostered by *samizdat* were aggregated in the collective ethnic perceptions as representing the "age-old aspirations" of the people.

We cannot ignore the "uneven development" of various ethnic movements, particularly their differing levels of intensity of assertiveness, and correspondingly, the different levels of advancement as expressed in their political platforms. This fact, that is, the level of political self-consciousness manifested by some dissident nationalist movements undoubtedly influenced, to no small degree, the assertiveness of fellow ethnic groups as political actors during *perestroika*. At the same time, during the period of dissident ethnic activism, certain universal standards of ethnic political behavior had been formulated. In the process of *perestroika*, these were automatically adopted by the mass nationalist movements (Popular or Peoples' Fronts and others) that emerged through 1987–1990, including movements among those peoples who had never before experienced dissident ethnic activism.

Throughout the "dissident period" of nationalist movements, ethnic politics, including ethnic demands, orientations, strategies, and the like, were elaborated upon in detail. Later, small informal groups and finally mass revivification movements that emerged during *perestroika* repeated the stages of political evolution as they had occurred in the dissident nationalist movements, adopting their platforms and utilizing their claims, historical myths, political vocabulary, references to legitimizing sources of demands, and so on.

The striking exactness with which the *samizdat* scenario of ethnopolitics was realized suggests that dissident ethnic activism during the "period of stagnation" gained a broader constituency than is generally thought, even though most people chose to demonstrate political passivity. Pointing to the "process of totalisation of 'infrastructural' dissent" in the former Baltic republics A. Shtromas indicates: "History was thus to prove that dissent in the Baltic states was total indeed and that the difference between conservationist and activist dissent was not of substance but only on methods.

When, because of *glasnost*, the difference in methods became irrelevant, nothing was left to draw a dividing line between the few activist dissidents and the rest of the people."[12]

No uniform role of ex-dissidents, *samizdat* activists, may be established regarding their personal practical involvement in the formation of influential nationalist opposition to the Communist regime in the course of *perestroika*. Thus, Ukrainian dissidents made a crucial contribution to "the development of informal opposition structures"[13] as well as to "the establishment of massive revivification movements" and "the launching of independent political parties."[14] Similarly, former authors and heroes of the *samizdat* accounts became indisputable leaders of the newly created Crimean Tatar and Jewish organizational structures. On the other hand, the practical participation of Estonian dissidents in the formation of popular movements and political parties seems to be rather modest. Anyway, nationalist dissidents, who for the first time were playing key roles in mass movements, could now formulate their politics as the new ethnic elite.

Even more important, during *perestroika* and particularly in the early post-Soviet period, was that the former Communist bureaucratic elite faced the classic dilemma of the traditional elite—whether to support a new elite or to resist. Former Communist functionaries seeking to mobilize support were forced to speak in the language of the former dissidents. When Viacheslav Chornovil, a dissident and political prisoner in pre-Gorbachev days, was asked during the presidential elections held in Ukraine on 1 December 1991 what the difference was between himself and his main rival, Leonid Kravchuk, he replied: "Nothing. Except that my program is thirty years old, and Kravchuk's three weeks old," T. Kuzio and A. Wilson pointed out.[15] Nevertheless, it was Kravchuk, not Chornovil who won the race for the Ukrainian presidency.

A broad consensus on the adoption of "the dissidents' scenario" signified the culminating point in attaining ethnic mobilization and reorientation of social-political thought. Simultaneously, the institutionalization of massive nationalist alliances indicated the beginning of the end of dissidents' coherence and solidarity. "The growing tendency toward political pluralism and internal disagreement"[16] within nationalist movements since the early 1990s rendered the disintegration of popular fronts and emergence of diverse competitor parties.[17] Correspondingly, dissident activists previously united in their struggle for common nationalist goals now found themselves divided by political, ideological and socio-economic orientations, by political strategies, by contemplation of past and future, and finally, by personal ambitions. For instance, two ex-dissidents, Chornovil and Luk'ianenko, ran for

Ukraine's Presidency in 1991, and two *Rukh*'s executive organs (Political Council and Grand Council) failed to reach agreement as to who of this duo should be supported by the *Rukh*.

The lack of cooperation and growing strife between ex-dissidents is cited as one of the explanations to their relatively poor achievements as political players. Another explanation is found in difficulty of ex-dissidents who used to act entirely within the space of civil society in adjusting to formal political institutions.[18] In this respect, former Communist party officials and Soviet managers in possession of nationalist slogans elaborated by dissidents have demonstrated outstanding performance in comparison with the "authentic architects" of the nationalist agenda. There is also a "behaviorist" explanation holding that a predominantly conservative constituency is most likely to approve radical alternative if the traditional leadership offers it.[19]

The years of *perestroika* can be described as the period in which ethnonationalist political ideas of dissidents were disseminated, adopted by the masses, and then implemented in the newly independent states. In effect, they form the yardstick of progress by which change in the post-Soviet era has come to be measured. As for the ex-dissidents, they have been successfully incorporated in post-Soviet ethnic mythology. They still enjoy great moral prestige, and their support tends to be regarded by competing political parties as undeniable electoral asset.[20]

The "modest charm" of nationalism (particularly if nationalist ideas are conveyed by "unfrocked communists") might have a "post-structuralist" explanation. After the first barriers of censorship had been removed, the Soviet populace to their great surprise revealed that accursed and persecuted by the Soviet authorities nationalism spoke rather in the same language that they used to be addressed by their communist bosses.[21] The democratic leaders of *perestroika* failed to offer serious alternative to ethnonationalism. Moreover, they introduced their appeal to democracy and liberal values into the framework of nationalist discourse. Basic ideas of nationalism and communism grounded on common foundations of collectivism and group solidarity appeared to be highly convertible. It was a matter of technique to accommodate the universal language of nationalism to specific needs of a specific ethnic group. The well-articulated ideology and politics of nationalism advanced by the dissident groups appears to have become the single serviceable counterpart to replace defunct Communism.

Appendix: The Relevant Nationalities—Basic Facts

Abkhazians

The Abkhaz Autonomous Republic (3,150 square miles) occupies the extreme northwest portion of Georga. Formerly a Georgian principality, Abkhazia was the home of the Abkhaz (Apkhaz) tribe. As a part of the Roman Empire, it adopted Christianity under Justinian (ca. 550). In the eighth century the Abkhazian Duke Leo conquered western Georgia and established his independent Kingdom of Abasgia, which later became part of the Georgian state. The Duchy of Abkhazia recovered its independence in 1463. Ottoman suzerainty was imposed in the sixteenth century and Islam supplanted Christianity. There are now both Muslim and Orthodox Christian Abkhazians, although paganism continues to influence both religious communities. In 1860, Prince George I of Abkhazia signed a treaty with Russia by which Abkhazia was made a Russian protectorate. In 1864, the country was annexed by Russia outright. In 1919, in the aftermath of the Russian Revolution, Abkhazia received autonomous status. The Abkhaz ASSR was proclaimed in 1921. The people of Abkhazia are a Circassian group belonging to the Western branch of the Paleo-Caucasian peoples. Their language belongs to the Abkhazo-Adygean group of the North Caucasian branch of the Japhetic languages. According to the 1989 census, there were 103,380 Abkhazians in the Soviet Union, an increase of 52.4 percent since 1959. A population of 96,000 lived in Georgia, mainly in the Abkhaz ASSR. There was also a small community in the Adzhar ASSR, 7,200 in the Russian Federation, and a sizeable community in Turkey. Of these, 93.5 percent listed Abkhazian as their native language. The Abkhazians are most closely related to the Adygei and the Abadzins.

Adygei

The Sunni Muslim Adygei comprise one element of the Circassian (Cherkess) ethnic group, a branch of the North Paleo-Caucasian group. The term includes the Kabardinians (390,814; 1989), Cherkess (52,363; 1989), Adygei (124,826; 1989), and Abaza (33,613; 1989). The overwhelming majority lives in the Russian Federation, where they are organized in the Kabardino-Balkar Autonomous Republic, the Karachai-Cherkess Autonomous *oblast* of the Stavropol *Krai*, and the Adygei Autonomous *oblast* of the Krasnodar *Krai*. The Adygei Autonomous *oblast*, formed in 1922, occupies 1,700 square miles. Of the 124,826 Adygei in the USSR in 1989, 122,908 lived in the Russian Federation (95,492, or 76.5 percent of all Adygei, in the Adygei Autonomous *oblast*). In their Autonomous *oblast* they comprise 22 percent of the total, predominantly Russian, population. From 1959 to 1989, the Adygei have increased 56.4 percent, although this does not compare with the Kabardinians, who increased 92.4 percent.

The Adygei language belongs to the Abkhazo-Adygean group of North Caucasian languages (see: Abkhazians). Around 94.7 percent of the Adygei population regarded Adygei as their native language.

A vast Circassian national area once existed throughout the entire western Caucasus zone, constituting a federation—"The Princes of Kabarda" in the sixteenth century. For over a century (1762–1864) the Circassians resisted Russia's southerly expansion.

R. Conquest notes that "By 1860, when the whole of the rest of the Caucasus had been subdued, there were still Circassians living in complete independence as far north as the Kuban River." (*The Nation Killers*, p. 20.) By 1864, about 600,000 Circassians were expelled from their lands, most of them to the Ottoman Empire. Today there are about 25,000 Circassians in Syria, 20,000 in Jordan, 10,000 in Iraq, and several hundred in Israel.

Armenians

Armenia is a highland country wedged between the mountains of Anatolia and Turkey. Modern Armenia occupies a territory of 11,175 square miles on the northern edge of the historic Armenian homeland, an area estimated by Armenians to comprise about 100,000 square miles. Armenians first arrived in these highlands in approximately the sixth century B.C. The first Armenian state, organized by the Artaxid dynasty in the second century B.C., ruled there until A.D. 428. Under their rule Armenian became both the official and spoken language. Armenia came under Roman domination in

A.D. 55 and in A.D. 301 Christianity was adopted by King Tiridates III as the official state religion. Since the sixth century, the Armenian Church has been distinct from both the Roman and Eastern Churches. Armenians refer to their Church as the Gregorian Church, after Saint Gregory Illuminator, under whose inspiration the religion was adopted.

A later Armenian state, established in the uplands by the Bagratid dynasty in the tenth century, fell to the Seljuk Turks in the eleventh century. Another Armenian principality, Cilicia, arose in the southeast corner of Anatolia in the late tenth–early eleventh centuries. This area, known as "Lesser Armenia," had a significant Armenian population until the massacres of 1915. Cilicia was conquered in the late fourteenth century, and the Armenian uplands were partitioned between the Ottoman Turks and Persia in 1639.

Modern Armenia was formed from the Persian share of the uplands. In 1828, it was conquered by Russia. From 1894 to 1898, several hundred thousand Armenians were massacred in eastern Turkey. In 1915, during a genocidal campaign conducted by Turks and Kurds, 1,500,000 Armenians were killed.

The independent Dashnaktsutiun Republic existed briefly in eastern Armenia from 1918 to 1920. In 1920, the Armenian SSR was proclaimed as part of the Transcaucasian Federation. The federation, which joined the USSR in 1922, was dissolved in 1936, and Armenia became a separate union republic.

Armenian constitutes a separate branch of the Indo-European family of languages. Its consonant system resembles that of Georgian and other languages of the Kartvelian family. An Armenian alphabet was created in A.D. 406 on the basis of the Greek alphabet. 91.7 percent of Armenians living in the Soviet Union in 1989 considered Armenian to be their native language.

In 1989, there were 4,623,232 Armenians in the Soviet Union, of whom 66.7 percent (3,084,000) lived in the Armenian SSR. In 1989, ethnic Armenians constituted 93.3 percent of the republic's total population, up from 88 percent in 1959. There has, in fact, been a decline in the number of non-Armenians living in the Armenian SSR: whereas 70,000 Russians lived there in 1979, this dropped to 51,600 in 1989; in the same period, the Azerbaijani population dropped from 161,000 to 85,000. From 1959 to 1989, the Armenian population in Armenia increased 98.7 percent, while in the rest of the USSR it grew to 65.9 percent. Another 391,000 Armenians lived in Azerbaijan in 1989 (down from 475,000 in 1979), and 523,000 in the Russian Federation. A large Armenian diaspora of about 2,000,000 people can be found mainly in the United States, France, Iran, Lebanon, Turkey, and Syria.

Byelorussians

The national territory of the Byelorussians lies in the western part of the Eastern European plain. The modern state of Belarus occupies 80,134 square miles. Between the thirteenth and the latter half of the eighteenth century Byelorussia was at the center of a medieval empire known as the Grand Duchy of Lithuania (from 1569 in political union with the Kingdom of Poland).

Modern Byelorussians are descended from the Kryvichy, Dryhavichy, and Radzimichy, East Slavic tribes who migrated to the present area from the west and southwest ca. A.D. 6, displacing or gradually assimilating the indigenous East Baltic tribes. The political organization of the Byelorussian lands dates back to the ninth century, when a vassal of Prince Rurik was granted the principality of Polotsk. The town became a major political and cultural center and by the late eleventh-early twelfth centuries, its feudal nobility had begun a struggle for political separation from Kiev.

The Byelorussian language came into use before the thirteenth century. In the Grand Duchy of Lithuania it was the language of official business, diplomatic correspondence, literature, religious polemics, and legal proceedings from the fourteenth century until 1697. In the eighteenth and nineteenth centuries it was replaced by Polish, although in some areas it was replaced by Russian. The development of the modern language dates from the nineteenth century.

As a result of the three partitions of Poland (1772, 1793, 1795) Byelorussia was incorporated into the Russian Empire. The country adhered to the Orthodox Church until the late sixteenth century, when most of the nobility embraced Catholicism and the Polish language. The establishment of the Uniate Church (1596) accelerated the process of polonization. By the late nineteenth century about one-quarter of all Byelorussians were Catholic.

The Byelorussian SSR was established in 1919. Large territories, including the cities of Vitebsk, Moghilev, and Gomel, were ceded to it by the Russian Federation in the 1920s. As a result of the Molotov-Ribbentrop accords, considerable tracts of Polish territory (Western Byelorussia) were also incorporated into the Byelorussian SSR, nearly doubling its size. In 1964, 8.7 square miles from the Smolensk *oblast*, populated primarily by Byelorussians, were transferred to Byelorussia by the Russian Federation. According to the 1989 census there were 10,036,251 Byelorussians in the USSR. Of these, 7,905,000 (78.8 percent) lived in the Byelorussian SSR, comprising 77.9 percent of the total population (81.1 percent in 1959). Over 2.1 million Byelorussians lived in the other republics, including

1,206,000 in the Russian Federation, 440,000 in the Ukraine, 183,000 in Kazakhstan, 120,000 in Latvia, and 63,000 in Lithuania. Between 1959 and 1989, the Byelorussian population increased 26.8 percent. In 1989, 70.9 percent of the Byelorussians listed Byelorussian as their native language.

Crimean Tatars

Crimean Tatars are a Turkic-speaking Muslim people, closely related to several other Turkic-speaking peoples. The South Crimean dialect is closest to Turkish and Turkmen; the North Crimean dialect is closest to Kazakh and Kirghiz.

As a part of the Golden Horde, the Crimean Tatars conquered the Crimean Peninsula from other nomadic peoples in the thirteenth century. The independent Khanate of the Crimea, established in 1425, was under Turkish suzerainty from 1470 to 1783, when it was annexed to the Russian Empire. In the 1860s, over 230,000 Crimean Tatars emigrated from the peninsula. In September 1917, in the wake of the February Revolution, a nationalist government was established in Bakhchisarai; however Russian (Soviet) rule was reestablished by February 1918. The Crimean ASSR was established on 18 October 1921. Just before World War II, the Crimean Tatar population numbered more than 202,000, but on the night of 18–19 May 1944 this population was forcibly deported from the Crimea to the Urals, Kazakhstan, and Uzbekistan. An estimated 46 percent of the population is believed to have perished in the year and a half immediately following the deportation.

According to the 1989 census, there were 271,715 Crimean Tatars in the USSR: 47,000 in the Climea (as opposed to 200 in 1959 and 6,600 in 1979); 189,000 in Uzbekistan; 21,000 in the Russian Federation, and 7,200 in Tajikistan. Some 93 percent of the Crimean Tatars have retained their vernacular.

Estonians

The ethnic territory of the Estonian people is situated between the Gulfs of Finland, to the north, and Riga, to the south. It includes the present-day territory of the Republic of Estonia (17,400 square miles) and the Petsery district of the Pskov *Oblast* of the Russian Federation. The Finnic forefathers of the Estonians arrived in this territory some five thousand years ago. The Estonian lands were subdued and baptized (although only superficially) ca. 1220 by German knights, who later joined the Teutonic Order. From the thirteenth to sixteenth centuries, the Estonian nobility, clergy, and urban elite spoke German. In the early sixteenth century, they adopted Lutheranism and worshiped in the vernacular. In the seventeenth century, Estonia was dominated by Sweden. It was conquered by Russia in the 1710s. Paganism survived among rural Estonians until the eighteenth century, when it was effectively supplanted by Christianity. Estonia declared its independence in 1918. The country was occupied, however, in June 1940, and in August of that year it was incorporated into the USSR.

The Estonian language, a member of the Finno-Ugric family of languages, utilizes the Latin alphabet. It is the native language of 96.1 percent of Estonians.

In 1989, there were 1,026,000 Estonians in the USSR. Of them, 963,000 (93.8 percent) lived in the Estonian SSR where they constituted 61.5 percent of the population and 46,390 lived in the Russian Federation. Between 1959 and 1989 the native population of Estonia increased by 7.2 percent, while the Russian population living in Estonia increased by 97.7 percent during the same period. Over 100,000 Estonians are believed to live abroad.

Georgians

The Georgian ethnic territory is situated in the western part of the Transcaucasus. Present-day Georgia consists of 29,400 square miles. In 1943, the Russian Federation ceded 2.5 square miles of territory along the northern slopes of the Greater Caucasus to Georgia after the liquidation of several autonomous units of peoples accused of collaboration with the Nazis.

Between the twelfth and seventh centuries B.C., various Georgian tribes (self-designation: Kartveli) that had settled in the Caucasus began a process of unification. In the sixth century B.C., the kingdom of Colchis, the first Georgian state, arose in western Georgia along the Black Sea coast. In the third century B.C., the kingdom of Kartli (Iberia), founded in eastern Georgia, united the main provinces of eastern, western, and southern Georgia into a single state. In the latter half of the first century A.D., Colchis and Kartli were conquered by the Romans. Christianity was established as the official religion in eastern Georgia in A.D. 330 and in western Georgia in ca. A.D. 520.

From the sixth to ninth centuries, Georgia was overrun in succession by Persians and Arabs. Arab rule ended in the late ninth century, when King Bagrat succeeded in bringing most Georgian lands under his control. In 1080, the kingdom fell to the Seljuk Turks. King David IV "the Restorer" regained independence (1120–1127) and reunited the Georgian lands.

During the reign of Queen Tamara (1184–1213) the Georgian kingdom included apart from Georgia proper, all of Armenia; however in 1235 the country was vanquished by Genghis Khan. The country was liberated and reunited for a brief period in the fourteenth century, however, from 1386 to 1403 it suffered from eight invasions led by Tamerlane. By the end of the fifteenth century, the Georgian state had disintegrated.

In the sixteenth century, Georgia was an area of friction between Ottoman Turkey and its rival, Safavid Persia. In the mid-eighteenth century two independent Georgian states were established, but in 1782, facing an Iranian and Turkish invasion, King Irakli II petitioned Catherine II of Russia for protection. As a result, a treaty of friendship was signed in 1783 between the Russian Empire and the Kingdom of Kartli-Kakhetia and in 1801 the kingdom was annexed to the Russian Empire. Other Georgian lands were also annexed to the Russian Empire in the nineteenth century as a result of the Russo-Turkish wars.

In May 1918, a sovereign Georgian republic was established. Despite the treaty recognizing Georgia's independence, the Soviet Red Army invaded the country in February 1921 and the country was placed under communist rule. From 1922 to 1936, Georgia was a member of the Transcaucasian Federation. On 5 December 1936, the Georgian SSR was established.

The Georgian language belongs to the Ibero-Caucasian group of the Caucasian family of languages. Together with Svanian and Mingrelo-Laz, it traces its descent to ancient Kartvelian. In 1989, 98.2 percent of ethnic Georgians listed Georgian as their mother tongue.

The 1989 census listed 3,981,045 Georgians in the USSR, of whom 3,787,000 (98.2 percent) lived in the Georgian SSR. Since 1959, the Georgian population in the Georgian SSR had increased by 45.6 percent. Similarly, the proportion of ethnic Georgians in the republic had increased from 64.3 percent (1959) to 70.1 percent (1989). Only a small minority of Georgians settled outside their republic, including 131,000 in the Russian Federation and 14,000 in Azerbaijan.

Germans

The first German inhabitants of Russia were a small group of townspeople who arrived there in the early czarist period. German peasant farmers began migrating there en masse following two decrees of Catherine the Great (1761, 1762), in which she called on foreigners to settle in the empty lands from which the khans had been driven. Scattered German settlements soon sprang up throughout the Russian southeast, stretching from the Ukraine to the Urals. The greatest concentration, however, was in the steppes of the Volga region, between the present-day regions of Saratov and Volgograd. Most of these German settlers were Protestants, although a few converted to Russian Orthodoxy.

In 1916, a law against "German dominance" was enacted. The expulsion of all Germans from the Volga region was set for April 1917. In October 1918, however, the autonomous German Volga Labor Commune was proclaimed by the new Bolshevik government. In February 1924, the commune received the status of an autonomous Soviet socialist republic. In 1926, there were 1,423,000 Germans throughout the Soviet Union. 382,000 lived in the Volga-German ASSR, where they constituted 66.4 percent of the total population. Throughout August 1941, the German population was deported from the Volga-German Republic, Ukraine, the Crimea, Moscow, the Caucasus, and other areas. Only the German population located between the Dnieper and Dniester rivers was able to remain. In March 1944, German survivors of the siege of Leningrad were deported to Siberia and Kazakhstan.

Postwar censuses in the Soviet Union gave the German population of the Russian Federation as 820,000 (1959), 791,000 (1979), and 842,000 (1989). In Kazakhstan, there were 660,000, 900,000, and 958,000 respectively. According to the 1989 census, there were also 38,000 Germans in Ukraine, 40,000 in Uzbekistan, 101,000 in Kirghizia, 33,000 in Tajikistan, and 3,500 in Estonia. The total German population of the Soviet Union was 2,038,603, showing an increase of 26 percent since 1959. In contrast, the number of people who listed German as their native language declined sharply. In 1959, 75 percent of all Germans claimed German as their mother tongue. This dropped to 66.8 in 1970 and 49 percent in 1989.

Jews

Although there was a Jewish presence in Kievan Rus' most Jews were incorporated in the Russian Empire during the eighteenth century, at the time of the three partitions of Poland. In 1772, Catherine the Great issued the first decree confirming the right of the Jews to settle in, what would later become the so-called Pale of Settlement, the western, southwestern, and southern parts of the Russian Empire. Jews were forbidden to settle in rural areas and they were a highly urbanized group (83 percent in 1887 and 97.8 percent in 1970).

According to the 1897 census, there were 5,215,000 Jews in Russia. Just before World War I there were an estimated 6,000,000 Jews there. (It must be noted that from 1897 to 1926 approximately 600,000 Jews emigrated from Russia.)

In May 1934, a Jewish Autonomous *oblast* with the capital Biro-Bidzhan was proclaimed in the Far East. However, the Jewish population of the region was always rather marginal: in 1989, Jews there constituted 4.2 percent of the total population of the *oblast* and only 0.65 percent of the total Jewish population of the USSR. In fact, Jews were spread throughout the country. They could be divided into two broad categories: Ashkenazi Jews and Oriental Jews.

Ashkenazi Jews

Most Ashkenazi Jews originated in the Polish territory to which they emigrated from Germany. They spoke Yiddish, a High German dialect written in Hebrew characters, and containing elements of Hebrew, Polish, and other Slavic languages. In 1989, 11.1 percent of the Ashkenazi Jews considered Yiddish their mother tongue and this dropped to only 9 percent in the Russian SFSR

Ashkenazi Jews could be found in all republics of the former USSR; however, there was a marked decline in the Jewish population in all regions. In 1959, there were 2,178,000 Ashkenazi Jews in the USSR, but in 1989 there were only 1,378,344—a decrease of 37 percent. At present, the largest Ashkenazi communities are in the Russian Federation (537,000), Ukraine (486,000), Byelorussia (112,000), and Moldova (66,000).

Oriental Jews

These arrived in the USSR from several Asian countries and the Mediterranean basin. There are several distinct communities, including Georgian Jews, Bukharan Jews, and Mountain Jews. Georgian Jews are a Georgian-speaking, urban community. Most reside in Georgia although there are smaller communities in nearby Baku (Azerbaijan) and Daghestan. In 1959, they numbered about 40,000, and in 1989, 16,054. Bukharan Jews live predominantly in the towns of Uzbekistan, mainly Tashkent, Samarkand, and Bukhara. They speak Jewish-Tajik, an archaic dialect of contemporary Persian. In 1959, there were an estimated 39,000 Bukharan Jews; in 1989, there were 36,152. Mountain Jews live in Daghestan and Azerbaijan. They speak Tat, an Iranian language heavily influenced by Turkic, and containing elements of Hebrew and several Caucasian dialects. In 1959, they numbered 33,000, in 1989–18,513. In 1989, 65 percent of Bukharan Jews, 76 percent of Mountain Jews, and 91 percent of Georgian Jews spoke their respective vernaculars.

From 1971 to 1991, approximately 850,000 Jews have emigrated from the former Soviet Union.

Latvians

Latvia (24,600 square miles) lies on the Baltic Sea coast between Estonia and Lithuania. Baltic tribes first entered the territory sometime during the last two millennia B.C., expelling or absorbing the indigenous Finno-Ugric tribes. In the latter half of the first millennium A.D., the region was subjected to constant invasion by Vikings and Slavs. In 1201, the city of Riga was founded by the German Teutonic Order. In 1290, the German Livonian Order conquered Latvia and established the Livonian Confederation. In 1561, Lithuania-Poland conquered eastern Latvia and the Duchy of Courland was established in the west. Sweden gained control over Riga and Livonia in the seventeenth century, but in 1721, as a result of Russia's victory in the Great Northern War, the territory was annexed to the Russian Empire. With the partitions of Poland (1772, 1793, 1795) the remainder of Latvia came under Russian domination.

Latvia was an independent state from 1918 to 1940. As a result of the Molotov–Ribbentrop pact, however, Soviet forces occupied the country in June 1940 and Latvia was incorporated into the USSR.

While the population of Livonia and Courland was predominantly Lutheran, Polish held Latgale, in the east, was reconverted to Catholicism. Before World War II 68 percent of the population adhered to the Evangelical Lutheran Church and 26 percent to the Roman Catholic Church.

Latvian and Lithuanian are members of the Baltic group of Indo-European languages. It employs a Latin alphabet with a number of diacritical marks 94.8 percent of Latvians consider Latvian their native language.

In 1989, there were 1,458,986 Latvians in the USSR 95.1 percent (1,388,000) lived in the Latvian SSR, where they constituted 52 percent of the population (62 percent in 1959). The eponymous population of Latvia had increased only 6.9 percent since 1959, although the overall population of the republic had increased 27.4 percent. In 1989, there were 46,829 ethnic Latvians in the Russian Federation.

Lezghians

Lezghians are a Paleo-Caucasian people inhabiting the mountainous region of the northeastern Caucasus. They are found mainly in the river valleys of southeastern Daghestan and adjacent areas of Azerbaijan. In antiquity, the Lezghians were known by their ethnic self-designation, Legez. Most are Sunni Muslims. The Lezghian language belongs to the eastern group of North Paleo-Caucasian languages and is related to Agul, Tabasaran, Rutul,

Tsakhur, Budukh, and Dzhek. A Latin script, adopted in 1928, was replaced by a Cyrillic one in 1938.

According to the 1989 census, there were 446,006 Lezghians in the USSR. Of these, 257,270 Lezghians lived in the Russian Federation (204,370, or 11.3 percent of the total population, in the Daghestan ASSR) and 171,000 in Azerbaijan. In the period 1959–1989, the Lezghian population of the Russian Federation increased as much as 200–300 percent. During the same period, the Lezghian population of Azerbaijan increased 74 percent. 91.5 percent of all Lezghians list Lezghian as their native language.

Lithuanians

Lithuania, the largest of the three Baltic republics, occupies 25,000 square miles. Until the fourth century A.D., Baltic tribes occupied a considerable part of modern Byelorussian territory, but they were forced north and west with Slavic expansion. By the early thirteenth century, a feudal noble social order had created a loose confederation of several Baltic tribes under the leadership of five main families. In the early fourteenth century, Gediminas organized the territory into a Grand Duchy. In 1323, he founded the city of Vilnius and declared it his capital. Gediminas's sons extended the dominion over Byelorussia and most of western Ukraine. In 1385, Grand Duke Jogaila married the Polish Queen and became king of Poland, however, in the early stages of the Lithuanian–Polish union the two states remained independent, although under a common sovereign.

Catholicism became fully entrenched as the national religion in the period 1390–1420. With Catholicism came the spread of Polish influence and the gradual polonization of the Lithuanian nobility. Polish became the official language of Lithuania in 1698, although Lithuanian survived among the lower classes until its revival in the nineteenth century.

Russia occupied Lithuania in 1796, except for Klaipeda and the area west of the city, up to the Neman River, all of which was annexed by Prussia. This area, along with Lithuanian-inhabited areas around the city of Koenigsberg (controlled by Germans since the fifteenth century), was known as Lithuania Minor. All of Lithuania was occupied by Germany in 1915. In February 1918, Lithuanian independence was restored.

Polish troops occupied Vilnius in 1918. Lithuania seized German-held Klaipeda in 1923, but was forced by Hitler to return it in 1939. In 1940, the Soviet troops occupied Lithuania and incorporated it into the USSR. Vilnius, which the Soviets had taken from Poland, was restored to Lithuania.

In 1940, 94 percent of the Lithuanian people were Catholic: the remainder were predominantly Lutheran. The Lithuanian language is one of the oldest surviving Indo-European languages. It and Latvian are the only surviving members of the Baltic group of the Indo-European family. It employs the Latin alphabet with the addition of certain diacritical marks. 2,996,858 Lithuanians (97.8 percent) listed Lithuanian as their native language.

According to the 1989 census, there were 3,067,390 Lithuanians in the USSR. 2,924,000 (95.3 percent) lived in Lithuania, where they constituted 79.6 percent of the total population (79.3 percent in 1959). In Lithuania, the eponymous population increased 36 percent since 1959: in contrast, the Russian population increased by 49 percent. Another 70,427 Lithuanians lived in the Russian Federation and 35,000 in Latvia. There is also a large Lithuanian diaspora of almost 2,000,000 (1,600,000 in the United States).

Meskhetians

The Meskhetians or Meskhi, are the indigenous Sunni Muslim inhabitants of Meskhetia, in southern Georgia. They are predominantly Turkish-speaking. Their native territory lay along the Soviet–Turkish border and originally included the valleys in the vicinity of the Upper Kura River. Meskhetia was inhabited mainly by Georgians, although there were significant Kurdish, Armenian (Khemshil), and Azerbaijani (Karapapakh) communities. The Georgians, islamicized and turkicized in the seventeenth century, together with the other ethnic groups there, were the forebears of the present-day Meskhetians. The 1926 census listed 137,921 "Turks" in Georgia (the figure did not include Khemshils and Kurds). Before World War II, Meskhetians lived in the Adzhar ASSR of the Georgian SSR, in the Akhaltsikhe, Akhalkalaki, Adigeni, Aspindza, and Bogdanovka districts.

On 15 November 1944, the entire Meskhetian population was deported to Central Asia. Although they have never since appeared in official Soviet censuses as a distinct ethnic group, *samizdat* documents of the 1970s estimated a Meskhetian population of 200,000 in the USSR. According to the 1989 census, there were 106,000 Turks in Uzbekistan, 50,000 in Kazakhstan, 18,000 in Azerbaijan, and 9,890 in Russia, for a total of 207,512. Over 91 percent listed Turkish as their native language.

A series of anti-Turkish pogroms in the Fergana Valley of Uzbekistan (1989) resulted in a considerable part of the Meskhetian population fleeing to Russia and Azerbaijan.

Moldovians

Contemporary Moldova (Moldavia, 13,680 square miles) lies in the extreme southwestern corner of the former USSR, between the Dniester and Prut rivers. It consists of central Bessarabia (90 percent of the total territory), and a small district on the east bank of the Dniester River, formerly the Moldavian ASSR of the Ukrainian SSR. Once part of Ottoman Empire, Bessarabia was annexed by Russia in 1812, restored to Romania in 1918, and annexed by the USSR in 1940, as a result of the Molotov–Ribbentrop accords.

The native population of Moldova consists of ethnic Romanians who have been officially designated Moldavians. After World War II, a regional dialect of Romanian (a Romance language) was proclaimed the Moldavian language and the Latin script was replaced by a Cyrillic one. Moldavians adhere to the Romanian Orthodox Church.

In 1959, there were 2,214,000 Moldavians in the USSR. This increased by 51.4 percent (in Moldavia, 48.1 percent), to 3,352,352 in 1989. In 1989, 83.4 percent of the Moldavians (2,795,000) lived in their titular republic, where they constituted 64.5 percent of the total population. Another 325,000 lived in Ukraine, mainly in those parts of the former Moldavian ASSR transferred to the Ukrainian SSR in 1940. 173,000 Moldavians lived in the Russian Federation.

In 1989, 3,070,389 (91.6 percent) listed Moldavian as their native language. This showed a slight decline from the 95.2 percent who did so in 1959.

Russians

Together with the Ukrainians and Byelorussians, Russians are part of the East Slavic peoples that adopted Christianity in the late tenth century. The formation of the Russians as a distinct group was intimately linked with the formation of the state of Muscovy. Their original ethnic expanse also included Vladimir, Suzdal, Novogorod, Smolensk, and Riazan. It was in this territory that a centralized Russian state began developing in the fifteenth and sixteenth centuries. Originally a loose confederation of principalities, in 1480 the Russian state became a centralized state, independent of the Tatars and governed from Moscow. Ivan IV was the first czar. In 1721, Russia was declared an empire.

At the same time as the Russian state began to emerge, distinctive Russian dialects consolidated and separated from other East Slavic dialects. A literary language was based on the Middle Russian dialect of Moscow.

Russian expansion began in the sixteenth and seventeenth centuries, when settlements began appearing in the Middle and Lower Volga Basin, the Don region, the Caucasus, and in the Caspian Basin along the Ya'ik River and northern Urals. Upon the annexation of Siberia in the late sixteenth–early seventeenth centuries, that vast region also became the target of Russian colonization, and ethnic Russians soon constituted the dominant ethnic group: the process repeated itself in the Kuban Basin in the late eighteenth–early nineteenth centuries. At the same time, Russians also moved east of the Volga River and to Transcaucasia; in the latter half of the nineteenth century, Russian settlements appeared in Central Asia, Kazakhstan, and the Far East.

At present, the Russian Federation occupies 6,501,500 square miles. Its population in 1989 was 147,022,000. In fact, the ethnic Russian population has doubled since the 1897 census. This can be attributed to two factors: natural increase and the assimilation of other ethnic groups such as Ukrainians in the Kuban Basin and the northern Caucasus, Mordvins, Karels, and so on. The 1989 census listed 145,155,489 Russians in the USSR (50.8 percent of the population). Of these, 119,866,000 lived in the Russian Federation, where they constituted 81.5 percent of the total population (a slight decline from 83.3 percent in 1959). Throughout the Soviet Union, 82.4 percent of all Russians lived in the Russian Federation: another 25,300,000 could be found in the other Soviet republics, where they often constituted a significant part of the population. They were 22.1 percent of the population of Ukraine (11,356,000); 13.2 percent of the population of Byelorussia (1,342,000); 37.8 percent of the population of Kazakhstan (6,228,000); 34 percent of the population of Latvia (906,000); 30.3 percent of the population of Estonia (475,000); and 21.5 percent of the population of Kyrghizia (917,000). On the other hand, Russians constituted only 1.6 percent of the population of Armenia (73,000). Furthermore, a significant decline in the ethnic Russian population was noted there, as well as in Turkmenistan, Tajikistan, Azerbaijan, Georgia, and Uzbekistan.

Russians had one of the lowest rates of natural increase for all the major national groups of the Soviet Union. From 1959 to 1989 their population increased by 21.2 percent (22.5 percent in the Russian Federation). From 1979 to 1989, the Russian population of the Russian Federation increased by only 5.6 percent. Nevertheless, in most regions of European Russia, Russians constitute 95 percent or more of the total population.

Russians in the Russian Federation are highly urbanized (76.7 percent). Russian was listed as the mother tongue of 99.7 percent of Russians in the former Soviet Union (99.95 in the Russian Federation).

Tatar–Bashkirs

The historical homeland of the Tatar–Bashkirs stretches from the Oka-Don lowlands and the Volga uplands in the west to the Siberian slopes of the Ural Mountains in the east. In the north it extends to the Viatka-Ural uplands and in the south its boundary runs along the southern section of the Volga uplands, on the Right Bank of the Volga River, to the Caspian lowlands and the city of Astrakhan. This territory approximates that of the Khanate of Kazan (early 1400–1552). Together, the present-day Tatar and Bashkir autonomous republics occupy about one-quarter of this historic homeland (the Tatar Autonomous Republic, 26,250 square miles, the Bashkir Autonomous Republic, 55,400 square miles).

The Tatars and Bashkirs are Turkic peoples, descended from the Volga Bulgars, the Qypchaq Turks of Central Asia, who arrived in the Volga–Ural region in the thirteenth century, and various turkicized Finnish tribes. The Bulgars appeared in the region in the seventh century and established a state in the ninth century. They adopted Islam in the tenth century. In the early thirteenth century, Mongol–Tatars invaded the area and established the Golden Horde. The Turkic Qypchaqs and Bulgars became the dominant ethnic element. In the first half of the thirteenth century, the Golden Horde broke up into several units, including the khanates of Kazan, Astrakhan, and Crimea. Kazan occupied the territory of the former Bulgar state. In the fourteenth and fifteenth centuries, the Bulgars migrated further north and west, merging with local Finns and Turks. They became known as the "New Bulgars" and later as the Kazan Tatars. In 1552, the Khanate of Kazan succumbed to Russian expansion.

In 1918, the Bolsheviks issued a decree creating the Tatar–Bashkir Soviet Republic, however, due to opposition from local Russian communists, two smaller federal units were established: the Bashkir ASSR (23 March 1919), and the Tatar ASSR (25 June 1920).

According to the 1989 census, there were 6,648,760 Tatars in the Soviet Union (5,522,000 in the Russian Federation), making them the seventh largest ethnic group in the country (the second largest in the Russian Federation). Since 1959, the Tatar population had increased 33.8 percent (35.5 percent in the Russian Federation). Tatars comprised 3.5 percent of the population of the Russian Federation and 48.5 (1,765,408) percent of the population of their titular republic. Another 1,120,702 Tatars lived in the Bashkir ASSR, constituting 28.4 percent of the total population. 26.5 percent of all ethnic Tatars lived in their titular republic and 16.8 percent in the Bashkir ASSR. 83.1 percent lived in the Russian Federation, while 468,000 lived in Uzbekistan and 328,000 in Kazakhstan.

The 1989 census also listed 1,449,157 Bashkirs in the USSR, of whom 1,345,0003 (92.8 percent) lived in the Russian Federation. 863,808 (59.6 percent) lived in their titular republic, where they constituted 21.9 percent of the total population.

Both Bashkir and Tatar belong to the northwestern (Qypchaq) group of Turkic languages. The vocabulary and grammar of the two are similar although there are certain phonetic differences. Until the late 1920s, both the Tatars and the Bashkirs used the Arabic alphabet, adopted by their forebears in the ninth century. In 1927, it was replaced by the Latin alphabet and in 1939–1940, by the Cyrillic alphabet. 83.2 percent of Tatars and 72.3 percent of Bashkirs listed their eponymous languages as their mother tongues.

Ukrainians

The modern Ukrainian state occupies an area of 223,089 square miles, extending 818 miles from east to west and 555 miles from north to south. Its border extends for 4,018 miles and its coastline stretches 654 miles.

The first state to exist in the present-day Ukraine was Kievan Rus', founded in the ninth century. Christianity was adopted in the tenth century. In the eleventh century, Kievan Rus' disintegrated into several principalities, two of which, Galicia and Volhynia, survived into the fourteenth century, when they were absorbed by Poland and Lithuania respectively. In 1569, Ukrainian lands were reunited under Polish rule. In 1667, the territory was partitioned between Poland and the Czardom of Muscovy. Most of the Ukrainian lands came under Russian rule as a result of the second and third partitions of Poland in 1793 and 1795; however, Galicia was ruled by Austria from 1772 to 1918. Following the defeat of Austria in World War I, a West Ukrainian republic was declared in Galicia (1918), but this was occupied by Poland the following year, receiving the sanction of the Allied powers in 1923. Eastern Ukraine was organized as the Ukrainian SSR in 1919 and in 1922, it became a constituent republic of the USSR.

As a result of the Molotov–Ribbentrop accords of 1939, the territory of the Ukrainian SSR was expanded to include Western Ukraine (from Poland), the Bessarabian districts of Northern Bukovina and Izmail (from Romania) and Transcarpathian Ruthenia (from Czechoslovakia). The Crimean Peninsula was transferred from Russia to Ukraine in 1954.

Traditionally, Ukrainians belonged predominantly to the Orthodox Church, however by the late sixteenth century the Uniate Church made major inroads, serving as the second principal church of Ukraine. The Uniate Church was dissolved in 1946.

Ukrainian, along with Russian and Byelorussian, belongs to the eastern branch of Slavic languages. Like them, it employs a Cyrillic script. Literary Ukrainian emerged from Church Slavonic, but also incorporated linguistic forms specific to the region. Polish and Latin also influenced the development of the language, particularly in the sixteenth–eighteenth centuries. Modern Ukrainian, based on the particular peasant dialect was first used in literature in the nineteenth century. Standard literary Ukrainian has made use of a number of dialectic forms as well as elements of Church Slavonic.

According to the 1989 census, there were 44,186,006 Ukrainians in the USSR, an increase of 18.6 percent since the 1959 census. 37,419,000 (84.7 percent) live in Ukraine, where they constitute 72.7 percent of the total population (76.8 percent in 1959). Approximately 6,800,000 ethnic Ukrainians lived in the other Soviet republics: the Russian Federation (4,363,000), Kazakhatan (896,000), Moldova (600,000), Byelorussia (291,000), Uzbekistan (153,000), Kirghizia (108,000), Latvia (92,000), and so on. Ukrainians could be found in all republics of the USSR. While in Ukraine, the increase of ethnic Ukrainians during the period 1959–1989 was 16.4 percent, in the Russian Federation it reached 29.9 percent. About 80 percent of ethnic Ukrainian regard Ukrainian as their native language.

There is also a large Ukrainian diaspora. According to data from the 1970s, there were 1,000,000 Ukrainians in the United States, 700,000 in Canada, 300,000 in Poland, and over 170,000 in other countries of Eastern Europe.

Sources for Appendix

1. *Bol'shaia entsyklopediia*. St. Petersburg: Prosveshcheniie.
2. *Chislennost' i sostav naseleniia SSSR*. Moskva: Finansy i statistika, 1984.
3. *The Encyclopedia Britanica*, 15th edition. Encyclopedia Britanica Inc., William Benton, Publisher, 1967.
4. Katz, Z. (ed.). *Handbook of Major Soviet Nationalities*. New York: Free Press, 1975.
5. *Natsional'nyi sostav naseleniia RSFSR po dannym vsesoiuznoi perepisi naseleniia na 1989 god*. Moskva: Respublikanskii Informatsionno-Izdatel'skii Tsentr, 1990.
6. Shabad, T. *Geography of the USSR*. New York: Columbia University Press, 1951.
7. *Vestnik statistiiki*, 1990, nos. 3–12; 1991, nos. 1, 4–6. "Vsesoiuznaia perepis' naseleniia1989 goda."
8. *Vsesoiuznaia perepis' naseleniia 1970 goda*. Moskva: Statistika, 1976.

List of Abbreviations

AS	*Arkhiv samizdata*
ES	*Evreiskii samizdat*
LLKS	The Movement of Struggle for Lithuanian Liberation
NEP	New Economic Policy
OUN	Organization of Ukrainian Nationalists
SPSUC	Central Committee of the Communist Party of the Soviet Union
UNF	Ukrainian National Front
VSKhSON	The All-Russian Social-Christian Union for the Liberation of the People

Notes and References

Preface

1. *Sovietology, Rationality, Nationality* (New York: Columbia University Press), 1990, p. 1.
2. Here the author alludes to the famous V. Havel's essay "The Power of the Powerless." See Havel, V. et al., *The Power of the Powerless: Citizens Against the State in Central-Eastern Europe* (Armork, N.Y.: M.E. Sharp, Inc.), 1985.
3. "Intellectuals, Nationalism, and the Exit from Communism: The Case of East Germany," *Comparative Studies in Society and History*, 37 (2), 1995, p. 213.

Chapter 1   Introduction: Theoretical Perspective and Focus of Inquiry

1. Rothschild, J., *Ethnopolitics: A Conceptual Framework* (New York: Columbia University Press), 1981.
2. Ibid., p. 6.
3. Gould, J. and W. Colb (eds.), *A Dictionary of the Social Sciences* (New York: The Free Press), 1965, p. 243.
4. Szporluk, R., *Communism and Nationalism* (New York: Oxford University Press), 1988, p. 157.
5. In this respect, Szporluk quotes P. Bruke (*Popular Culture in Early Modern Europe*. New York: Harper and Row, 1978) saying that "in 1800 craftsmen and peasants usually had a regional rather than a national consciousness" (Communism and Nationalism, p. 11).
6. On this issue see also Gellner, E., *Nations and Nationalism* (Oxford: Basil Blackwell), 1983; Anderson, B., *Imagined Communities* (London: Verso), 1983.
7. Szporluk, R., *Communism and Nationalism* (New York: Oxford University Press), p. 158.
8. Smith, A., *Nationalism in the Twentieth Century* (Oxford: Robertson), 1979, pp. 11–12
9. In Coakley, J. (ed.), *The Social Origins of Nationalist Movements: The Contemporary West European Experience* (London: SAGE Publications), 1992, p. ix.
10. Kohn, H., *The Idea of Nationalism: A Study of Its Origins and Background* (New York: Macmillan), 1944, p. 10. A similar definition was given by the

author in his later book, *Nationalism: Its Meaning and History*: "Nationalism is a state of mind, in which the supreme loyalty of the individual is felt to be due to the nation state" (Princeton, New Jersey: D. Van Nostrand), 1965, p. 9.

11. Snyder, L., *The Meaning of Nationalism* (New Brunswick, New Jersey: Rutgers University Press), 1954, p. 74.

12. Kedourie, E., *Nationalism* (London: Hutchinson), 1966, p. 9.

13. Hayes, C., *Nationalism: Historical Development*, 1933; reprinted in Snyder, L. (ed.), *The Dynamics of Nationalism* (Princeton, New Jersey: D. Van Company Inc.), 1964, p. 38.

14. Since the late 1970s, the discussion on ideological meaning and intellectual capacity of nationalism has been revived. On the one hand, some prominent students of nationalism pointed to simplistic rhetoric, ordinariness of nationalist doctrines, intellectual poverty of nationalism versus its political power. See, for example, Gellner, E., *Nations and Nationalism*, p. 124; Anderson, B., *Imagined Communities*, pp. 14–15; Seton-Watson, H., *Nations and States* (Boulder, Colo.: Westview Press), 1977, p. 445. On the other hand, R. Szporluk emphasizes "the original insights of major nationalist thinkers" (*Communism and Nationalism*, p. 80) stating that on the "early stages of the rise of modern nationalities" their "intellectual history was the history of those national movements, that is, of nations in the making" (ibid., p. 157).

15. Deutsch, K., *Nationalism and Social Communication* (Cambridge: MIT Press), 1966, p. 97.

16. Ibid., p. 102.

17. See also Deutsch, K., *Nationalism and Its Alternatives* (New York: Alfred Knopf), 1969.

18. See Ernest Gellner's *Thought and Change* (London: Weidenfeld and Nicolson), 1964; *Nations and Nationalism* (Oxford: Basil Blackwell), 1983; *Culture and Identity* (Cambridge: Cambridge University Press), 1986. See also Rokkan, S., "Models and Methods in the Comparative Study of Nation-Building," *Acta Sociologica*, 12 (2), 1969; "The Growth and Structuring of Mass Politics in Western Europe: Reflections on Possible Models of Explanation," *Scandinavian Political Studies*, 1970, 5; "Nation Building: A Review of Models and Approaches," *Current Sociology*, (3) 19, 1971, Brass, P., *Ethnicity and Nationalism* (New Delhi: SAGE Publications), 1991.

19. "National Movements and Social Factors: A Theoretical Perspective," in *The Social Origins of Nationalist Movements*, p. 42.

20. Gellner, E., *Nations and Nationalism*, p. 1.

21. Ibid., p. 1.

22. See Smith, A., *Theories of Nationalism* (London: Duckworth), 1971; *A Nationalism in the Twentieth Century* (New York: New York University Press), 1979; *The Ethnic Revival* (Cambridge: Cambridge University Press), 1981; The Ethnic Origins of Nations (Oxford: Basil Blackwell), 1986. See also *Nationalist Movements* (1976), ed. A. Smith (New York: St. Martin's Press).

23. *Nationalist Movements*, p. v.

24. Ibid., p. 2.
25. See Gellner, E., *Thought and Change* (1964), *Nations and Nationalism* (1983).
26. *Nationalism in the Twentieth Century*, p. 175.
27. *Nationalism and Social Communication*, particularly p. 103.
28. Eisenstadt, S., *Modernization: Protest and Change* (Cliffs, New Jersey: Prentice Hall), 1966, p. 1.
29. Bogratta, E.F. and M.L. Bogratta (eds.), *The Encyclopedia of Sociology* (New York: Macmillan Publishing Company), 1992, vol. 3, p. 1299.
30. Khazanov, A., *After the USSR* (Madison: The University of Wisconsin Press), 1995, p. 242.
31. *The Encyclopedia of Sociology*, p. 1303.
32. Hooghe, L., "Nationalist Movements and Social Factors," in *The Social Origins of Nationalist Movements*, p. 23
33. Deutsch, *Nationalism and Social Communication*, p. 103.
34. Ibid., p. 27. On this approach, see also: van den Berghe, P., *The Ethnic Phenomenon* (New York: Praeger), 1983; Schermerhorn, R., *Comparative Ethnic Relations: A Framework for Theory and Research* (Chicago, London: University of Chicago Press), 1970; Rothschild, J., *Ethnopolitics*; Francis, E., *Interethnic Relations: An Essay in Sociological Theory* (New York: Elsevier), 1976.
35. See Deutsch, K., *Nationalism and Social Communication*; "Social Mobilization and Political Development," *American Political Science Review*, 55 (3–4), 1961.
36. See Gourevitch, P., "The Reemergence of Peripheral Nationalism: Some Comparative Speculations on the Spatial Distribution of Political Leadership and Economic Growth," *Comparative Studies in Society and History*, 21, 1979; Rokkan, S. and D. Urwin, *Economy, Identity, Territory: Politics of West European Peripheries* (London: SAGE), 1983.
37. Hooghe, L., "National Movements and Social Factors: A Theoretical Perspective," in *The Social Origins of Nationalist Movements*, p. 25. Compare also Gellner's discussion on the emergence of nationalism: "Only when a nation became a class, a visible and unequally distributed category in an otherwise mobile system, did it become politically conscious and activist" (*Nations and Nationalism*, p. 121).
38. Keating, M., "Do the Workers Really Have No Country?" in *The Social Origins of Nationalist Movements*, p. 63. See also: Hechter, M., *Internal Colonialism: The Celtic Fringe in British National Development, 1536–1966* (London: Routledge and Kegan Paul), 1975.
39. See Nielsen, F., "Flemish Movement in Belgium after World War II," *American Sociological Review*, 45 (1), 1980; "Towards a Theory of Ethnic Solidarity in Modern Societies," ibid., 50 (2), 1985; Nagel, J. and S. Olzak, "Ethnic Mobilization in Old and New States: An Extension of the Competition Model," *Social Problems*, 30, 1982.
40. Petrosimo, D., "National and Regional Movements in Italy: The Case of Sardinia," in *The Social Origins of Nationalist Movements*, p. 141. Ethnic movements in the Basque country and Catatonia in Spain and in Croatia and Slovenia

in the former Yugoslavia exemplified the development of nationalism in economically advantaged regions.

41. See Coakley, J., "The Social Origins of Nationalist Movements and Explanations of Nationalism: A Review," and Hooghe, L., "Nationalist Movements and Social Factors," both in *The Social Origins of Nationalist Movements.*

42. Smith, A., *The Ethnic Revival*, p. 29.

43. Ibid., p. 28.

44. Ibid., p. 28.

45. Ibid., p. 28.

46. Such as Brand, J., *The National Movement in Scotland* (London: Routledge and Kegan Paul), 1978; Brooks, R., *Scottish Nationalism: Relative Deprivation and Social Mobility* (Ph.D. thesis, Michigan State University), 1973; Webb, K., *The Growth of Nationalism in Scotland* (London: Penguin Books), 1978.

47. Kellas, J., "The Social Origins of Nationalism in Great Britain: The Case of Scotland," in *The Social Origins of Nationalist Movements*, p. 173.

48. *Nationalism and the State* (Manchester: Manchester University Press), 1982, p. 11.

49. Smith, A., *Nationalism in the Twentieth Century*, p. 166.

50. Here I mean the general trend and not the universal rule. Certainly, the concept of state nationalism can hardly be applied to most nationalist movements in the Ottoman, Habsburg, or Romanov Empires. Even to a lesser degree, the anti-Dreyfuss *Ligue de la Partie Francaise* can be described in terms of state nationalism.

51. Schwartzmantel, J., "Nation versus Class: Nationalism and Socialism: Theory and Practice," in *The Social Origins of Nationalist Movements*, p. 55.

52. Gellner, E., *Nations and Nationalism*, p. 1.

53. On ethnic revival, see Allardt, E., *Implications of Ethnic Revival in Modern, Industrialized Society: A Comparative Study of the Linguistic Minorities in Western Europe* (Helsinki: Societas Scientarum Finnica), 1979; Elklit, J., J. Noach and O. Tonsgaard, "A National Group as a Social System: The German Minority in North Schleswig" in Torsvik, P. (ed.), *Mobilization, Center–Periphery Structures and Nation-Building* (Bergen and Oslo: Universitetsforlaget), 1981; Elklit, J. and O. Tonsgaard, "The Policies of Majority Groups towards National Minorities in the Danish–German Border Region: Why the Differences?" *Ethnic and Racial Studies*, 6 (4), 1983; "Elements for a Structural Theory of Ethnic Segregation and Assimilation," *European Journal of Political Research*, 12 (1), 1984; Rothschild, J., *Ethnopolitics*, 1981; Tagil, S. (ed.), *Region in Upheaval: Ethnic Conflict and Political Mobilization* (Lund: Esseble Studium), 1984.

54. Hooghe, L., "Nationalist Movements and Social Factors," in *The Social Origins of Nationalist Movements*, p. 21. See also: Enloe, C., *Ethnic Conflict and Political Development: An Analytical Study* (Boston: Little Brown and Co.), 1973; Horowitz, D., *Ethnic Groups in Conflict* (Berkeley: University of California Press), 1985.

55. Coakley, J. (ed.), *The Social Origins of Nationalist Movements*, p. ix.

56. *The Ethnic Revival*, pp. 15–17.
57. Elklit, J. and O. Tonsgaard, "The Absence of Nationalist Movements: The Case of the Nordic Areas," in *The Social Origins of Nationalist Movements*, p. 85.
58. Ibid., p. 85.
59. Schwartzmantel, J., "Nation versus Class: Nationalism and Socialism in Theory and Practice," in *The Social Origins of Nationalist Movements*, p. 54.
60. *Nations and Nationalism*, p. 1.
61. Rothschild, J., *Ethnopolitics*, p. 1.
62. Golovkov, A., *Ogonek*, no. 38 (14–21 September) 1991, p. 1.
63. Goble, P., "The Rise of Ethnic Politics," *Nationalities Papers*, 17 (1), 1989, p. 56.
64. Huttenbach, H., "Sources of National Movements," *Nationalities Papers*, 18 (1), 1990, p. 49.
65. See Dunlop, J., *The New Russian Nationalism* (New York: Praeger), 1985; *The Faces of Contemporary Russian Nationalism* (Princeton, New Jersey: Princeton University Press), 1983.
66. Saunders, G. (ed.), *Samizdat: Voices of the Soviet Opposition* (New York: Monad Press), 1974, p. 44.
67. Motyl, A., *Will the Non-Russians Rebel? State, Ethnicity, and Stability in the USSR* (Ithaca, N.Y.: Cornell University Press), 1987, p. 138.
68. Carrere d'Encausse, H., *The Great Challenge* (New York and London: Holmes and Meier), 1992, p. XI.
69. For a defense of this position, see: Zilberman, D., "Ethnography in Soviet Russia," *Dialectical Anthropology*, 1976, vol. 1, pp. 135–153; Motyl, A., *Sovietology, Rationality, Nationality* and *Will the Non-Russians Rebel?* See also Gitelman, Z., "The Nationalities," in White, S., A. Pravda, and Z. Gitelman (eds.), *Developments in Soviet Politics* (London: Macmillan Education, Ltd.), 1990.
70. Lanser, V., "A Sociological Approach," in Allworth, E. (ed.), *Soviet Nationality Problems* (New York: Columbia University Press), 1971, p. 209.
71. Kolarz, W., *Russia and Her Colonies* (New York: Praeger), 1952.
72. Ibid., p. 316.
73. Ibid., p. 316.
74. Ibid., p. 316.
75. Pipes, R., *The Formation of the Soviet Union* (Cambridge, Mass.: Harvard University Press), 1964, p. 296.
76. Ibid., p. 296.
77. In Allworth, E. (ed.), *Soviet Nationality Problems* (New York: Columbia University Press), 1971, p. 72.
78. Ibid., p. 73.
79. Ibid., p. 74.
80. Ibid., p. 165.
81. See Amalrik, A., *Will the Soviet Union Survive until 1984?* (New York: Harper and Row), 1980.

82. Carrere d'Encausse, H., *The End of the Soviet Empire* (New York: Harper Collins), 1992, p. x.

83. Thus, M. Qadhaffi in his 1974 treatise, *The Third Theory* stated that "a day will come when it [the USSR] will split," as a result of "the nationalist movement." Quoted from Azrael, J., "Emergent Nationality Problems in the USSR," in Azrael, J. (ed.), *Soviet Nationality Policies and Practices* (New York: Praeger), 1978, p. 382.

84. In Glazer, N. and D. Moynihan (eds.), *Ethnicity: Theory and Experience* (Cambridge, Mass.: Harvard University Press), 1975.

85. Ibid., p. 464.

86. The English edition was published in New York: Newsweek Books, 1979.

87. Ibid., p. 274.

88. Ibid., p. 218.

89. Carrere d'Encausse, H., *Decline of an Empire*, p. 268.

90. Coakley, J., "Nationalist Movements and Society in Contemporary Western Europe," in *The Social Origins of Nationalist Movements*, p. 28.

91. See Motyl, A., *Sovietology, Rationality, Nationality*.

92. Argyle, W., "Size and Scale as Factors in the Development of Nationalist Movements," in Smith, A. (ed.), *Nationalist Movements*, p. 52.

93. *Nationalism in the Twentieth Century*, p. 47.

94. Reddaway, P., *Uncensored Russia: Protest and Dissent in the Soviet Union* (New York: Index on Censorship), 1972; "Dissent in the Soviet Union," *Problems of Communism*, 6, 1983.

95. Rubenstein, J., *Soviet Dissidents: Their Struggle for Human Rights* (Boston: Beacon Press), 1980.

96. Schatz, M., *Soviet Dissent in Historical Perspective* (Cambridge, Mass.: Press Syndicate of the University of Cambridge), 1980.

97. Alexeyevam, L., *Soviet Dissent: Contemporary Movements for National, Religious, and Human Rights* (Middleton, Conn.: Wesleyan University Press), 1985.

98. Chiama, J. and J. Soulet, *Histoire de la dissidence: Opposition et revoltes en USSR et dans les democraties populaires de la mort de Stalin a nos hours* (Paris: Seuil), 1982.

99. Lewytzkyj, B., *Die Linke Opposition in der Sowjetunion* (Hamburg: Hoffmann und Campe Verlag), 1974.

100. Bilocerkowycz, J., *Soviet Ukrainian Dissent* (Boulder, Colo.: Westview Press), 1988.

101. Farmer, K., *Ukrainian Nationalism in the Post-Stalin Era* (The Hague: Martinius Nijhoff), 1980.

102. Bilinsky, Ya., "Politics, Purge, and Dissent in the Ukraine since the Fall of Shelest," in Kamenetsky, I. (ed.), *Nationalism and Human Rights in the USSR* (Littleton, Colo.: Libraries Unlimited), 1977.

103. Nahaylo, B., "Dissent and Opposition after Shelest," in Krawchenko, B. (ed.), *Ukraine after Shelest* (Edmonton: Canadian Institute of Ukrainian Studies), 1983.

104. Remeikis, T., *Opposition to Soviet Rule in Lithuania, 1945–1980* (Chicago: Institute of Lithuanian Studies Press), 1980.

105. Forgus, S., "The Manifestation of Nationalism in the Baltic Republics," *Nationalities Papers*, 7 (2), 1979.

106. Taagepera, R., "Inclusion of the Baltic Republics in the Nordic Nuclear-Free Zone," *Journal of Baltic Studies*, 16 (1), 1985.

107. Suny, R., "Transcaucasia: Cultural Cohesion and Ethnic Revival in a Multinational Society," in Hajda, L. and M. Beissinger (eds.), *The Nationalities Factor in Soviet Politics and Society* (Boulder, Colo.: Westview), 1989.

108. Dudwick, N., "Armenia: The Nation Awakens," in Bremmer, I. and R. Taras (eds.), *Nations and Politics in the Soviet Successor States* (Cambridge, Mass.: Cambridge University Press), 1993.

109. Jones, S., "Georgia: The Failed Democratic Transition," in Bremmer, I. and R. Taras (eds.), *Nations and Politics in the Soviet Successor States.*

110. Pinkus, B. and I. Fleischhauer, *Die Deutschen in der Sowjetunion* (Baden-Baden: Nomos), 1987.

111. Allworth, E. (ed.), *Tatars of the Crimea: Their Struggle for Survival* (Durham & London: Duke University Press), 1988.

112. Wimbush, S.E. and R. Wixman, "The Meskhetian Turks," *Canadian Slavonic Papers*, 17 (2/3), 1975.

113. Pinkus, B., *Tehiyyah u-tequmah le'ummit* (Sede Boker: The Ben-Gurion Research Center, Ben-Gurion University of the Negev Press), 1993. See also Pinkus's *The Soviet Government and the Jews* (Cambridge: Cambridge University Press), 1984.

114. See *Tehiyyah u-tequmah le'ummit*, pp. 678–698.

115. Schroeter, L., *The Last Exodus* (New York: Universe books), 1974.

116. Ettinger, S., "The National Revival of Soviet Jewry," *Forum*, 23, 1975.

117. Kowalewski, D., "Protests by Soviet Jews: Some Determinants of Success," *Soviet Jewish Affairs*, 3, 1980.

118. Shindler, C., *Exit Visa: Détente, Human Rights and the Jewish Emigration Movement in the USSR* (London: Bachman and Turner), 1978.

119. Zaslavsky, V. and R. Brym, *Soviet Jewish Emigration and Soviet Nationality Policy* (New York: St. Martin's Press), 1983.

120. Salitan, L., *Politics and Nationality in Contemporary Soviet Jewish Emigration, l968–1989* (New York: St. Martin's Press), 1992.

121. Drachman, E., *Challenging the Kremlin: The Soviet Jewish Movement for Freedom, 1969–1990* (New York: Paragon House), 1992.

122. Levin, N., *The Jews in the Soviet Union since 1917: Paradox of Survival* (New York: New York University Press), 1988, pp. 638–755.

123. Goldstein, Y., "The Jewish National Movement in the Soviet Union: A Profile," in Roi, Ya. and A. Beker (eds.), *Jewish Culture and Identity in the Soviet Union* (New York: New York University Press), 1991.

124. Dunlop, J., *New Russian Revolutionaries* (Belmont: Nordland Publishing Company), 1976; *The Faces of Contemporary Russian Nationalism*

(Princeton: Princeton University Press), 1983; *The New Russian Nationalism* (New York: Praeger), 1985.

125. Yanov, A., *The Russian Challenge and the Year 2000* (Oxford: Basil Blackwell), 1987.

126. Pospelovsky, D., "Resurgence of Russian Nationalism in Samizdat," *Survey*, 19 (1), 1973; "Russian Nationalist Thought and the Jewish Question," *Soviet Jewish Affairs*, 6 (1), 1976.

127. Lacqueur, W., *The Long Road to Freedom: Russia and Glasnost* (New York: C. Scribner's), 1989; *Black Hundred: The Rise of the Extreme Right in Russia* (New York: Harper and Collins), 1993; "Russian Nationalism," *Foreign Affairs*, winter, 1992/93, p. 120.

128. Carter, S., *Russian Nationalism: Yesterday, Today, Tomorrow* (New York: St. Martin's Press), 1990.

129. Parlan, T., *The Rejection in Russia of Totalitarian Socialism and Liberal Democracy* (Helsinki: Commentationes Scientarum Socialeiem), 1993.

130. See: Azrael, J., "Emergent Nationality Problems in the USSR," and Wimbush, S.E., "The Great Russians and the Soviet State: The Dilemmas of Ethnic Dominance," both in Azrael, J. (ed.), *Soviet Nationality Policies and Practices*; Misiunas, R. and R. Taagepera, *The Baltic States: Years of Dependence, 1940–1980* (Berkeley: University of California Press), 1983; Pospelovsky, D., "Ethnocentrism, Ethnic Tensions, and Marxism-Leninism," in Allsworth, E. (ed.), *Ethnic Russia in the USSR* (New York: Pergamon Press), 1980; Sakwa, R., *Soviet Politics* (London and New York: Routledge), 1989.

131. Nahaylo, B. and V. Swoboda, *Soviet Disunion: A History of the Nationalities Problem in the USSR* (New York: The Free Press), 1990.

132. Saunders, G. (ed.), *Samizdat: Voices of the Soviet Opposition* (New York: Monad Press), 1974, p. 7.

133. Ibid., p. 9.

134. Ibid., p. 7.

135. Ibid., p. 39.

136. In Hajda, L. and M. Beissinger (eds.), *The Nationalities Factor in Soviet Politics and Society*, p. 305.

137. *Tehiyyah u-tequmah le'ummit*, p. 153.

138. The method was elaborated by the prominent sociologist, S. Kracauer, in his book, *From Caligari to Hitler: A Psychological History of the German Film* (Princeton, New Jersey: Princeton University Press,), 1947, in which he ana-lyzed popular screen motifs in order to evaluate the collective perception of the German people during the period 1918–1945. I have modified Kracauer's methods so that they suit the particular objectives of my study.

139. As follows (in alphabetical order): 1. Abkhazians, 2. Adygei, 3. Armenians, 4. Byelorussians, 5. Crimean Tatars, 6. Estonians, 7. Georgians, 8. Jews, 9. Latvians, 10. Lezghians, 11. Lithuanians, 12. Meskhetian Turks, 13. Russians, 14. Tatar-Bashkirs, 15. Ukrainians, 16. Volga Germans.

140. *Tehiyyah u-tequmah le'ummit*, p. 9.

Chapter 2 Soviet Nationality Policy: Theory and Practice

1. Dunlop, J., *The New Russian Nationalism*, pp. 3–4.
2. Bokov, Kh., "Formirovat' internatsional'nyie ubezhdeniia," *Kommunist*, no. 2, 1988.
3. Zeimal, B., "Narody i ikh iazyki pri sotsializme," *Kommunist*, no. 15, 1988.
4. Conquest, R., *Soviet Nationalities Policy in Practice* (London: The Bodley Head, Ltd.), 1967, p. 16.
5. Cited from Conquest, R., ibid.
6. Lenin, V.I., *Sochineniia* (3rd ed.), vol. 17, p. 154.
7. Ibid., vol. 26, p. 408.
8. Ibid., vol. 17, p. 439.
9. Conquest, R., *Soviet Nationalities Policy in Practice*, p. 18.
10. Ibid., p. 21.
11. *Sobraniie uzakonenii i rasporiazhenii rabochego i krest'ianskogo pravitel'stva*, no. 2, art. 18, 19 December 1917.
12. Ibid., 2nd appendix.
13. See pp. 21–49 in *Soviet Nationalities Policy in Practice* (chapter 2).
14. *Sobraniie uzakonenii i rasporiazhenii rabochego i krest'ianskogo pravitel'stva*, no. 2, art. 18, 19 December 1917.
15. *Obrazovaniie SSSR*, Sbornik dokumentov (Moscow-Leningrad: The USSR Academy of Sciences), 1948.
16. *KPSS v postanovleniiakh i resheniiakh*, vol. 1, p. 443.
17. The autonomous republics and regions within the RSFSR were also able to elect deputies to the Council of Nationalities.
18. Conquest, R., *Soviet Nationalities Policy in Practice*, pp. 50–51.
19. Article six of the 1977 Constitution and Article 126 of the 1936 Constitution indicated the guiding role of the Communist Party in the Soviet political system.
20. Khazanov, A., *Soviet Nationality Policy during Perestroika* (Falls Church, Va.: Delphic), 1991, p. 9.
21. *Pravda*, 25 May 1945.
22. Volga Germans, Crimean Tatars, Chechens, Ingushi, Kalmyks, Karachai, and Balkars. Besides them there were Meskhetian Turks, Koreans, and Kurds, who were deported without any explanation.
23. The Volga Germans were rehabilitated in 1964, and the Crimean Tatars in 1967, by decrees of the Presidium of the Supreme Soviet of the USSR. However, their autonomous regions were not restored.
24. Conquest, R., *Soviet Nationalities Policy in Practice*, p. 149.
25. Ibid., p. 149.
26. Ibid., p. 148.
27. Ibid., p. 148.
28. Emerson, R., *From Empire to Nation* (Boston: Beacon Press), 1969, p. 229.
29. Kamenetsky, I. (ed.), *Nationalism and Human Rights: Processes of Modernization in the USSR* (Littleton, Colo: Libraries Unlimited), 1977, p. 9.

30. *A Sip of Freedom* was the title of a novel by B. Okudzhava.

31. In Lithuania, mass demonstrations were reported in Vilnius (1956) and Kaunas (1960). Similarly, in 1972 a two-day riot broke out in Kaunas after the self-immolation of a Lithuanian youth, Romas Kalanta, and some acts of violence were reported. Disturbances were reported in Tartu, Estonia, in 1977, as were a series of student demonstrations in Tallinn and several other cities. A violent anti-Russian riot was reported in Riga in 1985. Large-scale demonstrations took place in Georgia in 1956, 1978, and 1981 and in Armenia in 1965. An anti-Russian riot reportedly involving some 13,000 people apparently took place in Dushanbe, the capital of Tajikistan, in 1978. Mass gatherings and other acts of protest by Ukrainians, Crimean Tatars, Meskhetian Turks, Jews, Volga Germans, Chechens and Ingushi, and Abkhazians were reported regularly from the late 1960s to the 1980s. For a competent survey of protest actions by Soviet nationalities, see: Alexeyeva, L., *Soviet Dissent: Contemporary Movements for National, Religious, and Human Rights*, 1985; Azrael, J., "Emergent Nationality Problems in the USSR," in *Soviet Nationality Policies and Practices* (pp. 376–390); Nahaylo, B. and V. Swoboda, *Soviet Disunion*. Various *samizdat* documents that appeared in the 1960s and 1970s reported a pogrom organized by the Russian inhabitants of Groznyi in the summer of 1958 against the rehabilitated Chechens, who had returned from exile. An undisclosed number of Chechens were massacred during the three-day pogrom. For an account of these events, see *Soviet Disunion* (pp. 125–126).

32. "Emergent Nationality Problems in the USSR," in *Soviet Nationality Policies and Practices*, p. 376.

33. Brezhnev, L., "Report to the Twenty-Fourth Congress of the CPSU," *Pravda*, 31 March 1971, as cited by Hajda, L. and V. Swoboda in *Soviet Disunion*, p. 173.

34. Compared to 1959, the proportion of Russians decreased by 1.2 percent, of Ukrainians by 0.9 percent, and Byelorussians by 0.1 percent.

35. From 1959 to 1970, the percentage of Central Asian nationalities in the total population of the USSR increased by 2 percent.

36. *Soviet Disunion*, p. 202.

37. "Nationalism and Reform," in Hajda, L. and M. Beissinger (eds.), *The Nationalities Factor in Soviet Politics and Society*, p. 307.

38. Carrere d'Encausse, H., *Decline of an Empire*, p. 126.

39. "Nationalism and Reforms," in *The Nationalities Factor in Soviet Politics and Society*, p. 307.

40. *Decline of an Empire*, p. 128.

41. For a detailed survey, see Carrere d'Encausse, H., ibid., pp. 125–154.

42. Diuk, N. and A. Karatnycky, *The Hidden Nations: The People Challenge the Soviet Union* (New York: W. Morrow), 1990, p. 34.

43. Carrere d'Encausse, H., *Decline of an Empire*, pp. 212–213.

44. Nahaylo, B. and V. Swoboda, *Soviet Disunion*, p. 203.

45. Gellner, E., *Nations and Nationalism*, p. 122.

46. *Implications of the Ethnic Revival in Modern, Industrialized Society: A Comparative Study of the Linguistic Minorities in Western Europe* (Helsinki: Societas Scientiarium Fennica), 1979.

47. Khazanov, A., *After the USSR* (Madison: The University of Wisconsin Press), 1995, p. 17.

48. For a qualified analysis of statements made by Soviet leaders from 1982 to 1986 concerning the "nationality question," see *Soviet Disunion*, pp. 220–237.

49. Suny, R., "Transcaucasia," in Hajda, L. and M. Beissinger (eds.), *The Nationalities Factor in Soviet Politics and Society*, p. 232.

50. *Soviet Disunion*, p. 224

51. "Determinants and Parameters of Soviet Nationality Policy," in Azrael, J. (ed.), *Soviet Nationality Policies and Practices*, p. 54.

52. Motyl, A., *Will the Non-Russians Rebel?*, 1987, p. 43.

53. "Reflections on the Nationality Problem in the Soviet Union," in Glazer, N. and D. Moynihan (eds.), *Ethnicity: Theory and Experience* (Cambridge, Mass.: Harvard University Press), 1975, p. 461.

54. "The Social Origins of Nationalism in Great Britain: The Case of Scotland," in *The Social Origins of the Nationalist Movements*.

55. Only 3 percent of Russians living in the other republics spoke a Soviet language other than Russian.

56. "Nationalism and Reform," in *The Nationalities Factor in Soviet Politics and Society*, pp. 309–310.

57. *Decline of an Empire*, p. 127.

58. "Determinants and Parameters of Soviet Nationality Policy," in Azrael, J. (ed.), *Soviet Nationality Policies and Practices*, pp. 52–53.

59. Sakwa, R., *Soviet Politics* (London and New York: Routledge), 1989, p. 301.

Chapter 3   The Modernization Process and Ethnonationalism

1. *Communism and Nationalism*, p. 94.

2. For such an approach see Z. Gitelman, "Ethnopolitics and the Future of the Former Soviet Union," in Z. Gitelman (ed.), *The Politics of Nationality and the Erosion of the USSR* (New York: St. Martin's Press), 1992, p. 4.

3. On the correlation between perceived normative standards, expectations, partial improvement, and protest behavior see A. deCarufel, "Factors Affecting the Evaluation of Improvement," *Journal of Personality and Social Psychology*, 37, 1979, pp. 847–857; "Victims' Satisfaction with Compensation," *Journal of Applied Social Psychology*, 11, 1981, pp. 445–460.

4. *Sobraniie dokumentov samizdata/Materialy samizdata, Radio Svoboda, Arkhiv samizdata* (AS) no. 527, 1970.

5. Ibid.

6. Ibid.

7. *Molodezh v russkoi istorii* (Youth in Russian History), part I; AS no. 539, 1967–1968.

8. *Molodezh v russkoi istorii*, part II, AS no. 678, 1969–1970.
9. AS no. 527, 1970.
10. Anonymous author, *Iona (Leonid) Kolchinskii: Biographical Note*, AS no. 521, 1970.
11. See Iu. Glazov, *Iz Rossiiskoi diaspory*, 1971, *Evreiskii samizdat* (ES), vol. 8.
12. AS no. 149, 1967.
13. AS no. 110, 1969.
14. Ibid.
15. I. Kandyba, *Appeal to Shelest*, AS no. 904, 1966.
16. AS no. 912, 1964.
17. AS no. 70, 1968.
18. *Letter to Podgornyi*, AS no. 1509, 1973.
19. A speech in commemoration of the Ukrainian poet V. Symonenko, AS no. 914, 1965.
20. Ibid.
21. Maksym Sahaidak was a pseudonym of Stepan Khmara, who edited nos. 7 and 8 of the *Ukrainian Herald* after the arrest of its editor, V. Chornovil, in 1972.
22. "Chastkove spivrobitnytstvo I sptytna dyplomatiia," AS no. 2076, 1974.
23. The National Unification Party (NUP), an organization promoting Armenian independence, was formed in Yerevan in 1966.
24. AS no. 3119, 1976.
25. AS no. 987, 1967.
26. AS no. 3219, 1977.
27. AS no. 5225, 1983.
28. *Na pol'zu imperii*, AS no. 4327, 1980.
29. A nameless historical essay on events in Armenia during the period 1917–1921, written in the 1960s, AS no. 1219.
30. AS no. 3219.
31. See Iahot, V., "Razmyshlevniia o prichinah vyiezda evreev v Izrail"; Voronel, A., "Sostoianiie i predposylki natsional'nogo probuzhdeniia evreev," *Evrei v SSSR*, no. 1, ES vol. 4, 1972.
32. *Khronika soprotivleniia*, AS no. 411, 1970.
33. Ibid.
34. Later, speaking as representatives of the dominant ethnic majority, both, Voronel in Israel and Moroz in the independent Ukraine expressed anti-democratic, extreme nationalistic positions.
35. AS no. 5358, 1981.
36. AS no. 3012, 1977.
37. AS no. 4570, 1981.
38. *Chronicle of the Ukrainian Catholic Church*, no. 6, AS no. 5410, 1984.
39. Ibid.
40. AS no. 4452, 1980.
41. No. 8, AS no. 5431, 1984.

42. AS no. 2896, 1977.
43. "An Appeal to the President of Israel," *Chronicle of the Ukrainian Catholic Church*, no. 3, AS no. 5373, 1984. However, there is no evidence that the Israeli authorities have ever considered Terelia's application for citizenship.
44. Ibid.
45. *Information Bulletin Number 36 by the Representatives of the Crimean Tatar People*, AS no. 637, 1969.
46. I analyzed documents from 1969 published in *Arkhiv samizdata*.
47. An *Appeal* by the Initiative Committee of the Ukraine's Communists, 1969, was addressed to "all Communists in people's democracies and capitalist states, to the leaders of the Communist and Labor parties of the world" (AS no. 912). The *Open Letter Against Russification* by Seventeen Latvian Communists appealed to Communist leaders in Romania, Yugoslavia, France, Austria, and Spain, and personally to "comrades Aragon and Garaudy in France" (Saunders, ed., *Samizdat*, p. 427). A lengthy *Appeal*, 1969, by the Crimean Tatar people was addressed to "Communist and Labor parties and people of goodwill" (AS no. 137).
48. See *Appeal by Twenty-four Jews from the Northern Caucasus* to Golda Meir, Zalman Shazar, and others, AS no. 606 (early 1970s); *Letter by Eighteen Georgian Jews to the Israeli Ambassador to the United Nations I. Tekoa*, AS no. 267 (1969); *Letter of Congratulations* by Thirty-two Soviet Jews to Israeli Prime Minister Menachem Begin, Egyptian President Anwar Sadat, and American President Jimmy Carter on the occasion of signing the peace treaty between Israel and Egypt, AS no. 3532, 1979.
49. In letters *To Members of the Bundestag*, AS no. 4484, 1981; *To Leaders of the Federal Republic of Germany and the German Democratic Republic*, AS no. 2911, 1972.
50. *Letter to the Turkish Prime Minister*, AS no. 1248, 1972; see also: M. Niyazov, *Resolution by the Temporary Organizing Committee for the Return*, AS no. 1533, 1971.
51. AS no. 5405, 1984.
52. AS no. 5901, 1986.
53. AS no. 5036, 1983.
54. AS no. 5901, 1986.
55. *Ukrainian Herald*, nos. 7–8, AS no. 2076.
56. *Letter* by G. and I. Goldshtein and E. Tvaladze, AS no. 3177, 1977.
57. AS no. 3489, 1979.
58. AS no. 1042, 1971; also published in Saunders, G. (ed.), *Samizdat: Voices of the Soviet Opposition*.
59. AS no. 4164, 1980.
60. AS no. 4884, 1981.
61. Dunlop, J., *The New Russian Revolutionaries*, p. 243.
62. Ibid., pp. 245–246.
63. Ibid., p. 246.

64. Ibid., p. 247.
65. Ibid., p. 247.
66. Ibid., p. 278.
67. Ibid., p. 288.
68. J. Dunlop cited Russian philosophers G. Fedotov and N. Berdiaev as sources of VSKhSON's political ideals.
69. AS nos. 539, 678; the essay was published in *Grani*.
70. Ibid., part I, AS no. 539.
71. Ibid.
72. Ibid.
73. Ibid.
74. Ibid.
75. Ibid.
76. Ibid.
77. Ibid.
78. Ibid.
79. Ibid.
80. Ibid., part II, AS no. 678.
81. Ibid.
82. Ibid.
83. Ibid.
84. Ibid.
85. AS no. 196, 1969.
86. AS no. 590, 1970.
87. Ibid.
88. Ibid.
89. The *Manifesto* probably intended changes brought about by the February Revolution or even by Alexander II's reforms of 1861.
90. AS no. 590.
91. Ibid.
92. AS no. 1147, 1970.
93. Ibid.
94. Ibid.
95. AS no. 1468, 1972.
96. "Ucheniie Slavianofilov—vysshyi vzlet narodnogo samosoznaniia v doleninskii period," *Veche*, nos. 1–3, 1971, AS nos. 1013, 1020, 1108.
97. Ibid., *Veche*, no. 3, AS no. 1108, 1971.
98. Ibid.
99. "K voprosu o sfinkse," AS no. 1013, 1971.
100. *Veche*, no. 3, AS no. 1108, 1971.
101. Ibid.
102. *Piat' vozrazhenii Sakharovu*, AS no. 1696, 1974.
103. Ibid.

104. *Kak nam ponimat' nashu istoriiu i k chemu v nei stremitsa*, AS no. 1801, 1974.
105. Ibid.
106. *Veche*, no. 6, AS no. 1599, 1972.
107. "Pamiati Afanasiia Sakharova," *Veche*, no. 7, AS no. 1775, 1973.
108. "K voprosu o sfinkse," AS no. 1013, 1971.
109. "Po povodu pritiazanii Iaponii na Kuril'skiie Ostrova," *Veche*, no. 8, AS no. 1665, 1973.
110. *Letter to Soviet Leaders* (London, Index on Censorship), 1974.
111. *Piat' vozrazhenii Sakharovu*, AS no. 1696, 1974.
112. Ibid.
113. "*Pis'mo k vozhdiam* Aleksandra Solzhenitsyna," AS no. 1655, 1973.
114. Ibid.
115. AS no. 3256, 1978.
116. Ibid.
117. In his book *The Faces of Contemporary Russian Nationalism*, J. Dunlop described Soldatov's program as a kind of "democratic nationalism."
118. AS no. 3256.
119. See AS no. 1655.
120. AS no. 3256.
121. Dunlop, J., *The New Russian Revolutionaries*, p. 244.
122. Ibid., p. 248.
123. Ibid., p. 247.
124. Ibid., p. 247.
125. Ibid., p. 250.
126. Ibid., p. 261.
127. AS no. 677.
128. AS no. 1147, 1970.
129. *Molodezh v russkoi istorii*, AS no. 678.
130. AS no. 527, 1970.
131. AS no. 1147.
132. See AS no. 590.
133. *Veche*, no. 3, AS no. 1108.
134. Ibid.
135. Ibid.
136. *Veche*, no. 8, AS no. 1013.
137. "Obrashcheniie k pomestnomu soboru russkoi pravoslavnoi tserkvi," *Veche*, no. 3, AS no. 1108, 1971.
138. Ibid.
139. Ibid.
140. *Veche*, no. 6, AS no. 1599.
141. AS no. 1468, 1972.
142. "Sud skorui i nepravyi," *Veche*, no. 6, AS no. 1599, 1972.
143. *Kak nam ponimat' nashu istoriiu i k chemu v nei stremitsa*, AS no. 1801, 1974.

144. Ibid.
145. Ibid.
146. *Zaiavleniie po povodu vystupleniia V Osipova protiv zhurnala Veche*, AS no. 1787, 1974.
147. AS no. 1909, 1974.
148. Ibid.
149. ES vol. 10.
150. Ibid.
151. For a detailed analysis of the almanac's ideas, see Dunlop, J., *The New Russian Nationalism*, The Washington Papers (New York: Praeger), 1985.
152. AS no. 912, 1964.
153. As no. 64, 1968.
154. Ibid.
155. AS no. 1877, 1966.
156. AS no. 1216, 1965.
157. AS no. 906, 1964.
158. Ibid.
159. AS no. 914, 1965.
160. AS no. 969, May 1968.
161. Ibid.
162. AS no. 1219.
163. AS no. 1877.
164. AS no. 1776.
165. AS no. 1042.
166. AS no. 39, 1968.
167. AS no. 691, 1970.
168. AS no. 281, 1968.
169. In his book, B. Pinkus mentioned the 1970 statutes of the Leningrad Zionist organization (the written text was not found), according to which every member must adhere to the organization's political platform and ordinances, pay membership dues, and participate in at least one of the organization's activities. Note the obvious correspondence between these statutes and the 1903 statutes of the Bolshevik party (see *Tehiyyah u-Teqummah Le'umit*, p. 260).
170. AS no. 1877.
171. AS no. 45, 1968.
172. *Statement to the Party Central Committee, the Supreme Soviet, and the Soviet of Ministers*, AS no. 39, 1968; *Statement to the Party Central Committee, the Supreme Soviet, the Soviet of Ministers, and the Procurator General*, AS no. 77, 1968.
173. AS no. 137, 1969.
174. Ibid.
175. Kashka, Z. and I. Dugu, *Appeal to the United Nations Human Rights Committee*, AS no. 491, 1969.
176. *Dopolneniia i popravki Krymsko-Tatrskogo naroda k dokladam i recham na dvadtsat' chetvertom s'yezde KPSS (Additions and Corrections Suggested by the Crimean Tatars for Speeches at the Twenty-fourth Party Congress)*, AS no. 630.

177. Ibid.
178. AS no. 1629, 1973.
179. No. 10, AS no. 1085, 1974.
180. AS no. 3085, 1977.
181. AS no. 3086, 1977.
182. AS no. 3730, 1976.
183. Skochok, P., V. Chornovil, and L. Sheremet'eva, *Letter to the Ukrainian Satirical Journal "Perets"*, AS no. 945, 1966.
184. AS no. 3313, 1977.
185. AS no. 4164.
186. AS no. 3713, 1979.
187. *Pochemu ia podzheg iego*, AS no. 3076, 1975.
188. AS no. 3381, 1975.
189. AS no. 3219, 1977.
190. AS no. 3600, 1979.
191. AS no. 5044, 1982.
192 "Chastkove spivrobitnytstvo I sptytna dyplomatiia," *Ukrains'kyi Visnyk*, nos. 7–8, AS no. 2076, 1974.
193. AS no. 425, 1969.
194. *Statement to the Supreme Soviet of the USSR*, AS no. 5296, 1983.
195. M. Agurskii, *Russkiie evrei v otsenke svoiego proshlogo i v bor'be za svobodu, natsional'noie vozrozhdeniie i druzhbu narodov*: Sbornik statei i vystuplenii, 1974, AS no. 1690.
196. Kukshar, *A Short Article*, AS no. 3085, 1977.
197. AS no. 5391, 1983.
198. AS no. 291, 1968.
199. AS no. 188, 1969.
200. AS no. 5359, 1981.
201. No. 3, ES vol. 3, 1971.
202. Ibid.
203. Ibid.
204. AS no. 1485, 1973.
205. AS no. 46, 1968.
206. AS no. 4070, 1980.
207. AS no. 5405, 1984.
208. As reported in Allworth, E. (ed.), *Nationality Group Survival in Multi-Ethnic States*, 1977, p. 182.
209. Ibid.
210. AS no. 340, 1969.
211. Ibid.
212. See AS no. 76, 1968; AS nos. 152, 189 (1969).
213. See AS nos. 114, 100 (1968).
214. AS no. 520, 1969.
215. AS no. 101, 1969.
216. In *The Chronicle of Current Events*, no. 25, AS no. 1130, 1972.

217. AS no. 1725, 1974.
218. AS no. 625, 1971.
219. *Vestnik iskhoda*, no. 2, p. 115, ES vol. 3, 1971.
220. Cited in *The Chronicle of Current Events*, no. 22, AS no. 1038, 1971.
221. "O besprintsypnosti," *Democrat*, no. 6, 1972, AS no. 1152-E.
222. *Luch svobody*, no. 5, 1972, AS no. 1175-D.
223. AS no. 2633, 1976.
224. See AS nos. 2908, 2909, 3009 (all 1977).
225. AS no. 3051, 1977.
226. AS no. 2966, 1977.
227. AS no. 3755.
228. *The Chronicle of Current Events*, no. 13, AS no. 375.
229. AS no. 3730, 1976.
230. AS no. 4570.
231. AS no. 4479.
232. AS no. 5431, 1984.
233. AS no. 1829.
234. AS no. 1724.
235. Ibid.
236. 16 Political Prisoners, *Sbornik dokumentov o deakade solidarnosti*, AS no. 3647, 1978.
237. 6 Political Prisoners, *Zaiavleniie v sviazi so vtoroi dekadoi solidarnosti*, AS no. 3724, 1979.
238. Ibid.
239. AS no. 3064, 1977.
240. AS no. 2801, 1976.
241. AS no. 2932, 1976.
242. AS no. 5453, 1984.
243. Ibid.
244. No. 7, ES vol. 10, 1974.
245. "O vrednoi funktsii slov i probleme assimiliatsii evreev," *Evrei v SSR*, no. 7, ES vol. 10 (1974).
246. *The Last Exodus* (New York: Universe Books), 1974, p. 392.
247. In the early 1950s the so-called *Lishkat-ha-Kesher* (The Bureau of Relations), was established to maintain contacts with Soviet and East European Jewry. This organization has been responsible for the formulation and implementation of the Israeli policy toward the Soviet Jewry.
248. I first heard this story in 1981 from Leningrad *refusenik* Abba Taratuta. Together with some other refuseniks, Taratuta had been warned by representatives of *Lishkat-ha-Kesher* against both publicizing Lubman's case and participating in "non-Jewish affairs."
249. Dlaboha, I., "Rozdumy nad nepravdoiu," *Shlakh peremohy*, 14.2.93, pp. 3–4.
250. Dunlop, J., *The New Russian Revolutionaries*, p. 275.

251. AS no. 678.
252. *Veche*, no. 6, AS no. 1599.
253. AS no. 1760, 1974.
254. AS no. 590.
255. AS no. 2040, 1973.
256. Ibid.
257. "*Vestnik RSKhD i russkaia intelligentsia*," AS no. 1665.
258. *Veche*, no. 4, AS no. 1140, 1972.
259. *Zemlia*, no. 2, AS no. 2060, 1974.

Chapter 4   Relative Deprivation and the Politicization of Ethnic Groups

1. Guimond, S. and L. Dubè-Simard, "Relative Deprivation Theory and the Quebec Nationalist Movement: The Cognition-Emotion Distinction and the Personal-Group Deprivation Issue," *Journal of Personality and Social Psychology*, 144 (3), 1983, p. 526.
2. *The American Soldier: Adjustment during Army Life* (Princeton, NJ: Princeton University Press), 1949.
3. See Abeles, R., "Relative Deprivation, Raising Expectations and Black Militancy," *Journal of Social Issues*, 32 (2), 1976; Berkowitz, L., "Frustrations, Comparisons and Other Sources of Emotional Arousal as Contributors to Social Unrest," *Journal of Social Issues*, 28 (1), 1972; Crosby, F., "Model of Egoistical Relative Deprivation," *Psychological Review*, 83, 1976; Davis, J., "A Formal Interpretation of the Theory of Relative Deprivation," *Sociometry*, 22, 1959; "Toward a Theory of Revolution," *American Sociological Review*, 27, 1962; Gurr, T., *Why Men Rebel* (Princeton: Princeton University Press), 1970; etc.
4. *Relative Deprivation and Social Justice: A Study of Attitudes to Social Inequality in Twentieth-Century England* (Berkeley: University of California Press), 1966.
5. Guimond, S. and L. Dubè-Simard, p. 527.
6. Guimond, S. and L. Dubè -Simard, "Relative Deprivation and Social Protest," in Olson, J., C. Herman, and M. Zanna (eds.), *Relative Deprivation and Social Comparison: The Ontario Symposium*, vol. 4 (Hillsdale, NJ: Erlbaum), 1986, p. 202.
7. AS no. 912, 1964.
8. Ibid.
9. AS no. 4525, 1981.
10. AS no. 1219.
11. AS no. 3085, 1977.
12. AS no. 4871, 1982.
13. A founding member of the Ukrainian Workers and Peasant Union established in 1959. In 1961, he was tried and sentenced to fifteen years in prison and labor camps.

14. AS no. 904, 1967.
15. AS no. 1218, 1967.
16. AS no. 1042, 1971.
17. AS no. 1214, 1963.
18. AS no. 691, 1970.
19. Ibid.
20. AS no. 1669, 1974.
21. Born in 1950; sentenced to six years in a labor camp in 1974.
22. Ibid.
23. AS no. 1805, 1974.
24. *Declaration of Principles*, signed by founding members Ventslova, Gayauskas, Lukauskaite-Poskiene, Piatkus, and Finkelshtein.
25. AS no. 2841, 1977.
26. AS no. 1042.
27. AS no. 3007, 1977.
28. AS no. 5434, 1984.
29. AS no. 4779, 1982.
30. AS no. 1877, 1966.
31. Ibid.
32. AS no. 139, 1968.
33. Ibid.
34. AS no. 45, 1968.
35. AS no. 5224, 1983.
36. AS no. 1532, 1970.
37. AS no. 4884, 1981.
38. *Politicheskii dnevnik*, no. 9, AS no. 1002, 1972.
39. AS no. 1452, 1972.
40. AS no. 1448, 1969.
41. AS no. 5224, 1983.
42. AS no. 4755, 1980.
43. Census of 1979.
44. See *Appeal by Eighty-two Soviet Jews*, AS no. 554, 1970; Feigin, G., D. Zilberg, and R. Aleksandrovich, *Petition to the Central Committee of the KPSU*, AS no. 395, 1970.
45. AS no. 4270, 1981.
46. AS no. 912, 1964.
47. AS no. 907, 1964.
48. AS no. 198, 1966.
49. Ibid.
50. AS no. 954, 1967.
51. AS no. 963, 1967.
52. AS no. 2076, 1974.
53. AS no. 3087, 1977.

54. AS no. 1805, 1974.
55. AS no. 1042.
56. Ibid.
57. AS no. 3007, 1977.
58. AS no. 5906, 1986.
59. AS no. 5905, 1986.
60. AS no. 5906, 1986.
61. AS no. 5905, 1986.
62. Maksimov, G. (ed.), *Vsesoiuznaia perepis' naseleniia 1970 goda* (Moskva: Statistika, 1976), p. 203.
63. *Chislennost' i sostav naseleniia SSSR* (Moskva: Finansy i Statistika), 1984, p. 124.
64. *Vsesoiuznai perepis' naseleniia 1970 goda*, p. 203.
65. *Chislennost' i sostav naseleniia*, p. 134.
66. AS no. 3076, 1974.
67. AS no. 1830, 1974.
68. AS no. 214.
69. AS no. 218.
70. AS no. 4644, 1981.
71. AS no. 4636, 1978.
72. AS no. 4183, 1980.
73. AS no. 4184, 1980.
74. AS no. 2831, 1976.
75. AS no. 308, 1967.
76. AS no. 309, 1968.
77. AS no. 316, 1968.
78. AS no. 91, 1967.
79. AS no. 630, 1971.
80. AS no. 3170, 1977.
81. AS no. 1534, 1971.
82. Sixty-five families in 1960; 10 in 1964; 130 in 1965; and 500 in 1969.
83. Vukkert, K., *Some Thoughts on the State of the Germans, Citizens of the USSR*, AS no. 2811, 1976.
84. AS no. 1877.
85. AS no. 1532.
86. AS no. 2811.
87. See Ruppel, "An Appeal to Chairman of the Presidium of the Supreme Soviet, N. Podgornyi" (1971), "The Soviet Germans" (1974). Both in *Re-Patria*, AS no. 1776.
88. AS no. 64, 1968.
89. AS no. 404, 1970.
90. *Iton Alef* (May 1970), ES vol. 1.
91. AS no. 1877.
92. AS no. 91.

93. *Re-Patria*, AS no. 1776.
94. Ibid.
95. AS no. 335, 1969.
96. *An account of the trial*, AS no. 511, 1970.
97. AS no. 64.
98. AS no. 4270.
99. AS no. 5646, 1985.
100. AS no. 4270.
101. Masiutko, M., *Letter to the Supreme Soviet of the Ukrainian SSR*, AS no. 950, 1967.
102. See Kandyba, I., M. Horyn', and L. Luk'ianenko, *Appeal to the Human Rights Commission of the United Nations*, AS no. 261, 1969; *Letter by Friends and Members of Families of Jewish Prisoners of the Labor Camp in Potma* (Mordovia), ES vol. 3, 1971.
103. AS no. 963.
104. AS no. 3724, 1979.
105. The final plea at the trial, AS no. 5391, 1983.
106. M. Sahaidak, "Ethnocide of the Ukrainians in the USSR," AS no. 2076, 1974.
107. AS no. 974, 1968.
108. AS no. 904.
109. AS no. 2076.
110. AS no. 3314, 1975.
111. AS no. 3087.
112. AS no. 3086, 1977.
113. AS no. 5906.
114. *Letter to the UN Secretary General*, AS no. 4755.
115. AS no. 1214.
116. AS no. 4636.
117. AS no. 4183.
118. AS no. 1532.
119. AS no. 1877.
120. AS no. 1431, 1972.
121. *Zemlia* (no. 1, 1974), AS no. 1909.
122. AS no. 340, 1969.
123. AS no. 1042.
124. "Moreover, in July 1989, a group of Crimean Tatars protested against shooting film in the territory of Bakhchisaray Palace [Crimea] since they felt that this might threaten their unique historical environmental heritage" (Zisserman, D., *Environment Policy Review: Soviet Union and Eastern Europe*, 4 (3), 1990, p. 19). At that time the overwhelming majority of the Crimean Tatars population lived outside of Crimea.
125. AS no. 3085.
126. AS no. 1830.

127. AS no. 5822, 1986.
128. Ibid.
129. AS no. 198.
130. In 1979, in the Ulyanovsk *oblast* Tatars constituted 10.6 percent of the total population; in the Orenburg *oblast*, they constituted only about 7.2 percent of the population. In these two areas Russians constituted 75 and 72 percent of the population respectively.
131. M. Sahaidak, "Ethnocide of the Ukrainians in the USSR," AS no. 2076.
132. AS no. 1216, 1965.
133. *Commentary on a Letter by S. Khanzadian*, AS no. 3161, 1977.
134. AS no. 1830.
135. AS no. 4180, 1980.
136. AS no. 909, 1964.
137. AS no. 3220, 1977.
138. AS no. 2076.
139. A. Temkin, "Kto ia i chto ia?" ("Who Am I, and What Am I?"), *Evrei v SSSR*, no. 2, ES vol. 4, 1972.
140. AS no. 3120, 1977.
141. AS no. 3730, 1976.
142. No. 7, 1969, AS no. 196.
143. AS no. 3278, 1978.
144. AS no. 901. Ryl'sky's responses contained nothing but commonplace platitudes.
145. Ibid.
146. An analysis of the text seems to indicate that Lobko was one of or possibly the sole author of this leaflet.
147. AS no. 909.
148. AS no. 916, 1965.
149. AS no. 974, 1968.
150. AS no. 945, 1966. The letter was addressed to the Ukrainian satiric magazine, *Perets*.
151. AS no. 1147, 1971.
152. "Ethnocide of the Ukrainians in the USSR," AS no. 2076.
153. *Chislennost' i sostav naseleniia SSSR*, 1984.
154. Basic data in G. Maksimov (ed.), *Vsesoiuznaia perepis' naseleniia 1970 goda* (Moskva: Statistika, 1976).
155. AS no. 1042.
156. Ibid.
157. AS no. 5391.
158. Letter to Pope John Paul II, AS no. 5905, 1986.
159. AS no. 5391.
160. AS no. 3085.
161. AS no. 5391.
162. AS no. 1878, 1971.

163. Ibid.
164. AS no. 3076.
165. AS no. 4646, 1981.
166. M. Gamkharashvili and A. Otarashvili, *Letter*, AS no. 4636.
167. *The Review of Relations Between Moscow and Georgia Before and After 1917*, AS no. 1830.
168. AS no. 4184.
169. Ibid.
170. Ibid.
171. AS no. 4644.
172. AS no. 3085.
173. AS no. 3087.
174. Ibid.
175. AS no. 3086.
176. *Letter to the Procurator of the Ukrainian SSR*, AS no. 915, 1965.
177. AS no. 3086.
178. Unpublished manuscript, 1977.
179. The Crimean Tatars and Meskhetians were not included in the list of nationalities of the USSR.
180. Data in *Vsesoiuznaia perepis' naseleniia 1970 goda* (Moskva: Statistzka, 1976).
181. AS no. 1877.
182. AS no. 1185, 1972.
183. AS no. 3108, 1977.
184. AS no. 1534.
185. *Re-Patria*, AS no. 1776.
186. Ibid.
187. Ibid.
188. AS no. 395.
189. *Evrei v SSSR*, no. 4, 1973, ES vol. 6.
190. See P. Abramovich, *Letter to the Head of the Pervomaiskii Financial Department* (1977), AS no. 310; I. Begun, *Letter to the International Association of the Russian Language and Literature Teachers* (1977), AS no. 3275; etc.
191. AS no. 4270.
192. AS no. 987, 1967.
193. Ibid.
194. AS no. 954.
195. AS no. 1628, 1973.
196. Ibid.
197. AS no. 4167, 1980.
198. *Conspiracy of Silence*, AS no. 5427, 1983.
199. AS no. 2811.
200. AS no. 4270.
201. AS no. 3007.

202. AS no. 3161.
203. AS no. 1830.
204. AS no. 2510, 1976.
205. AS no. 4183.
206. AS no. 3161.
207. AS no. 4183.
208. *Additions and Corrections Suggested by the Crimean Tatars for Speeches at the Twenty-fourth Party Congress*, AS no. 630.
209. Ibid.
210. Ibid.
211. See *Letter by Twenty-nine Jews to the Central Committee of the Communist Party*, AS no. 4545; *Letter to L. Brezhnev*, signed by eighty Jewish activists, AS no. 4546 (both 1981).
212. AS no. 974.
213. AS no 3085.
214. AS no. 64.
215. AS no. 934, 1966.
216. Ibid.
217. Ibid.
218. AS no. 5759, 1986.
219. AS no. 2076.
220. *Concerning Debates in the Western Press on the State of the Georgian Church*, AS no. 2581, 1976.
221. *The Jewish Question in the USSR*, AS no. 404.
222. Christopher Doersam, "Sovietization, Culture, and Religion," in Allworth, E. (ed.), *Nationality Group Survival in Multi-Ethnic States*, p. 180.
223. AS no. 1091 (December 1971–January 1972).
224. *The Review of Relations Between Moscow and Georgia Before and After 1917*, AS no. 1830.
225. AS no. 3085.
226. AS no. 280, 1968.
227. Ibid.
228. Ibid.
229. Ibid.
230. AS no. 590, 1970.
231. Bilinsky, Ya., "Russian Dissenters and the Nationality Question," in I. Kamentsky (ed.), *Nationalism and Human Rights: Processes of Modernization in the USSR* (Littleton, Colo.: Libraries Unlimited, 1977).
232. Ibid., p. 85
233. AS no. 590.
234. Ibid.
235. Ibid.
236. Ibid.

237. AS no. 1140.

238. AS no. 775 (19 January 1973). The essay was written in response to the famous article by A. Iakovlev entitled "Against the Anti-historical Approach," published in *Literaturnaia Gazeta*, 15 November 1972.

239. *Veche*, no. 9, 1973, AS no. 2040.

240. D. Pospelovsky, "The Resurgence of Russian Nationalism in *Samizdat*," in *Survey* 19 (1), Winter 1973.

241. *Veche*, no. 9, 1973, AS no. 2040.

242. Ibid., "Response to Krasnov."

243. *Veche*, no. 1, AS no. 1013, 1971.

244. AS no. 1803, 1973.

245. Ibid.

246. AS no. 1013.

247. AS no. 4887.

248. Ibid.

249. A. Solzhenitsyn, *Letter to Soviet Leaders* (London: Index on Censorship), 1974.

250. A. Skuratov, "Po povodu polemiki mezhdu Sakharovym i Solzhenitsynym," in Agurskii, M. (ed.), *Chto zhdet Sovietskii Soiuz*, AS no. 2450, 1972.

251. V. Osipov, *The Last Day of Moscow*, AS no. 1803.

252. AS no. 1013.

253. He meant architects I. Rerberg, who built the Presidium of the Supreme Soviet in the 1930s, and K. Ton, the nineteenth-century architect of the Great Palace of the Kremlin.

254. AS no. 1665, 1973.

255. Mikhail Antonov, an architect and member of the so-called Fetisov group, the first known fascist organization in the USSR, was arrested in 1968, declared criminally insane and sent to the Special Psychiatric Hospital in Kazan, in which he has been interned for three years. He is currently a popular contributor to the Russian Communist and nationalist press.

256. Antonov, M., "Uchenie slavianoifilov—vysshyi vzlet narodnogo samosoznaniia Rossii v doleninskii period," *Veche* (nos. 1–3), AS nos. 1013, 1020, 1108.

257. AS no. 2040.

258. See "Bor'ba s tak nazyvaiemym russofil'stvom, ili put' gosudarstvennogo samoubiistva" (*Veche*, no. 7, 1973); "Otvet L'vu Andreevu" (*Veche*, no. 8, 1973); "Survey o russkom natsionalizme" (*Veche*, no. 9, 1973). See also Osipov, V., *Piat' vozrazhenii Sakharovu* (1974), AS no. 1696; Skuratov, A., "Po povodu polemiki mezhdu Sakharovym i Solzhenitsynym" (1974), AS no. 2450 (both dealt with Solzhenitsyn's *Letter to Soviet Leaders* and Sakharov's objections to Solzhenitsyn).

259. AS no. 1020 (citation from Ya. Bilinsky's article in *Nationalism and Human Rights*, pp. 84–85).

260. Osipov, V., *Piat' vozrazhenii Sakharovu*, AS no. 1696.

261. Ibid.

262. Iu. Osmanov, *Letter to Brezhnev*, AS no. 91, 1967.

263. AS no. 5943, 1984.
264. Authorship is attributed to B. Kochubievskii, AS no. 334, 1968.
265. AS no. 1610, 1973.
266. AS no. 950.
267. *Sredi snegov*, AS no. 596, 1970.
268. AS no. 1041, 1970.
269. Romaniuk, V. and O. Tyhyi, *Letter by Ukrainian Political Prisoners*, AS no. 3219, 1977.
270. The final plea, AS no. 1805.
271. AS no. 4779.
272. *Appeal to the World Public*, AS no. 45.
273. *Krymsko-Tatarskii narod osuzhdaet "Otzyv" Vahabova*, AS no. 1448, 1969.
274. See *Appeal to the Twenty-third Party Congress*, AS no. 1879, 1966; *Appeal to the Belgrade Conference on European Security*, AS no. 3170, 1977.
275. See I. Aharon, "Issledovaniia demograficheskih osobennostei evreiskogo naseleniia v Sovetskom Soiuze," in *Belaia kniga o simpoziume* (kniga vtoraia), 1976 (Evreiskii samizdat, vol. 15); Latvian Group Helsinki-86, *Appeal to the United Nations* (AS no. 5906, 1986).
276. AS no. 2040.
277. "Bor'ba s tak nazyvaiemym russofil'stvom...," AS no. 1775.
278. According to data cited by W. Kingkade (*USSR Estimates and Projections of the Population by Major Nationaliy*, 1979–2050, Center for International Research, U.S. Bureau of the Census, CIR Staff Paper no. 41, May 1988, p. 34) the Russian population during the period 1979–1985 increased by 3.6 percent; at the same time the total Slavic population rose by 3.3 percent, and other European nationalities, by 3.2 percent. The total increase during this period comprised 5.5 percent, due to the rapid increase in the population of the Central Asian nationalities.
279. "Po povodu polemiki mezhdu Sakharovym i Solzhenitsynym...," AS no. 2450.
280. Ibid.
281. AS no. 1787, 1974.
282. AS no. 901.
283. AS no. 4686, 1981.
284. AS no. 1830.
285. AS no. 1189, 1972.
286. AS no. 5842, 1986.
287. "Appeal to the Chairman of the Presidium of the Supreme Soviet of the USSR, N. Podgornyi," *Re-Patria*, AS no. 1776.
288. AS no. 335.
289. AS no. 4270.
290. AS no. 4755.
291. See Guimond, S. and L. Dubè-Simard, "Relative Deprivation Theory and the Quebec Nationalist Movement," *Journal of Personality and Social Psychology*, 144 (3), 1983; Vanneman, R. and T. Pettigrew, "Race and Relative Deprivation

in the Urban United States," *Race,* 13, 1972; Kinder, D. and D. Sears, "Prejudice and Politics: Symbolic Racism versus Racial Threats to the Good Life," *Journal of Personality and Social Psychology*, 40, 1981.

292. Guimond, S. and L. Dubè-Simard, ibid., p. 526.
293. See Festinger, L., "A Theory of Social Comparison," *Human Relations*, 7, 1954; Olson, J. and J. Hazlewood, "Relative Deprivation and Social Comparison: An Integrative Perspective," in *Relative Deprivation and Social Comparison: The Ontario Symposium.*
294. Olson, J. and J. Hazlewood, ibid., p. 6.
295. See Albert, S., "Temporal Comparison Theory," *Psychological Review*, 84, 1977, pp. 485–503.
296. deCarufel, A., "Factors Affecting the Evaluation of Improvement: The Role of Normative Standards and Allocator Resources," *Journal of Personality and Social Psychology*, 37, 1979, p. 856.
297. Ibid., pp. 847–857.
298. Ibid., p. 956.
299. *The Ethnic Revival*, p. 28.

Chapter 5   Ethnic Organizations, Programs, and Demands

1. AS no. 3219 (written after October 1977).
2. In Dunlop, J., *The New Russian Revolutionaries*, pp. 243–293.
3. AS no. 1878, 1971.
4. Dr. Galina Starovoitova, ethnographer, who served in 1991–1992 as an advisor to President Yeltsin on the nationality policy told that a few days before the meeting in Belovezhskaia Pushcha Yeltsin had asked her one question: How is Ukraine expected to vote if a referendum on independence takes place? Starovoitova answered that according to her estimation Ukraine would vote for secession. Then, Yeltsin ordered to prepare the documents on annulment of the Union Treaty (Starovoitova's oration at the conference *Soviet Society in Turmoil*, January 1992, Hebrew University, Jerusalem). Certainly, there are distinct accounts made by the "first-hand witnesses" on the decision-making process in this particular case. Anyway, the suggestion that the prospect of having Ukraine unilaterally seceded from the USSR has played an important role in the decision to disband the Soviet Union seems highly plausible.
5. The story of the Union was told in 1967 by Ivan Kandyba, then a political prisoner in the Mordovian labor camp, in his *Appeal*, addressed to the Ukrainian Communist leader, P. Shelest, AS no. 904.
6. Ibid.
7. Ibid.
8. Ibid.
9. AS no. 908, 1964.
10. AS no. 198, 1966.

11. AS no. 112 (December 1968).
12. AS no. 911. *Z pryvodu protsesu nad Pohruzhal'skym* (an anonymous letter), 1967.
13. *Complaint by 64 Citizens about the Conduct of Militiamen at a Meeting in Commemoration of T. G. Shevchenko*, addressed to L. Brezhnev, P. Shelest, and I. Golovchenko, AS no. 961, 1967.
14. On this issue see *Natsional'naia politika Rossii: istoriia I sovremennost'* (Moskva: Russkii mir), 1997, pp. 58–61.
15. AS no. 198.
16. Ibid.
17. Ibid.
18. AS no. 265, 1969.
19. AS no. 987, 1967.
20. AS no. 904, 1967.
21. Ibid.
22. AS no. 976, 1968.
23. The Organization of Ukrainian Nationalists (OUN), established in the Western Ukraine in 1929, championed the idea of an independent, authoritarian Ukrainian regime. By the late 1930s, the organization split into the extremist Bandera wing and the more moderate Melnyk wing.
24. Ibid.
25. Ibid.
26. In this document, Krasyvs'ky's name is given as Ivan. According to *The Chronicle of Current Events* (no. 17) his name is given as Zynovii.
27. AS no. 555. The same *Chronicle*'s issue mentioned that D. Kvets'ko was a historian, Z. Krasyvs'ky was a writer, and M. D'iak, a lieutenant in the militia.
28. AS no. 4233, 1980.
29. Ibid.
30. According to the report there were two issues of the almanac.
31. Wilson, A., *Ukrainian Nationalism in the 1990s: A Minority Faith* (Cambridge: Cambridge University Press), 1977, p. 55.
32. Kuzio, T. and A. Wilson, *Ukraine: Perestroika to Independence* (London: Macmillan), 1994, p. 230.
33. AS no. 2076, 1974.
34. AS no. 3219.
35. Ibid.
36. As cited by Bilinsky, Ya., in Kamenetsky, I. (ed.), *Nationalism and Human Rights*, p. 178.
37. AS no. 4164, 1980.
38. AS no. 5372, 1984.
39. Ibid.
40. Ibid.
41. Ibid.
42. AS no. 904.

43. AS no. 1214, 1963.
44. AS no. 1216, 1965.
45. Nora Dudwick, "Armenia: The Nation Awakes," in Bremmer, I. and R. Taras (eds.), *Nation and Politics in the Soviet Successor States* (Cambridge: Cambridge University Press), 1993, p. 272. Nora Dudwick described the first massive demonstration of Armenians with references to books by R. Suny, *Armenia in the Twentieth Century* (Chico, California: Scholars Press), 1983; and A. Alexeyeva, *Soviet Dissent.* Anatoly Khazanov commented that according to his Armenian informants, witnesses of the event, the militiamen apprehending possible casualties did not interfere in the procession. They merely attempted to block an entrance of demonstrators into the territory of governmental sites (personal communication with A. Khazanov).
46. AS no. 1217, 1965.
47. Ibid.
48. Ibid.
49. Ibid.
50. AS no. 1216.
51. The Union of Armenian Patriots mentioned in N. Dudwick's article appeared in 1956 in Yerevan State University. The Union of Armenian Youth was established in 1963.
52. AS no. 3119, 1976.
53. An article by Suny, R., "Transcaucasia: Cultural Cohesion and Ethnic Revival in a Multinational Society," in *The Nationalities Factor in Soviet Politics and Society* named Stepan Zotikian as the party's founder.
54. Ibid.
55. AS no. 3077, 1974.
56. AS no. 3119.
57. Ibid.
58. AS no. 3059, 1977.
59. AS no. 3060, 1977.
60. See *Report on the Persecution of Rtskhiladze*, AS no. 3116, 1977.
61. AS no. 4639, 1981.
62. AS no. 4636, 1978.
63. Ibid.
64. Ibid.
65. See also *Report on Georgian Unrest in March–April 1981*, AS no. 4415 (1981); *Appeal to Leonid Brezhnev* by Georgians of the Kakh, Zakataly, and Belokany *rayons* of the Azerbaijan SSR, AS no. 4183 (1980).
66. AS no. 1830, 1974.
67. AS no. 4871, 1982
68. Ibid.
69. Ibid.
70. Ibid.

71. Ibid.
72. AS no. 4167, 1980.
73. AS no. 4415, 1981.
74. Ibid.
75. *Claims of the Georgian People to Brezhnev and Shevardnadze*, AS no. 4639 (between 20 April 1981 and 18 May 1981).
76. Ibid.
77. See *Report on a Demonstration of Azerbaijanis in Marneuli in February 1983*, AS no. 5235.
78. AS no. 5225, 1983.
79. Ibid.
80. AS no. 5233, 1983.
81. As cited in AS no. 5233.
82. Ibid.
83. See AS no. 4415, AS no. 4639. See also *Letter by Georgian Writer Revaz Dzhaparidze to E. Shevardnadze on the Situation in Abkhazia*, AS no. 4638 (28 May 1979).
84. AS no. 4755, 1980.
85. Ibid.
86. Ibid.
87. My private archives.
88. Ibid.
89. Kukshar, *Short Article on the Suppression of the Tatar–Bashkirs*, AS no. 3085, 1977.
90. Ibid.
91. Ibid.
92. AS no. 3086, 1977.
93. Ibid.
94. AS no. 333, 1969.
95. AS no. 1155, 1972.
96. Ibid.
97. *The Chronicle*, no. 20, AS no. 675 (July 1971).
98. AS no. 70, 1979.
99. Extracts from the program were published in Russian in *The Chronicle*, no. 25, 5 July 1972; AS no. 1130. The full text was carried in *Esti Democrat*, no. 1, May 1972. This *samizdat* journal was jointly published by the Estonian National Front and the Estonian Democratic Movement, another underground dissident group.
100. As reported in Allworth, E. (ed.), *Nationality Group Survival in Multi-Ethnic States* (notes to: Ch. Doersam, "Sovietization, Culture, and Religion"), p. 187.
101. AS no. 1805-A.
102. Ibid.
103. The *Memorandum* was written December 1971–January 1972, AS no. 1091.

104. AS no. 1628, 1973.
105. As reported in Allworth, E. (ed.), *Nationality Group Survival*, pp. 165, 187.
106. AS no. 3755, 1979.
107. Ibid.
108. AS no. 4570, 1981.
109. AS no. 4779, 1982.
110. Ibid.
111. AS no. 5903, July 1986.
112. Ibid.
113. AS no. 5904, July 1986.
114. Ibid.
115. AS no. 5906, July 1986.
116. Ibid.
117. In Kamenetsky, I. (ed.), *Nationalism and Human Rights*, p. 228.
118. AS no. 1877, 1966.
119. AS no. 379, 1969.
120. AS no. 45, 1968.
121. AS no. 1884, 1973.
122. AS no. 39, 1968.
123. AS no. 1884.
124. Two members of this group were arrested and tried; dozens were expelled from the Komsomol and universities. AS no. 281, 1968.
125. AS no. 46, 1968.
126. Ibid.
127. AS no. 45.
128. AS no. 1884.
129. See: Asanov, S., *Information no. 70* on the work of the representatives of the Crimean Tatars in Moscow during the period 9–17 January 1979, AS no. 3527; *Information no. 15* on the work of the representatives of the Crimean Tatars in Moscow during the period 16–27 April 1983, AS no. 5224.
130. Reported in the *Appeal by the Crimean Tatar People to Communist and Workers Parties*, AS no. 137, July 1969.
131. AS no. 77, 1968.
132. AS no. 187, 1969.
133. AS no. 314, 1968.
134. Sarametov, K.A., *Petition to the Interior Minister and KGB of the USSR*, AS no. 320, 1968.
135. As reported in Asanov, S., *Information no. 70*, AS no. 3527, 1979.
136. AS no. 3528, 1977.
137. AS no. 3170, 1977.
138. Ibid.
139. AS no. 5310, 1984.
140. Ibid.

141. As reported in *Re-Patria*, A Collection of Material Devoted to the History, Culture, and Problems of the Soviet Germans, AS no. 1776, January 1974.
142. The text of the statement is reproduced in *Re-Patria*, ibid.
143. Ibid.
144. Ibid.
145. Ibid.
146. Ibid.
147. Ibid.
148. Reddaway, P., *Uncensored Russia*, p. 279.
149. *Re-Patria*, AS no. 1776.
150. AS no. 2811, 1976.
151. Ibid.
152. AS no. 4884, 1981.
153. AS no. 4487, 1981.
154. AS no. 5289, 1984.
155. AS no. 196 (translation from Reddaway, P., *Uncensored Russia*, p. 271).
156. Reddaway, P., ibid., p. 271.
157. Ibid., p. 272.
158. Ibid., p. 273.
159. Ibid., p. 276.
160. Ibid., p. 279.
161. Ibid., p. 270.
162. Ibid., p. 278.
163. Ibid., p. 279.
164. AS no. 1248, 1972.
165. Ibid.
166. Ibid.
167. AS no. 674, 1971.
168. AS no. 1248.
169. Ibid.
170. AS no. 2952, 1977.
171. Kh. Umarov-Gozalishvili, and others, AS no. 3001, 1977.
172. AS no. 6056, 1982.
173. AS no. 64, 1968.
174. ES vol. 1, *Iton Alef*, 1970.
175. Ibid., p. 85.
176. AS no. 322, 1969.
177. As reported in ES vol. 3, 1971, p. 14.
178. Ibid., pp. 118–121.
179. Ibid., p. 124.
180. AS no. 431, 1970.
181. *Uncensored Russia*, p. 317.
182. AS no. 64.

183. AS no. 430, 1970.
184. AS no. 322, 1969.
185. AS no. 595, 1970.
186. AS no. 1405, 1972.
187. AS no. 595.
188. The concept of national cultural autonomy is developed by Otto Bauer in his work "The Nationality Question and Social Democracy."
189. AS no. 1405.
190. "Sotsial'nyie predposylki natsional'nogo probuzhdeniia evreev," *Evrei v SSSR*, no. 1, 1972; ES vol. 4.
191. AS no. 334, 1968.
192. ES vol. 8, 1968–1975.
193. AS no. 404, 1970.
194. *Evrei v SSSR*, no. 9, ES vol. 11, 1974–1975.
195. Ibid.
196. Reprinted in ES vol. 15, 1977.
197. Lerner, A., "Emigratsiia ili tsivilizatsiia? Chto vazhneie?" (ES vol. 15).
198. Zubin, M., "Nekotoryie perspektivy evreiskoi natsional'noi kul'tury v SSSR" (ES vol. 15).
199. Ibid.
200. Ibid.
201. Fain, V., V. Prestin et al., "The Nearest Stage of Revival" (ES vol. 15).
202. "Nekotoryie perspektivy evreiskoi natsional'noi kul'tury v SSSR" (ES vol. 15).
203. "Emigratsiia ili tsivilizatsiia? Chto vazhneie?" (ES vol. 15).
204. AS no. 3038, September 1977.
205. AS no. 4664, 1982.
206. Ibid.
207. AS no. 5273, 1984.
208. AS no. 5569, 1985.
209. AS no. 5646, February 1986.
210. Belmont: Nordland Publishing Company, p. 13.
211. Ibid.
212. Ibid., p. 293.
213. Ibid., p. 247.
214. Ibid., p. 280.
215. Ibid.
216. Ibid., p. 281.
217. Ibid., p. 283.
218. Ibid., p. 284.
219. Ibid., p. 278.
220. Ibid., p. 280.
221. AS no. 280.
222. Ibid.

223. AS no. 340, 1969.
224. Ibid.
225. Ibid.
226 AS no. 590, 1970.
227. Ibid.
228. *Statement* by *Veche*'s editorial staff in connection with the Radio Liberty report on the first issue of *Veche*, AS no. 586, March 1971.
229. Ibid.
230. *Veche*, no. 6, AS no. 1599, 28 April 1972.
231. Ibid.
232. Ibid.
233. "Protiv antiistorizma," *Literatumaia gazeta*, 15 November 1972.
234. "Bor'ba s tak nazyvaiemym Rusofil'stvom ili put' gosudarstvennogo samoubistva," *Veche*, no. 7, AS no. 1775, 1973.
235. Ibid.
236. AS no. 1600. English translation by Ya. Bilinsky in *Sunday Times*, 3 March 1974.
237. *Sunday Times*, 3 March 1974.
238. *Letter to Soviet Leaders*, London, Index on Censorship, 1974, p. 23.
239. Ibid.
240. *Piat' vozrazhenii Sakharovu*, AS no. 1696, April 1974.
241. Ibid.
242. *K voprosu o tseli i metodakh legal'noi oppozitsii*, AS no. 1760, 1974.
243. "Separation or Reconciliation? The Nationalities Question in the USSR," in Solzhenitsyln, A. et al., *From Under the Rubble* (Boston, Mass.: Little Brown), 1975.
244. Bilinsky, Ya., "Russian Dissenters and the Nationality Question," in Kamenetsky, I. (ed.), *Nationalism and Human Rights*, p. 84.
245. AS no. 3256, 1978.
246. Ibid.
247. AS no. 3226, 1979.
248. AS no. 4887, 1982.
249. AS no. 5863, 1986.
250. "Nationalist Movements and Social Factors," in *The Social Origins of Nationalist Movements*, p. 22.
251. "The Absence of Nationalist Movements: The Case of the Nordic Areas," in *The Social Origins of Nationalist Movements*, p. 85.
252. Ibid., p. 85.
253. For a qualified analysis of consociationalism as a concept and political arrangement see Lijphart, A., *Democracy in Plural Societies: A Comparative Exploration* (New Haven: Yale University Press), 1977.
254. For a qualified analysis, see Alcock, A., *A History of the Protection of Regional Cultural Minorities in Europe from the Edict of Nantes to the Present Day*

(London: Macmillan), 2000. See also Esman, M., "Two Dimensions of Ethnic Politics: Defense of Homelands, Immigrant Rights," *Ethnic and Racial Studies*, 8 (3), 1985; Kymlicka, W. and W. Norman, *Citizenship in Diverse Societies* (Oxford: Oxford University Press), 2000; Kymlicka, W., *Multicultural Citizenship: A Liberal Theory of Minority Rights* (Oxford: Clarendon Press), 1995.

255. L. Gershtein, interview to Israeli TV.

Chapter 6   Legitimizing Sources of Ethnic Politics

1. See Ross, M., J. Thibaut, and S. Evenbeck, "Some Determinants of the Intensity of the Social Protest," *Journal of Experimental Social Psychology*, 7 (1), 1971.
2. AS no. 901, 1964.
3. *Our proposals*, AS no. 908, 1964.
4. AS no. 1877, 1966.
5. *Re-Patria*, AS no. 1776, 1974.
6. AS no. 950, 1966.
7. AS no. 1532, 1970.
8. Ronskaia, A. and A. Tovbas, AS no. 584, 1970.
9. AS no. 906, 1964.
10. *Petition to the Chairman of the Presidium of the Supreme Soviet of the Ukrainian SSR*, AS no. 987, 1967.
11. Ibid.
12. AS no. 397, 1968.
13. AS no. 424, 1969.
14. AS no. 1776.
15. AS no. 987, 1967.
16. AS no. 4755, 1980.
17. AS no. 425, 1969.
18. *Appeal by Twenty-eight Soviet Jews from Riga*, AS no. 390, 1970.
19. AS no. 3087, 1977.
20. AS no. 5451, 1985.
21. AS no. 4779, 1972.
22. AS no. 3219, 1977.
23. AS no. 4755, 1980.
24. As reported by three representatives of the Crimean Tatar movement in *Information*, no. 1, AS no. 3071, 1977.
25. AS no. 4167, 1982.
26. AS no. 3119, 1976.
27. AS no. 5904, 1986.
28. AS no. 3219.
29. *Letter to the Presidium of the Supreme Soviet*, AS no. 5445, 1983.
30. AS no. 3755, 1979.

31. *The Final Plea*, AS no. 5391, 1983.
32. *Veche*, no. 7, AS no. 1775, 1973.
33. AS no. 539.
34. Ibid.
35. "Ucheniie slavianofilov...," *Veche*, no. 1, AS no. 1013, 1971.
36. "K voprosu o sfinkse," *Veche*, no. 1, AS no. 1013.
37. *Veche*, no. 9, AS no. 2040, 1973.
38. AS no. 1665, 1973.
39. *Veche*, no. 6, AS no. 1599, 1972.
40. "Bor'ba s tak nazyvaiemym rusofil'stvom...," *Veche*, no. 7, AS no. 1775.
41. "K voprosu o sfinkse," *Veche*, no. 1, AS no. 1013.
42. Ibid.
43. *Kak nam ponimat' nashu istoriiu*, AS no. 1801, 1974.
44. AS no. 5290, 1983.
45. Ibid.
46. AS no. 1042, 1971.
47. Ibid.
48. AS no. 281, 1968.
49. AS no. 3219.
50. AS no. 3730, 1976.
51. AS no. 4755.
52. *Obzor otnoshenii mezhdu Moskvoi i Gruziei*, AS no. 1830, 1974.
53. Feigin, G. and others, *Letter to Brezhnev*, AS no. 595, 1970.
54. As reported in *The Chronicle of Current Events*, no. 7, AS no. 196, 1970.
55. AS no. 1214, 1963.
56. AS no. 4636, 1978.
57. AS no. 981, 1969.
58. *Statement to the Twenty-sixth Party Congress*, AS no. 4525, 1981.
59. AS no. 3219.
60. *Obzor otnoshenii mezhdu Moskvoi i Gruziei*, AS no. 1830.
61. *Re-Patria*, AS no. 1776.
62. AS no. 4884, 1981.
63. AS no. 5289, 1984.
64. Ibid.
65. "Vestnik RSKhD i Russkaia intelligentsiia," *Veche*, no. 8, AS no. 1665.
66. Manevich, G.M., *Letter to the Chief Rabbi of the Moscow Synagogue*, AS no. 1536, 1971.
67. AS no. 3730.
68. *Veche*, no. 8, AS no. 1665.
69. AS no. 4689, 1982.
70. AS no. 1805, 1974.
71. AS no. 5405, 1984.
72. *Aresty i sudy na Ukraine*, AS no. 976 (after July 1968).

73. *Letter* to the Russian-language journal *Vestnik RSKhD*, AS no. 1468, 1972.
74. *Letter* to the Jewish *samizdat* journal *Evrei v SSSR*, no. 8, 1974, ES vol. 10.
75. *Veche*, no. 8, AS no. 1665.
76. *Evrei v SSSR*, no. 8, ES vol. 10. 1974.

Chapter 7 The Problem of Orientation: Ethnocentrism–Polycentrism

1. *Volkways/Folkways* (Boston: Ginn), 1906, p. 1.
2. Smith, A., *Theories of Nationalism*, p. 158.
3. Ibid., pp. 158–159.
4. AS no. 590, 1970.
5. *Veche*, no. 7, AS no. 1775, 1973.
6. *Kak nam ponimat' nashu istoriiu . . .*, AS no. 1801, 1974.
7. Ibid.
8. *Evrei v SSSR*, no. 13, ES vol. 13, 1976.
9. Ibid.
10. Ibid.
11. *Veche*, no. 8, AS no. 1665, 1973.
12. *Veche*, no. 6, AS no. 1599, 1972.
13. Solzhenitsyn, A. et al., *From Under the Rubble*.
14. *Evrei v SSSR*, no. 13, ES vol. 13, 1976.
15. "Russkoie resheniie natsional'nogo voprosa," *Veche*, no. 6, AS no. 1599, 1972.
16. No. 5, AS no. 1230, 1972.
17. "Answer to the Letter by N.S.," *Veche*, no. 8, AS no. 1665.
18. N.B., "Fragments of a Diary," *Veche*, no. 4, AS no. 1140, 1972.
19. Ibid.
20. Ibid.
21. "V polemicheskom zadore," *Veche*, no. 4.
22. Ibid.
23. "Russian Dissenters and the Nationality Question," in Kamenetsky, I., *Nationalism and Human Rights*, p. 84.
24. AS no. 1978.
25. *Dvadstat' dva*, no. 63, Tel Aviv, 1989, pp. 124–125.
26. "Po povodu polemiki mezhdu Sakharovym i Solzhenitsynym," AS no. 2450, 1974.
27. Ibid.
28. Meanwhile, Yael Tamir argues against Setton-Watson's remark that the independent, nationally conscious and territorially satisfied nations no longer need nationalism, as well as against the tendency of liberal spokespersons to repudiate the majority nationalism. She believes that "national claims rest on theoretically sound and morally justified grounds . . . apply equally to all nations regardless of their power, their wealth, their history of suffering, or even the injustices they have inflected on others in the past" (*Liberal Nationalism*, Princeton University Press, 1995, p. 11).

29. "Lie Abramson," as cited in Dunlop, J., *The New Russian Nationalism*, 1985, p. 83.
30. Ibid.
31. Ibid.
32. *Evrei v SSSR*, no. 13, ES vol. 13.
33. Starodzubaiev, I., "Letter to *Veche*," *Veche*, no. 7, AS no. 1775.
34. *Veche*, no. 2, AS no. 1020, 1971
35. Ibid.
36. Ibid.
37. Ibid.
38. *Veche*, no. 4, AS no. 1140.
39. "K Soboru 1971 goda," *Veche*, no. 5, AS no. 1230.
40. "Kuril'skiie ostrova (istoriko-geograficheskaia spravka)," *Veche*, no. 8, AS no. 1665.
41. "Otvet L'vu Andreevu," *Veche*, no. 8, AS no. 1665.
42. "Russkii natsionalism i Sionizm," *Evrei v SSSR*, no. 14, ES vol. 16, 1977.
43. *Evrei v SSSR*, no. 8, ES vol. 10, 1974.
44. Dunlop, J., *The New Russian Nationalism*, p. 40.
45. AS no. 5414, l984.
46. AS no. 554, 1970.
47. AS no. 4779, 1982.
48. AS no. 4755, 1980.
49. "Kto ia i chto ia?" *Evrei v SSSR*, no. 2, ES vol. 4, 1972.
50. *Russkiie evrei v otsenke svoego proshlogo i v bor'be za svobodu, natsional'noie vozrozhdeniie i druzhbu narodov*, AS no. 1690, 1974.
51. AS no. 2289, 1975.
52. AS no. 2076, 1974.
53. AS no. 411, 1970.
54. Ibid.
55. *Nash Ivrit*, no. 3, 1980, ES vol. 22.
56. *Nash Ivrit*, no. 4, 1980, ES vol. 25.
57. *The Final Plea*, AS no. 3077, 1974.
58. AS no. 85, 1968.
59. AS no. 191, 1968.
60. *Nash Ivrit*, no. 2, 1979, ES vol. 17.
61. "Assimiliatsiia i svobodnyi vybor," *Evrei v SSSR*, no. 7, ES vol. 10, 1974.
62. AS no. 3119, 1976.
63. *Veche*, no. 4, AS no. 1140.
64. AS no. 316, 1968.
65. *Appeal by Forty Crimean Tatars to the Soviet Public and the Presidium of the Supreme Soviet*, AS no. 318, 1968.
66. AS no. 334, 1968.
67. *Evrei v SSSR*, no. 4, ES vol. 6, 1973.
68. AS no. 916, 1965.

69. AS no. 919, 1965.
70. AS no. 198, 1966.
71. AS no. 265, 1969.
72. AS no. 2076, 1974.
73. AS no. 5372, 1984.
74. AS no. 375, 1970.
75. AS no. 4638, 1979.
76. Ibid.
77. *Appeal to the Population of the Georgian SSR*, AS no. 5233, 1982 or 1983.
78. AS no. 5234, 1982.
79. AS no. 5233.
80. *Soobcheniie o demonstratsii Azerbaijantsev*, AS no. 5235, 1983.
81. Notadze, N. and others, AS no. 5225, 1983.
82. AS no. 4639, 1981.
83. AS no. 2757, 1976.
84. AS no. 2758, 1976.
85. For a detailed analysis of these debates see Khazanov, A., *After the USSR*, pp. 202–204.
86. AS no. 4639.
87. See AS no. 1532, AS nos. 1533, 1534 (1971).
88. *Claims of the Georgian People*, AS no. 4639.
89. AS no. 5905, 1986.
90. *Obzor otnoshenii mezhdu Moskvoi i Gruziei*, AS no. 1830, 1974.
91. *Letter to Newsweek*, AS no. 2757.
92. AS no. 3086, 1977.
93. *Letter to Pope John Paul II*, AS no. 5905.
94. AS no. 5094, 1983.
95. AS no. 4369, 1980.
96. Iakuskene, I., *Aushra*, no. 21, AS no. 4069.
97. *Petition to the Politburo*, AS no. 1449, 1972.
98. *Evrei v SSSR*, no.12, ES vol. 13, 1976.
99. As reported in Terliatskas, A., *Yeshcho raz o evreiakh i Litovtsakh*, AS no. 3621, 1978.
100. Ibid.
101. "On Attaining Sovereignty," in Smith, A. (ed.), *Nationalist Movements*, p. 134.

Chapter 8 Samizdat *and Ethnic Mobilization*

1. Motyl, A., *Sovietology, Rationality, Nationality: Coming to Grips with Nationalism in the USSR* (New York: Columbia University Press), 1990, pp. 187–188.
2. Ibid., p. 188.
3. Ibid., p. 196.
4. *Vilnius i vilniustsy glazami dissidenta*, AS no. 4142, 1979.

5. AS no. 3314, 1975.
6. In Gitelman, Z. (ed.), *The Politics of Nationality and the Erosion of the USSR* (New York: St. Martin's Press).
7. Vols. 22–24.
8. Personal communication with the producers of *samizdat*.
9. *Kievskii telegraf*, no. 35 (78), 2001, pp. 22–23.
10. In *Information*, no. 77, AS no. 291, 1968.
11. *Chronicle of the Catholic Church in Lithuania*, no. 51, 1982, AS no. 4706.
12. *Veche*, no. 6, AS no. 1599, 1972.
13. AS no. 3077, 1974.
14. An unpublished manuscript.
15. AS no. 4755, 1980.
16. For more details, see Zisserman-Brodsky, D. "Sources of Ethnic Politics in the Soviet Polity: The Pre-Perestroika Dimension," *Nationality Papers*, 22 (2), 1994.
17. Smith, A., *The Ethnic Revival*, pp. 28–29.
18. Ibid., p. 29.
19. "National Movements and Social Factors: A Theoretical Perspective," in *The Social Origins of Nationalist Movements*, 34.
20. See his *Struggle, Politics and Reform: Collective Action, Social Movements, and Cycles of Protest* (Ithaca: Western Societies Papers), 1989.
21. Hooghe, L., "Nationalist Movements and Social Factors: A Theoretical Perspective," in *The Social Origins of Nationalist Movements*, p. 34.
22. *Soziale Bewegungen: Ein historisch-systematischer Grundriss* (Frankfurt: Campus Verlag), 1985, p. 274.
23. This point concerns only those groups that experienced nationalist dissent.
24. Hooghe, L., ibid., p. 34.
25. Khazanov, A., *After the USSR*, p. 208. See also pp. 208–209 of this book for an analysis of Gamsakhurdia's policy toward minorities.
26. AS no. 1214, 1963.
27. AS no. 1218 (after 1967).
28. AS no. 1215 (after 1967).
29. AS no. 1218.
30. AS no. 1215.
31. AS no. 5235, 1983.
32. AS no. 4415, 1981.

Conclusion

1. *Sovietology, Rationality, Nationality*, p. 157.
2. Smith, A., *Theories of Nationalism*, 1971, pp. 124, 136.
3. Kogan Iasnui, V. and D. Zisserman-Brodsky, "Chechen Separatism," in Spencer, M. (ed.), Separatism: Democracy and Disintegration (Lanham, MD: Rowman and Littlefield), 1998, p. 222.

4. Ibid., p. 223.
5. Spencer, M., "When States Divide," in *Separatism: Democracy and Disintegration*, p. 9.
6. Ibid.
7. Walzer, M., *What it Means to be an American: Essays on the American Experience* (New York: Marsillo), 1992, p. 6.
8. See Smooha, S., "Minority Status in an Ethnic Democracy: The Status of the Arab Minority in Israel," *Ethnic and Racial Studies*, 13 (3), 1990; "Ethnic Democracy: Israel as an Archetype," *Israel Studies*, 2 (2), 1997.
9. On this issue see Smith, G. et al., "Statehood, Ethnic Relations and Citizenship," in Smith, G. (ed.), *The Baltic States* (New York: St. Martin's Press), 1996; Melvin, N., "Ethnic Democracy in Estonia and Latvia," in Stein, J. (ed.), *The Politics of National Minority Participation in Post-Communist Europe: State-Building, Democracy, and Ethnic Mobilization* (Armonk, N.Y.: Sharpe, M. E.), 1999.
10. Citizenship and naturalization laws of Latvia and Estonia de facto preclude most ethnic Russians, legal residents of these former Soviet republics from obtaining Estonian and Latvian citizenship. A Special Report by the Forced Migration Projects published by The Open Society Institute in 1997 indicates: "...Only about 100,000 of the approximately 550,000 Russian speakers living in Estonia in 1991 qualified for automatic citizenship. In Latvia, of the 900,000-plus Russian-speaking population, only about 200,000 qualified for immediate citizenship. The share of ethnic Russians in Latvia's overall population, including resident aliens, was 33 percent in 1994. But among the 1.77 million citizens of the country, ethnic Russians made up only a 16.2 percent share, or about 283,000 people. ...In Estonia in 1991, 78 percent of the ethnic-Russian population, or about 340,000 people, had lived in the country for at least 21 years. About 90 percent had lived in the country for at least 10 years."
11. "Ethnic Democracy: Israel as an Archetype," p. 199.
12. Shtromas, A., "The Baltic States as Soviet Republics," in Smith, G. (ed.), *The Baltic States: The National Self-Determination of Estonia, Latvia and Lithuania* (New York: St. Martin's Press), 1994, p. 108.
13. Kuzio, T. and A. Wilson, *Ukraine: Perestroika to Independence* (London: Macmillan), 1994, p. 63.
14. Rau, Z., "Four Stages of our Path out of Socialism," (cited in *Ukraine: Perestroika to Independence*, ibid.) For a competent account of the role of Ukrainian dissidents see also Wilson, A., *Ukrainian Nationalism in the 1990s* (Cambridge: Cambridge University Press), 1997, pp. 60–92.
15. *Ukraine: Perestroika to Independence*, p. 62.
16. Wilson, A., *Ukrainian Nationalism in the 1990s*, p. 75.
17. It's interesting (I am indebted to John Ishiyama for turning my attention to this point) that previously widely supported popular fronts such as *Sajudis* or *Atmoda* have quickly disappeared from the political arena. The fate of Ukrainian

popular movement is not much different from its Baltic counterparts. At the same time, *Rukh*, though it has been progressively splitting and shrinking still nominally remains on the political map. Thus, there were three competing factions of *Rukh* running in the 2002 elections to *Verkhovna Rada* (the Ukrainian parliament). People's *Rukh* of Ukraine and Ukrainian Popular *Rukh* both joined The Bloc of Viktor Yushchenko (which obtained the highest results), whereas independently running *Rukh* for Unity received 0.16% of the vote (for comparison, The Party for Rehabilitation of Seriously Ill Patients received 0.35%).

18. It's symptomatic that Zviad Gamsakhurdia in his capacity of Georgian president continued to behave as an uncompromising militant dissenter.

19. This theory may help to explain why not Sakharov, but Yeltsin was chosen to head the "democratic opposition" in the All-Union Congress of People's Deputies.

20. For example, Levko Luk'ianenko, veteran dissident and founder of The Ukrainian Republican Party, in the presentation of "our team" by The Bloc of Yuliia Timoshenko (in the 2002 elections the URP joined this bloc), was described as "living legend of the Ukrainian national-democratic movement" (available on internet http://www.tymoshenko.com.ua/eng/partners/). The Party of Estonian National Independence emphasized in the election campaigns that it was created in 1988 by former dissidents and political prisoners.

21. "Marxism won in Russia, it would seem, but it did so only by becoming a nationalism," Szporluk, R. concluded analyzing the Soviet variant of communism (*Communism and Nationalism*, pp. 230–231).

Selected Bibliography

Abeles, R., "Relative Deprivation, Raising Expectations and Black Militancy," *Journal of Social Issues*, 32 (2), 1976.

Agursky, M., *The Third Rome: National Bolshevism in the USSR* (Boulder, Colo.: Westview), 1987.

Alcock, A., *A History of the Protection of Regional Cultural Minorities in Europe from the Edict of Nantes to the Present Day* (London: Macmillan), 2000.

Alexeyeva, L., *Soviet Dissent: Contemporary Movements for National, Religious, Human Rights* (Middletown, Conn.: Wesleyan University Press), 1985.

Allardt, E., *Implications of the Ethnic Revival in Modern, Industrialized Society* (Helsinki: Societas Scientarum Finnica), 1979.

Allworth, E. (ed.), *Soviet Nationality Problems* (New York: Columbia University Press), 1971.

Allworth, E. (ed.), *The Nationality Question in the Soviet Central Asia* (New York: Praeger), 1973.

Allworth, E. (ed.), *Nationality Group Survival in Multi-Ethnic States* (New York: Praeger), 1977.

Allworth, E. (ed.), *Ethnic Russia in the USSR* (New York: Pergamon Press), 1980.

Allworth, E. (ed.), *Tatars of the Crimea–Their Struggle for Survival* (Durham & London: Duke University Press), 1988.

Allworth, E. (ed.), *The Tatars of Crimea: Return to the Homeland* (Durham: Duke University Press), 1998.

Alter, P., *Nationalism* (London: Edward Arnold), 1989.

Altshuler, M., *Soviet Jewry since the Second World War* (New York: Greenwood), 1987.

Amalrik, A., *Will the Soviet Union Survive until 1984?* (New York: Harper and Row), 1980.

Anderson, B., *Imagined Communities: Reflections on the Origin and Spread of Nationalism* (London: Verso), 1983.

Armstrong, J., *Ukrainian Nationalism* (Littleton, Colo.: Ukrainian Academic Press), 1980.

Armstrong, J., "Assessing the Soviet Nationalities Movements: A Critical Review," *Nationalities Papers*, 19 (1), 1991.

Axelbank, A., *Soviet Dissent, Intellectuals, Jews, and Détente* (New York: F. Watts), 1975.

Azrael, J. (ed.), *Soviet Nationality Policies and Practices* (New York: Praeger), 1978.

Bailey, H. and E. Katz (eds.), *Ethnic Group Politics* (Columbus, Oh.: E.F. Merrille), 1969.

Banks, M., *Ethnicity: Anthropological Constructions* (London: Routledge), 1996.

Banton, M., *Ethnic and Racial Competition* (Cambridge: Cambridge University Press), 1983.

Barghoorn, F., *Soviet Russian Nationalism* (New York: Oxford University Press), 1956.

Barth, F. (ed.), *Ethnic Groups and Boundaries* (Boston: Little, Brown and Company), 1969.

Belanger, S. and M. Pinard, *Ethnic Movements and the Competition Model: Some Missing Links, American Sociological Review*, 56 (4), 1991.

Bennigsen, A. and M. Broxup, *The Islamic Threat to the Soviet State* (London: Croom Helm), 1983.

Besancon, A., "The Nationality Issue in the USSR," *Survey*, 30 (4), 1989.

Bialer, S. (ed.), *Politics, Society, and Nationality Inside Gorbachev's Russia* (Boulder, Colo.: Westview), 1989.

Bilinsky, Ya., *The Second Soviet Republic: The Ukraine After World War II* (New Brunswick, N.J.: Rutgers University Press), 1964.

Bilinsky, Ya., "The Concept of the Soviet People and Its Implications for Soviet Nationality Policy," *Annals of the Ukrainian Academy of Arts and Science in the United States* (1979–1980), no. 14 (37–38).

Bilinsky, Ya., "Russian Dissidents' Attitudes towards the Political Strivings of the Non- Russian Nations," *Nationalities Papers*, 11 (2), 1983.

Bilocerkowicz, J., *Soviet Ukrainian Dissent: A Study of Political Alienation* (Boulder, Colo.: Westview), 1988.

Birch, A., "Minority Nationalist Movements and Theories of Political Integration," *World Politics*, 30 (3), 1978.

Birch, J., *The Ukrainian Nationalist Movement in the USSR since 1956* (London: Ukrainian Information Service), 1971.

Brass, P. (ed.), *Ethnic Groups and the State* (London and Sydney: Croom Helm), 1985.

Brass, P., *Ethnicity and Nationalism* (New Delhi: SAGE Publications), 1991.

Bremmer, L. and R. Taras (eds.), *Nations and Politics in the Soviet Successor States* (Cambridge: Cambridge University Press), 1993.

Breslauer, G., *Five Images of the Soviet Future: A Critical Review and Synthesis* (Berkeley: Institute of International Studies, University of California), 1978.

Breslauer, G., *Soviet Politics and Society* (St. Paul: West Publishing Company), 1978.

Breuilly, J., *Nationalism and the State* (Manchester: Manchester University Press), 1985.

Bromley, Iu., *Soviet Ethnology and Anthropology Today* (The Hague: Mouton), 1974.

Brooks, R., *Scottish Nationalism: Relative Deprivation and Social Mobility* (Ph.D. Thesis), Michigan State University, 1973.

Browne, M., *Ferment in the Ukraine* (New York: Praeger), 1971.

Brzezinski, Z., *The Grand Failure: The Birth and Death of Communism in the Twentieth Century* (New York: Charles Schribner's Sons), 1989.

Byrnes, R. (ed.), *After Brezhnev* (Bloomington: Indiana Univesity Press), 1983.

Carr, E.H., *Nationalism and After* (London: Macmillan), 1968.

Carrere d'Encausse, H., *Decline of an Empire: The Soviet Socialist Republics in Revolt* (New York: Newsweek Book), 1979.

Carrere d'Encausse, H., *The End of the Soviet Empire: The Triumph of Nations* (New York: Harper and Collins), 1992.

Carrere d'Encausse, H., *The Great Challenge: Nationalities and the Bolshevik State, 1917–1930* (New York and London: Holmes and Meier), 1992.

Carter, S., *Russian Nationalism: Yesterday, Today, Tomorrow* (New York: St. Martin's Press), 1990.

Chiama, J. and J.F. Soulet, *Histoire de la dissidence: Opposition et revoltes en USSR et dans les democrahes populaires de la mort de Stalin a nos jours* (Paris: Seuil), 1982.

Chislennost' i sostav naselniia SSSR (Moskva: Finansy i statistika), 1984.

Clem, R. (ed.), *The Soviet West Interplay Between Nationality and Social Organization* (New York: Praeger), 1975.

Coakley, J. (ed.), *The Social Origins of Nationalist Movements: The Contemporary West European Experience* (London, Newbury Park, New Delhi: SAGE Publications), 1992.

Cohen, S. et al. (eds.), *The Soviet Union Since Stalin* (Bloomington: Indiana University Press), 1980.

Cohen, S., *Rethinking the Soviet Experience: Politics and History Since 1917* (New York: Oxford University Press), 1985.

Connor, W., "The Politics of Ethnonationalism," *Journal of International Affairs*, 27 (1), 1973.

Connor, W., "Eco- or Ethno-nationalism," *Ethnic and Racial Studies*, 7 (3), 1984.

Connor, W., *The National Question in Marxist-Leninist Theory and Strategy* (Princeton: Princeton University Press), 1984.

Connor, W., *Ethnonationalism: The Quest for Understanding* (Princeton: Princeton University Press), 1994.

Conquest, R., *Soviet Nationalities Policy in Practice* (London: Bodley Head), 1967.

Conquest, R., *The Nation Killers: The Soviet Deportation of Nationalities* (New York: Macmillan Company), 1970.

Conquest, R. (ed.), *The Last Empire: Nationality and the Soviet Future* (Stanford: Hoover Institution Press), 1986.

deCarufel, A., "Factors Affecting the Evaluation of Improvement," *Journal of Personality and Social Psychology*, 37, 1979.

deCarufel, A., "Victims' Satisfaction with Compensation," *Journal of Applied Social Psychology*, 11, 1981.

Deutsch, K., "Social Mobilization and Political Development," *American Political Science Review*, 55 (3), 1961.

Deutsch, K., *Nationalism and Social Communication* (Cambridge, Mass.: MIT Press), 1966.

Deutsch, K., *Nationalism and Its Alternatives* (New York: Alfred Knopf), 1969.

Deutsch, K., *Tides Among Nations* (New York: Free Press), 1979.

Diamond, L. and M.F. Plattner (eds.), *Nationalism, Ethnic Conflict, and Democracy* (Baltimore: Johns Hopkins University Press), 1994.

Diuk, N. and A. Karatnycky, *The Hidden Nations* (New York: W. Morrow), 1990.

Drachman, E., *Challenging the Kremlin: The Soviet Jewish Emigration for Freedom* (New York: Paragon House), 1991.

Dunlop, J., *New Russian Revolutionaries* (Belmont: Nordland Publishing Company), 1976.

Dunlop, J., *The Faces of Contemporary Russian Nationalism* (Princeton: Princeton University Press), 1983.

Dunlop, J., *The New Russian Nationalism* (New York: Praeger), 1985.

Dziuba, I., *Internationalism or Russification? A Study in the Soviet Nationalities Problems* (New York: Monad Press), 1974.

Edwards, J., *Linguistic Minorities* (London: Academic Press), 1984.

Eisenstadt, S., *Modernization: Protest and Change* (Cliffs, NJ: Prentice Hall), 1966.

Elazar, D., *Federalism and Politcal Integration* (Ramat Gan, Israel: Turtledove), 1979.

Elklit, J. and O. Tonsgaard, "The Politics of Majority Groups towards National Minorities in the Danish-German Border Region: Why the Differences?" *Ethnic and Racial Studies* 6 (4), 1983.

Elklit, J. and O. Tonsgaard, "Elements for a Structural Theory of Ethnic Segregation and Assimilation," *European Journal of Political Research*, 12 (1), 1984.

Emerson, R., *From Empire to Nation* (Boston: Beacon Press), 1969.

Enloe, C., *Ethnic Conflicts and Political Developments* (Boston: Little Brown & Co.), 1973.

Esman, M., "Two Dimensions of Ethnic Politics: Defense of Homelands, Immigrant Rights," *Ethnic and Racial Studies*, 8 (3), 1985.

Ettinger, S., "The National Revival of Soviet Jewry," *Forum*, 23, 1975.

Farmer, K., *Ukrainian Nationalism in the Post-Stalin Era* (The Hague: Martinus Nijhoff), 1980.

Fisher, A., *The Crimean Tatars* (Stanford: Hoover Institution Press), 1987.

Fleischauer, I. and B. Pinkus, *The Soviet Germans: Past and Present* (London: C. Hurst and Company), 1986.

Forgus, S.P., "Manifestations of Nationalism in the Baltic Republics," *Nationalities Papers*, 7 (2), 1979.

Francis, E., *Interethnic Relations: An Essay in Sociological Theory* (New York: Elsevier), 1976.

Frankel, J., *Prophecy and Politics* (Cambridge: Cambridge University Press), 1980.

Freedman, R., *Soviet Jewry in the 1980s* (Durham, N.C.: Duke University Press), 1989.

Geller, M., *Utopia in Power* (New York: Summit Books), 1986.

Gellner, E., *Thought and Change* (London: Weidenfeld and Nicolson), 1964.

Gellner, E., *Nations and Nationalism* (Oxford: Basil Blackwell), 1983.

Gellner, E., *Culture, Identity and Politics* (Cambridge: Cambridge University Press), 1986.

Gellner, E., *State and Society in Soviet Thought* (Oxford: Basil Blackwell), 1987.

Gerstenmaier, C., *The Voices of the Silent* (New York: Hart), 1972.

Giddens, A., *The Nation-State and Violence* (Berkeley: University of California Press), 1987.

Gitelman, Z. (ed.), *The Politics of Nationality and the Erosion of the USSR* (New York: St. Martin's Press), 1992.

Glazer, N. and D. Moynihan (eds.), *Ethnicity: Theory and Experience* (Cambridge, Mass.: Harvard University Press), 1975.

Goble, P., "The Rise of Ethnic Politics," *Nationalities Papers*, 17 (1), 1989.

Goldhagen, E., *Ethnic Minorities in the Soviet Union* (New York: Praeger), 1968.

Gonzalez, N. and C. McComon, *Conflict, Migration, and the Expression of Ethnicity* (Boulder, Colo.: Westview), 1989.

Gourevitch, P., "Political Leadership, Economic Growth and the Reemergence of 'Peripheral' Nationalisms: Some Comparative Speculations," *Comparative Studies in Society and History*, 21 (3), 1979.

Greenfeld, L., *Nationalism: Five Roads to Modernity* (Cambridge, MA: Harvard University Press), 1992.

Guimond, S. and L. Dubè-Simard, "Relative Deprivation Theory and the Quebec Nationalist Movement: The Cognition-Emotion Distinction and the Personal-Group Deprivation Issue," *Journal of Personality and Social Psychology*, 144 (3), 1983.

Gurr, T., *Why Men Rebel* (Princeton: Princeton University Press), 1970.

Hajda, L. and M. Beissinger (eds.), *The Nationalities Factor in Soviet Politics and Society* (Boulder, Colo.: Westview), 1989.

Hall, J., "Nationalisms: Classified and Explained," *Daedalus*, 122 (3), 1993.

Hall, J. (ed.), *The State of the Nation. Ernest Gellner and the Theory of Nationalism* (New York: Cambridge University Press), 1998.

Hall, R. (ed.), *Ethnic Autonomy: Comparative Dynamics* (New York: Pergamon Press), 1979.

Hammer, D., *Russian Nationalism and Soviet Politics* (Boulder, Colo.: Westview), 1987.

Havel, V. et al., *The Power of the Powerless: Citizens against the State in Central-Eastern Europe* (Armork, N.Y: M.E. Sharp, Inc.), 1985.

Hayes, C.J.H., *Essays on Nationalism* (New York: Macmillan), 1926.

Hayes, C.J.H., *The Historical Evolution of Modern Nationalism* (New York: Richard R. Smith), 1931.

Hazan, B., *From Brezhnev to Gorbachev* (Boulder, Colo.: Westview), 1987.

Hechter, M., *Internal Colonialism: The Celtic Fringe in British National Development, 1536–1966* (London: Routledge and Kegan Paul), 1975.

Hechter, M., "Group Formation and the Cultural Division of Labor," *American Journal of Sociology*, 84 (2), 1978.

Hechter, M., *Principles of Group Solidarity* (Berkeley: University of California Press), 1988.

Hobsbaum, E.J., *Nations and Nationalism Since 1980: Programme, Myth, Reality* (Cambridge: Cambridge University Press), 1982.

Hoffman, E., *The Politics of Economic Modernization in the Soviet Union* (Ithaca: Cornell University Press), 1982.

Hooghe, L., *Separatism: Conflict tussen: Twee projecten voor nativorling* (*Leuven*: Afdeling Politologie), 1989.

Horowitz, D., "Patterns of Ethnic Separatism," *Comparative Studies in Society and History*, 23 (2), 1981.

Horowitz, D., *Ethnic Groups in Conflict* (Berkeley: University of California Press), 1985.

Hroch, M., *Social Preconditions of National Revival in Europe* (Cambridge: Cambridge University Press), 1985.

Huttenbach, H. (ed.), *Soviet Nationality Policies: Ruling Ethnic Groups in the USSR* (London: Mansell), 1990.

Huttenbach, H., "Sources of National Movements," *Nationalities Papers*, 18 (2), 1990.

Jones, E. and F. Grupp, "Modernization and Equalization in the USSR," *Soviet Studies*, 36 (2), April 1984.

Joppke, Ch., "Intellectuals, Nationalism, and the Exit from Communism: The Case of East Germany," *Comparative Studies in Society and History*, 37 (2), 1995.

Joppke, Ch., *East German Dissidents and the Revolution of 1989* (New York: New York University Press), 1995.

Kamenetsky, I. (ed.), *Nationalism and Human Rights* (Littleton, Colo.: Libraries Unlimited), 1977.

Karklins, R., *Ethnic Relations in the USSR: The Perspective from Below* (Boston: Allen & Unwin), 1986.

Katz, Z. (ed.), *Handbook of Major Soviet Nationalities* (New York: Free Press), 1975.

Keating, M., *State and Regional Nationalism: Territorial Politics and the European State* (Hemel Hempstead: Harvester-Wheatsheaf), 1988.

Kedourie, E., *Nationalism* (London: Hutchinson), 1979.

Kerblay, B., *Modern Soviet Society* (New York: Pantheon), 1983.

Kessler, L., *The Dissident Press* (Newbury Park, Calif.: SAGE Publications), 1984.

Khazanov, A., *Soviet Nationality Policy during Perestroika* (Falls Church, Va.: Delphic), 1991.

Khazanov, A., *After the USSR* (Madison: the University of Wisconsin Press), 1995.

Kingkade, W., *Estimates and Projections of the Population of the USSR: 1979 to 2025* (Washington: Center for International Research, U.S. Bureau of the Census), 1987.

Kohn, H., *The Idea of Nationalism: A Study of Its Origins and Background* (New York: Macmillan), 1944.

Kohn, H., *The Age of Nationalism* (New York: Harper and Row), 1962.

Kohn, H., *Nationalism: Its Meaning and History* (Princeton, NJ: D. van Nostrand), 1965.

Kolarz, W., *Russia and Her Colonies* (New York: Praeger), 1952.

Kowalewski, D., "National Dissent in the Soviet Union: The Crimean Tatar Case," *Nationalities Papers*, 2 (2), 1974.

Kowalewski, D., "National Rights Protests in the Brezhnev Era: Some Determinations of Success," *Ethnic and Racial Studies*, 4 (2), 1981.

Kowalewski, D. and C. Johnson, "The Ukrainian Dissident: A Statistical Profile," *Ukrainian Quarterly*, 40 (1), 1984.

KPSS v rezoliutsiiakh i resheiiakh, 7th ed. (Moscow: State Publishing House of Political Literature), 1954.

Kracauer, S., *From Caligari to Hitler: A Psychological History of the German Film* (Princeton, NJ: Princeton University Press), 1947.

Kravchenko, B. (ed.), *Ukraine after Shelest* (Edmonton, Alta.: Canadian Institute of Ukrainian Studies), 1983.

Kriesberg, L. (ed.), *Research in Social Movements: Conflict and Change* (Greenwich: JAI Press), 1985.

Kuzio, T. and A. Wilson, *Ukraine: Perestroika to Independence* (London: Macmillan), 1994.

Kymlicka, W. *Multicultural Citizenship: A Liberal Theory of Minority Rights* (Oxford: Clarendon Press), 1995.

Kymlicka, W. and W. Norman, *Citizenship in Diverse Societies* (Oxford: Oxford University Press), 2000.

Kymlicka, W., *Politics in the Vernacular: Nationalism, Multiculturalism, and Citizenship* (Oxford: Oxford University Press), 2001.

Lacqueur, W., *The Long Road to Freedom: Russia and Glasnost* (New York: C. Scribner's), 1989.

Lacqueur, W., *Black Hundred: The Rise of the Extreme Right in Russia* (New York: Harper and Collins), 1993.

Lang, D., *A Modern History of Soviet Georgia* (New York: Grove Press), 1962.

Lenin, V.I., *Sochineniia* (3rd ed., 30 vols.), Publishing House of the Central Committee of the VKP(b), 1925–1932.

Lenin, V.I., *Sochineniia* (4th ed., 35 vols.), Moscow Marx-Engels-Lenin Institute, 1941–1950.

Letter to a Russian Friend: A Samizdat Publication from Soviet Byelorussia (London: Association of Byelorussians in Great Britain), 1979.

Levin, N., *The Jews in the Soviet Union Since 1917: Paradox of Survival* (New York: New York University Press), 1988.

Lewis, R. and R. Rowland, *Population Redistribution in the USSR* (New York: Praeger), 1979.

Lewytzkyi, B., *Die sowjetische nationalitaten Politik nach Stalins Tod (1953–1970)* Munich, 1970.

Lewytzkyi, B., *Politics and Society in the Soviet Ukraine, 1953–1980* (Edmonton, Alta.: Canadian Institute of Ukrainian Studies), 1984.

Lijphart, A., *Democracy in Plural Societies: A Comparative Exploration* (New Haven: Yale University Press), 1977.

Linden, C. et al., *Nationalities and Nationalism in the USSR: A Soviet Dilemma* (Washington D.C.: Center for Strategic and International Studies), 1977.

Linden, C., *The Soviet State: The Politics of Ideocratic Nationalism* (New York: Praeger), 1983.

Low, A., *Soviet Jewry and Soviet Policy* (Boulder, Colo.: East European Monographs), 1990.

Matossian, M., *The Impact of Soviet Policies in Armenia* (Leiden: Brill), 1962.

Milne, R., *Politics in Ethnically Bipolar States* (Vancouver: University of British Columbia Press), 1982.

Misiunas, R. and R. Taagepera, *The Baltic States: Years of Dependence, 1940–1980* (Berkeley: University of California Press), 1983.

Motyl, A., *Will the Non-Russians Rebel? State, Ethnicity, and Stability in the USSR* (Ithaca, N.Y.: Cornell University Press), 1987.

Motyl, A., *Sovietology, Rationality, Nationality* (New York: Columbia University Press), 1990.

Motyl, A., *Thinking Theoretically about Soviet Nationalities: History and Comparison in the Study of the USSR* (New York: Columbia University Press), 1992.

Motyl, A. (ed.), *The Post-Soviet Nations. Perspectives in the Demise of the USSR* (New York: Columbia University Press), 1992.

Nagel, J. and Olzak, S. "Ethnic Mobilization in Old and New States: An Extension of the Competitive Model," *Social Problems*, 30 (2), 1982.

Nagel, J., "The Ethnic Revolution: The Emergence of Ethnic Nationalism in the Modern State," *Sociology and Social Research*, 68 (4), 1984.

Nahaylo, B. and V. Swoboda, *Soviet Disunion: A History of the Nationalities Problem in the USSR* (New York: The Free Press), 1990.

Natsional'nyi sostav naseleniia RSFSR po dannym vsesoiuznoi perepisi naseleniia na 1989 god (Moscow: Respublikanskii Informatsionno-Izdatel'skii Tsentr), 1990.

Nielsen, F., "The Flemish Movement in Belgium after World War II," *American Sociological Review*, 45 (1), 1980.

Nielsen, F., "The Ethnic Revolution: The Emergence of Ethnic Nationalism in the Modern State," *Sociology and Social Research*, 68 (4), 1984.

Nielsen, F., "Towards a Theory of Ethnic Solidarity in Modern Societies," *American Sociological Review*, 50 (2), 1985.

Nove, A., *Stalinism and After: The Road to Gorbachev*, 3rd ed. (Boston: Unwin Hyman), 1989.

Oberschall, A., *Social Conflict and Social Movements* (Englewood Cliffs, NJ: Prentice Hall), 1973.

Olson, M., *The Rise and Decline of Nations* (New Haven: Yale University Press), 1982.

Olson, J., C. Herman, and M. Zanna (eds.), *Relative Deprivation and Social Comparison: The Ontario Symposium*, vol. 4 (Hillsdale, NJ: Erlbaum) 1986.

Olzak, S. "Contemporary Ethnic Mobilization," *American Review of Sociology*, 9, 1983.

Olzak, S. and J. Nagel (eds.), *Competitive Ethnic Relations* (Orlando Fla.: Academic Press), 1986.

Orridge, A., "Uneven Development and Nationalism," *Political Studies*, 29 (2), 1981.

Parland, T., *The Rejection in Russia of Totalitarian Socialism and Liberal Democracy* (Helsinki: Commentationes Scientarum Socialeiem), 1993.

Patterson, O., *Ethnic Chauvinism* (New York: Stein and Day), 1977.

Peterson, W. (ed.), *The Background of Ethnic Conflict* (Leiden: Brill), 1979.

Pinkus, B., *The Jews of the Soviet Union* (Cambridge: Cambridge University Press), 1988.

Pinkus, B., *Tehiyyah u-tequmah le'umit: Ha-Ziyyonut ve-ha-tenu'ah ha-ziyyonit bi-vrit ha mo'atzot, 1947–1987* (Sde Boqer, Israel: Ben Gurion University of the Negev Press), 1993.

Pipes, R., *The Formation of the Soviet Union: Communism and Nationalism, 1917–1923* (Cambridge, Mass.: Harvard University Press), 1977.

Pospelovsky, D., "The Resurgence of Russian Nationalism in *Samizdat*," *Survey*, 19 (1), 1973.

Pospelovsky, D., "Nationalist Thought and the Jewish Question," *Soviet Jewish Affairs*, 6 (1), 1976.

Potichnyi, P., (ed.), *The Soviet Union: Party and Society* (Cambridge: Cambridge University Press), 1988.

Potichnyi, P. and M. Aster (eds.), *Ukrainian-Jewish Relations in Historical Perspective* (Edmonton, Alta: University of Alberta Press), 1988.

Raschke, J., *Sociale Bewegungen: Ein historisch-systematischer Grundriss* (Frankfurt: Campus Verlag), 1985.

Raun, T., *Estonia and Estonians* (Stanford: Hoover Institution Press), 1987.

Reddaway, P., *Uncensored Russia* (New York: American Heritage), 1972.

Reddaway, P., *Soviet Policy Towards Dissent and Emigration: The Radical Change of Course Since 1979*, Occasional Paper no. 192 (Washington D.C.: Kennan Institute), August 1984.

Remeikis, T., *Opposition to Soviet Rule in Lithuania, 1945–1980* (Chicago: Institute of Lithuanian Studies Press), 1980.

Rockett, R.L., *Ethnic Nationalities in the Soviet Union* (New York: Praeger), 1981.

Roeder, P.G., "Soviet Federalism and Ethnic Mobilization," *World Politics*, 43 (2), 1991.

Ro'i, Ya., *The Struggle for Soviet Jewish Emigration, 1948–1967* (Cambridge: Cambridge University Press), 1991.

Ro'i, Ya. and A. Beker (eds.), *Jewish Culture and Identity in the Soviet Union* (New York, London: New York University Press), 1991.

Rokkan, S., "The Growth and Structuring of Mass Politics in Western Europe: Reflections and Possible Models of Explanations," *Scandinavian Political Studies*, 5, 1970.

Rokkan, S., "Nation-Building: A Review of Models and Approaches," *Current Sociology*, 19 (3), 1971.

Rokkan, S. and D. Urwin (eds.), *The Politics of Territorial Identity: Studies in European Regionalism* (London: SAGE Publications), 1982.

Rokkan, S. and D. Urwin, *Economy, Territory, Identity: Politics of West European Peripheries* (London: SAGE Publications), 1983.

Rorlich, A., *The Volga Tatars: A Profile in National Resilience* (Stanford: Hoover Institution Press), 1986.

Ross, J. et al. (eds.), *The Mobilization of Collective Identity: Comparative Perspectives* (Lanham, MD: University Press of America), 1980.

Ross, M., J. Thibaut, and S. Evenbeck, "Some Determinants of the Intensity of the Social Protest," *Journal of Experimental Social Psychology*, 7 (1), 1971.

Rothschild, J., *Ethnopolitics: A Conceptual Framework* (New York: Columbia University Press), 1981.

Rothschild, J., *Return to Diversity: A Political History of East Central Europe Since World War II* (Oxford: Oxford University Press), 1989.

Royal Institute of International Affairs, *Nationalism A Report* (London: Oxford University Press), 1939.

Rubenstein, J., *Soviet Dissidents: Their Struggle for Human Rights* (Boston: Beacon Press), 1980.

Rudolph, J. and R. Thompson (eds.), *Ethnoterritorial Politics, Policy, and the Western World* (Boulder, Colo.: L. Reinner), 1989.

Runciman, W., *Relative Deprivation and Social Justice: A Study of Attitudes to Social Inequality in Twentieth-Century England* (Berkeley: University of California Press), 1966.

Ryvkin, M., *Moscow's Muslim Challenge* (Armonk, N.Y.: M.E. Sharpe), 1982.

Sakwa, R., *Soviet Politics* (London and New York: Routledge), 1989.

Salitan, L., *Politics and Nationality in Contemporary Soviet Jewish Emigration, 1968–1989* (New York: St. Martin's Press), 1992.

Saunders, G. (ed.), *Samizdat: Voices of the Soviet Opposition* (New York: Monad Press), 1974.

Schapiro, L., *The USSR and the Future* (New York: Praeger), 1963.

Schapiro, L., *Totalitarianism* (New York: Praeger), 1972.

Schapiro, L., *Russian Studies* (New York: Penguin Books), 1988.

Schermerhorn, R., *Comparative Ethnic Relations* (Chicago, London: University of Chicago Press), 1970.

Schroeter, L., *The Last Exodus* (New York: Universe Books), 1974.

Setton-Watson, H., *Nations and States: An Enquiry into the Origins of Nations and the Politics of Nationalism* (Boulder, Colo.: Westview Press), 1977.

Shabad, T., *Geography of the USSR* (New York: Columbia University Press), 1951.

Shafarevich, I. "Rusofobiia," *Dvadtsat' Dva*, nos. 63–64, 1989.

Sharpe, L.J. (ed.), *Decentralist Trends in the Western Democracies* (London: SAGE Publications), 1979.

Shatz, M., *Soviet Dissent in Historical Perspective* (Cambridge: Press Syndicate of the University of Cambridge), 1980.

Sheehy, A., *The Crimean Tatars and Volga Germans: Soviet Treatment of Two National Minorities* (London: Minority Rights Group), 1971.

Shindler, C., *Exit Visa: Détente, Human Rights and the Jewish Emigration Movement in the USSR* (London: Bachman and Turner), 1978.

Shtromas, A. and M. Kaplan (eds.), *The Soviet Union and the Challenge of the Future* (New York: Paragon House), 1989.

Simmonds, G. (ed.), *Nationalism in the USSR and Eastern Europe in the Era of Brezhnev and Kosygin* (Detroit: University of Detroit Press), 1977.

Simon, G., *Nationalism and Policy towards Nationalities in the Soviet Union* (Boulder, Colo.: Westview), 1991.

Smith, A., *Theories of Nationalism* (London: Duckworth), 1971.

Smith, A. (ed.), *Nationalist Movements* (New York: St. Martin's Press), 1976.

Smith, A., *Nationalism in the Twentieth Century* (New York: New York University Press), 1979.

Smith, A., *The Ethnic Revival* (Cambridge: Cambridge University Press), 1981.

Smith, A., *The Ethnic Origins of Nations* (Oxford: Basil Blackwell), 1986.

Smith, A., *Nations and Nationalism in a Global Era* (Cambridge: Polity Press), 1995.

Smith, A., *Nationalism and Modernism: A Critical Survey of Recent Theories of Nations and Nationalism* (London & New York: Routledge), 1998.

Smith, G. (ed.), *The Baltic States: The National Self-Determination of Estonia, Latvia and Lithuania* (New York: St. Martin's Press), 1996.

Smooha, S., "Minority Status in an Ethnic Democracy: The Status of the Arab Minority in Israel," *Ethnic and Racial Studies*, 13 (3), 1990.

Smooha, S., "Ethnic Democracy: Israel as an Archetype," *Israel Studies*, 2 (2), 1997.

Snyder, L., *The Meaning of Nationalism* (New Brunswick, NJ: Rutgers University Press), 1954.

Snyder, L. (ed.), *Dynamics of Nationalism: Readings in Its Meanings and Development* (Princeton: D. van Nostrand), 1964.

Solzhenitsyn, A., *Letter to Soviet Leaders* (London: Index on Censorship), 1974.

Solzhenitsyn, A. et al., *From Under the Rubble* (Boston: Little Brown), 1975.

Spencer, M. (ed.), *Separatism: Democracy and Disintegration* (Lanham, MD: Rowman and Littlefied), 1998.

Stein, J. (ed.), *The Politics of National Minority Participation in Post-Communist Europe: State-Building, Democracy, and Ethnic Mobilization* (Armonk, N.Y.: Sharpe, M.E.), 1999.

Stouffer, S., E. Suchman et al., *The American Soldier: Adjustment during Army Life* (Princeton, NJ: Princeton University Press), 1949.

Sugar, P.F. (ed.), *Ethnic Diversity and Conflict in Eastern Europe* (Santa Barbara, Oxford: ABC-Clio), 1980.

Sumner, W.G., *Volkways/Folkways* (Boston: Ginn), 1906.

Suny, R., *Armenia in the Twentieth Century* (Chico, California: Scholars Press), 1983.

Suny, R., *The Revenge of the Past: Nationalism, Revolution, and the Collapse of the Soviet Union* (Stanford: Stanford University Press), 1993.

Suny, R. (ed.), *Transcaucasia, Nationalism and Social Change: Essays in the History of Armenia, Azerbaijan, and Georgia* (Ann Arbor: University of Michigan Press), 1996.

Szporluk, R., *Communism and Nationalism* (New York, Oxford: Oxford University Press), 1988.

Tagil, S. (ed.), *Region in Upheaval: Ethnic Conflict and Political Mobilization* (Lund: Esseble Studium), 1984.

Tamir, Y., *Liberal Nationalism* (Princeton: Princeton University Press), 1993.

Tarrow, S., *Struggle, Politics and Reform: Collective Action, Social Movements and Cycles of Protest* (Ithaca: Western Societies Papers), 1989.

Tarrow, S., *Power in Movement* (New York: Cambridge University Press), 1994.

Taylor, C., *Multiculturalism and "the Politics of Recognition"* (Princeton: Princeton University Press), 1992.

Thompson, D. and D. Ronen (eds.), *Ethnicity, Politics, and Development* (Boulder, Colo.: Lynne Reinner, 1986.

Tilly, C., *The Formation of National States in Western Europe* (Princeton: Princeton University Press), 1975.

Tishkov, V., "Narody i gosudarstvo," *Kommunist*, 1, 1989.

Tokes, R. (ed.), *Dissent in the USSR: Politics, Ideology and People* (Baltimore: Johns Hopkins University Press), 1975.

Torsvik, P. (ed.), *Mobilization, Center–Periphery Structures and Nation-Building: A Volume in Commemoration of Stein Rokkan* (Bergen, Oslo: Universitetsforlaget), 1981.

Van den Berghe, P.L., *The Ethnic Phenomenon* (New York: Praeger), 1981.

Vardys, S. (ed.), *Lithuania under the Soviets* (New York: Praeger), 1965.

Vardys, S., "Modernization and Baltic Nationalism," *Problems of Communism*, 5, 1975.

Vardys, S., *The Catholic Church, Dissent and Nationality in Soviet Lithuania* (New York: Columbia University Press, East European Monographs, 43) 1978.

Vsesoiuznaia perepis' naseleniia 1970 goda (Moscow: Statistika), 1976.

Walzer, M. et al., *The Politics of Ethnicity* (Cambridge, Mass.: The Belknap Press of Harvard University Press), 1982.

Walzer, M., *What it Means to be an American: Essays on the American Experience* (New York: Marsillo), 1992.

Webb, K., *The Growth of Nationalism in Scotland* (London: Penguin Books), 1978.

White, S., A. Pravda, and Z. Gitelman (eds.), *Developments in Soviet Politics* (London: Macmillan Education, Ltd.), 1990.

Wilson, A., *Ukrainian Nationalism in the 1990s: A Minority Faith* (Cambridge: Cambridge University Press), 1997.

Wimbush, S. and R. Wixman, "The Meskhetian Turks: A New Voice in Soviet Central Asia," *Canadian Slavonic Papers*, no. 17 (2–3), 1975.

Yanov, A., *The Russian Challenge and the Year 2000* (New York: Basil Blackwell), 1987.

Zaslavsky, V. and R. Brym, *Soviet Jewish Emigration and Soviet Nationality Policy* (New York: St. Martin's Press), 1983.

Zisserman, D., "The Politicization of the Environmental Issue within National Movements in the USSR," *Environment Policy Review*, 4 (2), 1990.

Zisserman-Brodsky, D. "Sources of Ethnic Politics in the Soviet Polity: The Pre-Perestroika Dimension," *Nationalities Papers*, 22 (2), 1994.

Index

Note. Since Soviet Union, USSR, *samizdat*, dissidents are mentioned on almost every page of this book, they have not been indicated separately.